International Migration in Southeast Asia

The **Institute of Southeast Asian Studies (ISEAS)** was established as an autonomous organization in 1968. It is a regional centre dedicated to the study of socio-political, security and economic trends and developments in Southeast Asia and its wider geostrategic and economic environment.

The Institute's research programmes are the Regional Economic Studies (RES, including ASEAN and APEC), Regional Strategic and Political Studies (RSPS), and Regional Social and Cultural Studies (RSCS).

ISEAS Publications, an established academic press, has issued more than 1,000 books and journals. It is the largest scholarly publisher of research about Southeast Asia from within the region. ISEAS Publications works with many other academic and trade publishers and distributors to disseminate important research and analyses from and about Southeast Asia to the rest of the world.

International Migration in Southeast Asia

Edited by
Aris Ananta & Evi Nurvidya Arifin

LSEAS INSTITUTE OF SOUTHEAST ASIAN STUDIES
Singapore

First published in Singapore in 2004 by ISEAS Publications
Institute of Southeast Asian Studies
30 Heng Mui Keng Terrace
Pasir Panjang
Singapore 119614

E-mail: publish@iseas.edu.sg
Website: <http://bookshop.iseas.edu.sg>

The responsibility for facts and opinions in this publication rests exclusively with the authors and their interpretations do not necessarily reflect the views or the policy of the publisher or its supporters.

ISEAS Library Cataloguing-in-Publication Data

International migration in Southeast Asia / edited by Aris Ananta and Evi
    Nurvidya Arifin
   1.   Asia, Southeastern—Emigration and immigration—Economic aspects.
   2.   Asia, Southeastern—Emigration and immigration—Government policy.
   I.   Ananta, Aris.
   II.   Arifin, Evi Nurvidya.
JV8753.7 I61   2004

ISBN 981-230-279-4 (soft cover)
ISBN 981-230-278-6 (hard cover)

Typeset by Superskill Graphics Pte Ltd
Printed in Singapore by Utopia Press Pte Ltd

Contents

List of Tables

List of Figures

Message from the Director

Rapid population dynamics, economic development, and globalization have brought and been affected by the rising population mobility — along with other factors such as increasing international trade and capital flow. Also what happens in one country, or one region, becomes inter-related to developments in other countries or regions.

Southeast Asia is no exception. An event in one of the countries in Southeast Asia is very likely to have implications in other countries in Southeast Asia, and even, beyond Southeast Asia. On the other hand, events outside Southeast Asia may also affect the situations in Southeast Asia. International trade and capital flow, for example, have transformed the economies and lives in Southeast Asia.

In the last ten years, we have witnessed an increase in migration within and from Southeast Asia. This migration — involving people with different social, economic, and political backgrounds — certainly has as much implications as international trade and capital flow. It is therefore very timely for this book to be published. Edited by two ISEAS researchers, the book examines the migration issue from economic, social, and political perspectives.

I commend the contributors and the two editors of this volume and hope that it is beneficial to a better understanding of the complex issues of population dynamics, economic development, and globalization in Southeast Asia.

K. Kesavapany
Director
Institute of Southeast Asian Studies
Singapore

Acknowledgements

First of all we would like to thank the Konrad Adenauer Stiftung for their financial support of the ISEAS research project that resulted in this book. Thanks also to Professor Chia Siow Yue for suggesting the workshop. The title of the project and ensuing workshop was "International Migration in Southeast Asia: Impacts and Challenges", held at ISEAS on 31 October–1 November 2002. Second, we really appreciate the collaboration with all authors, discussants, and observers during the workshop and are particularly grateful for the willingness of the authors to revise their papers after the workshop. Third, we are very fortunate to work in the conducive environment that ISEAS has provided to finish editing this book — a special note of thanks goes to Mr K. Kesavapany, the current Director of ISEAS, for his constant encouragement to publish books. Fourth, we owe the Publications Unit our thanks for making this manuscript publishable. Finally, any remaining errors are solely the responsibility of the editors and authors.

Contributors

Aris Ananta
Senior Research Fellow, Institute of Southeast Asian Studies, Singapore.

Evi Nurvidya Arifin
Visiting Research Fellow, Institute of Southeast Asian Studies, Singapore.

Maruja M.B. Asis
Director of Research and Publications of the Scalabrini Migration Center (SMC), Manila, the Philippines.

Yongyuth Chalamwong
Research Director for Labour Development, Human Resources and Social Development Programme, Thailand Development Research Institute Foundation, Bangkok, Thailand.

Carl Grundy-Warr
Senior Lecturer, Department of Geography, National University of Singapore, Singapore.

Abdul Haris
Research Staff of the Centre for Population and Policy Studies, Gadjah Mada University, Yogyakarta, Indonesia.

Graeme Hugo
Federation Fellow, Professor of the Department of Geographical and Environmental Studies and Director of the National Centre for Social

Applications of Geographical Information Systems at the University of Adelaide, Adelaide, Australia.

Bilson Kurus
Executive Director of the Institute for Indigenous Economic Progress or INDEP, Sabah, Malaysia.

Nimfa B. Ogena
Director of the University of the Philippines Population Institute (UPPI), Diliman, Quezon City, the Philippines.

P. Ramasamy
Professor of Political Economy, Centre for History, Political Science and Strategic Studies, National University of Malaysia, Bangi, Selangor.

Elan Satriawan
Research Staff of the Centre for Population and Policy Studies, Gadjah Mada University, Yogyakarta, Indonesia.

Amy Sim
Ph.D. Candidate in Anthropology at the Department of Sociology, The University of Hong Kong, People's Republic of China.

Sukamdi
Director of the Centre for Population and Policy Studies, Gadjah Mada University, Yogyakarta, Indonesia.

Leo Suryadinata
Senior Research Fellow, Institute of Southeast Asian Studies, Singapore. Formerly, Professor, Department of Political Science, National University of Singapore.

Riwanto Tirtosudarmo
Senior Research Associate, Research Centre of Society and Culture, Indonesian Institute of Sciences.

Pan-Long Tsai
Professor at the Department of Economics, National Tsing Hua University, Hsin-Chu, Taiwan.

Ching-Lung Tsay
Professor at the Institute of Southeast Asian Studies, Tamkang University in Tamshui, Taipei, Taiwan; and an adjunct professorial fellow at the Institute of Economics, Academia Sinica in Nankang, Taipei, Taiwan.

Vivienne Wee
Associate Director of the Southeast Asia Research Centre (SEARC) and Associate Professor of the Department of Applied Social Studies, City University of Hong Kong, Hong Kong Special Administrative Region, China.

1

Should Southeast Asian Borders be Opened?

Aris Ananta and Evi Nurvidya Arifin

The international networks of wealth, technology, and power have resulted in globalization and informationalization, and in turn have rapidly transformed all societies in the world. Productive capacity has increased, cultural creativity has expanded, and communication potential has multiplied. However, these same forces have also disfranchised the societies. The sudden transformations have led to the crumbling of existing mechanisms of social control and political representation (Castells 1997).

Castells argues that globalization and informationalization have brought increasing economic integration and governments have lost some controls within their own borders. International economic integration and political sovereignty have been in conflict. In the area of international labour mobility, as part of the globalization and informationalization, policies on labour market in one country may be of concern for other countries. A policy can stimulate the flow of migration to other countries and dampen wages in the receiving countries. Political problems arise because the gain from migration is not equally shared by all groups of people in a country. There are losers and winners.

Carl Gundry-Warr, in Chapter 8, posits that global migration has changed the way people think about their political, cultural, and economic maps. Moving has been much easier today and the states have become "borderless". Yet, many of them have been trapped between or within borders simply because they have crossed the borders.

It is not surprising then, that there are two opposing views on the relationship between international labour mobility and economic development. As mentioned by Tapinos (1994), the first one sees immigrants as a positive contribution to the economic development of the receiving countries. With this view, international labour mobility should be enhanced, and permitted to follow the nature of the labour market. The second view considers the non-economic, negative, implications of immigrants. This view, therefore, suggests that liberalization of trade, capital flow, relocation of activities, and co-operation should be enhanced rather than encourage in-migration.

Brettel (2000) argues that international migrants can be part of transnationalism, defined as "a social process whereby migrants operate in social fields that transgress geographic, political, and cultural borders". This construct is very appropriate where modes of transportation and communication in general have shortened the social distances between sending and receiving countries. The migrants can easily maintain their contact with others in their home countries. Home and host countries become "one", integrated. They are not uprooted, but they move back and forth freely between different cultures, social, economics, and political system. Migrants not only send economic remittances, but also social, cultural, and, perhaps political remittances.

Fundamental tensions have been found in all efforts to manage international population mobility in this globalizing world. On the one hand, business is transnational and international business necessitates the unrestricted flow of people internationally. On the other hand, politics is still national. The existence of supranational institutions and international organizations cannot supersede the importance of politics, which prioritizes the security and protection of the citizens in a country and hence demands restriction on the international flow of people. This dilemma becomes evident, as we have witnessed wars, internal conflicts, prosecution of minorities, and global terrorism (Jordan and Duvell 2002).

Migration has also been part of the globalization which has shaped the inter-dependence among nations, including those within Southeast

Asian countries and between Southeast Asian countries and other countries. Hugo (1998) has shown that international labour mobility in Asia is also a complex process of inter-relationship among economic, political, and social changes, especially with the emerging trend of globalization. However, the mechanism of international migration in Asia is much more complicated than that in nineteenth-century Europe, when international migration was relatively much easier. The Asian countries face many restrictions that the European countries did not have. It is not surprising therefore that, as pointed out by Graeme Hugo in Chapter 2, international migration has been an increasingly important topic in Southeast Asia among those both in the governments and outside the governments. International migration has become public consciousness as the mass media have reported it almost daily.

In an integrated world economy, trade, flow of capital, flow of labour, flow of raw materials and technology are inter-related. Therefore, studies of international migration should be seen in the context of an integrated world economy. From this point of view, in this book we examine the socio-economic and political impacts and challenges of international migration within Southeast Asia, to Southeast Asia, and from Southeast Asia, with particular emphasis on migration within and from Southeast Asia. The theme consists of four sub-themes. The first sub-theme discusses the history of migration in modern Southeast Asia. The second examines the linkage between international migration and economic development, particularly with respect to investments, remittances, and welfare. The third investigates the excesses of the lucrative business of sending unskilled workers — with a focus on the vulnerability of the workers. The fourth theme focuses on the national policies regarding international migration of two sending countries (the Philippines and Indonesia) and two receiving countries (Malaysia and Thailand). Finally, the fifth sub-theme provides some recommendations on approaching the problem of irregular migrants.

History of Migration in Modern Southeast Asia

There have been several rapid transformations sweeping across Southeast Asia in the last half century. Rapidly rising international population mobility is one of the transformations and it has been a cause and a consequence of extraordinary changes in the social, economic, and political life in the region. (Graeme Hugo, in Chapter 2). Yet, as argued by Maruja M.B. Asis, in Chapter 7, this international migration has actually been part of the history and culture of Southeast Asia. It is not a recent phenomenon. In maritime Southeast Asia, the current Indonesia, the Philippines, Malaysia, and Singapore used to be part of the *Dunia Melayu* (Malay world) and there had been extensive contacts through migration and trade. In the Philippines, the Tagalogs came from Malacca through Kalimantan (Indonesia), the Pampangos from Sumatra (Indonesia), and the Bicols and Visayans from Makasar in Sulawesi (Indonesia). In the mainland Southeast Asia, Thailand and its neighbouring countries (such as Yunnan and China) had had a lot of exchanges. Riwanto Tirtosudarmo, in Chapter 11, shows that people used to move from the present West Sumatra, Indonesia, to the present West Malaysia and people from what is now called South Sulawesi, Indonesia, to Australia's Northern Territory. Carl Grundy-Warr, in Chapter 8, reveals that Mae Hong Son province in north-western Thailand has received many Tai Yai or Shan migrants from Myanmar for a long time. The Tai Yai has constituted the majority of the population in the Mae Hong Son province and therefore the historical, cultural, and social ties have transcended the political spaces.

However, spontaneous population mobility stopped when countries came under the colonial administration. The mobility became even more limited when the countries had their independences as they started delineating national borders.

Initially, according to Hugo, the emigration of indigenous groups in the region was very limited. Migration was mainly from European countries. Later, the Japanese occupation in most of the region had pushed the Europeans out of the region. In the early years of independence, international migration was still limited to the main movements consisting of flows of Europeans either to their colonial countries or to Australia. Groups strongly associated with the European colonialists also returned to their home countries. Although small, flows of students from the Southeast Asia to Euro-American nations under the Colombo Plan occurred and gave rise to concerns about "brain drain". Limited international labour migration from the region also started to emerge. For example, during the 1960s, substantial workers from Thailand and Korea were recruited to work on U.S. military contracts and reconstruction projects in the then South Vietnam.

Since the 1970s, and particularly the 1980s, migration within, from, and to, Southeast Asia has rapidly multiplied. Asis argues that this emergence of international migration may seem as a resumption of the old pattern of population mobility in the region. However, she also notes that the rising population mobility in Southeast Asia since the 1970s is different from that in East Asia — which consists mostly of countries of destination, except China, and those in South Asia — which consists mostly of countries of origin. The Southeast Asian region consists of countries of origin (the Philippines, Indonesia, Myanmar, Vietnam, Laos, and Cambodia), countries of destination (Singapore and Brunei), and countries of both origin and destination (Malaysia and Thailand).

Hugo maintains that international migration has been increasing with different flows, from South to North, and also from North to South. The migrants could be refugees, overseas contract workers and students. However, the complexity of the region in many aspects — such as the culture, ethnic and religious composition, and political and economic structure — makes generalization difficult. Furthermore, the data relating to international migration is incomplete and totally absent for most nations in the region.

He also states that the revolution in global transport and communications and the proliferation of radio, television and other mass media are some of the factors that contribute to the rising international movement of workers out of, in to, and between Southeast Asian countries. The shift in immigration policy from the racially based policies to the ones based more on skills and family connections increased the opportunity to migrate. On the other hand, the developments in the region succeeded in increasing the level of education of Southeast Asians who therefore had the skills and qualifications to qualify for settlement in other countries. The uneven progress of demographic transition across countries in the world resulted in differences in the number and growth of the workforces of the countries. This further creates a cleavage between labour-deficit and labour-surplus countries. Labour-deficit countries tend to have rapid growing economies which enhances the demand for labour. Labour-surplus countries are likely to have limited economic opportunities but are endowed with a great number of working-age population.

The development of global education markets was the momentum for the more developed countries to offer training and programmes for students from developing countries. Hugo gives the example of the increasing number of overseas students studying in Australia during 1983–2000, half of whom were from Southeast Asia. On the other hand, there is evidence of a rising number of students migrating within Southeast Asian countries.

He notes that until the time of writing, Asia had more refugees than any other region in the world. In the year 2000, half of the refugees were in Asia. The peak was reached in 1991. Southeast Asia contributed the most in the 1970s and 1980s. The picture was dominated by the outflow from Vietnam.

Smaller flows of refugees, but significant to the locals, have also been observed in Southeast Asia. First is the flow of refugees from Myanmar to Bangladesh. Second is the migration from Myanmar to Thailand, though it is not exactly known how many of them are refugees and how many are labour migrants. Third is the flow of refugees to Indonesia from the former Indonesian province of East Timor.

Hugo also mentions that migration of the Chinese has the longest lasting impact on the society of each of the ten Southeast Asian countries. Along with the Indians, Persians, and Arabs, the Chinese had settled in the port cities of Southeast Asia before the Europeans came, but in the last century of colonial occupation, the Chinese had been permitted, and encouraged, to settle in the destination areas. P. Ramasamy, in Chapter 9, describes that during the British colonial period, a great number of Indians and Chinese came to Malaysia, to work in plantation and tin mines. They were brought in as temporary workers. However, after many years of living in Malaysia, they could uproot themselves from their original cultures and started settling in Malaysia. Malaysia then became a multi-racial and multi-religious society.

Leo Suryadinata, in Chapter 3, focuses on the migration of the ethnic Chinese. He shows that mass migration of the Chinese from China took place in the mid-nineteenth century after the defeat of the Qing dynasty and the establishment of the colonial power in Southeast Asia. He argues that turbulence and poverty in China — as the push factors — and the economic opportunities in Southeast Asia — as the pull factors — can still be used to explain the situation in the twentieth century and beyond. However, China itself possessed both the push and pull factors. Traditionally, the sources of Chinese migrants were from the two southern provinces: Fujian and Guangdong. He uses the term ethnic Chinese to include those who are "of Chinese descent" and "ethnic Chinese proper". During the colonial period, the number of ethnic Chinese in the region increased remarkably. They numbered about four million, consisting of 2.88 per cent of the total Southeast Asian population in the 1930s. In Singapore, they formed 75 per cent of the population but in other countries in the region they were always a minority group, ranging from 0.3 per cent in Laos to 33.9 per cent in Malaya. The number increased drastically to about 20 million in 2000. The proportion in the region increased to 3.84 per cent, but in some countries the percentage declined.

During the Cold War period, the emigration of the Chinese was affected because the documented migration from China to Southeast Asian countries was stopped. After the end of the Cold War, along with the rapid globalization process, migration from China recurred. Suryadinata suggests that other push factors for this migration might be the modernization of China, the return of Hong Kong to the mainland, and also the uncertainty of Taiwan's future. A new wave of Chinese migrants from the Mainland, Hong Kong and also Taiwan forms what is known as the *xin yi ming* (Chinese new migrants). Unlike in the last century and earlier, the destination of Chinese migration was more to developed countries than to developing countries. The background characteristics of the migrants were also different from those in the past. Many of these migrants were not from rural but urban China. These new migrants consisted of businessmen, professionals and a large number of Chinese students. Some came to the region with not only skills but also capital. They became the links between China and Southeast Asia.

Suryadinata argues that the changes in the percentage of the Chinese in each country in the region may be explained in terms of the domestic situation, that is, government policy, especially since each country became independent and started the nation-building process. Nevertheless, different policies toward ethnic Chinese are observed in Southeast Asian countries. Some countries have adopted integrationist, yet others have introduced assimilation and accommodation policies. Occasionally expulsion has also been used. A government may adopt more than one policy towards the Chinese during a certain period. Suryadinata gives an example, the government of Indonesia, which introduced more integrationist policy after its independence in 1945. It gradually became more assimilationist since 1959. However, the expulsion policy also occurred during Sukarno's period in the early 1960s. When Suharto was in power, it became assimilationist. After 1998, when Suharto stepped down, the policy was reversed back to pluralism.

International Migration and Economic Development: Investment, Remittances, and Welfare

In the world of free market mechanism, people produce goods and services following the demand signalled by the prices. Factors of production (especially labour, capital, and technology) will go to where they can get the best rewards. If migration is an equilibrating force in the labour market, then people move to where they can be better off. The history of the now advanced countries in Europe and North America has confirmed this pattern. On the other hand, the rise of nations with its consequent nationalism has greatly reduced the flow of capital and labour. Therefore, the next best solution is to have free international trade which, it has been argued, will enhance the welfare of all nations despite the political inability to move capital and labour.

However, in the last three decades, capital, technology, and even labour have migrated with rising rates. Zlotnik (1998) notes that freedom of movement had been an important aspiration for the establishment of the European community. The freedom of movement became a reality in 1992. Furthermore, since 1960 some countries have liberalized their emigration policies and as a result, they have welcomed migrants who had not been previously welcome.

In Chapter 4, Pang-Long Tsai and Ching-Lung Tsay focus their study on the close relationship between foreign direct investment, labour mobility, and economic development in four Southeast Asian countries: Indonesia, Philippines, Thailand and Malaysia. They employ the IMDP (investment-migration-development path) model as shown in Figure 1.1. They argue that differentials in economic development and economic growth are the source of income disparity and various stages of labour market transformations. In stage 1 of the model, when the real per capita income of the country is usually still below US$500, countries usually send more than receive labour. At the same time they receive more than send capital. In the early part of stage 1, the magnitude of labour sent abroad and capital received is usually small. Probably, they even almost do not receive

FIGURE 1.1
Investment-Migration-Development Path

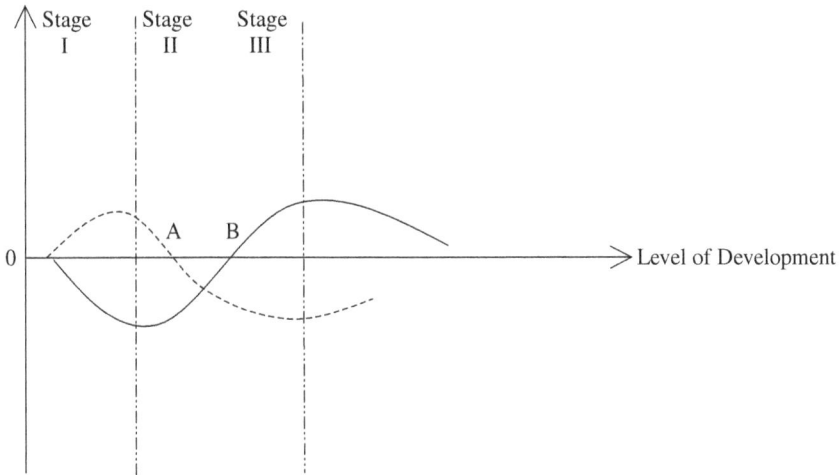

Net Outward ILM (------)
Net Outward FDI (___)

Source: Figure 4.1 in Chapter 4.

foreign labour and do not send capital abroad. As the countries enjoy better economic development, shown by higher per capita income, the magnitude of labour sent and capital received increases. Indonesia and the Philippines are in this later part of stage 1.

Later on, the magnitude of labour sent and capital received decreases and they are in stage 2 of the model. A turning point will be reached at point A, where the countries receive more than send labour. This turning point is usually reached at per capita income in the range of US$1,500 and US$2,000. Thailand is already in the second stage and they may have passed the first turning point before the 1997 crisis. The crisis had brought them back to the earlier stages but they may now have just passed the first turning point again. The second turning point, at point B, will be attained at per capita income above $5,000. After passing the turning point, countries will send more than receive capital. Malaysia has certainly been between points A and B. They have shifted to receive more than send labour; but they still receive more than send capital though the net amount is approaching zero.

Tsai and Tsay maintain that countries will follow the IMDP model and as they go to a higher level of development, they cannot escape the problems faced at that level of development — for example, problems of shortage of unskilled workers and too much capital in the country. Thailand and Malaysia cannot escape from the problem as Japan and Taiwan have experienced it. "Exceptionalism" is only temporary for the market forces. Nevertheless, foreign direct investment and international migration have received asymmetrical treatment both in the global/regional and national contexts.

Following efforts to liberalize trade through WTO, there has been an equally important attempt to liberalize investment through the framework of GATT in the last two decades. Yet, there are no such institutions to liberalize international migration. Tsai and Tsay do not even foresee such an effort in the near future.

Such asymmetry is even worse at the national level. People in countries receiving foreign capital are often worried that the foreign capital competes with their own domestic capital and hence endanger the domestic investment. At the same time, Tsai and Tsay also find public hostility toward foreign workers. Particularly, discussions about receiving unskilled foreign workers are sometimes still a politically taboo subject in some countries.

Taking a legal approach alone will not solve the issue of the rising number of foreign workers. Asis shows that Malaysia and Thailand have used the legal approach to provide jobs for the locals during the crisis. They repatriated foreign workers, particularly those who entered without legal documents. However, repatriation did not solve the domestic labour market problems. Ramasamy posits that the nature of the economic structure has made it difficult for the government of Malaysia to get rid of the foreign workers, especially in the areas of domestic services, plantation, manufacturing, and construction. Without the foreign workers, the economy could have stagnated. In Chapter 13, Yongyuth Chalamwong shows that hiring illegal migrants may have saved employers in Thailand about US$0.3 billion per firm per year.

Bilateral agreement between the sending and receiving countries may not solve the problem of foreign workers either. Ramasamy argues that though the sending countries may take the initiative to reduce the flow of migrants, the impact may be insignificant. Long and porous borders between Indonesia and the Philippines on one hand, and Malaysia on the other, for example, along with the very lucrative nature of the labour recruitment business, have rendered bilateral agreements ineffective.

Tsai and Tsay, therefore, recommend that labour-receiving countries should view international migration more pragmatically along economic terms. In the integrated world economy, unskilled workers will keep coming if there are big differentials in income between countries of origin and destination countries. If they cannot enter through legal channels, they will breach the law as illegal workers as long as the market still indicates a need for unskilled workers.

The rising number of international migrants has also meant a rising number of remittances sent internationally and that the remittances may have improved the balance of payments of the sending countries. Indeed, as pointed out by Nyberg-Sorenson et al. (2002), worldwide remittances have constituted a very large portion of the world financial flow and their number is even greater than the amount of money for global overseas development. In the case of the Philippines, Nimfa B. Ogena, in Chapter 12, shows that remittances contributed about 21 per cent of the country's gross national product in 1999. The remittances have been the largest contributor to the foreign earnings of the country. The government considers the overseas workers as the "modern-day heroes" of the national economy.

Sukamdi, Elan Satriawan, and Abdul Haris, in Chapter 6, warn that a large amount of remittances may produce inflationary pressure, raise the imports and then reduce the benefit from foreign exchange, unless the government implements a conducive economic environment to invest the remittances in the sending countries. Remittances are neither a reliable source for investment. Sending workers abroad should not replace sound macroeconomic policies. They also emphasize that the statistics on remittances may be highly under-estimated, as shown with the cases in Indonesia. They find that unofficial remittances in some regions in Indonesia may be higher than those officially recorded. Yet, based on official statistics alone, the remittances per capita (per migrant) in Indonesia have risen, and it is higher than the average wages in Indonesia. In some provinces such as West Nusa Tenggara and East Java, the remittances are relatively much larger, especially compared to the income of the province. Detailed studies on some districts in Indonesia show the very significant contribution of remittances to the local economies.

However, as elaborated by Sukamdi, Satriawan, and Haris, measured as a percentage of the Gross Domestic Product (GDP), remittances have played a small role in the Indonesian economy, with a percentage of less than 1.5 per cent. The contribution is also small, always below 2.7 per cent, if measured as a percentage of exports and imports.

They also mention that the 1997 crisis has been a "blessing" for the Indonesian economy and migrants. The much weaker Indonesian rupiah has resulted in a quick jump in the earnings of the migrants, measured in rupiah. However, how do the migrants spend the money? More importantly, does the migration improve the welfare of the migrants and/ or the families of the migrants?

Bretell (2000) finds that unskilled migrants do not necessarily experience upward mobility after they return to their sending countries. They tend to spend their savings on conspicuous consumption, rather than for investment. The skills learned abroad are not easily applicable in the countries of origin. Hence, migration may not be an aid for local development. Rather, it may create a community which depends so much on migration. The returning migrants are likely to migrate again.

Furthermore, Stalker (1994) notes that the returning migrants may drive prices in the rural areas up. The poorest, who cannot migrate, then suffer. On the other hand, the migration may reduce the disparity between the lower and the middle-classes.

Using results of studies in some regions in Indonesia, Sukamdi, Satriawan, and Haris conclude that the migrants first use the remittances to fulfil their subsistent needs, including the paying of debts. After that, they spend the money on luxury goods, to raise the socio-economic status of the remittance-receiving households. They build new houses, as monuments of their success in working abroad. They spend most of the remittances locally, rather than in the country of destination, and hence the remittances help to stimulate the local economies. They conclude that remittances have raised the welfare of the migrant families. The remittances have also significantly changed the consumption patterns of the families, and perhaps, the community where they live.

However, Sukamdi et al. do not see that expenditure for paying debts and luxurious goods as "unproductive" and they do not "blame" the migrants for not using the remittances efficiently. It is the national and local governments who should actively find ways to channel the great amount of remittances for more "productive" activities. Furthermore, they also emphasize that the government should not see the workers as merely a source for high economic growth. The first criteria of whether to send workers abroad should be whether it will improve the welfare of the migrants and the families; rather than whether it will help increase the economic growth.

A similar case is seen in the Philippines. Asis (1995) shows how international female migration has produced significant transformations in the sending communities in the Philippines. Whether it is merely a survival strategy or social mobility, working abroad has provided golden economic opportunities, at least for a short period of time. Social changes have also occurred and they may be bad or good. Yet, these social changes have provided the communities with alternatives to fulfilling individual and social needs. Ogena notes however, that the returning workers may take a longer time to find the desired jobs. While waiting for the jobs, their savings from working abroad may become depleted and this may force them to work overseas again.

Excesses of a Lucrative Business: Vulnerable Migrants

Asis argues that the economic situation of the sending countries is not sufficient to generate a big supply of workers. Intermediaries (brokers or agents) step in to help would-be migrants follow certain requirements and procedures — and only with the "help" of the intermediaries does the supply of workers become very large. On the other hand, neither is the economic situation of the receiving countries sufficient to generate a big demand for foreign workers. The employers do not have sufficient knowledge to recruit workers — hence, they cannot produce a sufficiently large demand for foreign workers. So, intermediaries intervene and provide the employers with the services to facilitate the hiring of the migrants. Therefore, sending workers abroad has been a very lucrative industry. Many individuals and parties — in both the sending and receiving countries — have benefited greatly from the international migration of unskilled workers.

At the same time, the rising supply of and demand for unskilled workers is also accompanied by the tendency of receiving countries to tighten the borders. The existence of regulations to intervene in the labour market — through migration control — is likely to result in the rising number of cases in breach of migration laws (Jordan and Duvel 2002). Irregular migration occurs as a "black market" when the market mechanism has been intervened. As with other black markets, abuses can take place relatively easily. Yet, the existence of the black market may have indeed made the business of overseas labour recruitment more attractive.

Martin, Mason, and Nagayama (1996) reveal that many migrants in Asia have relied on the frequently shadowy network of labour brokers, contractors, and transporters. Today's system of recruitment is different from the one in the 1960s and early 1970s. Stalker (1994) notes that in those days, employers had to find their own workers overseas. They paid for the travel and other expenses. Today, the majority of migrants pay their own travel expenses and other costs such as for the passport and fees to the syndicates.

Asis finds that brokers and social networks facilitating the international migration exist in both the sending and receiving countries. Ramasamy observes that this business (involving many individuals, including corrupt officials in both sending and receiving countries) has played a crucial role in the migration process. Without this business, the magnitude of international migration would not be the size we see today. Chantanavich and Germershausen (2000) recommend deception-free recruitment procedures to the Thai Government.

It is not surprising therefore that recruitment organizations have been mushrooming in Asia, particularly for finding jobs in the Middle East and prosperous Asian countries such as Japan, Singapore, and Taiwan. It is a business and terminologies such as "export" and "import" have been widely used in discussing foreign workers.

In Chapter 6, Vivienne Wee and Amy Sim argue that this transnational network has functioned as a bridge between the workers, especially female workers, and international labour markets. Recruitment always involves three stages: pre-employment, employment, and post-migration. Guzman (1996) shows that in each stage migrants from Southeast Asia are vulnerable to exploitation. This vulnerability is observed regardless whether the recruitment process is legal or illegal. Legal recruitment is through licensed recruitment agencies, and illegal recruitment utilizes intensive social networking.

There are many unregistered companies in Asia. Migrants going abroad through these illegal agencies face much higher risks. They have to pay higher fees yet their condition in the destination country remains uncertain. These agents may suddenly disappear. Tirtosudarmo indicates that the unskilled migrants, with no political power and limited economic opportunities, are easy preys to both legal and illegal labour recruiting agencies, which strongly control the lucrative industry.

Jones (2000) notes that the distinction between what is legal and illegal is often not clear. In Indonesian villages, the same agents may employ both legal and illegal procedures to recruit migrants. Indonesian corrupt police, immigration officials and others play important roles in sending undocumented workers abroad. At the same time, Malaysian marine police often receive money to pretend not to know about the arrival of the undocumented migrants. These workers also often find ways to pay the fees so that they are not arrested or deported. From the perspective of Indonesian migrants, it is much cheaper and easier to work in Malaysia with good employers, though without proper documents, rather than pay the fees for passport, visa, and work permit.

As described by Ananta et al. (1998), the legal recruitment in Indonesia was through a legal intermediary, the so-called PJTKI (*Perusahaan Jasa Tenaga Kerja Indonesia*-Indonesian Labour Sending Firms). The applicants had to fill in twenty different documents and follow ten processes before they could leave Indonesia. Filling each document and going through each process is very time consuming, complicated, and costly. Therefore, many preferred to go through the much less complicated illegal recruitment. In the case of going to Malaysia, the illegal recruitment was a collusion of Indonesian *calo* and Malaysian *tekong*, supported by security personnel from both Indonesia and Malaysia.

Wee and Sim show that the networking has enabled millions of women to migrate back and forth from various countries — from a sending country to a receiving country, and then returning to the sending country and staying for a while before she moves to another (or the same) receiving country. The transnational network has significantly "helped" the workers to find jobs overseas though the female workers are usually prone to being vulnerable at all points of the migration stages.

They illustrate the discussion by comparing cases of Filipino and Indonesian workers, especially those who work in Hong Kong where Filipino workers constitute the largest group of foreign workers, followed by the Indonesians. The Filipino workers came before the Indonesian workers did, meaning that the Indonesians entered a labour market already dominated by Filipino workers. The Filipinos have better education, speak English and hence they have higher wages and greater autonomy of choice and decision-making. The Filipino workers are luckier and better treated than the Indonesian counterparts.

For example, almost all Filipino domestic workers received at least the minimum wage in 2001, but only half of the Indonesian domestic workers received the minimum wage. Many Indonesian workers did not know about the minimum wage and they found out about it only after they signed the contract. The Filipino workers pay all the fees for the entire process of working abroad before the agents begin the processing. On the other hand, the Indonesian workers repay all the fees after they work in the destination countries. It may take up to seven months of wages out of the standard twenty-four-month contract. The workers may also first borrow the money with interest to pay the fees after they arrive in the destination country.

Chain-migration (migration using the network of previous migrants) is another way of migrating and it has been much more dominant in the case of workers from Indonesia to Malaysia than those from Myanmar to Thailand. Once they arrive in the destination country, social network becomes very important for Indonesians in Malaysia, because the Indonesians do not know any NGOs who can help them. Families and friends have emerged as the most cohesive element in the migration process in Southeast Asia (Asis 2000).

Findings by Asis in Indonesian and the Philippine surveys have found that about 40 per cent of the respondents in the Philippines had claimed to be victimized by illegal recruiters. The percentage could be higher if the number of victims included respondents who had heard of cases of victimized overseas workers. In contrast, only about 13 per cent of the Indonesian respondents admitted that they had been victimized. The lower percentage in Indonesia may be partly because the intermediaries were members of the migrants' social network.

Wee and Sim also find that the Indonesian labour recruiters monopolize the labour market, in contrast to the Philippine recruiters who tend to be service providers who have to compete to get clients among Filipino workers. The system of mutual help in finding jobs is much stronger among the Filipinos than Indonesians in Hong Kong.

The vulnerability of Indonesian female workers is also observed in Indonesia. Jones (2000) reported that extortion occurs right from the time the migrants leave the villages until the time they arrive in the Sukarno-Hatta international airport in Jakarta. Sukamdi, Satriawan, and Haris have shown that extortion of the migrants when they arrive in the airport has been made possible by the establishment of "Terminal 3", specially designed for the returning migrants. The extortion may continue during the bus ride home.

The workers are in very weak positions. Wee and Sim demonstrate that the networking — from the recruitment until the return to the villages in Indonesia — has greatly facilitated the rising supply of unskilled workers, but at great cost to the workers at almost all points of the migration stages. The Filipino cases show that empowerment of the women is very important to avoid the abuses on the female domestic workers.

A closely related issue to the excesses of the lucrative labour recruitment business is the trafficking of human beings. IOM (1999) reports that Southeast Asia, especially in Cambodia, Vietnam, China, Myanmar, and Laos, has suffered a serious problem of human trafficking, particularly of women and children. For example, there has been a rising trend of trafficking in women and children from Vietnam to its neighbouring countries for marriage, workers, and prostitution. On the other hand, Thailand has been the main destination for trafficking. Traffickers seeking economic profit have illegally recruited people for exploitation, abuse, and hardship. They seem to work with impunity. Ahtukorala, Manning, and Wickramasekara (2000) claim that the trafficking is organized by powerful vested interests and it has a wide social implication, including the spread of HIV.

As in trade and narcotics, Skeldon (2000) describes the trafficking as an illicit exchange of goods. However, unlike the trading of goods, trafficking involves a moral dimension because it deals with human beings. Any effort to limit labour migration in Asia is doomed to failure. Trafficking is expected to continue to rise as long as governments attempt to intervene in the market mechanism of the dynamics of labour migration. Trafficking will even increase during recession. The elimination of trafficking should not be through legislation and declaration of intent.

It must be through betterment of the socio-economic status of the population.

National Policies[1]

Tirtosudarmo posits that cross-border migration has become one of the important demographic phenomena in the history of population mobility in Southeast Asia. The national boundaries — land or sea — are always porous and therefore it is very easy for people to migrate across borders. Indonesia is a very large country and covering wide, and porous, sea and land borders.

As described by Chalamwong, Thailand (as a country which sends and receives unskilled workers) has also hundreds of points of entry along the very long borders with Myanmar, Laos and Cambodia. These points of entry are also often in the form of undeveloped forested terrain that is very difficult to monitor. It is almost impossible to completely close these points. The cost would be too prohibitive. Worse, the institutions to patrol the borders are often understaffed and underfunded. The difficulty in controlling the borders is compounded by the sensitive political issues raised by the irregular workers from the minorities at the borders.

Chalamwong describes how Thailand faces the dilemma of providing the foreign, and especially the irregular, workers with their basic human rights and maintaining the national culture and identity. On the one hand, the cheap foreign workers may have solved the problem of shortage of workers in 3-D jobs, stimulated new labour intensive industries, and encouraged Thai workers to obtain better paid jobs. The migrants may also reduce the demand for higher-cost local labour. On the other hand, Thailand may become so dependent on foreign unskilled labour that the established family and community network may make it very difficult to stop the influx. The irregular workers may also contribute to criminal activities, bring diseases and stateless babies, and compete for social infrastructure such as public health and schooling.

The dilemma will still be seen in the foreseeable future because Thailand still encourages the migration of both unskilled and semi-skilled workers to find new markets abroad and therefore, there will be opportunities in Thailand to be filled by workers from outside Thailand. Some business persons have pressured the government to bring in foreign unskilled workers, for example for the fishery sector and rubber plantation in the southern part of Thailand. This pressure is to maintain high profitability and competitiveness in labour-intensive industries.

Furthermore, the issue of irregular migrants is also politically sensitive both domestically and internationally, especially because of the history of refugees from war and ethnic persecution, involving politicians, military, and stateless minorities. In other words, the influx of irregular migrants also poses a threat to national security, which may strain the diplomatic relationship between Thailand and the sending countries, particularly Myanmar.

Grundy-Warr explains that the human landscape of the Myanmar-Thai borderlands has been characterized by decades of low-level warfare, warlord politics, and huge human suffering. He recommends effort to understand the complex geopolitics of international migration — to find out the underlying mechanisms that bring about, and necessitate, the large scale of international migration. With this understanding, the solution to the issues of international migration can then consider the elements of security and human dignity.

The policy in Thailand must therefore be able to balance the positive and negative impacts of foreign workers. Chalamwong argues that Thailand needs to produce a thorough migration policy, accommodating both the emigrants and immigrants. Thailand should learn from the experiences of the Philippines in protecting their workers abroad through bilateral and multilateral agreement; and learn from Singapore in managing the foreign workers based on the industries' projected trends and needs. As shown by Asis, Singapore is the only destination country in Southeast Asia which has been successful in managing irregular migration. It is the first Asian country which is aware of its needs for foreign workers and has proceeded to produce a migration policy to respond to these needs. Brunei is another country in Southeast Asia which has recognized migrants as an essential component of its labour force and has followed pragmatic policies.

Chalamwong also maintains that if Thailand implements a highly controlled migration policy, it must be ready to face a situation of marginalization and conflicts in the society. However, if the country applies a policy of some measure of control and respect of human rights simultaneously, it must be willing to accept significant transformation in Thailand's culture and identity. With the rising democracy, Thailand should take a compromising approach by respecting the human rights of the irregular workers, as it also expects the same to be extended to its overseas workers.

Malaysia has also received a lot of foreign workers and has also become a transit point in international migration flows. Though Malaysia still sends workers abroad, the numbers migrating into exceed those migrating out of Malaysia. Bilson Kurus in Chapter 12 finds that the foreign workers are very crucial to the Malaysian economy, especially in the manufacturing, plantation, and domestic sectors. Nationally, more than 70 per cent of the foreign workers are Indonesians. However, most of the workers are concentrated in Sabah and Labuan, in East Malaysia. Sabah is also known as the largest concentration of foreign unskilled workers in Southeast and East Asia. Furthermore, Sabah is the centre of attention whenever issues relating to Filipino workers emerge. Sabah also shares borders with Kalimantan, Indonesia, and it has been directly affected by the flow of migrants from Indonesia.

Kurus argues that the high contribution in the domestic sectors also reflects the support given to the two-income households, the rising middle-class, in Malaysia. These situations are anticipated to remain in Malaysia unless the economy has been successfully restructured to be non-labour intensive economy and the local workers are willing to do the jobs currently performed by the foreign workers.

Malaysia, too, has attempted to control the migration, especially with the rising cross-border crimes and extremist activities (after September 11). The number of irregular migration has become a special concern for the government and society. Malaysia's tougher immigration policies can be viewed as an effort to better manage the undocumented workers, rather than to force the migrants out of the country. Ramasamy observes the government's fear that inability to systematically check the irregular migration may worsen the social and political problems in Malaysia. Further, its policy regarding foreign workers must also take into consideration the bilateral relations between Malaysia and the sending countries such as the Philippines and Indonesia.

It is interesting to note the findings of Asis' study on Indonesian workers in Malaysia. The close proximity between Indonesia and Malaysia has brought a large inflow of Indonesians to Malaysia. At the same time, this close proximity also means that the Indonesians face higher risks of being deported. Yet, Indonesians are still going to Malaysia and are not deterred by the higher risks of deportation.

A diplomatic tension between Malaysia and Indonesia can emerge if problems involving Indonesian migrants in Malaysia are not properly handled. Tirtosudarmo provides an example of the Nunukan (Indonesia), at the border between Indonesia and Malaysia. Because of the large mass deportation of Indonesian workers in Malaysia, many of them found shelter in the Nunukan, Kalimantan, where a high death toll had been claimed among them.

Interestingly, as noted by Tirtosudarmo, the flow of Indonesian migrants to Malaysia has attracted little attention in Indonesia, although it has become a political issue in Malaysia. Though the issues of overseas workers have received greater attention after the fall of Suharto, they are usually still limited to the margins of political discourse. Labour politics is a marginal issue in the mainstream Indonesian politics. Furthermore, under Megawati's presidency — with heavy emphasis on economic development and political stability — the issues of overseas workers have become much less important.

On the other hand, the impact of the mass deportation in Malaysia has concerned the government and society of the Philippines more than the government and society of Indonesia. Asis shows how, in the Philippines, the treatment of Filipino deportees from Malaysia has ignited outrage. Ogena mentions that the deportation has resulted in an anti-Malaysian sentiment in the Philippines. It has therefore strained the diplomatic relationship between the two countries. The president of the Philippines, Gloria Macapagal Arroyo, made a personal call to the then prime minister of Malaysia, Mahathir Mohamad, to solve the problems.

Kurus recommends greater regional co-operation towards the facilitation and management of agreeable and beneficial flows of migrant workers within the region. He is also aware, however, that the implementation of such a policy may be hampered by political and psychological difficulties in all countries involved.

Chalamwong's and Kurus' recommendations for Thailand and Malaysia respectively are consistent with the demographic imperatives usually found in many developed countries. Asis, for example, mentions that the ageing problem may push receiving countries to adopt migration as a solution which necessitates social, cultural, and political transformation of the receiving countries.

In contrast to Thailand and Malaysia, the Philippines is a sending country. As described by Ogena, not only does the Philippines send workers abroad to improve the economy, but the government also pays attention to the interest and well being of the workers and their families. The government created Overseas Workers Welfare Administration (OWWA), with funding from employer contributions, to implement programmes and services for the migrants and their families. The government has also provided a reintegration programme to assist returning workers in finding jobs in the domestic economy. However, in Indonesia, as mentioned by Tirtosudarmo, non-government organizations have provided many kinds of training to empower the overseas workers — to strengthen their political consciousness, to voice their aspirations to the government, recruiting agencies, and employers.

As pointed out by Ogena, the government of Arroyo has also encouraged the rising number of workers sent abroad. Indeed, the Philippines is the second largest country in the world, after Mexico, in sending workers abroad. The president mentioned that the economy of the Philippines will not be able to absorb the returning overseas workers; unless they can be resent abroad, their return will deepen the problems at home. This policy has stimulated debate in the Philippines. It has heightened the fear of the civil society that the government will do away with the protection of the migrants.

Ogena also raises the issue of human rights of migrants, particularly the irregular migrants. In 1990 the Migrant Workers Convention was adopted, to guarantee human rights protection to everyone entering and staying in a territory, regardless of the legal status. However, after twelve years since the adoption of the convention, only nineteen additional countries have ratified it. Receiving countries such as the United States and Canada seem to be unwilling to join the convention. This unwillingness reflects political, rather than technical issues, of the countries. Ogena argues that the tragedy of the mass deportation from Malaysia is an important case to show the necessity for the global ratification and adoption of the convention.

Interestingly, Indonesia is also reluctant to adopt the international convention. Tirtosudarmo argues that the strong vested interest of the bureaucratic staff in profiting from the lucrative overseas labour recruitment business has contributed much to the low priority of the political agenda on the issue of overseas workers. He mentions that the tragedy in Nunukan is just an example of the results of the performance of corrupt and ignorant Indonesian state bureaucracies in regulating the lucrative business of sending workers abroad. The Nunukan tragedy should be used as a golden opportunity to push the government of Indonesia to do more on its long-neglected homework — the protection of its overseas workers.

The need to protect workers, particularly the undocumented workers, in the receiving countries is even greater when the receiving countries, as argued by Chantavanich and Gemershausen (2000), view the workers as sources of trouble, crimes, and threat to national security. There is no law which protects these workers and the workers obtain insufficient legal assistance and protection when they are prosecuted and put to trial.

In short, international migration has posed a very complex and difficult question of justice in the management of migration in many migrant-receiving countries. Globalization has made international migration an inescapable topic in politics and policy-making. Migration may reflect the larger forces in the global economy and how governments optimally deal with the migrants, considering the socio-political conditions in their countries (Jordan and Duvel 2002). Kurus posits that migration becomes an important vocabulary in government policies when countries start being concerned with their own national borders and security even as globalization penetrates almost all regions in the world. In ASEAN states, as described by Grundy-Warr, international migration has become a truly transnational phenomenon — beyond the capacity of states to contain the issues domestically — and really challenges the state institutions. Yet, he argues that the ASEAN states see the issue of international, particularly unskilled, migration primarily from the perspective of sovereignty and security. The political landscape of the region is dominated by realist, pragmatist, and state-centred geopolitics.

Concluding Remarks

According to an economic theory, everybody will gain if we have free trade, free capital movement, and free labour movement. However, this theory is not applicable, because each country has its own interests. What is good for one country may be considered bad for another country. The theory does not consider the role of the political and social factors within and among countries. Politically, free international trade may hurt some segments of one society and yet more and more countries have argued for the long-run benefit of free trade for all involved in the free trade agreements. A similar reasoning is for the free international capital movement. Nevertheless, the most difficult and sensitive area is the discussion on free international labour movement. It involves human beings, and human beings bring with them their myriad aspects which may affect the social and political life of the receiving countries.

Yet, talks have been conducted to have free movement of skilled labour along with free trade and free capital movement. On the other hand, it is still politically impossible to have free movement of unskilled labour. It is simply unimaginable if a large number of unskilled labour with different religions and cultures suddenly or slowly overwhelm the receiving communities. Social and political tensions may arise and it may sweep away the economic advantage of having foreign unskilled workers.

At the same time, free trade, free capital movement, and free movement of skilled labour may bring the developing countries to the international market. Therefore, the populations in the developing countries are likely to enter the relatively more expensive international market to satisfy the demand from the more advanced countries. The cost of living in developing countries may rise, and the rise will become another push factor for the people, including those unskilled workers in developing countries to work overseas.

Furthermore, growth brought about by free trade, free capital movement, and free movement of skilled labour will also raise the income of some of unskilled workers. Hence, they have greater capacity to go abroad, to work overseas. This becomes another push factor for the migration of unskilled workers.

With this condition, tension will keep rising because of both the rising supply of unskilled workers — thanks to free trade, free capital movement, and free movement of skilled labour — and resistance from the receiving communities against the large number of unskilled foreign workers, despite the continuous strong demand for unskilled workers in the receiving countries.

As Hollified (2000) concludes, the issue is on the abundance-scarcity of resources, the social-human capital of the migrants, and the integration of the migration to the receiving societies. Migration need not be a threat to both sending and receiving countries. It provides remittances and employment for the sending countries, and factors of production for the receiving countries.

The solution is to address both the demand and supply sides. The developed countries must change the demand. They must restructure the economy so that they do not depend on unskilled workers, including not depending on maids (and foreign maids). On the supply side, the developing countries should continue creating investments that can absorb unskilled workers. Free trade, free capital movement and free movement of skilled labours should be directed toward the creation of much more attractive jobs for the unskilled workers so that they would prefer to work in their own countries.

The government of each country should also work hard to "clean" all migration stages — from the recruitment, during the employment, until the return — from any possibility of corruption and collusion between government officials and business persons dealing with the lucrative business of sending workers abroad.

As concluded by Asis, the existence of irregular migration has forced us to see international migration from an alternative perspective — that is, to view migration as part of the globalization and integration of the world economy. This is especially true in Southeast Asia, where cross-border movements consist of mostly irregular migration.

Within the context of globalization, the question may not be whether the border should be open or closed, but how open or how restrictive should the government be with respect to the inflow of international migrants. This is a very inter-connected issue requiring careful examination from many perspectives such as economic, cultural, and political conditions.

Though very delicate and sensitive, discussions on international labour movement should not be avoided. Both sending and receiving countries can discuss the issue amicably with cool heads, considering all aspects (not only economic) in both countries. The receiving countries have the demand, and the sending countries have the supply. Friendly discussions will benefit all countries. By having friendly agreements, considering the market forces and social-political conditions, labour forces in all countries in Southeast Asia can be more competitive.

Note

[1]   The discussion focuses on two sending countries (Indonesia and the Philippines) and two receiving countries (Malaysia and Thailand).

References

Athukorala, Prema-chandra, Chris Manning and Piyasiri Wickramasekara. *Growth, Employment and Migration in Southeast Asia*. Cheltenham, UK: Edward Elgar, 2000.

Ananta, Aris, Daksini Kartowibowo, Nurhadi Wiyono, and Chotib "The Impact of the Economic Crisis on International Migration: The Case of Indonesia". *Asian and Pacific Migration Journal* 7, nos. 2–3 (1998).

Asis, Maruja M.B. "Overseas Employment and Social Transformation in Source Communities: Findings from the Philippines". *Asian and Pacific Migration Journal* 4, nos. 2–3 (1995).

Asis, Maruja M.B. "Imagining the Future of Migration and Families in Asia". *Asian and Pacific Migration Journal* 9, no. 3 (2000).

Brettell, Caroline B. "Theorizing Migration in Anthropology. The Social Construction of Networks, Identities, Communities, and Globalscapes". In *Migration Theory: Talking across Disciplines*, edited by Caroline B. Brettell and James F. Hollifield. New York and London: Routledge, 2000.

Castells, Manuel. "The Power of Identity". In *The Information Age: Economy, Society and Culture* II. Massachusetts: Blackwell Publishers, Inc., 1997.

Chantavanich, Supang and Andreas Germershausen. "Introduction: Research on Thai Migrant Workers in East and Southeast Asia". In *Thai Migrant Workers in East and Southeast Asia, 1996–1997*, edited by Supang Chantavanich, Andreas Germershausen and Allan Beesey. Bangkok: Asian Research Centre for Migration, Institute of Asian Studies, Chulalongkorn University, 2000.

Ehrenberg, Ronald G. *Labor Markets and Integrating National Economies*. Washington, D.C.: The Brooking Institutions, 1994.

Hugo, Graeme. "Undocumented International Migration in Southeast Asia". In *International Migration in Southeast Asia. Trends, Consequences, Issues, and Policy Measures*. Jakarta: The Southeast Asian Studies Regional Exchange, the Toyota Foundation, and the Southeast Asian Studies Programme, the Indonesian Institute of Sciences, 1998.

Hollifield, James F. "The Politics of International Migration". In *Migration Theory: Talking across Disciplines*, edited by Caroline B. Brettel. New York: Routledge, 2000.

IOM (International Organization for Migration). *Migration Initiatives. The Bangkok Declaration and IOM Programmes in Southeast Asia.* Geneva: International Organization for Migration, 1999.

Jones, Sidney. *Making Money off Migrants: The Indonesian Exodus to Malaysia.* Hongkong: Asia 2000 Ltd and Australia: Centre for Asia Pacific Social Transformation Studies, 2000.

Jordan, Bill and Franck Duvell. *Irregular Migration: The Dilemmas of Transnational Mobility.* Cheltenham: Edward Elgar, 2002.

Martin, Philip, Andrew, Mason and Toshikazu Nagayama. "Introduction". *Asian and Pacific Migration Journal* 5, nos. 2–3 (1996).

Nyberg-Sorensen et al. "The Migration-Development Nexus: Evidence and Policy Options State-of-the-Art Overview". *International Migration Quarterly Review.* Special issue: The Migration Development Nexus 40, no. 5 (2000*a*).

Skeldon, Ronald. "Trafficking: A Perspective from Asia". *International Migration Review* 38, no. 3 (2000). Special issues.

Stalker, Peter. *The Work of Strangers: A Survey of International Labour Migration.* Geneva: International Labour Office, 1994.

Tapinos, George. "Regional Economic Integration and its Effects on Employment and Migration" in *Migration and Development. New Partnership for Co-operation.* Paris: OECD, 1994.

Zlotnik, Hania. "International Migration 1965–96: An Overview". *Population and Development Review* 24, no. 3 (September 1998).

2

International Migration in Southeast Asia since World War II

Graeme Hugo

Introduction

Southeast Asia's population has trebled in the post-World War II era, growing from 178 million in 1950 to 522 million in 2000 (United Nations 2001, p. 70). However, over this period it is not just in terms of size that the region's population has been transformed but also the fertility, mortality and migration processes shaping that growth have changed massively as have the characteristics and distribution of the population. This chapter focuses on just one of these processes, that of international migration which has not been as great an influence as fertility and mortality in shaping the population growth of the ten countries of the region but has become an increasingly important factor in the demography of Southeast Asia, especially in the last decade. Moreover, it is not only with respect to regional demography that international migration has had an increasing impact; it is both a cause and effect of much of the dramatic economic and social changes which has swept across the region over the last half century, especially in recent years.

This chapter argues that one of the most fundamental changes over the last half-century has been that in every country in the Southeast Asian region, personal mobility has increased greatly. As part of this, movement between nations inside and beyond the region is now part of the calculus of choice of many millions of Southeast Asians as they respond to change and consider their life chances. Many labour markets in Southeast Asia now overlap national boundaries, not just for highly skilled workers but also unskilled workers. While the expansion of international migration has not matched the expansion of flows of capital, traded goods and information between nations it has nevertheless increased substantially. All countries in the region are now influenced to some degree by international migration although the nature and level of that impact varies greatly. International migration is a topic of unprecedented interest in the region among both governments and the population. With newspapers and other media reporting on it daily, the issue is constantly in the public consciousness.

This chapter seeks to trace the evolution of trends in international migration in the region. The first half of this period was one of quite limited international movement in the region as most of the nations of the region made the transition from colonial rule to Independence. The first section of the paper attempts to summarize the main trends in international migration in Southeast Asia during that period. The bulk of the paper, however, focuses on the last thirty years and discusses, in turn, developments in a number of types of international migration influencing the people of Southeast Asia. The main forces shaping international migration in the region during this period are then briefly discussed. It then argues that there are elements in the existing international migration system of the region, including the increasing pervasiveness of globalization, namely migrant social networks and the proliferation of an immigration industry, as well as rapid social, economic and political change, which will lead to the perpetuation and enhancement of international migration in the region to some extent regardless of political and economic development and the interventions of government.

An analysis of the kind attempted here confronts a number of difficulties. Firstly, the vast size and cultural, ethnic, political, religious and economic complexity of the Southeast Asian region makes it difficult to generalize. Secondly, the data relating to international migration is incomplete or totally absent for most nations in the region (*Asia Pacific*

Migration Journal 8, no. 4 (1995); Bilsborrow *et al.* 1997) and there is a very limited empirical research base.

International Migration in Southeast Asia, 1945–70

In 1972 the United Nations Economic Commission for Asia and the Far East[1] convened the Second Asian Population Conference in Tokyo. These events are held each decade to assess the major population trends and issues in the region and assist Asian governments to develop effective population policies. The summary paper produced for the meeting (United Nations 1972) does not mention international migration, reflecting the fact that in the 1950s and 1960s, there was very limited migration in and out of the countries of the region. During the era of European colonial rule in Southeast Asia, international mobility was relatively limited but included some flows of major significance. The largest account, and that with the most long lasting effects in the region, was the immigration and settlement of Chinese in each of the areas which were to become the ten independent Southeast Asian countries. Chinese traders settled in port cities of the region before European contact along with Indians, Persians and Arabs. However, in the final century of colonial presence in the region exploitation reached unprecedented levels and the Chinese were permitted (and, at times, encouraged) to settle in the region. They were often given separate formal status within the colonial system. Table 2.1 shows that the Chinese population of Indonesia, for example, doubled between 1860 and 1900 and again between 1900 and 1930 so that they comprised more than two per cent of the total population of the Netherlands East Indies (NEI). The colonial system tended to channel the Chinese and other non-indigenous Asian groups into employment as foremen and white collar workers in Western industrial enterprises (Skinner 1963, p. 98), small and medium scale internal retail trade and provision of internal credit facilities and community services (Vries and Cohen 1938, p. 269) and service industry (Aten 1952, p. 1). Consequently, the non-indigenous Asian segment of the population was strongly concentrated in urban areas as Table 2.2 shows.

The rapid development of colonialism also saw a significant influx of Europeans into the Southeast Asian region as again the Indonesian case (Table 2.1) exemplifies. The international migration of indigenous groups in Southeast Asian countries during the colonial period was very limited. In the Indonesian case, for example, a small number of Java-born persons

TABLE 2.1
Indonesia: Increase of Indigenous and Non-Indigenous Population, 1860–1930

Year		Indigenous	Europeans	Chinese	Other Asians
1860		15,409,944	43,876	221,438	8,909
1900		34,666,659	91,142	537,316	27,399
1930		59,138,067	240,417	1,233,214	115,535
Average Annual	1860–1900	2.05	1.86	2.23	2.85
Rate of Increase	1900–1920	1.78	3.28	2.80	4.91

Source: Volkstelling 1936, VIII.

TABLE 2.2
Percentage Distribution of Indigenous and Non-Indigenous Population:
Indonesian Rural and Urban Areas, 1930

	Indigenous	Europeans	Chinese	Other Asians
Netherlands East Indies				
Large Cities	3.7	63.7	27.5	36.2
Towns	2.7	11.8	16.6	21.0
Rural Areas	93.7	24.5	55.9	42.9
Java				
Urban	7.4	79.9	58.7	40.8
Rural	92.6	20.1	41.3	59.2
Outer Islands				
Urban	4.0	58.1	31.0	41.4
Rural	96.0	41.9	69.0	58.6

Source: Volkstelling 1936, VIII.

moved out of Indonesia during the last century of colonial rule, mostly under "contract-coolie" recruitment programmes to obtain cheap labour for plantations. In 1930 there were 89,735 Java-born persons (Bahrin 1967, p. 280) and 170,000 ethnic Javanese (Volkstelling 1936, VIII, p. 45) in Malaya, 31,000 emigrants in the Dutch colony of Surinam and 6,000 in New Caledonia (Volkstelling 1933, VIII, p. 45). Smaller numbers moved to Siam (3,000 Java-born persons in 1920), British North Borneo (5,237 in 1922) and to a lesser extent Sarawak, Cochin China and Queensland, Australia (Scheltema 1926, p. 874). There were also some small flows of more spontaneous movement of peoples across what later became international borders. For example, there are reports of Javanese resettling in Peninsular Malaysia more than five centuries ago.

Labour movements from the NEI to Malaya increased in the 1930s (Bahrin 1967) and the major patterns are depicted in Figure 2.1. The diagram also shows the distribution of the birthplaces of Indonesia-born residents of Malaya recorded at the 1947 Malaya census. The number of Java-born recorded was 189,450 (an increase of 111 per cent over the 1930 figure). There were also 52,400 Banjarese from South Kalimantan and 26,300 Sumatrans, predominantly from Minangkabau from West Sumatra and Mandailing Batak from North Sumatra. The Minangkabau movement was a longstanding one with many settling in the Negri Sembilan area (Hadi 1981). There were also 20,400 Bawean-born and 7,000 Celebes-born people identified (Bahrin 1965, p. 53). These figures, of course, only apply to Peninsular Malaysia and it needs to be mentioned that there was significant movement from the NEI into British Borneo and, to a lesser extent, Sarawak.

The so-called "Boyanese" group presents an interesting case. They come from the tiny island of Bawean which currently has a population of around 66,000 and is frequently known as the "Island of Women". In almost all households on the island the male head or a son are away working in Malaysia or Singapore (Anon 1982). This movement has become a *rite de passage* in a society for young men to the extent that a woman is reported to have sought to divorce her husband because he "isn't really an adult man because he has never gone *merantau* (migrated temporarily)" (Subarkah, Marsidi and Fadjari 1986, p. 2). This migration is said to date back to links established with Palembang in the early seventeenth century when the Sultan of Bawean was converted to Islam by a missionary from the southern part of Sumatra. In any case they were recorded as a distinct group in the Singapore census of 1894 and had increased to 22,000 by the 1957 census (Vredenbregt 1964). They also appear to have established a Kampung Boyan in Saigon (now Ho Chi Minh City), Vietnam at the end of the nineteenth century (Anon 1982, p. 62). To many (perhaps the majority) of Bawean men, the Malaya Peninsula or Singapore has become a *tanah air kedua* (Anon 1982, p. 62) or second native country.

The Japanese occupation of most of the region ejected the European colonial powers and did produce some substantial displacements of population due to the forced labour *romusha* schemes which they initiated. In the early years of independences, however, there was limited

FIGURE 2.1

Pre World War II Labour Migrations from Indonesia to Malaysia

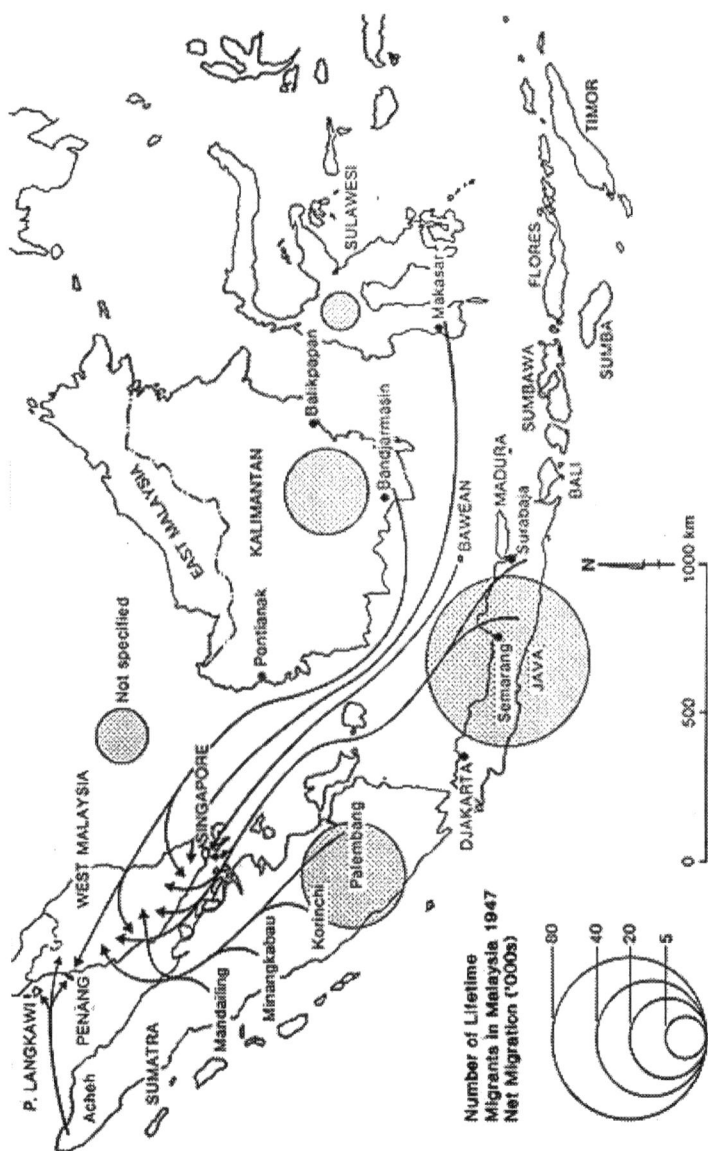

Source: 1947 Census of Malaya; Hugo 1993.

international migration. The main movements are briefly summarized as the following.

One flow was of Europeans who were repatriated as part of the decolonization process. This movement was exacerbated in situations such as occurred in 1957 in Indonesia when many of the main activities in which Europeans were engaged, such as plantations, were nationalized. The Dutch exodus continued throughout the Sukarno period and between 1952 and 1961 there was a net out-migration of 100,565 Dutch nationals, a peak outmigration of 29,842 being reached in 1957.

The repatriation process not only involved the return of Europeans to the colonial country but many British from Malaysia-Singapore and Dutch from Indonesia immigrated to Australia rather than went back to the home countries. In addition, in some cases groups who were strongly associated with the European colonialists accompanied them back to their home countries and set up communities there. The best-known case of this was the Moluccans of Ambon and other islands in the contemporary province of Maluku in Indonesia. With the expansion of colonial exploitation in the late nineteenth and early twentieth centuries there was a corresponding increase in the demand for soldiers, police and low level administrative staff recruited from among the indigenous population. In this recruiting, the Dutch had a policy of concentrating on particular Outer Islands ethnic groups, especially those who had been Christianized. Fisher (1964, p. 265) points out that the educational medical work carried out by Christian missionaries was invariably superior to that provided by the colonial government so that the ethnic groups influenced by missionaries were, from the government's viewpoint, far better equipped and trained to take up skilled and semi-skilled employment in the colonial service than were Javanese, Malays and other Muslim groups. Accordingly, many of these Christians emigrated out of their home areas to various parts of the archipelago in which European investment and colonial activity were concentrated.

> In particular, Menadonese (from North Sulawesi) have gone to Java as officials, clerks and accountants, and have provided a major component in the Netherlands Indies army in modern times, while Ambonese (from Maluku), besides serving in the army, have found employment as teachers and hospital attendants all over the country, and many Bataks have gone as clerks and overseers to the Cultuugebied (Plantations in Northeast Sumatra) and as domestic servants to Batavia (Fisher 1964, p. 265).

Many of these colonial functionaries developed considerable loyalty to the Dutch and a substantial number, especially those from Ambon, followed them back to the Netherlands where for most of the subsequent period they harboured the wish to liberate their home area. The Moluccans in the Netherlands currently number around 120,316.[2]

Notwithstanding the last group, the extent of so-called "south-north" migration during this period was very limited. Immigration to the former colonial provinces was heavily restricted and even though "traditional" immigration nations of the United States, Canada, Australia and New Zealand were taking in unprecedented numbers of settlers, their immigration policies largely excluded non-Europeans. There was a very small flow of students to Euro-American nations under schemes like the Colombo Plan. The flows of students, although small, gave rise to concerns about a "brain drain", especially to the United States.

The achievement of Independence largely saw an end to the long history of Chinese immigration into most countries in the region. In Indonesia there was a net outmigration of 142,653 Chinese over the 1952–1961 period. The peak outflow of Chinese of 102,297 persons occurred in 1960 following the passage of laws which forced Chinese residents holding dual nationality to choose between Indonesian and Chinese nationality and which prevented the Chinese from operating businesses in rural areas in several provinces.

One pattern of international mobility, which re-emerged in the region, was among Muslims (largely from Indonesia, Malaysia, Thailand, Philippines and Brunei) who undertook the Haj to Mecca (for example, Vredenbregt 1964).

There was also some limited international labour migration involving the deployment under contract of workers, usually for a period of two years in a foreign country. During the 1960s, for example, substantial numbers of workers from Thailand and Korea were recruited by Korean and United States companies to work on US military contracts and reconstruction projects in the then South Vietnam.

Increasing International Migration in the 1970s

There were a number of elements which contributed to an increase in international population movement out of, in to and between the ten countries of Southeast Asia in the 1970s. Some of these elements were global while others were relatively specific to the region. Among the more general patterns, there are several important ones. First is the revolution in global transport which dramatically lowered the real cost of international travel and enhanced the ease of such movement and in communications with the proliferation of radio, television and other mass media which greatly enhanced Southeast Asians' knowledge of other countries.

Second is the shift in immigration policy in the "traditional" immigration nations that saw the abolition of the racially based exclusionist immigration policies such as Australia's notorious White Australia Policy. Instead, immigrant selection became more based on skills and family connections.

Third is the initiation and uneven progress of the demographic transition across the world which exacerbated differences in the growth of the workforces of countries so that the gap between labour deficit and labour surplus economies began to increase (Hugo 1998a). Such differences combined with the fact that the countries with the smallest fertility levels tended also to have the most rapidly growing economies so that the demand for workers was enhanced in those countries while in the higher fertility countries labour surpluses increased. In addition, the increasing levels of education meant more Southeast Asians had the skills and qualifications to qualify for settlement in "north" countries.

Fourth is the initial impact of globalization seen in international flows of goods, finance, information etc., encouraging the growth of international population mobility. The development of global education markets began to gather momentum with more developed countries offering training to students from less developed areas, both through development assistance programmes and increasingly through full fee paying programmes.

There also were a number of developments which were more specific to the Southeast Asian region which also favoured the development of international migration. For example, the reunification of Vietnam and its aftermath created one of the world's largest ever flows of refugees. Another case is the massive increases in oil prices in 1973 which resulted in a massive demand for workers in the Middle East where there was a proliferation of development of large scale infrastructure projects. Several Southeast Asian countries were targeted to send workers, predominantly unskilled, to work on these projects. This was partly because some of the companies working on these projects in the Middle East had previously worked with Southeast Asian labour on the projects in Vietnam referred to earlier.

Several Southeast Asian countries also began to experience rapid economic growth as part of the Asian Miracle. This influenced international migration in several ways. On the one hand it encouraged immigration of higher skilled technicians, managers etc. from more developed areas. It also created jobs in unskilled areas which in places like Singapore could not be met fully by the local workforce which was growing more slowly due to fertility decline but also becoming less willing to work in low status, poorly paid manual occupations.

These changes resulted in an upswing of international population movement in the Southeast Asian region. Over the next three decades the movement increased in scale and complexity. More of the ten nations became involved and both high and low skilled groups moved. Women came to outnumber men in some types of international mobility. Some of the major developments are summarized below.

South-North Migration

For more than two centuries the United States, Canada, Australia and New Zealand have been receiving substantial numbers of immigrants and are among the very few countries in the world to have active immigration programmes. Until the late 1960s, however, these programmes discriminated in favour of Europeans and against Asians. Since the removal by the early 1970s of discrimination on the basis of race, ethnicity or birthplace, immigration selection is now based mainly on skills and family reunion, and Southeast Asian immigration has increased substantially. Moreover, Europe has also become a significant destination for Southeast Asian migrants, with movement partly being associated with previous colonial linkages. The change is readily apparent in Table 2.3 which shows the number of the Southeast Asia-born population in Australia over the last fifty years. It is noted that the numbers of Southeast Asia-born in Australia numbered only 2,827 in 1947. Although they had increased to 16,863 in 1961 the majority of these were not ethnic Southeast Asians.

Following decolonization in Myanmar, Malaysia-Singapore and Indonesia, many Europeans of English and Dutch origin instead of returning to their countries of origin immigrated to nearby Australia. This

TABLE 2.3
Population Born in Southeast Asia: Australia, 1947–2001

Birthplace	1947	1961	1971	1981	1991	2001
Burma/Myanmar	na	1,492	4,932	7,294	8,266	10,973
Thailand	na	371	1,004	3,346	14,023	23,600
Malaysia }	1,768	5,793	14,945	31,598	72,566	78,858
Singapore		2,759	5,532	11,990	26,000	33,485
Indonesia	918	6,018	7,981	16,166	35,400	47,158
Philippines	141	430	2,550	15,431	74,100	103,942
Cambodia	na	na	717	3,589	17,629	22,979
Laos	na	na	na	5,352	9,658	9,565
Vietnam	na	na	na	41,097	124,800	154,831
Brunei	na	na	na	na	1,643	2,069
Total	2,827	16,863	37,661	135,863	384,085	487,460

Source: ABS Censuses.

also was a factor in the growth of the Southeast Asia-born in the 1960s. There was a small but growing component of ethnic Southeast Asian students moving from Southeast Asia to study in Australia and some married Australians. Also in the 1960s the White Australia Policy began to be dismantled and for the first time a few skilled independent immigrants from the region entered Australia. The policy was finally dismantled in the 1970s and for the first time there was a significant influx of ethnic Southeast Asian groups. The Australian immigration policy, as it evolved in the 1970s, had a number of separate components all of which were channels for the Southeast Asians to settle in the country. Firstly, the refugee and humanitarian component of the policy was the main vehicle by which people from the former Indo-China entered Australia, especially the Vietnamese who became the largest single Southeast Asian birthplace group in Australia and by 2001 were the fourth largest non-Australian group in the country.

A second plank of the immigration policy involved family reunion which allowed residents to bring in family members. Many Vietnamese who entered Australia as refugees brought family members to the nation under this criteria. Many Southeast Asians qualified for immigration to Australia under one of the "economic" categories. A points test was used to select people with skills in shortage in the labour market. There was also a category of business migration whereby entrepreneurs who were prepared to invest a substantial sum of money could gain entry. In addition, student migration began increasing. The movement of Southeast Asians to Australia apart from the refugees flow was strongly selective of high skill groups. In some of the flows (for example, from Indonesia, Malaysia and Singapore) there was a strong selectivity of ethnic Chinese.

The migration from Myanmar had a strong "Indian Ocean focus" being directed predominantly to Perth (Hugo 1996a), and while being predominantly made up of Europeans and Eurasians, has recently included many refugees. Movement from Thailand has been relatively limited and in fact a large number of the Thai-born in 1981 and 1991 were children of Indochinese parents born in refugee camps in Thailand. Malaysia-Singapore has been a major source of economic migrants and students, especially in the 1980s. Indonesian migration to Australia has been slower to develop. It has been selective of Chinese Indonesians and skilled migrants (Penny 1993). There has been a large student movement and the migration increased following the economic crisis of 1997.

The migration of Filipinos to Australia has been substantial with the Philippines-born population increasing almost seven times in the last two decades. It has been a distinctive movement with predominance of family migration and females outnumbering males. The mail order bride phenomenon has drawn considerable attention from researchers (for example, Robinson 1996). As a result, the sex ratio of the Philippines-born population in 2001 was 52.6. Thailand, too, has been an important source of brides for Australia-born men with a sex ratio of 62.1. The Indochinese migration to Australia has largely been of people settling under the refugee-humanitarian scheme and subsequent family migration.

The patterns depicted for Australia are repeated with some minor modifications by the other traditional immigration countries. Figure 2.2 demonstrates how south-north movement out of Asia has increased substantially in recent years. Table 2.4 presents a summary of the available information on the Southeast Asia-born populations in the main destination areas. The large Philippines-born population in the United States reflects a long history of movement reflecting the colonial links between the two countries. The table clearly shows that the Philippines and Vietnam have the largest communities established in "north" nations among Southeast Asian nations.

FIGURE 2.2
Average Annual Number of Immigrants to Developed Countries
from East and Southeast Asia, 1960–94

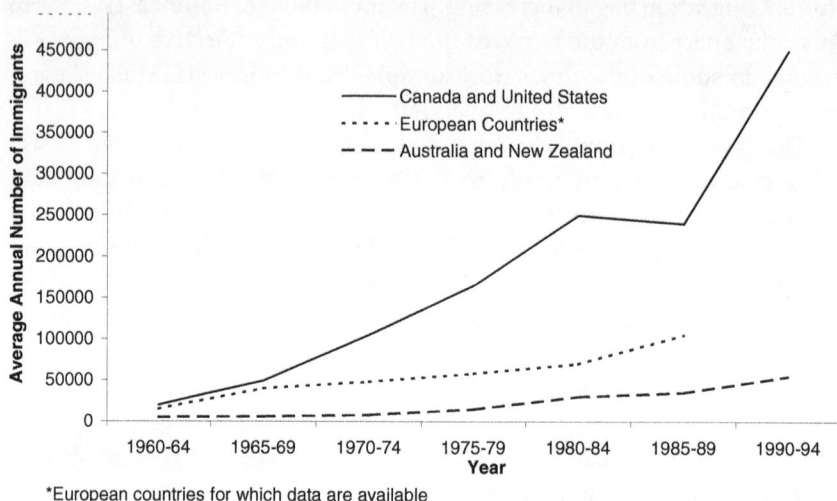

*European countries for which data are available

Source: United Nations, Population Division.

Refugees

Until recently Asia had more refugees than any other world region, reaching a peak in 1991 of 8.5 million UNHCR recognized refugees. However, the numbers have since declined to 4.8 million in 1996 and risen slightly to 5.8 million in 2002 (United Nations 2002) — nearly half of the world total. Southeast Asia was a major element in this during the 1970s and 1980s. This has been predominantly from the former Indochinese nations (for example, see Figure 2.3). The total refugee picture in Southeast Asia has been dominated since the reunification of Vietnam in 1975 by outflows from these countries. Between reunification and the early 1990s, some two million had landed in neighbouring countries. However, as Billard (1983, p. 24) points out, "it is possible to count those who finally arrived ... no one will ever know how many were lost at sea. The wrecks and human remnants washed ashore on the beaches of Southeast Asian countries give only a faint idea of the extent of the tragedy". In any case more than two

TABLE 2.4
Traditional Migration Countries: Southeast Asian Populations Around 2000

Source Country	Europe/Japan 1998	Australia 2001	U.S. 2001	Canada 1991/96	New Zealand 1996	Total
Brunei	na	2,069	na	4,425*	na	6,494
Myanmar	na	10,973	22,000	2,435*	513	35,921
Cambodia	47,400	22,979	92,000	17,965*	3,678	184,022
Indonesia	185,300	47,158	72,000	7,610*	2,715	314,783
Laos	31,800	9,565	117,000	14,445*	1,008	173,818
Malaysia	6,600	78,858	39,000	16,100*	11,889	152,447
Philippines	105,300	103,942	1,273,000	184,550	7,002	1,673,794
Singapore	na	33,485	23,000	6,285*	3,477	66,247
Thailand	25,100	23,600	142,000	5,220*	3,348	199,268
Vietnam	98,700	154,831	758,000	139,300	3,465	1,154,296
Total Southeast Asia	500,200	487,460	2,538,000	408,985**	37,095	3,961,090

Notes: * 1991
      ** 1996

Sources: ABS 2001 Census; US Census Bureau Current Population Survey 2001; New Zealand 1996 Census; Statistics Canada 20 per cent Sample Data; Statistics Canada 1992; OECD 2001.

FIGURE 2.3
Refugees by Country of Asylum: Southeast Asia, 1980 to 2000

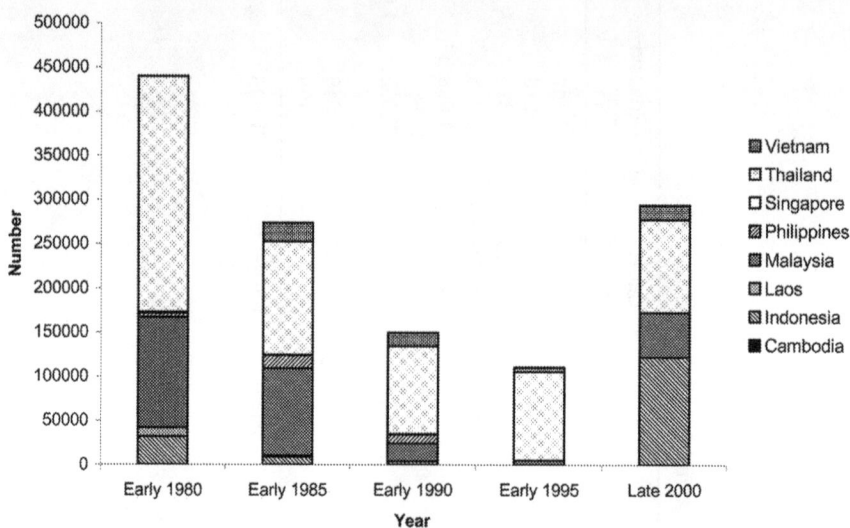

Source: United Nations 1997; UNHCR 2002.

per cent of Vietnam's total population left the country since 1975. During that period the outflow from Laos and Cambodia has made up more than five per cent of their total combined national populations.

Although almost all of these refugees landed in an Asian country of first asylum, the majority has been resettled in a third country outside of Southeast Asia. The initial flow of refugees was associated with the displacement of South Vietnamese during the reunification of the nation but the outflows were at their peak in the late 1970s and during the 1980s. There was controversy over those who were genuinely refugees and others who were refused refugee status and repatriated. The drying up of the refugee flows began with the UNHCR's Comprehensive Plan of Action (signed in 1989 by Western countries, countries of first asylum such as Indonesia, Malaysia, etc. and Vietnam) which reduced the number of Indo-Chinese refugees leaving their home countries. Nevertheless, there was a residual group in camps for most of the 1990s.

There are also smaller but locally significant flows that have been important in Southeast Asia. Perhaps the most substantial of these has been the refugee outflow from Burma. There have been longstanding flows of Rohinga Muslims into Bangladesh due to persecution in predominantly Buddhist Myanmar. In 1992, some 300,000 entered Bangladesh (Rogge 1993, p. 4). There has been movement across the Myanmar-Thailand border for many years, but crackdowns by the military government in Burma caused large-scale movements into Thailand in 1991–92, involving especially students and intellectuals and focusing on Bangkok. There are now more than a half million Burmese in Thailand, many of them refugees, and they were the target of government attempts to repatriate them in light of the financial crisis of 1997–98. Nevertheless, the migration of Burmese into Thailand has continued and while the number who are refugees and the number whose movement is labour related is not known, a recent estimate puts the number of Burmese in Thailand at more than 500,000 (*Asian Migration News*, 15 April 2002).

It will be noted in Figure 2.3 that there were 123,000 refugees recognized by the UNHCR in Indonesia in 2002. These were associated with the substantial flows out of the former Indonesian province of East Timor in the aftermath of the 30 August 1999 vote for independence. The outflow included two groups. On the one hand were people from Java who filled many of the government positions and the Bugis from South Sulawesi who dominated small-scale private sector economic activity. On the other, were over 200,000 Timorese who were placed in camps in several parts of Indonesia but especially across the border in West Timor[3] and near the West Timor capital of Kupang. With the restoration of order by a United Nations force there was some repatriation of the latter group. Nevertheless, in late 2001 there were still 143,471 East Timorese refugees in the adjoining province of East Nusa Tenggara (*Asian Migration News*, 16–30 November 2001). The bulk of them located in West Timor "awaiting repatriation in the face of protests of pro-Jakarta militia groups which continue to resist the refugees' return home" (Djalal 2001, p. 58). Other refugees were in Bali, West Nusa Tenggara, Southeast Sulawesi, South Sulawesi, East Java and Central Java.

Other significant refugee flows have included the movement of as many as 200,000 Muslim Filipinos from Southern Mindanao into Sabah in East Malaysia. The bulk of this movement occurred in the 1970s and early 1980s which was associated with the activities of groups like the Moro

National Liberation Front to achieve an independent state in Mindanao for the Muslim minority and the efforts by the Philippines Government to repress them. The large Filipino community remains in Sabah. There have been some smaller flows like that of perhaps 10,000 people from Irian Jaya/Papua in Indonesia to adjoining Papua New Guinea.

One crucial point about the large numbers of Southeast Asian refugees who have settled in "third nations" is that they have provided a basis for creating networks between the Asian region and North American, European and Australasian countries along which non-refugee migrants have subsequently flowed. These have included some 500,000 people who left Vietnam under the Orderly Departure Programme. These settlers have established communities which have been the "anchors" around which subsequent non-refugee migration has been attracted, especially via family reunion elements of the immigration programmes of countries like Australia and Canada.

Overseas Contract Workers

The largest international migrations influencing contemporary Southeast Asian countries are those involving largely non-permanent labour movements. These types of migrations have a long history in Southeast Asia (Hugo 1997a) but entered a new era in scale and complexity with the 1973 increase in oil prices and the associated massive demand for workers in the Middle East with the development of infrastructure projects. This demand was partly met from Southeast Asia, especially the Philippines. Table 2.5 shows the trajectory that official deployment of Overseas Contract Workers (OCWs) took over the 1975–94 period in the four main labour supplier nations in the region. In addition to the official movements of OCWs there has been substantial undocumented labour migration in the area. The largest single flow of undocumented migration has been from Indonesia to Malaysia (Hugo 1993), a flow which is second only to the Mexico-U.S. movement in terms of the scale of longstanding undocumented migration. There have also been substantial undocumented flows into Thailand from Myanmar and from Thailand into Malaysia.

Table 2.5 shows the increasing tempo of OCW movement out of the Philippines, Indonesia and, to a lesser extent, Thailand. It also shows the increasing significance of Intra-Asian movement with Japan, South Korea, Taiwan, Hong Kong, Singapore, Malaysia, Brunei and Thailand being

Average Annual Number of Migrant Workers Originating in the Major Labour
Exporting Countries of Southeast Asia and Distribution by Region of Destination,
1975–94 (Percentages)

	1975–79	1980–84	1985–89	1990–94
Indonesia				
Western Asia	73.7	64.9	78.0	40.6
Other Asia	8.5	20.5	13.1	55.5
Outside Asia	17.8	14.6	8.9	3.9
Number of clearances	10,400	24,400	63,500	118,000
Myanmar				
Number of clearances	–	8,100	8,700	9,100
Philippines				
Western Asia	67.4	84.8	71.8	61.0
Other Asia	17.7	11.2	22.5	30.7
Outside Asia	14.9	4.0	5.7	8.3
Number of clearances (land-based)	42,400	274,000	353,900	498,000
Thailand				
Western Asia	75.5	81.7	72.4	24.4
Other Asia	7.7	5.3	14.6	71.9
Outside Asia	16.9	13.1	13.0	3.7
Number of clearances	6,300	60,100	89,600	86,800

Source: United Nations 1997, pp. 80–81.

particularly important destinations for OCWs from Southeast Asia. The growing diversity of destinations of contract workers from Southeast Asia is well illustrated in Figure 2.4 which shows the distribution of overseas contract workers from the Philippines, one of the world's leading countries of emigration.

The scale of labour migration out of Southeast Asian countries, especially the major labour surplus nations, has continued to increase and Table 2.6 presents the author's estimates of the current stocks of labour migrants overseas. This suggests that at any one time there are several million Southeast Asians working overseas. The significance of Asian destinations is in evidence.

There are broadly two systems of labour migration involving Southeast Asian OCWs. The first and by far the largest involves mainly unskilled and semi-skilled workers who are employed in low paid, low status, so-called 3-D (dirty, dangerous and difficult) jobs that are eschewed by local

FIGURE 2.4
Main Destinations of Labour Migrants: Philippines, 1994

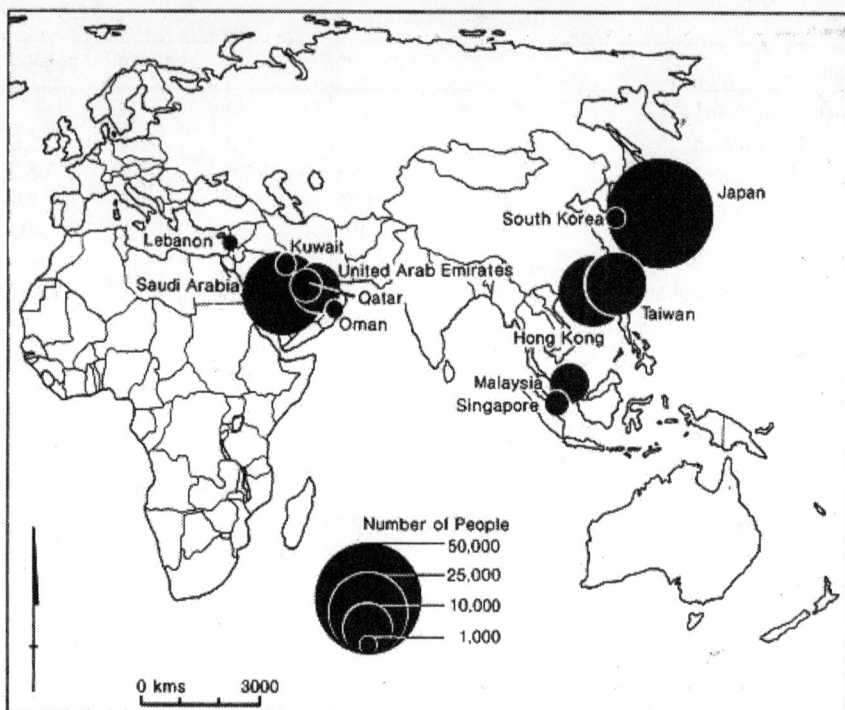

Source: Compiled from data in Rimban 1995.

workers in fast growing labour short nations of Asia and the Middle East. These are drawn predominantly from Indonesia, Thailand, Philippines, Myanmar and Vietnam. The second group are much smaller in number but still significant and involve highly skilled professionals drawn mainly from Singapore, Malaysia and the Philippines and are drawn not only to fast developing labour-short Newly Industrializing Countries (NICs) and near NICs but also to labour-surplus nations like Indonesia where there is a mismatch between the products of the education and training system and the skilled labour demands of a rapidly restructuring and growing economy.

TABLE 2.6
Southeast Asian Countries: Estimates of Stocks of Migrant Workers in Other Countries

Origin Countries	Number	Main Destinations	Source of Information	Year
Southeast Asia				
Burma/Myanmar	1,100,000	Thailand	*Migration News*, December 2001	2001
Thailand	340,000	Saudi Arabia, Taiwan, Myanmar, Singapore, Brunei, Malaysia	*Migration News*, March 2002, Scalabrini Migration Centre 1999	2002
Laos	100,000 [b]	Thailand	Asian Migrant Centre 1999, Scalabrini Migration Centre 1999	1998
Cambodia	200,000	Malaysia, Thailand	Scalabrini Migration Centre 2000	1999
Vietnam	300,000	Korea, Japan	Nguyen 2002	2001
Philippines	7,300,000	Middle East, Malaysia, Thailand, Korea, Hong Kong, Taiwan	*Asian Migration News*, June 2002	2002
Malaysia	250,000	Japan, Taiwan	Asian Migrant Centre 1999	1995
Singapore	5,000 [a]		Asian Migrant Centre 1999	1998
Indonesia	2,000,000 [a]	Malaysia, Saudi Arabia, Taiwan, Singapore, South Korea, United Arab Emirates	*Migration News*, November 2001	2001
Total	11,495,000			

a) Documented
b) Undocumented

In the contemporary situation it is possible to classify the nations of Southeast Asia according to whether they have significant gains or losses of migrant workers to other Asian destinations. This classification is presented in Table 2.7 and shows the larger nations of Asia in which the transition to low fertility did not commence until the 1970s or later hence remain labour surplus areas. On the other hand, in Japan and the NICs fertility decline was much earlier and economic growth has been more rapid and sustained over a long period. Despite strict immigration regulations the shortage of labour in these countries has led to major inflows of workers both documented and undocumented. These countries were mainly regions of emigration in the first three decades of the post-war period but have been through a rapid transition to become substantial immigration nations. This transition has been much more rapid than the similar transition in Europe and is a distinctive feature of the Asian international migration situation (Martin 1993, 1994; Fields 1994; Skeldon 1994; Vasuprasat 1994).

Two countries in the region currently are mid-way through this transition, Malaysia and Thailand, who are both recording substantial emigration over a long period but also significant immigration of workers from nearby labour-surplus nations (Indonesia, Bangladesh and Myanmar especially). In passing, however, it should be mentioned that in the

TABLE 2.7
Classification of Southeast Asian Nations on the Basis of Their International Migration Situation in the Late 1990s

Mainly Emigration	
Philippines	Indonesia
Cambodia	Myanmar
Laos	Vietnam
Mainly Immigration	
Singapore	
Brunei	
Both Significant Immigration and Emigration	
Malaysia	
Thailand	

contemporary situation all Asian nations are to some extent both emigration and immigration nations with highly skilled workers moving in to even labour-surplus nations because of shortages of skills in fast growing economies and the spread of Multi-National Corporations (MNCs). Brunei, in many ways, is more like the Middle East destinations of Asian migrants in that it has vast foreign exchange earnings which have meant that there are not enough local workers to meet the labour demands of the economy so that more than a third of the population are foreigners (Hiebert 1995).

Turning to the destinations of labour migrants within Southeast Asia, Table 2.8 shows that there are significant numbers of migrant workers in Malaysia, Thailand, Singapore and Brunei. In these countries the tempo of inmovement of workers has gradually increased over the last twenty years. This was interrupted by the onset of the Asian financial crisis in 1997 which especially influenced movement of workers to Thailand, and a lesser extent, Malaysia. Malaysia in recent times (*Asian Migration News*, August 2002) has introduced strong measures to detect and deport illegal workers. While Malaysia and Thailand have a larger number of workers than Singapore, the island republic now has one of the highest ratios of migrants to native workers of any country, certainly the highest in Asia. An issue of increasing importance in these destination countries has been growing labour market segmentation. Most migrant workers in the four main destination areas are unskilled and fill jobs which, because of their low pay and low status, are eschewed by local workers. Hence, even at times of economic downturn and high unemployment, the labour migration continues.

TABLE 2.8
Estimated Stocks of Foreign Labour
in Southeast Asian Countries Around 2000

Country	Year	Stock
Singapore	2000	530,000
Malaysia	2002	1,200,000
Thailand	2000	1,160,000
Brunei	1999	91,800
Total		2,981,800

Source: *Migration News*, June 2000; February 2000; September 2000; March 2002.

One of the major evolving trends in labour migration of Southeast Asians over the last fifty years has been the increasing involvement of women in that movement. This is especially the case in the Philippines and Indonesia where women outnumber men in the official outmigration of workers. The results of a survey of Florenese (Eastern Indonesian) undocumented workers to Sabah (Hugo 1998*b*) are shown in Figure 2.5. This movement was overwhelmingly of males from East Flores to work in the plantation and forestry industries in Sabah. Local custom strictly prohibited female outmigration (Titu-Eki 2002). However, over time

FIGURE 2.5
Number of Migrants by Sex: East Flores Survey Village, 1976–96

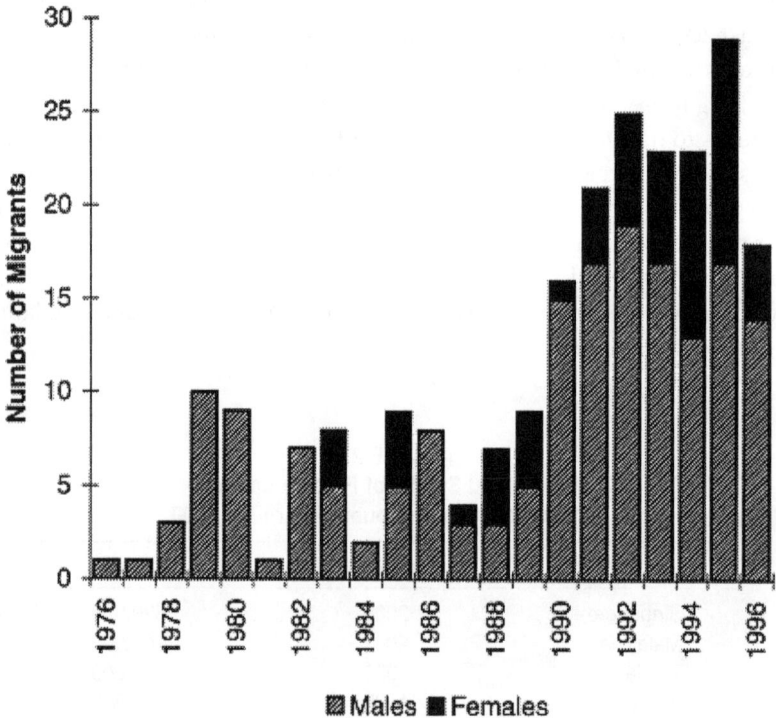

Source: Hugo 1998*b*.

women started to accompany husbands and brothers and eventually began to move independently to Sabah where they mainly worked in domestic service, as cooks, and in cleaner types of occupations. There is a great deal more occupational segregation among Southeast Asian female labour migration than is the case for males. They are especially concentrated in the domestic service areas (Hugo 2002) and, to a lesser extent, in the so-called entertainment industry and in factory work. The faster pace of growth of female labour migration than that of males is depicted in Figure 2.6.

FIGURE 2.6
Number of Indonesian Overseas Workers Processed
by the Ministry of Manpower by Sex, 1983–84 to 2001*

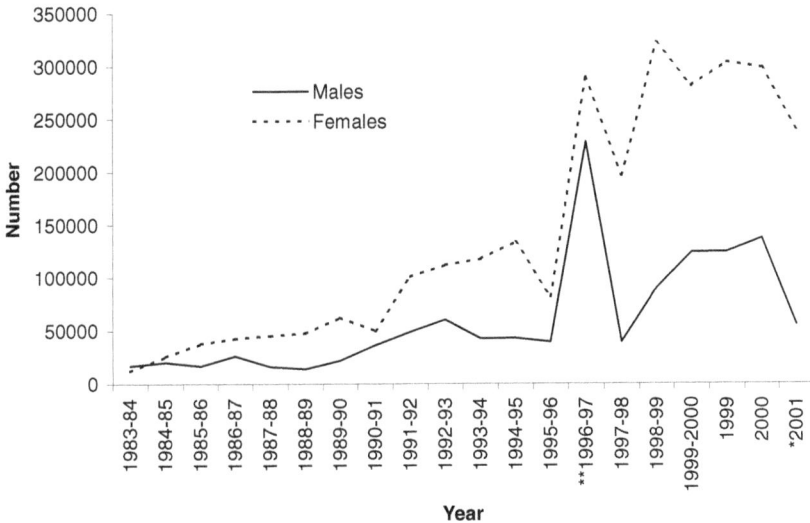

Notes: * To 30 November 2001.
         ** Year in which 300,000+ Malaysian labour migrants were regularized (194,343 males and 127,413 females).
         In 2000 the Indonesian Government transferred to a calendar year system of accounting from previously using 1 April–31 March.
Sources: Suyono 1981; Singhanetra-Renard 1986, p. 52; Pusat Penelitian Kependudukan, Universitas Gadjah Mada 1986, p. 2; AKAN Offices, Bandung and Jakarta; AKAN (Antar Kerja Antar Negara); Departemen Tengara Kerja, Republic of Indonesia 1998, p. 14.

The increasing feminization of Southeast Asian international labour migration over the last half century then has been an important trend. Another is the significance of undocumented migration. It is apparent that there are very substantial such flows in the region. They are partly a function of barriers to labour migration in many potential destinations but also are influenced by the high costs, delays and difficulty of some official systems in labour origin nations, especially in Indonesia. They are also influenced by the existence of a well-organized international migration industry which is important in both documented and undocumented migration. Over the last half century the industry has expanded exponentially. It involves not only recruiting companies, travel agents, travel providers etc. but a myriad of local sub-agents, small scale transporters etc. Moreover, over the year strong linkages have been developed between origin and destination areas which have contributed increasingly to the flow of labour migrants.

A crucial question relating to the burgeoning international labour migration impinging upon Asia is the extent to which the migration will remain temporary. At present the bulk of OCWs return to their homeland. However, the policy makers in destination nations are conscious of the experience with guest workers in Europe in the 1950s and 1960s whereby temporary labour migration became transformed into permanent settlement (Castles, Booth and Wallace 1984). There are signs that some Asian labour migrants are settling more or less permanently at their destinations (for example, the Indonesians in Malaysia; Hugo 1998b). However, it is not clear as yet how widespread this pattern is.

North-South Migration

In contemporary Southeast Asia the rapid growth and restructuring of national economies has been accompanied by an increasing influx of skilled workers and business people from Europe, North America and Australasia on a mostly temporary, but long-term, basis. This has been in addition to significant movement of professionals and other highly skilled workers within the Asian region largely from countries with education systems producing larger numbers of such workers than their own economies can currently absorb especially India, the Philippines, Pakistan, Sri Lanka and Bangladesh. The influx of professionals, business people and technical workers from More Developed Countries (MDCs) is associated with two factors.

First is the massive growth of investment by multinational operations in the region which has seen the MNCs transfer large numbers of MDC origin staff into Asia. Hence by 1994 there were 689,895 Japanese citizens officially living overseas, many in Southeast Asia (Okunishi 1995, p. 141). Second is the mismatches between the education and training systems and labour market skill needs in rapidly growing economies like Indonesia whereby, notwithstanding high levels of under-employment and educated unemployment, substantial numbers of expatriate engineers, technicians, accountants, finance and management experts, etc. have had to be imported (Hugo 1996b). The result has been a substantial influx from MDCs of highly trained people into the rapidly growing economies of the Southeast Asian region.

In addition to documented overseas workers, there are also many expatriates who enter Asian nations under tourist visas but subsequently engage in some work (*Manila Chronicle*, 16 December 1994). The media in the region are increasingly carrying stories opposing the impact of foreign skilled workers for individual projects (for example, *Economic and Business Review Indonesia*, 24 September 1994). However, in a survey of 3,000 *Far Eastern Economic Review* readers in April–June 1994, only in Malaysia was there a predominantly positive response to the statement "There are too many foreigners in my country".

An important element in this north-south flow of migrants is a reverse flow to the south-north migration considered earlier. A common phrase used in contemporary Asian countries with fast growing economies in recent years is "reverse brain drain". It refers to the phenomenon of a repatriation of nationals and former nationals who have spent a considerable period living and working overseas in an MDC. This movement has been gathering momentum throughout the late 1980s and 1990s and is partly associated with the burgeoning opportunities in the rapidly growing, restructuring and labour shortage economies of their home country. Moreover, the dynamism of the economies of their home countries has contrasted with the low growth and economic downturns experienced by some MDCs in the early 1990s. In addition, in several countries in the region there has been a deliberate policy to attract back former emigrants who have particular technical, professional and business skills (Hugo 1996c).

The reverse brain drain is only one part of a complex pattern of return migration from MDCs, although the scale is difficult to establish since most MDCs do not keep comprehensive emigration statistics (Hugo 1994).

Australia is one of the few such nations which keep accurate and comprehensive data sets on all persons leaving the country so we will concentrate here on those data. In the case of more permanent emigrants from Asian countries, two patterns of return migration appear to be occurring. First is return migration of the conventional type whereby migrants return to settle in their country of origin. Second is "astronauting" whereby migrants shuttle between their origin and destination countries, often keeping business interests in both countries.

The pattern of return migration of Southeast Asian migrants from Australia over the last decade is depicted in Table 2.9. This shows the origins of the 299,386 immigrants from Southeast Asia settling in Australia between 1984 and 2000 and the number of emigrants from Australia flowing in the opposite direction. The highest rate of return from Australia is among Thai and Singapore settlers, suggesting that many of these groups moving to Australia do so on transfer with a multinational company and after a few years' service in Australia they return home. However, for the bulk of Asian birthplaces the backflow is very small indeed.

TABLE 2.9
Immigration From, and Emigration To, Southeast Asian Countries:
Australia, 1984–85 to 1999–2000

Country of Origin/ Destination	Immigrants to Australia	Overseas-Born Emigrants		Australia-Born Emigrants	Ratio of Overseas to Australia-Born Emigrants
		Number	As Percentage of Immigrants		
Southeast Asia					
Indonesia	23,626	2,488	10.5	2,731	0.91
Malaysia	47,939	2,108	4.4	2,388	0.88
Philippines	79,171	1,575	2.0	1,127	1.40
Singapore	16,511	3,245	19.7	5,338	0.61
Thailand	11,695	2,184	18.7	1,446	1.51
Vietnam	98,904	1,547	1.6	688	2.25
Other	21,540	594	2.8	921	0.64
	299,386	13,159	4.4	14,399	0.91

Sources: Calculated from Department of Immigration, Multicultural and Indigenous Affairs sources and ABS *Migration Australia*, various issues.

Student Migration

The exponential increase in temporary international labour movements in the Southeast Asian region has been more than matched by expansion of other moves associated with tourism, business and education. Some indication of this can be gained by examining the tourist flows into Indonesia shown in Table 2.10. One type of short-term movement of particular significance is the increasing tempo of migration of Asian students (Shu and Hawthorne 1996). Again the pattern in Australia is indicative. Figure 2.7 shows that over the 1983–2000 period the number of overseas students studying in Australian universities increased from 13,674 to 95,607. Half of these are from Southeast Asia. It is estimated that in 1994 Malaysia paid out M$49.9 billion for education of its nationals, most of it flowing to MDCs (*Far Eastern Economic Review*, 27 April 1995, p. 44). Moreover, there is little evidence of a reduction in student migrations out of Southeast Asia, although there is increasing evidence of increasing student migration between Southeast Asian countries.

There is undoubtedly a strong connection between student migration and eventual settlement of Southeast Asian origin groups in MDCs. It may occur through students who overstay their education visas, gain a change of status to a resident, or return to their home country on completion of their studies and subsequently immigrate officially to the country where they studied. Indeed, Australian immigration policy now makes it easier for many overseas students graduating from Australian universities to qualify for permanent residence in the country.

TABLE 2.10
Foreign Visitor Arrivals: Indonesia, 1979–2000

1979	494,366	1987	1,060,347	1995	4,069,478
1980	566,402	1988	1,301,049	1996	4,258,136
1981	598,715	1989	1,625,965	1997	5,185,200
1982	592,046	1990	2,177,566	1998	3,764,700
1983	638,855	1991	2,584,570	1999	3,920,300
1984	700,910	1992	3,060,197	2000*	3,084,100
1985	749,351	1993	3,403,138		
1986	825,035	1994	4,006,312		

Note: * Estimate.
Source: BPS 2000; Indonesia Department of Tourism Posts and Telecommunications 1992.

FIGURE 2.7
Overseas Students in Australian Universities, 1983 to 2000

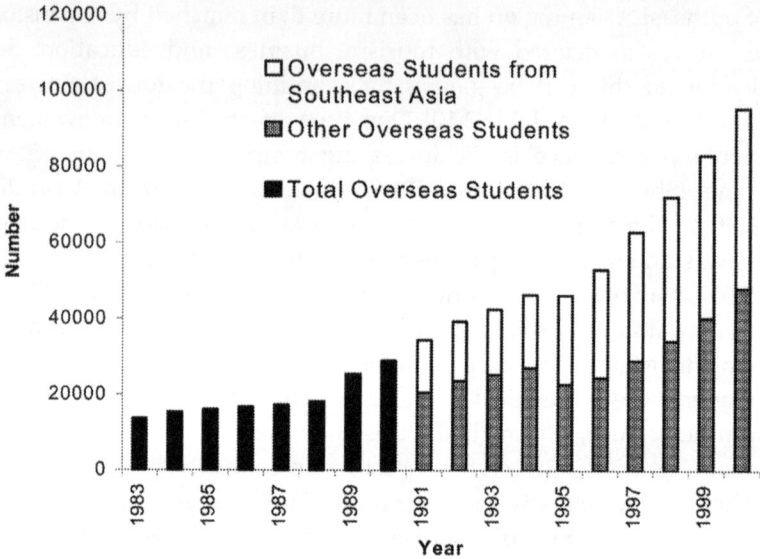

Source: DETYA Selected Higher Education Student Statistics, various issues.

Emerging Issues in International Migration in Southeast Asia

The earlier part of this chapter has demonstrated that the last thirty years has seen an increase in the scale and complexity of international migration in Southeast Asia. However, the data systems which have been put in place to measure and analyze the phenomenon have not kept pace with the development. Of the demographic processes shaping the region, it is the one which we know least about in terms of its scale, composition, causes and implications. No country in the region has included appropriate questions in its population census to establish the stock of immigrants in the country and the numbers of citizens currently working overseas. Flow data is little better with overseas arrival and departure data collection being of limited value for research and policy development. Labour migration data collection systems also remain underdeveloped.

The last thirty years, however, have seen an increasing involvement of governments in the region to influence international flows. However, while ASEAN has from time to time considered migration, no regional agreements regarding population movement have been conducted. Undoubtedly, one of the issues which has galvanized government attention, especially in the labour sending countries, has been the issue of remittances. Figure 2.8 shows the trends in remittances received in the three major labour exporting nations of the region. It must be commented that official data on remittances are substantial under-estimates of the actual flows since they do not capture money and goods brought home by migrants on their return and those sent home with friends. Nevertheless, the diagram shows that the remittance flows are substantial and increasing in significance. In the Philippines, for example, by 1994 official foreign exchange remittances of migrants was US$3.28 billion — a third the size of total merchandise exports from the country. However, by 2001 they had almost doubled to $6.234 billion (*Asian Migration News*, 15 May 2002).

There is considerable debate about the impact of remittances in the countries of origin. Table 2.11 indicates official remittance earnings relative to total merchandise exports and imports in the three major labour exporting regions. Again, it must be reiterated that these data greatly under-estimate the actual flows. The significance of remittances in the Philippines economy is especially in evidence. However, examination of remittances at a national level doesn't always reflect their true impact. Labour migrants are not drawn from randomly from across a nation's territory. Most come from particular regions and particular localities within those regions. Hence the impact of remittances is large in those particular areas. This has particular significance when it is considered that many migrant workers come from the poorest parts of their nations.

Government concern about international migration has heightened in both countries of origin of migrants and in destination countries. However, in international migration research generally attention has been most focused on countries of destination. However, one of the most distinctive developments in the Southeast Asian region has been in the development of policies in some nations to encourage, facilitate and initiate international migration, usually non-permanent international labour migration. Labour export has become an important part of

FIGURE 2.8
Growth of Remittances to the Philippines, Thailand and Indonesia, 1980–2001

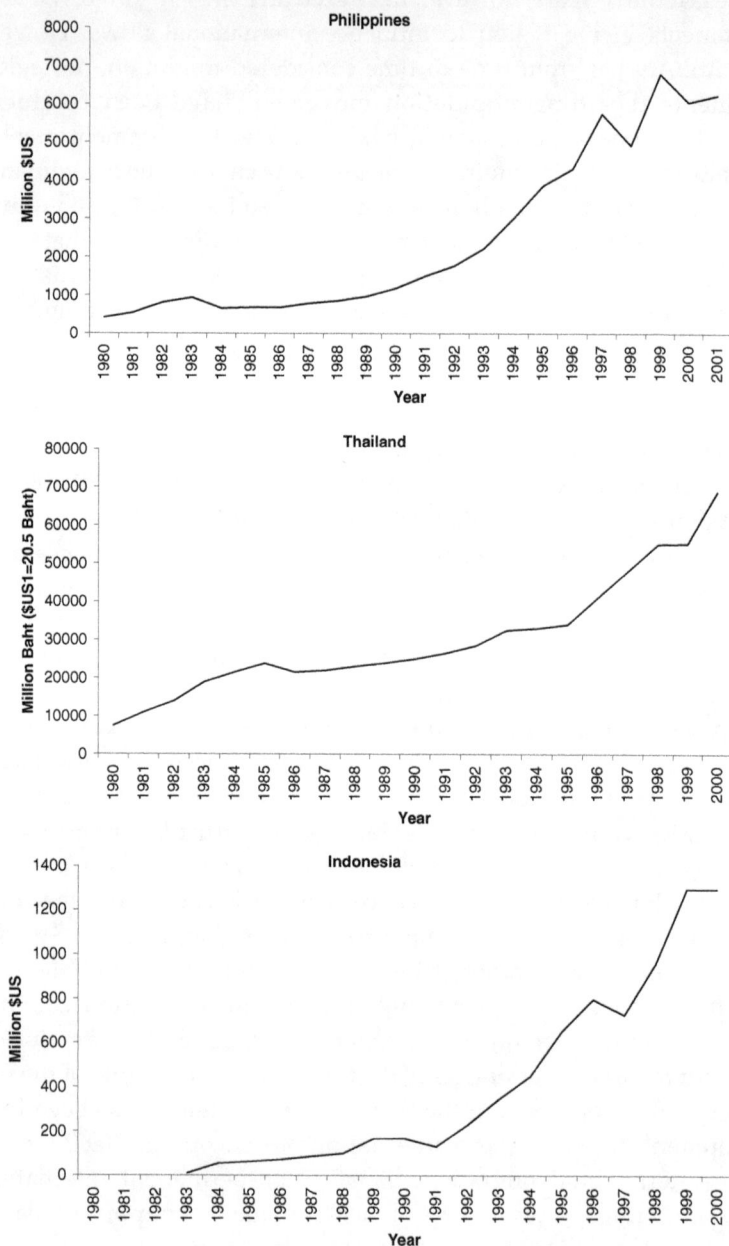

Sources: Scalabrini Migration Centre 1999; Go 2002, p. 12; *Asian Migration News*, 15 May 2002; Bank of Thailand; Chalamwong 2002, p. 16; IMF Balance of Payments Statistics Yearbook; Soeprobo 2002, p. 5.

economic planning in countries such as the Philippines and Indonesia with the objectives of reducing pressure upon national and regional labour markets, enhancing foreign exchange earnings, and in some cases, providing its workers with skills and training.

Indeed, as was pointed out earlier, sending labour abroad has become the largest single foreign exchange earning activity, outweighing commodity exports, in the national economy in a number of Asian labour-surplus nations. To maximize the scale and benefits of sending labour abroad, national governments have put in place a number of policies and programmes. The first example is that they establish labour export agencies within the government bureaucracy. Almost all labour-surplus nations within the region have such agencies although the functions they have vary between regulating the flow, controlling recruitment, training of potential migrants to exploring new markets for labour and active encouragement of nations to obtain work overseas. Second, they initiate special programs to maximize remittances — tax breaks, special banking facilities at destinations, forced remittance of a share of weekly earnings. Third, they seek out bilateral arrangements with destination countries to supply labour, to protect workers, and to provide support services. Fourth, they assist in re-adjustment back into

TABLE 2.11
Workers' Remittances Relative to Exports and Imports in US$ Million:
Main Southeast Asian Labour Exporting Countries, 1980–99

| Country | Year | Workers' Remittances | Total Merchandise | | $\frac{R}{X}$ | $\frac{R}{M}$ |
			Exports (X)	Imports (M)	X	M
Indonesia	1980	33	21,908	10,834	0.1	0.3
	1992	264	33,815	27,280	0.8	1.0
	1997	1,261	63,238	62,830	2.0	2.0
	1998	1,252	48,848	27,337	2.6	4.6
	1999	1,295	55,741	42,071	2.3	3.1
Philippines	1980	421	5,744	8,295	7.3	5.0
	1992	2,222	9,790	15,465	22.7	14.4
	1997	5,742	40,365	50,477	14.2	11.4
	1999	6,795	39,012	36,767	17.4	18.5
Thailand	1979	191	5,240	7,158	3.6	2.7
	1992	1,500	32,473	40,466	4.6	3.7
	1997	1,306	72,415	72,437	1.8	1.8
	1999	1,346	65,903	48,704	2.0	2.8

Sources: Hugo 1995; Battistella and Asis 1999; *Asian Migration News*, 30 June 1999; World Bank 2000, 2001; Soeprobo 2002, p. 5; Go 2002, p. 12; Chalamwong 2002.

the home community after migration. Fifth, they create special programmes to attract back former nationals, especially those with high-level skills or wealth, to return to their home country.

Some countries have built in to their national and provincial economic planning target levels of international labour migration, the composition of the flows and levels of remittances (Hugo 1995). Hence governments in some nations of Asia are not only facilitating and regulating international migration but also actively initiating and encouraging that movement.

Undoubtedly, one area of most concern relates to the protection of nationals overseas, especially temporary labour migrants. The Philippines over time has developed the most comprehensive regulations and infrastructure in the world to protect its diaspora of workers. However, even in this case there remain problems, especially with undocumented migrants. In Indonesia, NGOs report a high level of mistreatment and abuse of migrant workers abroad, especially among women and especially in Saudi Arabia (Hugo 2002). Throughout the region there is a pressing need for improving the protection of workers and encouraging the wider ratification of the relevant ILO conventions.

The increasing role of women in international migration in the region is of particular note. The role and status of women in Asia is undergoing rapid and profound change especially with the spread of education, increasing participation in the workforce outside of the home and increased use of contraceptives. However, little is known about the impact of these changes on population mobility and whether migration is associated with an improvement in the status of women. Much research into international migration in the region remains gender-blind or relegates migration of women to being predominantly associational. However, it is clear that the independent migration of women is gathering pace in the region but understanding of its implications for women and their families is limited. The fact that many Southeast Asian women move to other nations for marriage, to work as domestics or in the entertainment and sex industries means that they are often vulnerable to abuse and exploitation.

The sex trade has also become a significant element in female international migration in Southeast Asia. Women are recruited to work as entertainers or prostitutes in other Asian countries or in MDCs such as Japan and Australia. Thailand and the Philippines are important source countries of this movement. Brockett (1996) has shown how for Thai women there are a pattern of a circuit of movement to Japan, Taiwan and

Australia and social networks link the sex industry across several nations. One insidious element in this is the increased scale of trafficking of women. Figure 2.9 shows some of the major flows of women involved in such trafficking in the Southeast Asian region. This trade is largely in the hands of organized crime, some of it involving diversification from the drug trade. There are an estimated 150,000 foreign sex workers in Japan alone, most of them Thais and Filipinos (Sherry, Lee and Vatikiotis 1995, p. 24).

Although international movements out of Asian countries which are predominantly made up of women and place them in particularly vulnerable work situations are striking and of major policy significance, one of the most important trends has been in women becoming involved in the full gamut of international movements which have in the past not only been much smaller in scale but have been heavily dominated by males. Hence Asian women are now heavily represented in the massive numbers of students now spending several years in MDCs undertaking training of various kinds. This reflects the changing roles and status of women in LDCs. In Flores in Eastern Indonesia young men have been travelling for several decades to Sabah in East Malaysia to work on plantations and construction works. If women were involved at all it was to accompany or join their husbands. In the 1990s, however, young women from Flores are also migrating to Malaysia on an autonomous basis to work as domestic servants, mess cooks or housemaids, etc. In the Flores study mentioned earlier, for example, 24.1 per cent of contemporary migrants were women.

Increasingly, governments are becoming involved in facilitating or controlling the international migration of women. The Philippines has long had training institutions to train nurses to a standard acceptable in the United States so that they can work overseas upon graduation. The Indonesian Government has initiated a similar training programme and has long provided a compulsory course that women going to work as domestic servants in the Middle East have had to take before being given an exit permit. Mail order bride schemes involving Filipino (and, to a lesser extent, Thai) women in Australia, Japan, Germany, the United States, Italy and elsewhere have come under increasing scrutiny of governments, both at the origin and destination (Cahill 1990). There were 20,000 mail order brides from the Philippines to Japan in 1996.

The greatly increased scale of female international migration in Asia would appear on the surface to offer considerable opportunity for women

FIGURE 2.9
Trafficking of Women and Children: Southeast Asia

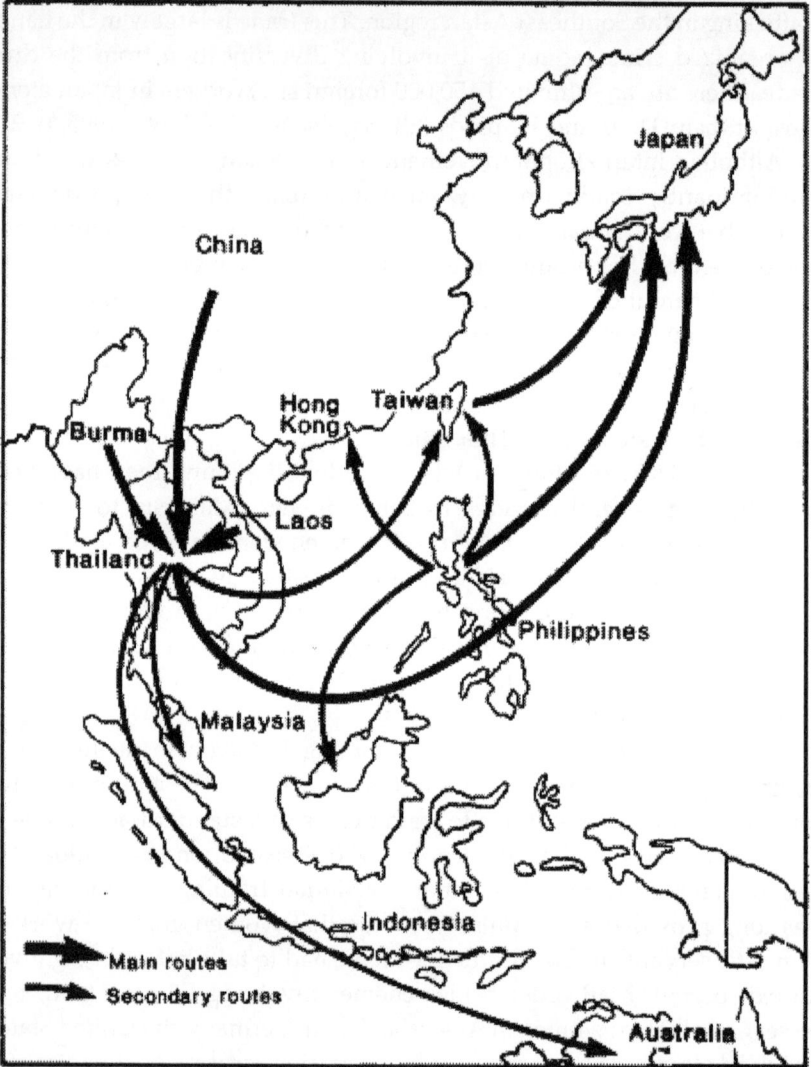

Source: Far Eastern Economic Review, 14 December 1995, p. 26.

to improve their economic and social situation. It frequently involves movement between contexts which, other things being equal, one would expect some empowerment to occur. Hence movement often involves a transition from a rural to an urban context, from a familial mode of production to an enterprise mode and from a "traditional" situation to a "modern" situation. It often involves women moving away from the immediate control of traditional forms of authority which are often patriarchal and in moving to a situation where they receive money for their work and where they have control over that money. For the first time they may be living in a situation which is not with their family. They are likely to be exposed to a range of experiences and influences different to the traditional way of life maintained in their village origins. They will probably meet people from a wider range of backgrounds and experience than would be the case in the home village. However, while such transitions can and do result in empowerment of the women involved, it is by no means an automatic result of migration. Indeed, as is shown elsewhere, migration can also operate so as to preserve, and even strengthen, the *status quo* with respect to gender position and relations (Hugo 1997*b*). Indeed, many female international migrants from Asia move into vulnerable situations and there is a pressing need for appropriate policies and programmes to protect their rights (Lim and Oishi 1996).

    In the early post-war decades there can be little doubt that several countries of Southeast Asia experienced a significant brain drain. International emigration from Southeast Asia was very limited in scale and had little demographic effect in origin countries, but most of the movement involved highly qualified personnel moving to MDCs, especially the United States (Hugo 1996*c*). This movement often involved Asian nationals who had previously studied in the country which they eventually settled in. The brain drain to the United States was greatly facilitated by the 1965 amendments to the Immigration Law (Pernia 1976, p. 63; Fortney 1972). In the 1980s and 1990s, however, when the scale of migration has greatly increased, the degree of educational selectivity of migration has decreased. The diversification of flows out of Southeast Asian nations has resulted in uneven brain drain effects. On the one hand it appears that refugee movements, family migration and contract labour (legal and illegal) have generally had limited impacts in depriving Asian nations of scarce talent crucial to their economic and social progress. On the other hand losses of skilled nationals through "economic" and business migration to MDCs and "leakage" of students remaining overseas after completing their courses undoubtedly represents a brain drain to some nations (Hugo 1996c). Hence, in the Philippines there is concern that a substantial proportion of the best quality science graduates emigrate (*Manila Chronicle*, 24 March 1994).

In Singapore the overall labour shortages have been exacerbated by a significant outflow of highly educated people. For example, the number of Singapore-born people resident in Australia has increased from 12,400 in 1981 to 32,700 in 1994 and 33,485 in 2001. Beng (1990) shows that there was an increase in the number of emigrants leaving Singapore from 5,040 in 1986 to 11,770 in 1988 and shows why this is of concern to the government. In addition, around 30,000 Singapore citizens were living abroad in 1990 — mainly students, professionals and managers (Fong 1993, p. 78).

It has been argued elsewhere (Hugo 1996c) that loss of highly trained personnel in some Asian contexts can have beneficial impacts upon the sending countries because of a mismatch between the origin country's supply of such labour and its economy's capacity to absorb them, the inflow of remittances from the migrants, the significant return migration of this group to their origin countries with enhanced skills and capacities, the other economic linkages which these migrants forge between their origin and destination countries, migrants can act as beachheads for origin country goods to be sold in the destination countries, and migrants in influential positions in destination based MNCs can direct investment to their home country.

One of the most controversial issues associated with international migration in countries of destination is its impact upon social cohesion. Some established groups at destinations fear that an influx of migrants with different ethnic, cultural, language and religious backgrounds represents a threat to the existing social system. The extent to which change occurs among the migrants and among the community they join of course depends upon the scale and nature of the migration, the characteristics of the migrants, their degree of permanency and upon the socio-cultural systems of the migrants and the host community. In each of the countries of destination the main intention is for their international labour migrants' stay in their country to be a temporary one.

However, the experience in Europe has been that many guest workers who originally in the 1950s and 1960s were recruited on a temporary basis, have tended to settle in their host countries (Castles, Booth and Wallace 1984). It is unclear as to whether this will happen to the same degree in Asia and indeed, there are already some indications of labour migrants becoming more or less permanently settled in some destination countries. This applies especially to Indonesians and Filipinos in Malaysia, although in both cases there are strong cultural and ethnic similarities between the migrant workers and the dominant Malay group. In Singapore too, some concessions have been made to Hong Kong Chinese workers and some highly qualified workers from elsewhere.

However, in general, the overwhelming attitude of governments and communities is for labour migration to be a temporary phenomenon. To this end, migrant workers tend to live separately from the local communities in destination countries and not be offered access to government-provided services made available to citizens of the country. With a likely continuation of economic growth and lack of growth in the local workforce however, it may well be that more labour migrants will establish themselves permanently in destination countries regardless of the wishes and policies of host governments and communities, as has been the case in Europe.

As is the case worldwide, migrant workers in Asia often find themselves accused of misdeeds by the host populations. Hence Indonesian migrants in Malaysia are stereotyped as criminals although the relevant data do not show any above average involvement in crime. They have been accused of spreading the HIV AIDS virus and other infectious diseases, although again the evidence of this is at best inconclusive. The experience with international labour migration in the Asian region is that a backlash against migrant workers seems to occur when there are some signs that the OCWs are settling permanently at the destination, establishing families, marrying locals, etc.; when the migrants begin to compete with local population by seeking work outside of the labour market segments originally set aside for migrant workers in low paid, low status dirty jobs; and when the migrants begin to compete with the local population for services such as health, education, etc.

Conclusion

Among all of the massive transformations which have swept across Southeast Asia in the last half-century, the increase in population mobility has been one of the most striking. There has been an increase in both scale and complexity of population movement both as a cause and a consequence of the dramatic social, economic, political and demographic changes. International migration has been an important part of this change. The scale, spatial patterning and composition of international movements have ensued with rapid economic transformation, globalization, political change, development of education, etc. Our understanding of these developments remains limited and in the last half century the research effort in this area remains meagre. If researchers are to contribute to the effect which is needed to modify international migration to maximize its beneficial effects and minimize its negative impacts, a considerable expansion of effort is required.

Notes

[1] Now the Economic and Social Commission for Asia and the Pacific (ESCAP).
[2] This was supplied by Dr. Philip Muus, the former Netherlands SOPEMI correspondent. The source of the data is Netherlands Statistics (Central Bureau Voor de Statistiek Voorburg, The Netherlands).
[3] An estimated 250,000 East Timorese fled or were forced to West Timor in 1999 (*Asian Migration News*, 16–30 November 2001).

References

Anon. "Mencari Lingdungan Datuk Musa (Seeking a Shelter for Moses)". *Tempo* xi, February (1982): 60–68.
Asian Migrant Centre. *Asian Migrant Yearbook 1999*. Hong Kong: Asian Migrant Centre Ltd., 1999.
Aten, A. "Some Remarks on Rural Industry". *Indonesie* 6 (1952–53): 19–27, 193–216, 330–45, 411–22, 536–59.
Australian Bureau of Statistics (ABS). *Migration Australia*. Canberra: ABS, various issues.
Bahrin, T.S. "Indonesian Labor in Malaysia". *Kajian Ekonomi Malaysia* 11, no. 1 (1965): 53–70.
Bahrin, T.S. "The Pattern of Indonesian Migration and Settlement in Malaya". *Asian Studies* 5, no. 2 (1967): 233–57.
Battistella, G. and M.B. Asis. *The Crisis and Migration in Asia*. Quezon City: Scalabrini Migration Centre, 1999.
Beng, C.S. "Brain Drain in Singapore: Issues and Prospects". *Singapore Economic Review* 35, no. 2 (1990): 55–77.

Billard, A. "The Largest Concentration of Kampuchean Refugees in Thailand". *Refugees* 3 (1983): 12–13.

Bilsborrow, R.E., G. Hugo, A.S. Oberai and H. Zlotnik. *International Migration Statistics: Guidelines for Improving Data Collection Systems.* Geneva: International Labour Office, 1997.

Biro Pusat Statistik (BPS). *Indonesia in Figures.* Jakarta: Biro Pusat Statistik, 2000.

Brockett, L. "Thai Sex Workers in Sydney". Unpublished M.A. thesis, Department of Geography, University of Sydney, 1996.

Cahill, D. *Intermarriages in International Contexts: A Study of Filipino Women Married to Australian, Japanese and Swiss Men.* Quezon City: Scalabrini Migration Centre, 1990.

Castles, S., H. Booth and P. Wallace. *Here for Good: West Europe's Ethnic Minorities.* London: Pluto Press, 1984.

Chalamwong, Y. "Economic Stagnation, Labour Market and International Migration in Thailand". Paper presented at Annual Conference on Economic Labour Market and International Migration, organized by the Japan Institute of Labour, Tokyo, Japan, 4–5 February 2002.

Departemen Tenaga Kerja, Republic of Indonesia. *Strategi Penempatan Tenaga Kerja Indonesia Ke Luar Negeri.* Jakarta: Departemen Tenaga Kerja, Republic of Indonesia, 1998.

Department of Education, Training and Youth Affairs (DETYA). *Selected Higher Education Student Statistics.* Canberra: AGPS, various issues.

Djalal, D. Strangers in Our Own Land. *Far Eastern Economic Review,* 18 January (2001): 56–59.

Fields, G.S. The Migration Transition in Asia. *Asian and Pacific Migration Journal* 3, no. 1 (1994): 7–30.

Fisher, C.A. *Southeast Asia.* London: Methuen, 1964.

Fong, P.E. *Regionalisation and Labour Flows in Pacific Asia.* Paris: OECD, 1993.

Fortney, J. "Immigrant Professionals: A Brief Historical Survey". *International Migration Review* 6, no. 1 (1972): 50–62.

Go, S.P. "Recent Trends in Migration Movements and Policies: The Movement of Filipino Professionals and Managers". Paper presented at the Workshop on International Migration and Labour Markets in Asia, Japan Institute of Labour: Tokyo, Japan, 4-5 February 2002.

Hadi, A.S. "Population Mobility in Negri Sembilan, Peninsular Malaysia: Evidence from Three Villages in Kuala Pilah". Unpublished Ph.D. thesis, School of Social Sciences, Flinders University of South Australia, Adelaide, April 1981.

Hiebert, M. "Give and Take". *Far Eastern Economic Review,* 25 May (1995): 54–59.

Hugo, G.J. "Indonesian Labour Migration to Malaysia: Trends and Policy Implications". *Southeast Asian Journal of Social Science* 21, no. 1 (1993): 36–70.

Hugo, G.J. *The Economic Implications of Emigration from Australia*. Canberra: AGPS, 1994.

Hugo, G.J. "Labour Export from Indonesia: An Overview". *ASEAN Economic Bulletin* 12, no. 2 (1995): 275–98.

Hugo, G.J. *Atlas of the Australian People — 1991 Census: Western Australia*. Canberra: AGPS, 1996a.

Hugo, G.J. "Economic Impacts of International Labour Emigration on Regional and Local Development: Some Evidence from Indonesia". Paper presented at the Annual Meeting of the PAA, New Orleans, May 1996b.

Hugo, G.J. "Brain Drain and Student Movements". In *International Trade and Migration in the APEC Region*, edited by P.J. Lloyd and L.S. Williams, pp. 210–28. Melbourne: Oxford University Press, 1996c.

Hugo, G.J. "International Migration in the Asia-Pacific Region: Emerging Trends and Issues". Paper prepared for the Conference on International Migration at Century's End: Trends and Issues, organized by the International Union for the Scientific Study of Population, Barcelona, Spain, 7–10 May 1997a.

Hugo, G.J. "Migration and Female Empowerment". First draft of a paper prepared for International Union for the Scientific Study of Population's Committee on Gender and Population's Seminar on Female Empowerment and Demographic Processes: Moving Beyond Cairo, Lund, Sweden, 21–24 April 1997b.

Hugo, G.J. "The Demographic Underpinnings of Current and Future International Migration in Asia". *Asian and Pacific Migration Journal* 7, no. 1 (1998a): 1–25.

Hugo, G.J. "International Migration in Eastern Indonesia". Paper prepared for East Indonesia Project, January 1998b.

Hugo, G.J. "Women's International Labour Migration". In *Women in Indonesia: Gender, Equity and Development*, edited by K. Robinson and S. Bessell. Singapore: Institute of Southeast Asian Studies, 2002.

Indonesia, Department of Tourism, Posts and Telecommunications. *Statistical Report on Visitor Arrivals to Indonesia, 1991*. Jakarta: Department of Tourism, Posts and Telecommunications, Centre for Research and Development, 1992.

Lim, L.L. and N. Oishi. "International Labor Migration of Asian Women: Distinctive Characteristics and Policy Concerns". *Asian and Pacific Migration Journal*, 5, no. 1 (1996): 85–115.

Martin, P.L. *Trade and Migration: NAFTA and Agriculture*. Washington D.C.: Institute for International Economics, 1993.

Martin, P.L. "Migration and Trade: Challenges for the 1990s". *Work and Family Life of International Migrant Workers* 4, no. 3 (1994): 1–21.

Nguyen, N.X. "International Migration of Highly Skilled Workers in Vietnam". Paper presented at the Workshop on International Migration and Labour Markets in Asia, Japan Institute of Labour: Tokyo, Japan, 4–5 February 2002.

Okunishi, Y. "Japan". *ASEAN Economic Bulletin* 12, no. 2 (1995): 139–62.

Organization for Economic Co-operation and Development (OECD). *Trends in International Migration: Continuous Reporting System on Migration: Annual Report.* Paris: OECD, 2001.

Penny, J. "Indonesians in Australia: From Migration to Integration, 1947–1986". Unpublished Ph.D. thesis, Department of Social Work, School of Behavioural Sciences, LaTrobe University, Victoria, 1993.

Pernia, E.M. "The Question of the Brain Drain from the Philippines." *International Migration Review* 10, no. 1 (1976): 63–72.

Pusat Penelitian Kependudukan, Universitas Gadjah Mada. *Mobilitas Angkatan Kerja ke Timur Tengah.* Yogyakarta: Gadjah Mada University, 1986.

Rimban, L. "Tales of Woe Don't Deter Pinays' Quest for Jobs Abroad". *The Manila Chronicle*, 3 November 1995.

Robinson, K. "Of Mail Order Brides and 'Boy's Own' Tales: Representations of Asian-Australian Marriages". *Feminist Review* 52 (1996): 53–68.

Rogge, J.R. "Refugee Migration: Changing Characteristics and Prospect". Paper presented at Expert Group Meeting on Population Distribution and Migration, Santa Cruz, Bolivia, 18–22 January 1993.

Scalabrini Migration Centre. *Asian Migration Atlas 1999.* <http://www.scalabrini. asn.au/atlas/amatlas.htm>

Scalabrini Migration Centre. *Asian Migration Atlas 2000.* <http://www.scalabrini. asn.au/atlas/amatlas.htm>

Scheltema, A.M.P.A. "Doe Groe Van Java's Bevolking". *Koloniale Studien* 10, no. 2 (1926): 849–83.

Sherry, A., M. Lee and M. Vatikiotis. "For Lust or Money". *Far Eastern Economic Review*, 14 December (1995): 22–23.

Shu, J. and L. Hawthorne. "Asian Student Migration to Australia". *International Migration* 24, no. 1 (1996): 65–96.

Singhanetra-Renard, A. "The Middle East and Beyond: Dynamics of International Labour Circulation Among Southeast Asian Workers". Mimeographed, 1986.

Skeldon, R. "Turning Points in Labour Migration: The Case of Hong Kong". *Asian and Pacific Migration Journal* 3, no. 1 (1994): 93–118.

Skinner, G.W. "The Chinese Minority". In *Indonesia,* edited by R.T. McVey, pp. 91–117. New Haven: Human Relations Area Files, 1963.

Soeprobo, T.B. "Recent Trends of International Migration in Indonesia". Paper presented at the Workshop on International Migration and Labour Markets in Asia, Japan Institute of Labour, Tokyo, Japan, 4–5 February 2002.

Subarkah, A.W., D. Marsidi and E. Fadjari. "Tidak Merantau Bisa Jadi Alasan Cerai". *Minggu,* April (1986): 2.

Suyono, M. "Tenaga Kerja Indonesia di Timur Tengah Makin Mantap". *Suara Karya,* h.v.k. (1981): 2–6.

Titu-Eki, A. "International Labour Migration from Eastern Flores to Sabah: A

Study of Patterns, Cause and Consequences". Unpublished Ph.D. thesis, Department of Geographical and Environmental Studies, University of Adelaide, 2002.

United Nations. The Demographic Situation in the ECAFE Region, in United Nations. *Population Strategy in Asia: The Second Asian Population Conference, Tokyo, November 1972*, Asian Population Studies Series no. 28 (E/CN.11/1152), New York: United Nations, 1972.

United Nations. *World Population Monitoring, 1997: Issues of International Migration and Development: Selected Aspects*. New York: United Nations, 1997.

United Nations. *World Population Prospects: The 2000 Revision 1: Comprehensive Tables*. New York: United Nations, 2002.

United Nations High Commissioner for Refugees (UNHCR). *Refugees and Others of Concern to UNHCR, 2000 Statistical Overview*. Geneva: UNHCR, 2002.

Vasuprasat, P. "Turning Points in International Labour Migration: A Case Study of Thailand". *Asian and Pacific Migration Journal* 3, no. 1 (1994): 93–118.

Volkstelling (Population Census). *Definitieve Uitkomsten van de Volkstelling 1930*. 8 volumes, Batavia: Depatement van Landbouw, Nijverheid en Handel, 1933–36.

Vredenbregt, J. "Bawean Migrations". *Bijdragen tot de Taal-Land-en Volkenkunde*, 120 (1964): 109–30.

Vries, E. de and Cohen, H. "On Village Shopkeeping in Java and Madura". *Bulletin of the Colonial Institute of Amsterdam* 1, no. 4 (1938): 263–73.

World Bank. *Entering the 21st Century: World Development Report 1999/2000*. New York: Oxford University Press, 2000.

World Bank. *World Development Report 2000/2001: Attacking Poverty*. New York: Oxford University Press, 2001.

3

Chinese Migration and Adaptation in Southeast Asia: The Last Half-Century

Leo Suryadinata

Introduction

This chapter examines briefly the migration of ethnic Chinese to Southeast Asia with special reference to the last half century, their numbers in Southeast Asia, their process of adaptation, the government policies towards them and their present situation. It will also discuss the challenges of Chinese new migrants as a result of globalization and the re-migration of the ethnic Chinese in the Southeast Asian region.[1] A general question on the patterns of Chinese migration will also be addressed towards the end of this chapter.

The Chinese in China have had contacts with Southeast Asia since the Han dynasty (second century), or even earlier, but mass migration of the Chinese only took place in the mid-nineteenth century when the West defeated the Qing dynasty. The upheaval in China coincided with the exploitation of Southeast Asia by the West, which offered new opportunities. The presence of the pull factors (economic opportunity in Southeast Asia) and push factors (turbulence and poverty in China) have been used to explain Chinese migration in the past which can still be used to explicate the situation in the twentieth century and beyond. However, in the late twentieth century, China possessed both the pull and push factors. Many first generation Chinese in the West and Southeast Asia, have returned, if not re-migrated, to China (Mainland and Taiwan). Nevertheless, many Mainland Chinese, especially from the coastal areas, continue to go overseas for new opportunities. They have formed some sort of identifiable patterns of migration.

The above are the factors, which contributed to Chinese migration from China to Southeast Asia and beyond. However, did the ethnic Chinese really intend to immigrate, in the sense that they planned to settle in the other countries permanently? Are the Chinese different from other ethnic groups in their intention to "go overseas"? Do they really intend to settle down? These academic questions are interesting and relevant to this chapter. However, due to space constraints, the discussions on these questions are only brief.

In traditional Chinese, there is no concept which is equivalent to "immigration". The Chinese term *"yimin"*, which is used to mean "immigration" today, is a new concept. In traditional Chinese, *"yimin"* refers to the action of the state to move people from one area to another within the territory of China.[2] The original Chinese term, which is "equivalent" to the Western concept of "immigration" is *qiaoju* or roughly translated as "sojourning".[3] The Chinese did not intend to settle overseas but to return to the homeland once they made enough money. However, I would maintain that the first generation Chinese migrants might have such notion but in reality many did not return to China. Also, it has to be pointed out that for subsequent generations, especially those who were the springs of inter-marriages, their chances of "returning" to the ancestral land became more remote as their culture is no longer "pure Chinese". The *peranakan* or local-born Indonesian-speaking Chinese are a case in point. Even during the 1929 economic crisis, many of the migrant Chinese, who were often called "birds of season", in reality stayed and did not return to the Mainland China. Nevertheless, the notion of settling down for the "migrant" Chinese in general and the first generation Chinese in particular took place only after the emergence of the nation-states after World War II and the ethnic Chinese decided to settle down.

The original intention not to settle down does not solely apply to the ethnic Chinese but also other Asian "immigrants". The Indians, for instance, were also "temporary" and only after World War II that they decided to settle down. In this sense the ethnic Chinese are not unique. Relevant to this sojourning attitude is the preservation of ethnic identity overseas, the Chinese appeared to retain their Chinese culture overseas and were not prepared to assimilate themselves into the local and non-Chinese population. This is a complex subject and the answer depends on the length of their stay and the country of residence. It should also be pointed out that once they stayed over an extended period of time, they had to adapt to life in the new land and the process of change had also taken place. This point will be discussed later.

The Number of Ethnic Chinese in Southeast Asia

The traditional sources of Chinese migrants were from the two southern provinces: Fujian (Fuchien) and Guangdong (Kwangtung). In Southeast Asia where approximately eighty per cent of the Chinese overseas stay, no comprehensive statistics on ethnic Chinese are available. The problem is complex but the difficulty of defining "Chinese" is certainly a factor. The majority of ethnic Chinese in Southeast Asia are not recent migrants, many have been in this region for many generations, and they have undergone the process of integration, if not assimilation. It is often problematic to identify "ethnic Chinese" in Myanmar, Vietnam and Thailand who have been there more than one generation.[4] Some have been "assimilated" or "acculturated" while many are partially assimilated. They are often no longer considered as ethnic Chinese by the country concerned, at least in their statistics. In Thailand (Siam), for instance, Chinese of Thai citizenship is considered Thai and will not show in the population census as Chinese. Many countries such as the Philippines and Indonesia (before 2000) did not include ethnic background in their population censuses at all. Therefore, there were no official figures on ethnic Chinese population. Only in Malaysia, Singapore and Brunei did they include ethnic (racial) categories in their censuses and hence it is easier to count the numbers of ethnic Chinese.

Who are the ethnic Chinese in Southeast Asia? In some countries it is easy to identify them as those people with Chinese surnames who still speak Chinese. However, in some countries such as Thailand, the

Philippines and Indonesia, there are many people of Chinese descent who no longer have Chinese surnames and do not speak and write Chinese. In the local context, these residents are still considered to be Chinese by non-Chinese members of the population and may also choose to identify themselves as ethnic Chinese.

For discussion purposes, the term ethnic Chinese is used here to refer to those people who have or had Chinese surnames, and who claim to have a common Chinese ancestry, whether real or imagined. Some even possess a form of "double identity" such that they are both Chinese and Thai, and the categorization "of Chinese descent" is more appropriate than "ethnic Chinese". However, I still use the term ethnic Chinese to include those who are "of Chinese descent" and "ethnic Chinese proper". Due to the complexity of the definition, it is therefore difficult, if not impossible, to give a precise number of ethnic Chinese. With the exception of Singapore, Malaysia and Brunei, the numbers of Chinese population presented in Table 3.1 are based on an educated guess.[5]

TABLE 3.1
Chinese Population in Southeast Asia, 1930s

Country	Total Population	Ethnic Chinese	% of Ethnic Chinese
Brunei (1931)	30,135	2,683	8.9
Cambodia (1937)	3,046,000	106,000	3.48
Indonesia (1930)	60,727,000	1,233,000	2.03
Laos (1937)	1,012,000	3,000	0.3
Malaya (1931)*	3,788,000	1,285,000	33.92
Myanmar (Burma 1931)	14,667,146	193,594	1.32
Philippines (1939)	16,000,000	117,487	0.73
Singapore (1931)	557,745	418,640	75.1
Thailand (1937)#	14,464,105	154,118	10.66
Vietnam (1931)	18,972,000	217,000	1.14
Total	133,264,431	3,730522	2.88

Notes: * Excluding Sarawak and North Borneo (Sabah).
#The official figure for ethnic Chinese was 534,062 (3.69%). But I use William Skinner's estimate here for the number of ethnic Chinese in Thailand. See Skinner (1957, p. 186).
Source: Purcell (1965, pp. 43, 173, 223, 504); Landon (1940, p. 22).

During the colonial period, the number of ethnic Chinese in Southeast Asia increased remarkably. In the 1930s, the number of ethnic Chinese was about four million, consisting of 2.88 per cent of the total Southeast Asian population. Apart from Singapore, the Chinese have always formed a minority group, ranging from 0.3 per cent (Laos) to 33.92 per cent (Malaya). However, the Chinese constituted a significant minority. They are especially important in terms of the economic and social life of the countries. In the past, they have always been identified as the trading minority of Southeast Asia.[6] They served as the middlemen between the Europeans and the indigenous population. The middle distributive trade was in the hands of the Chinese. However, recent studies reveal that as late as the eighteenth century, the sea trade in the region was still controlled by the Chinese. European scholars called Southeast Asia of the eighteenth century as the "Century of the Chinese".

As a matter of fact, the role of the Chinese went beyond trading to cover mining, the arts, the press, and film industry. They often served as pioneers in many Southeast Asian countries. However, the focus on the economic activities often blurred the role of the ethnic Chinese in other areas.

Through natural increase and migration (both legal and illegal), the number of Chinese in Southeast Asia has increased drastically. There were about 20 million ethnic Chinese in Southeast Asia in 2000 (Table 3.2), five times larger than the figures of the 1930s. However, in proportion to the total local population, in Southeast Asia as a whole it increased from 2.80 per cent to 4.04 per cent, but in some countries the actual percentage of the Chinese declined. The decline in the total percentage of the Chinese may be explained in terms of the domestic situation in the country concerned. The individual government policy is an important factor.

After World War II, Southeast Asian countries, which were mainly colonies of the West, became independent. The Chinese who were born in Southeast Asia faced a new situation. In the past, they were claimed by both China and the colonial governments as their subjects, hence these Chinese often possessed dual "citizenship". However, after independence, the Chinese were faced with the challenge of nation-building. They had to choose between local citizenship and that of China. While the first-generation Chinese were not given a choice, the second-generation Chinese were often offered local citizenship. It is safe to say that the majority of the

TABLE 3.2
Chinese Population in Southeast Asia, 2000

Country	Total Population	Ethnic Chinese	% of Ethnic Chinese
Brunei	323,600	48,600	15.0
Cambodia	10,946,000	109,000	1.0
Indonesia*	201,000,000	4,020,000	2.0
Laos	5,297,000	212,000	0.4
Malaysia	21,889.900	5,691.900	26.0
Myanmar (Burma)	46,400,000	324,800	0.7
Philippines	74,454,000	968,000	1.3
Singapore	3,263,209	2,505,379	76.8
Thailand	60,606,947	5,234,000	8.6
Vietnam	78,705,000	1,181,000	1.5
Total	502,895,656	20,292,679	4.04

Note: * The Indonesian Chinese figure is based on our estimate of 1.5% to 2.0%. I have used 2% for this table, in light of the 2000 Census. See Leo Suryadinata, Evi Nurvidya Arifin and Aris Ananta, *Indonesia's Population: Ethnicity and Religion in a Changing Political Landscape*, Singapore: ISEAS, 2003.
Source: Amstrong (2001, p. 2), and various statistics.

Chinese in Southeast Asia are now Southeast Asian citizens. The Southeast-Asianization of ethnic Chinese has taken place.

It should be noted that I do not have information on the number of ethnic Chinese who are non-citizens in all Southeast Asian countries (See Table 3.3). But from the figures of the four countries, it is clear that the number of foreign Chinese constitutes only between 0.83 per cent (Singapore) to 4.15 per cent (Thailand) of the total Chinese population. I believe that with the possible exception of Indonesia, these foreign citizens are likely to be foreign-born rather than local-born, as many Southeast Asian countries offered local citizenship to their local-born Chinese. Also, naturalization was made easier in most of the Southeast Asian states in the last few decades.

The Cold War and Half-Century of Nation-Building

Since independence, Southeast Asian states have started the nation-building process. Local citizenship is the first step for the Southeast Asian

TABLE 3.3
Foreign Chinese in Southeast Asia

Country	No. of Foreign Chinese	% of Chinese Population
Brunei	N.A.	N.A.
Cambodia	N. A.	N.A.
Indonesia	93,717 (4,020,000)	2.33
Laos	N.A.	N.A.
Malaysia	N.A.	N.A.
Myanmar (Burma)	45,898 (324,800)	1.41
Philippines	N.A.	N.A.
Singapore	220,762 (2,505,379)	0.83
Thailand	217,135 (5,234,000)	4.15
Vietnam	N.A.	N.A.

Sources: *Statistical Year Book 2000* (Myanmar), p. 26; *Statistical Year Book Thailand* (2000, pp. 64–65); *Population Census 2000 Indonesia.*

governments to integrate the ethnic Chinese. It is safe to say that generally all countries in Southeast Asia have adopted an integrationist approach towards their Chinese population. However, if we examine the policies more closely, behind this integrationist approach, some have adopted values integration but others have introduced assimilation and accommodation policies. Occasionally expulsion has also been used as a drastic measure to reduce the Chinese population, with the aim of creating a more "homogeneous" nation.

Different policies often produce different types of ethnic Chinese in Southeast Asia. Some appear to be more "acculturated" than others, while some have been assimilated. There has been a change of identity among the Chinese in Southeast Asia. Referring to those who have not been assimilated, Wang Gungwu discerns three stages of changing identities for "Chinese overseas: *huaqiao* (overseas Chinese), *huaren* (ethnic Chinese) and *huayi* (Chinese descent)." Through half of a century of nation-building, Southeast Asian Chinese have indeed been transformed into *huaren* and *huayi*.

In recent years, Southeast Asian governments have faced the challenge of globalization, democratization, and economic crisis. These challenges have profound implication on the Chinese in Southeast Asia as the governments in the region have been forced to change their policies towards ethnic Chinese.

The size of the local Chinese community and the nature of the political system often influence, if not determine, the policies of the government towards ethnic Chinese. In general, a democratic government is unlikely to adopt an assimilationist policy, as assimilation — one ethnic group assumes the identity/culture of the other ethnic group — is against the democratic principle. However, many Southeast Asian governments in the past were authoritarian or semi-authoritarian, therefore some assimilationist policies had been introduced provided that the size of the Chinese communities was small. Suharto's Indonesia and Thailand are two examples. However, in some cases, China's relations with the country concerned also serves as another independent variable. The expulsion policy was introduced during Sukarno's period in the early 1960s and Vietnam in the second half of the1970s.

A government may adopt more than one policy towards the Chinese during one period. For instance, in the 1970s, Vietnam adopted both assimilationist and expulsion policies towards its Chinese population. A country may also introduce two different policies during different periods. For example, Indonesia after independence introduced a more integrationist policy, and since 1959 it gradually became more assimilationist. When Suharto came to power, the policy was assimilationist. However, after the fall of Suharto (1998), the policy was reversed to pluralism. In the case of Vietnam, it was assimilationist prior to the Sino-Vietnamese War (1978). During and after the war, it was assimilationist combined with expulsion. Only after the end of the Cold War in the 1990s, has the policy been reverted back to integrationist.

Nevertheless, Thailand has continued to adopt the assimilationist policy. But with the end of the Cold War, the assimilationist policy was not abandoned but it was somewhat relaxed. The only Southeast Asian state which has adopted "multi-racialism" (multi-culturalism) is Singapore. But it does not mean that Singapore is not interested in integrating its population. Through the English language and common values, the government wants to build a Singapore nation. It is safe to say that no matter what the policy is adopted, all countries cannot afford not to integrate its multi-ethnic and multi-cultural population. Various types of national integration programmes have been adopted and the citizenship law has been used to build a nation.

Throughout the Cold War period, the documented migration from Mainland China to Southeast Asia was stopped. Only undocumented migration took place and the number was small. Without the influx of new migrants, the ethnic Chinese communities in the region became more stable. They became more localized and identified themselves with the local governments and population. It is also worth noting that the PRC government since 1955 adopted a new policy, encouraging the local Chinese to take up local citizenship and integrate themselves with the people where they resided. The PRC wanted to solve the historical problem of the so-called overseas Chinese.

After the end of the Cold War and rapid globalization process, Chinese migration recurred. In the 1960s and 1970s, many observers argued that the "overseas Chinese" would eventually disappear from Southeast Asia as all Chinese children who are foreign-born would have become citizens of a Southeast Asian country. They cease to become *huaqiao* (Chinese citizens overseas) but *huaren* (ethnic Chinese) or *huayi* (of Chinese descent).[7] In other words, there will be no more *huaqiao*. Many did not foresee the influx of Chinese migrants from outside the region, nor did they predict the re-emigration of Southeast Asian Chinese to other regions. The modernization of China, the return of Hong Kong to the Mainland, and the uncertainty of Taiwan's future served as new push factors for the Chinese to emigrate. The economic pressure and the rise of globalization also compelled many Southeast Asian states to change their policies towards Chinese migration and began to accept them or were unable to stop them. A new wave of Chinese migration from Mainland China, Hong Kong and Taiwan occurred, forming what is known as the *xin yi ming* (Chinese new migrants). Some Southeast Asian countries (for example, Vietnam and Indonesia) encountered major upheaval, resulting in the re-migration of some *huaren* and *huayi* to either neighbouring countries or to the West. Some also re-entered China.

New Chinese Migration

The territorial source of new Chinese migration is no longer confined to Mainland China, but also Taiwan and Hong Kong. The so-called *xin yimin* is also a new phenomenon, it occurred after the re-emergence of Deng Xiaoping who introduced the Four Modernization Programmes and an open-door policy in the late 1970s. Since then, many Chinese from Mainland China have migrated to other countries. Unlike in the last century and earlier, the focus of Chinese migration was no longer the "under-developed"

Southeast Asia but the "developed" West, which include the United States, Canada and Australia. According to one estimate, there were 2,830,000 new Chinese migrants in the United States and 960,000 new Chinese migrants in Canada (Zhuang 2001, p. 353). In Australia, in 1999 alone, there were about 380,000 new Chinese migrants (Table 3.4).

The reasons for new migrants to go to the West rather than to Southeast Asia are complex, and there is no doubt that this is due to the opportunities provided by these countries to new migrants as well as the background of these new migrants. In the past the West was reluctant to accept Chinese migrants. Therefore the Chinese were only able to go to under-developed countries. In addition, there was difficulty in the transportation from China to the West. The situation changed after World War II, especially since the 1960s. The West welcome Chinese migrants. The living standards of the Western countries are higher and are the dreams of many Chinese migrants. Unlike Chinese migrants in the past, it appears that many of these migrants are not from rural areas but urban China.

These new migrants consist of businessmen, professionals and migrants, with a large number of Chinese students. For instance, during 1989 soon after the Tiananmen Affair, it was reported that there were at least 70,000 Mainland Chinese students in the United States. However, in 1996 there were 84,333 Chinese students in the United States, of which 39,613 students were from the PRC, 32,702 from Taiwan and 12,018 from Hong Kong.[8] It

TABLE 3.4
1981–1999 Chinese Migrants to Developed Countries (Thousands)

Country	1981	1992	1999	Non-official Estimate
U.S.	806	1,800	2,830	3,000
Canada	292	750	960	100
Australia	123	250	380	400
U.K.	91	250	250	270
France	150	–	200	250
Netherlands	40	60	130	150
Germany	20	70	110	130
Italy	3.5	50	70	170
Japan	60	180	250	260

Source: Zhuang (2001, pp. 353–54).

should also be noted that there were a large number of illegal migrants from Mainland China to the above three countries and Europe. According to one estimate, from the 1970s to the end of the 1990s, between 50,000 and 70,000 Chinese undocumented migrants entered those countries. (Zhuang 2001, p. 353).

It is not true that there is no more Chinese migration to Southeast Asia. In fact, there have been new Chinese migrants, both legal and illegal, from Mainland China, Hong Kong and Taiwan to this region. However, their number is believed to be much smaller when compared to those who have gone to the West. Perhaps from the table of foreign Chinese (See Table 3.3), one can argue that these foreigners are actually new Chinese migrants. The number of new Chinese migrants coincided with the individual country policy towards immigration. Singapore is a "migrant state" and it introduced an open door policy, especially towards "foreign talents". It welcomed both Chinese and non-Chinese to immigrate. In 1989, the Singapore Government introduced a new policy to offer 25,000 Hong Kong skilled workers (with their families) to reside in Singapore. If the offers were taken, more than 100,000 Hong Kong Chinese would have been in Singapore now (Skeldon 1995, pp. 227–28). The offer coincided with the return of Hong Kong to China in 1997. I do not have the actual figures of the Hongkongers who eventually migrated to Singapore, but according to an estimate, more than 50 per cent took the offer. With regard to the Chinese from Mainland China in Singapore, again, I do not have the figure but there is a significant new Mainland Chinese migrant community here. Even the Singapore sportswomen who were gold medallists in the recent Commonwealth Games were imported from China.

New Chinese migrants were spread all over Southeast Asia but some countries have more Chinese new migrants than others. Even in Indonesia, which was closed to the Chinese migrants, one can see a significant number of new arrivals. They came in during the end of Suharto rule, and many were from Fujian rather than other provinces. In fact, many new migrants were undocumented migrants. However, there are not yet book-length studies on the topic.[9] According to one estimate, between 1980s and 1990s, there were 50,000 to 60,000 new Chinese migrants, mainly from Mainland China, to Myanmar, the Philippines, Indonesia, Singapore, Malaysia and Thailand (Zhuang 2001, p. 353). The illegal migrants from China have not alarmed Southeast Asian governments yet, but they have drawn the attention of the media in Western Europe.

These new Chinese migrants who are legal are generally well educated. Many are professionals. Some came to the region with not only skills but also capital. They became the links between China and Southeast Asia. Like in the past, there is also friction, if not conflict, between new migrants and old migrants. This conflict in culture and values is not new — that had happened in the late nineteenth century and early twentieth century.

Re-migration of Southeast Asian Chinese, Especially Chinese Indonesians

The Chinese in Southeast Asia have been transformed from sojourners to settlers. They have also become part of the newly established Southeast Asian nations. Nevertheless, because of government policies and socio-political situations, some Southeast Asian Chinese were forced to leave their adopted country and re-migrate to another country. The destinations of re-migration can be China or elsewhere. Before the mid-1960s many re-migrants "returned" to China, but others moved to the West. Good examples of this re-migration are the Indonesian Chinese in 1960 and 1998 and the Vietnamese Chinese between 1976–78. But even in the case of Indonesia and Vietnam, many of them also re-migrated to other Southeast Asian countries (such as Singapore and Malaysia) and the West (Australia, United States and Canada). If we visit the above three countries, we will find many Chinese communities originating from Malaysia, Indonesia and Singapore.

In Australia, for instance, the Chinese from Malaysia, Vietnam, Singapore and Indonesia formed a significant number of their Asian population. According to the 1986 census, out of 185,237 persons who stated "Chinese as main ancestry", 15.6 per cent were born in Malaysia, 15.4 per cent born in Vietnam, 3.8 per cent born in Singapore, and 2.6 per cent in Indonesia (Kee 1995, p. 295). In 1998 out of 18,751,000 Australian residents, 92,100 were born in Malaysia, 55,000 were born in Indonesia, 35,900 were born in Singapore, and 168,600 were born in Vietnam (Hugo 2001, p. 163). I would argue that the majority of these people are of Chinese descent.

The re-migration of ethnic Chinese in the last decade was caused by many factors, economic difficulty, political instability and anti-Chinese sentiments being the most important ones. Nevertheless, the Asian economic crisis, which started in 1997, is often cited as a major factor of the re-migration of many Southeast Asian Chinese, especially to the West.

In this chapter, I would like to use the Indonesian Chinese example as a case of re-migration. I use the term re-migration to mean population movements. It includes migrating (internal and international), taking refuge, working and studying overseas. In May 1998 there were major anti-Chinese riots, which caused the exodus of Chinese Indonesians.[10] It is not true that the Chinese only left Indonesia during the 1998 May anti-Chinese riots, which was a major event in Indonesian Chinese history. After Indonesia achieved political independence in 1949, there were at least three "Chinese exoduses". The first "exodus" was in 1960 following the banning of the retail trade in the rural areas, where about 100,000 Chinese left and the majority went to China.[11] In 1963 there was another anti-Chinese riot but fewer people migrated. But this cannot be called an exodus, as it was small in number and not nationwide. The second exodus took place in 1965 after the abortive coup. However, less than 10,000 people left Indonesia and few went to China.[12] The latest was in the 1998 May riots, and the number was estimated to be about 70,000 Chinese and very few went to China. As to the nature of the exodus, there are similarities and differences. While all of these exoduses are connected with political violence in Indonesia,[13] the most recent one appeared to be somewhat different. The PRC policy towards the ethnic Chinese[14] and the ethnic Chinese condition in Indonesia also affect the recent movement of the ethnic Chinese population.

First of all, let us look at the May riots. There are many interpretations of the May riots. Many believed that they were not spontaneous but engineered. Both Suharto and Prabowo were involved.[15] The major purposes were to divert people's attention in order to save the Suharto's regime and benefit Prabowo personally. It is also possible that the anti-Chinese group used the riots to frighten the Chinese so that they would leave the country and never return.

Power struggles among the indigenous elite are not new, but the May riots appear to be different from the previous ones where Chinese women were systematically raped. In the past there were lootings, arson but not much raping. Different from the 1965 anti-Chinese campaign, the May 1998 riots were non-ideological but "ethnic" or "racial". The riots had identifiable patterns and were quite well organized. The attacks on ethnic

Chinese, especially the rape of Chinese-Indonesian women and terror imposed upon the community were "unique". The May riots received worldwide attention.[16] The Chinese communities all over the world paid attention to the riots. Reports in both the print and electronic media were widely available. Many pictorials and booklets were also published and circulated among the Chinese communities beyond Indonesia. There was a controversy in terms of the number of Chinese women raped and killed. The earlier estimate or rumour was too high and some victims were fictitious. Some also questioned the authenticity of some pictures but the basic story of horror was unchallenged[17] and the impact on the ethnic Chinese in Indonesia was tremendous.[18]

Because of the notoriety of the riots, many Chinese ran for their lives, especially those who had young girls in the family. According to the Indonesian immigration report, before and after the May riots, about 152,000 people fled Indonesia through Jakarta, Sumatra, Bali and Surabaya airports and seaports.[19] Of these 70,800 were Indonesian citizens, where the majority were presumably ethnic Chinese rather than indigenous Indonesians. These Chinese went to Singapore, Malaysia, Hong Kong, Taiwan, Mainland China, Australia and the United States.

However, according to the report made by the *Forum Pengusaha Reformasi*, an indigenous businessmen organization, there were 110,000 Chinese families who left Jakarta during the upheaval.[20] The same report also said that 72.7 per cent of these Chinese expressed their desire to return to Indonesian once the situation got back to normal. Only 18.2 per cent hesitated and another 9.1 per cent expressed their decision not to return.[21]

Nevertheless, if 70,800 people who left Indonesia were Chinese-Indonesians, this only constituted slightly more than 2.3 per cent of the Chinese population. If there were 110,000 Chinese who left Indonesia, they constituted only less than 3.7 per cent of the Chinese population. In other words, the majority of the ethnic Chinese had to continue to stay in Indonesia. Even those who left Indonesia eventually returned to their birthplace, as it was difficult for them to live overseas in a new environment.

Chinese-Indonesian "refugees" after the fall of Suharto can be divided into two large groups — those who migrated to "safer areas" in Indonesia and those who went overseas.

The term refugee is problematic as many of them are not really "refugees". They fled Indonesia to escape the riots but returned when the situation became normal. Chinese-Indonesian students were also involved in this "population movement", as many may not want to return to Indonesia, especially girls.

In 1998, the number of Chinese Indonesians who left Indonesia might have been large in number but the majority appeared to be temporary. Those who left for China were small in number. This was due to two reasons. Firstly, unlike in 1960 and 1965, Beijing no longer encouraged ethnic Chinese to "return" to China, as most of them were local citizens. Secondly, there was a profound change among the Chinese-Indonesian communities during the thirty-two years of Suharto's rule. Chinese-Indonesians had been highly Indonesianized and were no longer oriented toward Mainland China but towards the region and the West. It is also worth noting that the economic situation of Chinese-Indonesians in the New Order had improved and many could afford to go overseas. Their first choice was the West (United States, Australia and Canada). Second choice was Singapore and Malaysia, and third choice was Hong Kong, Taiwan and Mainland China. Those who could not afford to go overseas preferred to migrate to safer areas within Indonesia.

Perhaps, the exodus of the Chinese Indonesians may be compared with the exodus of the Vietnamese Chinese in the 1970s. The security issue was a major problem. However, it is not without an economic overtone. The re-migration of the Chinese in other Southeast Asian countries might be caused more by the economic rather than security factors. Nevertheless, one important point which should be kept in mind is this: the number of ethnic Chinese who re-migrated are small in terms of their percentage of the overall Chinese population in their respective countries.

New Migrants, Re-emigrants and Southeast Asian Societies

Earlier I have proposed that globalization, democratization and economic crisis have posed challenges to Southeast Asia. These challenges have forced Southeast Asian governments to democratize their policy, including those towards the ethnic Chinese. Many Southeast Asian states have now adopted more liberal policies towards the Chinese; many countries, including Indonesia, have abandoned the assimilationist policy, at least officially. The Chinese have now enjoyed more freedom in the socio-cultural spheres. The three pillars of Chinese culture overseas (that is,

Chinese organizations, Chinese media and Chinese-medium schools), with the exception of the full-fledged Chinese schools, are now permitted. There is a revival of Chinese ethnicity, not only in Indonesia but also in other Southeast Asian states. To establish a homogeneous nation has become more difficult, if not impossible. Many even maintain that the era of nation-state is over; it is going to be replaced by a multinational state. I am of the view that the nation-state has not demised but many states are redefining (or liberalizing) the concept of nation in order to keep up with globalization.

New Chinese migrants and re-emigrant Chinese have posed challenges to Southeast Asian governments. But the challenges have not come from the ethnic Chinese alone. In fact, the influx of non-Chinese migrant workers challenges the emerging nations such as Malaysia and Thailand and affect international relations in the region. Malaysia has two million migrant workers; many are from Indonesia and the Philippines, while Thailand has one million migrant workers who are mainly from Myanmar. Their presence has presented social and economic problems for the host countries. This makes the nation-building process more difficult than ever.

Even in Indonesia, the "problem" is no longer confined to ethnic Chinese but indigenous minorities who felt suppressed by the dominant Javanese groups. Globalization and democratization have given new impetus to ethnic friction, if not conflict. However, it may also be true that the influx of ethnic Chinese and democratization may offer an opportunity to ethnic Chinese to strengthen their economic position since in general, ethnic Chinese are economically better off than the indigenous masses.

In Singapore, globalization has made Singapore "an immigrant society" again. Brigadier-General George Yeo, Minister for Trade and Industry, in one of the interviews stated:

> "We are seeing large numbers coming in now. I can give you one statistic you may not be aware of. For every two babies that are born in Singapore, we bring in one foreign permanent resident. Also among one of the four marriages among Singaporeans is to a foreigner. This has doubled in the last ten years. We have become a migrant society all over again." (*Straits Times*, 11 June 2000).

The case of Singapore may be a bit extreme as this is a migrant city-state. However, the challenges of migration and re-migration to many Southeast Asian countries are real.

Patterns of Chinese Migration: Continuity and Change

At this juncture, it is relevant to address the question relating to patterns of Chinese migration. Are there identifiable patterns that we can apply to Chinese migration over a longer period of history, not only for the Southeast Asian region but also beyond? Professor Wang Gungwu, a leading authority on the subject,[22] in his thought-provoking paper written in 1985 and published in 1989 after revision (re-published in 1991), has divided Chinese migration into four major patterns: *huagong* (Chinese coolies), *huaqiao* (Chinese sojourners), *huayi* (Chinese descent or Chinese re-migrant) and *huashang* (Chinese traders). He maintains that the *huagong* pattern, which lasted between the nineteenth century and 1920s, is gone, the *huaqiao* pattern is insignificant and the *huayi* pattern is still uncertain. Only the *huashang* pattern, which is the basic pattern, still remains.[23] In his words, "only the basic *huashang* pattern remains — the foundation for Chinese migration from ancient times to present, the most resilient pattern for us to study through the ages".

Wang's historical patterns are very useful for us to understand Chinese migration in general and in Southeast Asia particularly. However, as for most historical patterns, it also suffers some limitations because it often stresses continuity rather than change. Although in broad terms, his arguments are still valid, some profound changes in the last half century, especially in the last two-and-a-half decades, have taken place. There is therefore a need to re-examine the *huashang* pattern.

The usual translation of *huashang* is "Chinese traders" or "Chinese businessmen". However, Wang defines the *huashang* pattern very liberally. He said that "the trader pattern refers to merchants and artisans (including miners and other skilled workers) who went abroad, or sent their colleagues, agents and members of their extended families or clans (including those with little or no skills working as apprentices or lowly assistants) abroad to work for them and set up bases at ports, mines or trading cities. When this proved successful, the business abroad, or the mining business, could expand and require more agents or young family members to join it; or new businesses and mines were established into a network, also requiring more agents or family members to be sent out to help the new ventures. Over a generation or two, the migrants, mostly male, would settle down and bring up local families".[24]

Wang maintained that the *huashang* pattern had been "established by traders, artisans and miners within China since at least the Song dynasty". "Excellent examples were those merchants of Shanxi, Anhwei, Fujian and Guangdong, who dominated the long-distance trade within China for several centuries." He noted that this *huashang* pattern of migration "was an extension abroad of this traditional practice, most notably among the Hokkien (South Fujian) merchants in Japan, the Philippines, Java, the Hakkas in West Borneo and the Teochius in Thailand".[25]

I have two observations. Firstly, it seems that the pattern is more applicable to Southeast Asia, and secondly, it seems that his definition is too liberal and inclusive, and that the boundaries between trade and non-trade become blurred. In fact, Wang did not use the term very rigidly and his "trader pattern" is a form of "trading network". In other words, everyone who is connected with this "trading network", either in the mainstream or on the periphery, is called *huashang*. This division is understandable when applied to the period prior to industrialization/ modernization, as in a traditional society, the social structure is simpler and the division of labour is not very clear. However, when we look into the pattern of Chinese migration throughout the world in the late twentieth century and beyond, the *huashang* model may need further refinement. In my view, it may not be very useful to lump capitalists, students, professionals and skilled and unskilled labourers into the same *huashang* pattern.

Even if we do accept the *huashang* pattern to be inclusive of the above, it remains to be proven whether or not those Chinese professionals (from Hong Kong, Taiwan and Mainland China) and the students are linked to the "trading network". No doubt many are still working within the Chinese trading network, but it is also possible that a significant number worked or formed partnerships with non-Chinese, that is, outside the *huashang* pattern. More research is needed on these aspects.

In addition to the *huashang* pattern, there have also been legal and illegal migrants to the West as well as to Southeast Asia. In the West there were illegal migrants known as the "human snakes" (*renshe*), which were similar to the coolie trade in the nineteenth and early twentieth centuries. One can argue that in fact the coolie trade in the modern form still exists.

Let us re-examine the nature of the four patterns of migration suggested by Wang. They consist of two types, one type is by occupation, that is, *huashang* and *huagong*; the other type is non-occupational (more precisely, based on "citizenship"), i.e. *huaqiao* refers to Chinese nationals who are sojourners while *huayi* refers to those of Chinese descent but holding foreign citizenship. Wang maintains that in the historical period, *huashang* and *huagong* were all *huaqiao*, while *huayi* is a new phenomenon as it has emerged only with the establishment of nation-states. As a result, the first three patterns, when they are put together, tended to overlap and hence became less useful as an analytical tool.

Wang himself in his more recent article addressed the issue of the new migrants (*xin yimin*) and pointed out certain "recurrent themes". He highlighted the different backgrounds of new migrants in terms of family, work, education and religion.[26] Yet, he did not re-visit his earlier models (patterns) and incorporate these new developments and findings. I am looking forward to reading his new articles on the subject matter.

Conclusion

It is clear that mass migration of the Chinese from China only took place after the defeat of the Qing dynasty and the establishment of the colonial power in Southeast Asia. However, the migration patterns differ between the late nineteenth century/early twentieth century and the late twentieth century. The majority of the earlier migrants were less educated and they came to Southeast Asia while the new migrants (*xin yimin*) were better educated and went to the West. Also the sources of the migrants were not confined to Mainland China but also include Taiwan and Hong Kong. However, Chinese migration to Southeast Asia has never really stopped. The *xin yimin* phenomenon has happened in Southeast Asia as well but the presence of the new migrants differs from country to country. Nevertheless, they have posed a challenge to nation-building in Southeast Asia.

Chinese migration is not a one-way traffic. The Chinese overseas have invested in Mainland China, and in the last two decades, it seems that they had invested more in Mainland China than before. Some had even moved back to China but the number was not large. Moreover, there has been re-migration among the Chinese in Southeast Asia to other Southeast Asian countries or the West. Their favourite places are the United States, Canada and Australia.

Due to this new migration of the Chinese and the rise of globalization, some have begun to speak of the emergence of a new "Overseas Chinese" community. However, the "Chinese overseas" remains divided. The *xin yimin* are different from the *lao yimin* (old migrants) in their language and values. As in the past, the new migrants would have to adapt to the local situation, just like their forefathers, if they want to be accepted by the locals and *lao yimin*.

Many Southeast Asian Chinese, particularly those from Indonesia, have lost their command of the Chinese language. They use local Southeast Asian languages, English or a mixture of languages to communicate. Increasingly, English has been the major medium of communication among the educated Southeast Asian Chinese. This "Chinese overseas" community is different from that of the *xin yimin* from China or Taiwan whose major medium of communication is still Mandarin.

Due to the economic crisis and resurgence of China as an economic giant, many Chinese who have lost their command of the Chinese language have begun to learn Chinese again. However, if they continue to live in Southeast Asia, they will not be transformed into Mainland Chinese or Taiwanese Chinese. Though the influence of Mainland China has begun to be felt in the region and the number of Chinese tourists has increased remarkably, it appears the number of Chinese new migrants remains small. If this persists, the process of adaptation for the new migrants will continue.

This chapter is confined to Chinese migration. It has therefore highlighted the challenges posed by Chinese migration. In fact, migration challenges in Southeast Asia are not confined to the Chinese. Non-Chinese migration has often posed equally serious, if not more, challenges to Southeast Asian countries. The chapter should therefore be put into a larger context of migration if we want to have a more comprehensive ethnic picture of Southeast Asia.

Notes

[1]   Professor Wang Gungwu has published numerous articles and books on Chinese migration (please see References), however, I would like to highlight his three thought-provoking articles: Wang Gungwu, "Patterns of Chinese Migration in Historical Perspective", in Wang (1991: 3–21); "Sojourning: The Chinese Experience", in Wang (2001: 54–72); Wang (2002), "New Migrants: How New and Why New?" in *Asian Culture*, no. 26. I have benefited from these articles in writing this chapter.

2   See Wang Gungwu's article, "Sojourning: The Chinese Experience," p. 56.

3   For a discussion of the Chinese sojourning experience in a historical context, see Wang Gungwu, "Sojourning", pp. 54–47. Wang defined sojourning as "longer visit or even extended period of stay", see ibid., p. 55.

4   Mainland Chinese scholar, Chen Bisheng, also raised this problem in his book, *Shijie huaqiao huaren jianshi*, Xiamen: Xiamen University Press, 1991.

5   I would like to note here that it is time for us to form a team to examine the number of Chinese in Southeast Asia and beyond so that we will be able to obtain more reliable data.

6   W.F. Wertheim uses the term a "Trading Minority" to refer to the Chinese in Southeast Asia.

7   For a discussion on this development, see Wang Gungwu, "Upgrading the Migrant: Neither Huaqiao nor Huaren", *Chinese America: History and Perspectives, 1996*. San Francisco (1996), pp. 1–18, reprinted in his *Don't Leave Home: Migration and the Chinese*, Singapore, Times Academic Press, pp. 143–64.

8   "Meiguo Yazhou liuxuesheng renshu xiajiang", *Zhiliao yu Yanjiu* (Malaysia) no. 25 (March 1997), p. 110.

9   They are some papers which deal with this issue, see James K. Chin (unpublished and 2000) and Chen Tianxi (2000).

10 The information included here is based on my paper entitled "Ethnic Chinese Population Movement after the Fall of Suharto: Some Remarks", presented to the colloquium on "Chinese Emigrants and Refugees: Recent Population Movements in East and Southeast Asia, Australia, and New Zealand", Department of History, University of Melbourne, Australia, 1 June 2001. (Unpublished)

11 According to Mary Somers Heidhus, about 136,000 Chinese left Indonesia in the course of 1960. See her dissertation, Peranakan Chinese Politics in Indonesia (Cornell University, 1966) pp. 208–09; cited in J.A.C. Mackie, "Anti-Chinese Outbreaks in Indonesia, 1959–68", in J.A.C. Mackie, ed. *The Chinese in Indonesia: Five Essays*. The University Press of Hawaii, Honolulu, in association with the Australian Institute of International Affairs, 1976, p. 95. According to the Indonesian source, in 1960 alone, 102,297 Chinese left Indonesia. See *Statistical Pocket Book on Indonesia 1962*, p. 14.

12 According to David Mozingo, "fragmentary reports indicate that apparently no more than ten thousand availed themselves of the option to leave Indonesia". See David Mozingo, *Chinese Policy toward Indonesia, 1949–1967*. Ithaca and London: Cornell University Press, 1976, p. 250. The figure is rather low. However, according to Garth Alexander, from 1966 to 1969, every year an average of 17,000 Chinese left Indonesia. He claimed that he got the figure from the Indonesian Immigration Department. See his book, *The Invisible China: The Overseas Chinese and the Politics of Southeast Asia*. New York: Macmillan, 1973, p. 196.

13   For a detailed study of the anti-Chinese riots up to 1968, see J.A.C. Mackie's article, cited in footnote 11.
14   While Beijing encouraged Chinese Indonesians to leave Indonesia in 1960, it changed its attitude in 1966. See David Mozinggo, op. cit. The same non-intervention attitude was also adopted during 1998. See Leo Suryadinata, "China's hands-off on Indonesia", *FEER*, 16 April 1998, p. 31.
15   For various interpretations of the May riots, see Leo Suryadinata, *Elections and Politics in Indonesia*. Singapore: Institute of Southeast Asian Studies, 2002, pp. 53–55.
16   For a reaction of the world Chinese communities to the May riots (between 23 May and 3 August 1998), see *Huayi de beiqing* (the sorrow of the people of Chinese descent), Hong Kong, Zhongguo yu Shijie Zazhi she, August 1998, pp. 77–79.
17   The earliest and most well documented reports on the victims and the events were by the Tim Relawan.
18   *Heise de wuyue* (The black May), published in October 1998 in Beijing by China's Broadcasting Corporation. I also bought a Video-CD in Chinese showing the May riots in Indonesia. It should be pointed out that some pictures and reports were fabricated in order to discredit the whole "anti-Chinese events", but the impact of the May riots on the Chinese community, both in Indonesia and beyond, was tremendous.
19   *Tempo Interaktif*, 9 June 1998.
20   *Pikiran Rakyat*, 6 June 1998; *Waspada*, 6 June 1998.
21   Ibid.
22   Wang Gungwu, "Patterns of Chinese Migrations", pp. 3–21.
23   Ibid., p. 21.
24   Ibid., p. 5.
25   Ibid.
26   Wang, "New Migrants: How New? Why New?" See also footnote 1.

References

Amstrong, M. Jocelyn, et al., eds. *Chinese Population in Contemporary Southeast Asian Societies*. Curzon, 2001.

Chen Tianxi, "Huaren feifa yimin de xianzhuang yu fashi", *Shijie Jingji Luntan* (Hong Kong), no. 6 (2000), pp. 79–84.

Chin, James K. "Gold from the Lands Afar: New Fujianese Emigration Revisited". (Unpublished paper).

——— (Qian Jiang) "Zhenjing shijie de Fujian feifa yimin", in *Shijie Jingji Luntan* (Hong Kong), no. 6 (2000), pp. 70–77.

Hugo, Graeme. "International Migration and the Labour Market in Australia". In *International Migration in Asia*. Tokyo: OECD, 2001.

Kee Pookong. "The New Nanyang: Contemporary Chinese Populations in Australia". In *Crossing Borders: Transmigration in Asia Pacific*, edited by Ong Jin Hui, Chan Kok Bun and Chew Soon Beng. New York and Singapore: Prentice Hall, 1995.

Landon, Kenneth Perry. *The Chinese in Thailand*. New York: Russell and Russell, 1941. (Reissued in 1973).

Purcell, Victor. *The Chinese in Southeast Asia*, second edition. London and Kuala Lumpur: Oxford University Press, 1965.

Skeldon, Ronald. "Singapore as a Potential Destination for Hong Kong Emigrants before 1997". In *Crossing Borders: Transmigration in Asia Pacific*, edited by Ong Jin Hui, Chan Kwok Bun and Chew Seen Kong. Singapore: Prentice Hall, 1995, pp. 227–28.

Skinner, G. William. *Report on the Chinese in Southeast Asia*. Ithaca: Cornell University Southeast Asia Programme, Department of Far Eastern Studies. December 1950.

———, *Chinese Society in Thailand: An Analytical History*. Ithaca: Cornell University Press, 1957.

———, "The Chinese Minority". In *Indonesia*, edited by Ruth McVey, New Haven: Yale, 1961.

Suryadinata, Leo. *China and the Asian States: the Ethnic Chinese Dimension*. Singapore: Singapore University Press, 1985.

———, ed. *Ethnic Chinese as Southeast Asians*. Singapore: ISEAS, 1997.

———, *Chinese and Nation-Building in Southeast Asia*. Singapore: Singapore Society of Asian Studies, 1997. (Reprinted with new appendix, 1999).

———, Evi Nurvidya Arifin, Aris Ananta. *Indonesia's Population: Ethnicity and Religion in a Changing Political Landscape*. Singapore: ISEAS, 2003.

Wang, Gungwu. *China and the Chinese Overseas*. Singapore: Times Academic Press, 1991.

———, ed. *Global History and Migrations*. Boulder, Colorado: Westview Press, 1997.

———, *The Chinese Overseas* (The Edwin O. Reischauer Lectures 1997). Cambridge, Mass. And London: Harvard University Press, 2000.

———, *Don't Leave Home: Migration and the Chinese*. Singapore: Times Academic Press, 2001.

———, "New Migrants: How New? Why New?" *Asian Culture*, no. 26 (June 2002) pp. 1–12.

Zhuang Guotu. *Huaqiao, huaren yu Zhongguo de guanxi*. Guangzhou: Guangdong Gaodeng jiaoyu chubanshe, 2001.

4

Foreign Direct Investment and International Labour Migration in Economic Development: Indonesia, Malaysia, Philippines and Thailand

Pan-Long Tsai and Ching-Lung Tsay

Introduction

Foreign direct investment (FDI) and international labour migration (ILM) have been continuing parts of the world development process. Most Western developed countries experienced problems related to FDI and ILM policies during various stages of economic growth. With the surge of FDI and ILM in the mid-1960s, the problems emerged as crucial and sensitive topics in both the domestic and international political agenda. The East and Southeast Asian "flock of flying geese" is no exception to this general trend (Freeman and Mo 1996).

The unprecedented upsurge of FDI and ILM among East and Southeast Asian countries since the mid-1980s has reflected the working of the market mechanism. Differential levels of economic development and different speeds of economic growth lead to growing income disparity as well as diverging labour market transformations. The "pull" and "push" forces are generated to equalize capital and labour rewards across the markets in different countries. In this sense, it is clear that the acceleration of FDI and ILM in East and Southeast Asia is basically of economic origin. Indeed, the phenomena could be well understood as integral parts of the flying geese pattern of economic development. In general, it is expected that the economies in the leading group tend to be the net outward foreign investors and the net foreign labour importers whereas those in the following group, the net importers of FDI and the net labour exporters.

This chapter intends to explore the development-FDI-ILM nexus by examining the experiences of Indonesia, Malaysia, the Philippines and Thailand. For that purpose, an Investment-Migration-Development Path (IMDP), which was constructed by integrating two strands of literature on international factor movements, will be introduced. The basic argument is that both FDI and ILM are outcomes of market forces generated to equilibrate factor rewards across countries at different stages of economic development. It should be noted that the discussion is confined to the stylized phenomena of FDI and ILM in East and Southeast Asia, in particular those occurring after the mid-1980s. The major focus is placed on the temporary, and economically motivated ILM as it is most relevant to the four countries during the past two decades. Likewise, the FDI refers to the part flowing from more developed economies to developing ones in search of lower labour costs.

The remainder of the chapter is organized as follows. The theoretical relationship between development, FDI and ILM is sketched in the next section followed by empirical evidence of FDI and ILM for Indonesia and the Philippines, which are in Stage I of the IMDP. The two countries in Stage II, Thailand and Malaysia, are also discussed in parallel. For each of the four cases, some relevant policy issues are addressed. The last section summarizes the research findings and provides concluding remarks.

Economic Development, FDI, and ILM:
The Nexus between Economic Development and FDI[1]

The impact of FDI on economic development may be examined from the home country's or the host country's point of view. While there are concerns on unemployment and the hollowing out of industries in some home countries, most studies focus on the development effects in the host countries. The debate between dependency and modernization schools during the 1960s and early 1970s are well documented. However, this debate has become virtually irrelevant since the 1980s when the East Asian newly industrializing economies (NIEs) demonstrated that FDI could indeed contribute to growth and development of the host countries via channels such as transfers of technology, management skills and access to export markets.

There are two relevant theories on how economic development affects FDI. To the extent that there is a positive relationship between wage level and the level of economic development, Vernon's product cycle theory (Vernon 1966) predicts that developed countries tend to be the sources of FDI, while the developing ones, the host countries. A more direct and sophisticated description is Dunning's "investment development path (IDP)" thesis (Dunning and Narula 1996). Built on the eclectic paradigm, the IDP hypothesizes how economic development interacts with ownership advantage and location advantage of both domestic and foreign firms, and thus the patterns of inward and outward FDI.

The IDP thesis argues that, at a very low level of development, a country cannot possibly have any outward FDI. At the same time, factors such as limited market size, inadequate infrastructure, and an under-educated labour force would fence off inward FDI, except in some industries of natural resources. Only when economic development reaches a minimum level will outsourcing or market-seeking FDI from abroad appear. In general, outward FDI, if it exists at all, remains insignificant at this stage. As a result, the net outward FDI is typically negative in countries with a low level of development.

When economic development brings about changes in ownership advantage and location advantage, countries may see a slowdown of inward FDI along with increasing outward FDI. Indeed, outward FDI would eventually catch up with inward FDI and turn the net outward investment into positive, as witnessed in the East Asian NIEs after the 1980s. As development continues, the outward and the inward FDI tend to balance each other so that the net outward investment fluctuates around zero.

Economic Development and ILM

The ILM could affect economic development of both the sending and the receiving countries. From a sending country's point of view, out-migration influences its economic development mainly through remittances and the potential loss of human capital. The migrants' remittances could alleviate the foreign exchange constraint of a country and, at the same time, contribute to national savings. Unfortunately, with a few exceptions such as Bangladesh, Pakistan, Sri Lanka and the Philippines, available data indicate that the scale of remittances is too low to have practical significance.[2] As for the loss of human capital, it occurs to the extent that the workers have accepted various levels of education and training in the sending countries. The loss would be very substantial if the migrant workers comprise well-trained professionals. However, this could hardly be the case in the migration from Southeast Asia, of which the great majority is unskilled labour.

The obvious benefit for the labour-receiving country is the relief of labour shortage, which is particularly important for countries depending on labour-intensive exports as the engine for economic growth. The importation of foreign workers is especially useful when domestic workers become reluctant to take up menial tasks because of rising living standards. Nevertheless, the acceptance of labour forces from abroad is not without concern. Not only is it likely to have an adverse income distribution effect, but it also could retard technology upgrading and therefore long-run economic development. Moreover, the long-run social costs could be very substantial.

Since economically motivated ILM is caused by differences in employment opportunities and wage rates between the sending and the receiving countries, the relative level and speed of economic development in the two countries play critical roles in the whole migration process. This relationship is best captured by the open economy Lewis-Fei-Ranis model (Athukorala and Manning 1999). According to the model, as the growth process continues to the point where domestic surplus labour is depleted, the increase in labour costs ultimately threatens a country's international competitiveness. To avoid losing the export market, importing cheap foreign workers becomes a direct extension of what the firms used to do in the domestic market. The model therefore nicely depicts how economic development drives a country to become a labour importing country.

In a potential labour-sending country, the out-migration of workers is limited at a stage of low development level simply because of high migration costs. Out-migration would gradually gain momentum with the improvement in the financial capacity of potential migrants due to economic development. However, the trend of rising out-migration would reach a turning point and then taper off once the country attains a higher level of economic development (Pang 1994). The transition occurs since economic growth generates sufficient employment opportunities and better economic perspectives. If the economy keeps growing, it eventually becomes a net labour importer as depicted by the open economy Lewis-Fei-Ranis model.

FDI and ILM

FDI could influence ILM directly through employment creation in the short-term, and indirectly through economic development in the long term (Sauvant et al. 1993; UN 1996). The previous two sub-sections have discussed the long-term effects of FDI on economic development and the impact of economic development on ILM. The short-term effects of FDI through employment creation could affect potential migrants in the developing countries either positively or negatively. In a country at a lower level of economic development, FDI (through employment creation) is likely to reduce the financial constraints and thus facilitate poverty-driven workers to go abroad. Therefore, FDI might induce out-migration for lower-end developing countries. On the other hand, FDI (by providing better opportunities) might reduce the immediate pressure for poverty-driven workers to migrate.

The opening of possibilities for upward mobility and career advancement, which are not available without FDI, provides strong incentives for potential opportunity-seekers to remain at home. Moreover, the presence of FDI could have crucial psychological effect. By its very characteristics, FDI inflows represent a commitment to a national economy and provide a sense of economic opportunity and hope in the host country. This confidence-building effect could be no better captured by the following passage:

> "FDI inflows are to economic hope as capital flight is to economic despair: opportunity-seeking migration declines with the former while it increases with the latter" (UN 1996, pp. 53–54).

The relationship between economic development, FDI and ILM can be illustrated by Figure 4.1, which is referred to as the investment migration development path (IMDP). As shown by the Net Outward Migration (NOM) and Net Outward Investment (NOI) curves, a country starts as a net labour exporter as well as a net capital importer, and may expect to rise in both during the first stage of development (Stage I). When a certain level of economic development is attained, the development *per se*, along with the endogenous interaction between FDI and ILM, work to reduce net labour export as well as the net stock of inward investment. This is what happens in the early portion of Stage II. The IMDP further predicts that a country's net FDI and net ILM position would reverse as its economic development exceeds some level in Stage II, namely point A for ILM and point B for FDI.[3] Depending on the speeds of adjustment of FDI and ILM, it is perfectly likely that a country becomes a net importer of both foreign workers and foreign capital. This possibility is represented by the portion between points A and B and can be identified with some second-tier NIEs like Malaysia and Thailand today. The country eventually becomes a net labour importer and net outward investor if it develops beyond a point like B in Figure 4.1.

FIGURE 4.1
Investment-Migration-Development Path (IMDP) Model

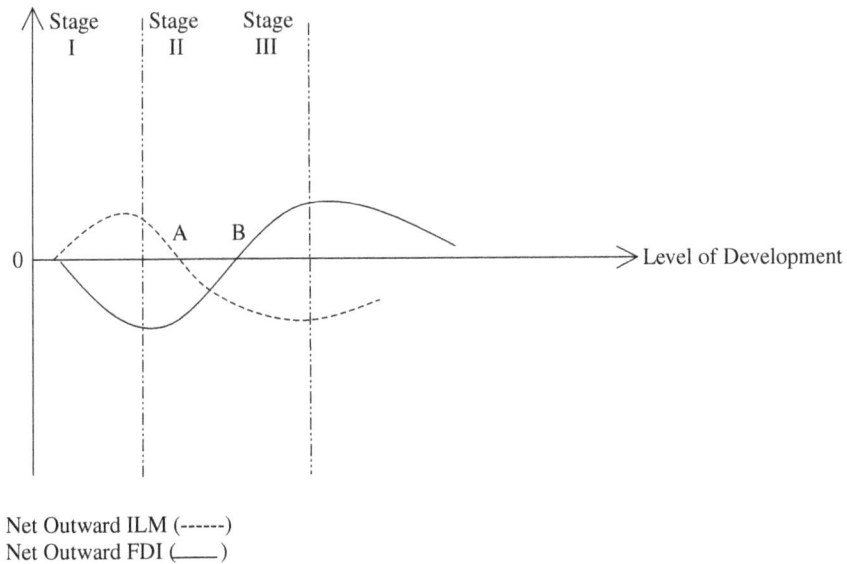

Net Outward ILM (------)
Net Outward FDI (___)

It should be cautioned that the IMDP illustrated above assumes an idealized situation without any impediments to FDI or ILM. Both FDI and ILM arise to equilibrate disparities in factor rewards driven by different levels of economic development across countries. In reality, FDI and ILM are constrained by complex economic, institutional and policy variables. The interaction of these variables jointly determines the shape and position of the two curves in Figure 4.1 and explains the diverse trajectories of FDI and ILM among countries. In the following two sections, the experiences of four Southeast Asian countries will be examined by utilizing the IMDP framework. Indonesia and the Philippines are countries in Stage I, while Thailand and Malaysia represent countries in Stage II.

Indonesia (Country in Stage One)

Economic Development

The Indonesian economy was in great chaos under the "guided democracy and guided economy" of President Sukarno beginning in 1959. By 1965, inflation accelerated to 1000 per cent whereas per capita income was 15 per cent lower than that of 1958. Extensive nationalization, increasing disintegration from the international society, and widespread social unrest and violence eventually brought General Suharto into power in 1965.

The year 1966 was a watershed in Indonesia's economic history, marking a decisive change in policy priorities and economic fortunes (Hill 1996). To curb hyperinflation and to reduce budget deficit, the New Order government of Suharto moved swiftly to announce a macroeconomic stabilization and rehabilitation programme. The economy recovered surprisingly quickly; double-digit growth was recorded for the first time in 1968 and average annual growth rate reached 7.2 per cent during 1967–72.

Indonesia benefited greatly when the oil prices quadrupled in the second half of 1974. The massive increase in oil revenue gave the government an opportunity to intensify development efforts and brought in a period of sustained economic growth. Real GDP increased at an average annual rate of 7.7 per cent during 1971–81, as a result of strong expansion of public and private investment (World Bank 1993; Hill 1996). Ironically, the oil windfall and the ensuing economic success also resulted in the resurgence of nationalism. Over this period, the government policy strongly favoured *pribumi* business interests. The trade and investment regime became increasingly restrictive and inward oriented.

When the oil prices declined in the early 1980s, the decade-long oil-financed growth and abundance also ended. The slump in economic growth in 1982 sparked a debate and reassessment of development policies. However, the overall policy response was ambivalent. While the government was relatively successful in terms of macroeconomic adjustment, trade and industrial policies became even more inward oriented and subject to government intervention. It was only in 1986, when petroleum prices fell sharply, that this interventionist trend was arrested. In response to this situation, the government launched a wide-ranging microeconomic reform in addition to maintaining macroeconomic stability. Packages of deregulation and liberalization were introduced in 1986–88, which opened the way for a shift towards export promotion. The strong recovery began in 1987. It lasted about a decade, with average annual growth rate over 7 per cent during 1987–96 and real per capita GDP reaching its all-time high of US$1,155 (in 1995 dollar) by the eve of the Asian financial crisis.

Indonesia was hit harder than any other country throughout the crisis. In less than a year this high-performing Asian economy turned into dust. Real GDP growth contracted more than 13 per cent in 1998 and real GDP per capita plummeted nearly 60 per cent of its 1996 level to US$477 (in 1995 dollar) in 1998. Seven out of nine economic sectors collapsed during the crisis; the worst-hit construction sector contracted up to 40 per cent, followed by 27 per cent in the financial sector. While the economy has relatively recovered by 2000, its real per capita GDP is still lower than that of 1992.

Foreign Direct Investment

Indonesia is the second largest FDI receiving country among the ASEAN countries, next only to Singapore. However, over the past three or four decades, the Indonesian Government's attitude towards FDI has been at best ambivalent, and at worst outright hostile. Dancing to the tune of oil revenue and the domestic economic situation, the FDI policy has swung back and forth between liberal and restrictive regimes.

The colonial history provided Indonesia with sufficient reasons to be sceptical towards FDI after its independence in 1945. It was not until 1966 did the New Order government reverse the political and economic priorities of the Old Order regime. In desperate need of foreign capital and technology as well as restoring the country's credibility abroad, the government adopted a very favourable stance towards FDI. In 1967, the Foreign Investment Law (FIL) No. 1 was promulgated which, among others, allowed 100 per cent foreign ownership, provided a period of thirty years guarantee of non-nationalization and compensation, guaranteed foreign investors unrestricted repatriation of profits and capital, and offered incentives such as tax holidays.[4] For the administration of the FIL, the Technical Team for Foreign Investment (PTPM) was organized. However, the PTPM was so ineffective that it was replaced by the Investment Co-ordinating Board (BKPM) in 1974. Being directly under and responsible to the President, the BKPM screens incoming investment proposals before sending to the President for final approval.[5]

The relatively open regime lasted about six years. As the economy gradually recovered from the chaos of the early 1960s, and fuelled by the surge in oil revenue after the first oil crisis, nationalistic sentiment reasserted itself. Restrictions on FDI began to proliferate, and culminated in the aftermath of the 1974 Malari protest against the Japanese economic predominance. As a result, 100 per cent foreign ownership was prohibited for new investments, at least 20 per cent local participation was required in a new joint venture, and more sectors were closed to FDI. This hostile posture affected the investment climate so adversely that approved FDI projects plummeted in the following years (Hill 1996). The total approved FDI dropped from US$542.4 million in 1974 to US$221 million in 1976, and further to US$167 million in 1977. Similarly, the realized FDI inflows decreased to US$235 million in 1977 from its 1974 level of US$476 million (Table 4.1).

In response to the slowdown of capital inflows, the government implemented the new regulations less vigorously on the one hand, and introduced administrative reforms to simplify FDI approval process on the other. The BKPM was re-organized as a "one-stop-service centre" in 1977, which subsequently published for the first time the Investment Priority List (DSP). However, the policy pendulum quickly swung back to greater restrictions as the second oil price boom brought Indonesia another bumper oil revenue. The majority Indonesian ownership was reiterated; more sectors were closed to FDI in the 1980 and 1981 DSPs; local content requirements as well as labour regulations were tightened. As a result,

TABLE 4.1
Realized Foreign Direct Investment, Indonesia (US$ Millions)

Year	Flow		Stock	
	Inward	Outward	Inward	Outward
1963	10			
1964	25			
1965	18			
1966	−44			
1967	−10			
1968	−2			
1969	32			
1970	83		405	
1971	139		785	
1972	207		1,252	
1973	15		1,917	
1974	−49		3,108	
1975	476		4,380	
1976	344		5,572	
1977	235		6,431	
1978	279		7,429	
1979	226		8,492	
1980	183		10,274	
1981	133		12,764	
1982	225		15,922	
1983	292		19,161	
1984	222		21,558	
1985	310		24,971	55
1986	258		27,787	
1987	385		30,094	
1988	576		32,656	
1989	682		35,125	
1990	1,093		38,883	77
1991	1,482			
1992	1,777			
1993	2,004	356		
1994	2,109	609		
1995	4,346	1,319	50,601	1,295
1996	6,194	600		
1997	4,677	178		
1998	−356	44		
1999	−2,745	72		
2000	−4,550	150	60,638	2,339
2001	−3,277	125	57,361	2,464

Sources: a. International Financial Statistics and Balance of Payments Yearbook, various years.
b. World Investment Report, various years.

approved FDI plunged to US$1,097 million in 1984 and US$ 853 million in 1985, which were far below the US$2.4 billion in 1982 and 1983. Deterioration of the investment climate reached a climax in 1985 and early 1986 when two large U.S. multinationals, National Semiconductor and Fairchild, stopped production in Indonesia.

The continuing decline of international petroleum prices along with the rise in international interest rate in the first half of the 1980s brought the trend towards active intervention to an end. A milestone in deregulating FDI was the replacing of the long and complicated DSP in 1989 with a much shorter "negative list", which contained those sectors that were absolutely closed and those that were regulated for investment entries. To attract the growing small scale FDI from the Asian NIEs, the minimum amount of investment was lowered for labour-intensive export-oriented sectors.

The FDI policy has wavered again since the early 1990s. The annual inflows of FDI in 1991–94 decreased to the lowest level since 1981 (Table 4.1). This was partly caused by the decline in Japanese outward FDI, which was one of the major sources of Indonesia's inward FDI. In addition, there was the perception that Indonesia's investment climate was deteriorating relative to its competitors such as China and Vietnam. This led to the sweeping investment deregulation package of June 1994, in which 100 per cent foreign ownership was permitted in all cases, the minimum investment requirement were abolished and the divestment regulation was essentially removed. In response, FDI inflows soared in 1995 and 1996. Unfortunately, the Asian financial crisis, together with the accompanying political unrest, has struck such a devastating blow to the Indonesian economy that there has been massive divestment in the recent four years.

International Labour Migration

Available records indicate that Indonesia has been sending labour abroad since 1969 and formally introduced foreign workers in 1973. The inflows of foreigners are very small and most of them are capital-assisted skilled migrants, which differ from the low-end workers considered in this chapter. The following discussion will be limited to the labour export from Indonesia. It should also be cautioned that the official data of Indonesian workers abroad seriously under-estimate the actual numbers, because the great majority of the workers went abroad through illegal channels (Stahl and Appleyard 1992). For instance, in 1997, the total number of legal overseas workers was 305,774 according to the official statistic of Indonesia, whereas the estimated illegal Indonesian workers in Malaysia alone were about one million (Firdausy 2001).

The number of labour export was miniscule initially, totalling 5,624 in 1969–74. The out-migration gained momentum in the following years. Over 17,000 workers were recorded to go abroad during 1974–79 (Nazara 2000). In the period 1969–93, the total outflow of Indonesian workers reached 877,310. The great majority of these workers went to Saudi Arabia (63 per cent), followed by Malaysia (19.7 per cent) and Singapore (6 per cent) (Firdausy 2001). The number of overseas workers through official channels grew significantly since the early 1980s. As Table 4.2 shows, it exceeded 100,000 for the first time in 1991.

The export of labour from Indonesia has been greatly encouraged by the government for two reasons. First, it is one of the solutions to the unemployment problem, which is a potential source of social and political unrests. This reason was particularly important after the 1997 financial crisis. According to the Manpower Department, the number of unemployed workers in 1999 was about 36 million or 38 per cent of the total employment. Because of the sluggish recovery of the Indonesian economy, it is widely believed that the number has in fact increased to forty million by 2001 and onward. Therefore, to provide sufficient work opportunities for those unemployed becomes an urgent job for the government. As a promising alternative, exporting workers overseas increased markedly after the financial crisis. It was estimated that the flow of Indonesian migrant workers was around 2.1 to 3.2 million in 1994–98, though the official number recorded in the Manpower Department was only 1,461,236 during this period (Firdausy 2001; Soeprobo 2002).

The second reason for the encouragement is to obtain badly needed foreign exchange through remittances. Admittedly, remittances are less important to the Indonesian economy than other countries such as the Philippines. However, for a country deep in economic slump, this is an invaluable source for foreign exchange. During 1996–99, the total remittances sent back by Indonesian overseas workers was estimated to be US$2.72 billion. The government has planned to export up to 1.95 million workers between 2001–03, expecting the total remittances to reach US$9.2 billion (Firdausy 2001).

TABLE 4.2
International Labour Migration: Indonesia and the Philippines

Year	Indonesia		Philippines	
	Inward	Outward	Inward	Outward
1975				36,035
1976		1,900		47,726
1977		3,675		70,375
1978				88,241
1979		10,378		137,337
1980		16,186		214,990
1981		17,604		266,243
1982		21,152		305,422
1983		28,960		434,207
1984		37,857		425,081
1985		56,678		372,784
1986		46,384		378,214
1987		59,353		449,271
1988		63,998		471,030
1989		72,000		458,626
1990		86,264		446,095
1991		149,777		615,019
1992		172,197		686,461
1993	37,817	159,995		696,630
1994	41,442	141,287		719,602
1995	57,159	134,719		654,022
1996	48,658	418,716		660,122
1997	24,868	305,774		747,696
1998	24,359	367,526		831,643
1999	21,307	427,619		837,020
2000	14,863	435,219		841,628
2001	16,836	338,992		

Sources: a. Indonesia: Athukorala (1993), Huguet (1995), Stahl and Appleyard (1992), Soeprobo (2002), Nazea (2000).
b. Philippines: Tan (2000), Hayase (2002).

The Philippines (Country in Stage One)

Economic Development

Compared to most of its neighbours, the Philippines has had much more staggering development experience. With an average annual growth rate 6.5 per cent in GDP, the import substitution development strategy adopted in the post-war decades (1950–70) was successful at first (1950–60). However, the biases in favour of large-scale capital-intensive industries, which run against the comparative advantage of a labour-surplus economy, along with the gradual exhaustion of the domestic market took its toll in terms of a slowdown of economic growth after 1960. The average annual growth rate of GDP decreased to 5.1 per cent during 1960–70, implying a stagnation of per capita GDP in the face of comparable growth of the population.

While the debt-driving growth strategy (1970–83) brought about the best decade of the country's post-war development, it still lagged behind all the other four original ASEAN countries. Its per capita income was overtaken by Thailand in the 1970s, and even by Indonesia once in the 1980s. The situation was exacerbated by a series of political crises, culminating in the Aquino assassination in 1983 and the deposition of Marcos in 1986. As a result, the largest economic contraction in the country's post independence history set in and GDP per capita plunged by nearly 20 per cent in 1985–86 (Hill and Balisacan 2003). Although the condition improved as the political turmoil petered out, economic recovery was generally slow and patchy.

Only in the mid-1990s was there a return to moderately good growth, which was facilitated by a series of decisive reforms under the Ramos administration, especially in the trade regime. Trade was liberalized through the elimination of import restrictions and tariff reduction. By 1995, the average level of effective protection was 24 per cent, significantly lower than its 1983 level of 44 per cent. While the Philippines weathered the Asian financial crisis relatively well, the performance of the economy has been far less than satisfactory due to continuing political malaise and the ensuing economic uncertainty.

Foreign Direct Investment

The up and down economic growth as well as political instability augur ill for any direct investment from abroad. The fact that Philippine regulations are more extensive and complex than those prevailing in other neighbouring countries has further weakened its attractiveness to foreign investors. As a consequence, the Philippines is a veritable laggard in terms of attracting FDI, relative to other ASEAN countries. Total stock of inward FDI in 2000 in the Philippines was around 50 per cent of that in Thailand, less than 25 per cent of that in Malaysia, and only 20 per cent of that in Indonesia.

Despite lack of reliable data, available evidence suggests that FDI was small prior to 1970.[6] Inflows of FDI were discouraged by factors including, *inter alia*, uncertain political situation, domestic opposition to a large foreign presence, regulations stipulating at least 50 per cent Filipino ownership, with phase-out provisions requiring the sale of foreign equity after twenty years, and the uncertain status of American-owned investment after the expiration of the Laurel-Langley Agreement in 1974.[7] In addition, the prolonged import substitution strategy might have also inhibited export-oriented foreign firms from taking advantage of the surplus labour to produce for the world market.

The climate changed with the enactment of the Investment Incentives Act and the Export Incentives Act in 1970. The Board of Investment vigorously promoted export and investment, including FDI. However, as is usually the case, it is the general political and economic climate which is the key determinant of FDI, not fiscal incentives. While increasing, FDI remained constantly at low levels during the 1970s. While there was a mild surge in 1981–83, FDI decreased sharply until 1986 due to the well-known political and economic chaos (Table 4.3).

After the revolution of February 1986 the democratic institutions were gradually restored. Business confidence returned and the government initiated pump priming measures to boost overall economic activity. The Omnibus Investments Code of 1987 aligned the Philippine incentive scheme to those of other ASEAN countries. New foreign investments and re-invested earnings flowed once more into the country. In 1991, the Omnibus Investments Code of 1987 was amended to become the Foreign Investment Act, which allowed foreign investors to hold up to 100 per cent ownership in all areas not on the Foreign Investment Negative List. With trade liberalization and deregulation being pursued rigorously in the 1990s, and aided by the easing of political tensions, FDI, especially those in services sectors and export-oriented industries, increased rapidly. A phenomenal growth in its post-war history notwithstanding, the Philippine still lagged behind Malaysia and Thailand in terms of receiving FDI.

International Labour Migration

The Philippines has a rich and unique experience in ILM. It is currently the world's second largest labour exporting country, next only to Mexico. Today, there are approximately seven million Filipinos working or living in more than 130 foreign countries, of which some three million are temporary contract workers. Every day, about 2,300 workers are deployed

TABLE 4.3
Realized Foreign Direct Investment, the Philippines (US$ Millions)

Year	Flow		Stock	
	Inward	Outward	Inward	Outward
1970	4	5		
1971	3	5		
1972	2	9		
1973	83	6		
1974	64	3		
1975	116	4	485	29
1976	158	6	486	35
1977	208	5	671	40
1978	130	9	831	49
1979	130	40	1,028	89
1980	114	86	1,281	171
1981	243	47	1,486	212
1982	193	61	1,718	257
1983	247	27	1,596	224
1984	137	15	1,209	164
1985	64	24	2,061	171
1986	89	2	1,346	158
1987	374	1	1,429	158
1988	917	2	1,461	156
1989	505		1,619	
1990	530		3,268	155
1991	544			
1992	228	5		
1993	1,238	374		
1994	1,591	302		
1995	1,459	98	6,084	1,220
1996	1,520	182		
1997	1,246	136		
1998	1,752	160		
1999	578	30		
2000	1,241	107	12,440	1,965
2001	1,792	161	14,232	2,126

Sources: a. International Financial Statistics and Balance of Payments Yearbook, various years.
b. World Investment Report, various years.
c. Dunning and Cantwell (1987).

overseas. As a matter of fact, in every year between 1994 and 2001 more Filipinos have found jobs abroad than those that were added to the number of employment in the domestic market (Go 2002). In 1997, at least 6 per cent of Filipino families receive income from abroad, the remittances through the banking system reached $5.7 billion, amounting to 23 per cent of the country's export earnings and 70 per cent of services income (Go 2002; Yoshida 2002; Hill and Balisacan 2003).

Overseas deployment of contract workers in the Philippines started after the Second World War, mainly in the American bases and enterprises in the Pacific region (Tan 2001; Yoshida 2002). The opening of the labour market in Middle East after the oil crisis proved to be a watershed in the development of overseas contract workers (OCWs). The number of land-based OCWs jumped more than ten times from 12,501 in 1975 to 157,394 in 1980, and double again to 320,494 in 1985. To some extent, this was facilitated by the institutionalization of the overseas employment programme.

In 1974 the Labour Code of the Philippines was promulgated, which created the Overseas Employment Development Board and the National Seamen's Board to supervise overseas employment. The Labour Code was amended in 1978 to permit the participation of the private sector in the "overseas employment industry". This turned out to be a critical development; today most workers prefer private recruiters because of their richer information and stronger overseas networks. The Overseas Employment Development Board and the National Seamen's Board were merged into the Philippine Overseas Employment Administration (POEA) in 1982, which has since then the single most important agency in making and implementing overseas employment policies in the Philippines.

The mass overseas deployment triggered by the Middle East market has, expectedly or unexpectedly, evolved into a permanent feature, even a culture of the Philippine labour market since the mid-1970s. There are of course complex factors responsible for this phenomenon. The IMDP introduced in Section 2, however, predicts that the failure of the economy to generate sufficient employment opportunities, and thus the low wage rate and disparity in income level, in the face of the rapidly growing labour force, is the main culprit. People, and the government as well, gradually treated foreign labour markets as part of the total market (Tan 2001).[8] Through "learning by doing", many Filipinos become repeat foreign workers toiling in country after country.

The rapid expansion of deployment in the Middle East market turned out to be short-lived as the construction boom came to an end. The first negative growth of OCWs to the Middle East appeared in 1984; negative growth was also recorded in four of the following six years. On the other hand, while starting small, the East Asian market has grown quickly since the mid-1980s and compensated for the slowdown of the Middle East market. The share of OCWs in the Middle East decreased from 79 per cent in 1985 to 44 per cent in 2000, whereas that of the East Asia increased from 16 per cent to 45 per cent (Yoshida 2002). In 1999–2001, the average share of Filipino workers to East Asia and Middle East was the same at 45 per cent each (Go 2002). Saudi Arabia, which absorbs more than 180,000 Filipino workers in 2000, remains the most important destination. Hong Kong comes in as the second, and Taiwan has increasingly become a popular destination for overseas Filipino workers since 1995.

Thailand (Country in Stage Two)

Economic Development

The transition from the lower to the higher rate of economic growth in the period of 1960–63 marked the beginning of the modern economic development in Thailand. The GNP grew by an annual average of 4.7 per cent in 1951–58, whereas it reached 8.6 per cent in 1959–69 (Dixon 1999). Despite some efforts in promoting export during the 1970s, Thailand had remained very much an agriculture-based, inward-looking economy by the early 1980s. However, in the early 1980s some Thai producers, in particular textile producers, were able to take over the markets of labour-intensive products left by Asian NIEs that were losing their comparative advantage in such activities. The reorientation of indigenous firms, and to some extent joint ventures, towards the export markets presaged dramatic structural adjustments. The upsurge of FDI in labour-intensive manufacturing from Japan and the NIEs after 1987 helped Thailand to achieve an unprecedented economic prosperity, which came to a sudden death only with the advent of the 1997 financial crisis.

In the period of 1960–95, the Thai economy registered an average annual growth rate at 7 per cent or higher. The records of 9.9 per cent for 1985–90 and 8.3 per cent for 1990–95 are most remarkable (Chalamwong 1998). As a result, Thailand became one of the most rapidly growing economies in the world, and has been recognized as a new NIE or little dragon in Asia. The kingdom, however, is more similar to other developing countries than to the four Asian NIEs of Hong Kong, South Korea, Singapore and Taiwan. Thailand is neither a city-state, nor a former Japanese colony. Furthermore, unlike in Taiwan and South Korea, the industrial development in Thailand has been much attributed to foreign investors and transnational corporations. In terms of the extent of state intervention in economic development, Thailand is less aggressive than each of the four Asian NIEs (Dixon 1999).

The rapid economic development in Thailand in the decade of 1985–95 did not spread evenly across national sub-divisions and over economic sectors. The manufacturing industry, especially medium- and high-technology manufacturing, has been concentrated in and around the capital city of Bangkok. Economic development has benefited mostly the well educated elite, while the improvement in earnings has been much slower for the mass of workers with little education. The wage gap between Bangkok and other *changwats* (provinces) widened substantially and the rural-urban income difference increased in the 1980s and early 1990s (Sussangkarn 1995).

With a high proportion engaged in the agricultural sector, rural Thais commonly suffered from seasonal unemployment, under-employment, and labour under-utilization. As a result, the problem of poverty has been long existing in Thailand. In the early 1960s, almost 60 per cent of the national population lived under the poverty line. While the proportion decreased to 40 per cent in the late 1960s, one-third in late 1970s and in the 1980s, it stood at 27 per cent in 1990 before reaching 13 per cent in 1998 (Soonthorndhada 2001). The high poverty rate in the early years, especially in rural Thailand, created strong pressure for young adults to migrate out. The low-income Thais, mostly the less educated rural workforce, have been motivated to search for overseas jobs promising higher pay. Despite the remarkable performance of the national economy, working abroad is a goal for many who want to improve their economic position and social status.

Foreign Direct Investment

Thailand has been a country scarce in capital. Before the mid-1980s, there was virtually no outward FDI from Thailand, even though it once exceeded US$800 million by the eve of the 1997 financial crisis. In 1991–98, however, the average annual outward FDI was only 15 per cent of the inward FDI.

Given the insignificance of outward FDI, the following discussion will focus on the inward FDI.

Compared to other developing countries, Thailand has traditionally maintained a relatively liberal and open attitude towards FDI. The regulations and restrictions have always been minor. Of course, the focus of FDI policy has evolved with the transformation of the Thai economy. In the 1960s and 1970s, the government's intention to encourage import-substituting industries was reflected in policies favouring FDI producing for the domestic market. While the country experienced rapid economic growth in 1961–71, the import-substitution development strategy quickly ran into formidable structural problems.[9] This was manifested by the balance of payments deficits appearing in 1969 after several years of surplus. As a consequence, the FDI regime turned more restrictive and selective. Notwithstanding, FDI seemed not to be affected to any noticeable extent. In fact, the amounts of FDI inflows more than doubled from 1972 (US$68 million) to 1974 (US$188 million).

The disappointing economic performance precipitated by the second oil shock (1979) fully exposed the weakness of the import-substitution policy followed since the 1960s. In 1981, the government shifted its development strategy decisively towards export promotion. As part of the policy reorientation, the focus of the Board of Investment also changed to favour export-oriented, labour-intensive manufacturing projects. Several measures were initiated to improve the investment climate and to enhance competitiveness. Among others, ownership restrictions and local content requirements were greatly relaxed, foreign exchange control was liberalized, priority activities for promotion were expanded, and more lucrative incentives were offered.

The changes, along with its relatively stable economic and political environment, have indeed prepared Thailand as a strong competitor for FDI. It became an ideal host country for Japanese and Taiwanese investors after the mid-1980s when they suffered from the double blows of labour shortages and currency appreciation. The amount of FDI increased from US$190 million in 1980 to US$352 million in 1987, and shot up to US$1,105 million in 1988 (Table 4.4). A whole decade of rapid FDI-assisted, export-led economic growth thus set in and led Thailand to be heralded as one of the high-performing Asian economies. The inward FDI surged to US$2,444 million in 1990 and has stayed above US$2,000 to date except for 1993 and

TABLE 4.4
Realized Foreign Direct Investment, Thailand (US$ Millions)

Year	Flow		Stock	
	Inward	Outward	Inward	Outward
1963	21			
1964	18			
1965	42			
1966	27			
1967	43			
1968	60			
1969	51			
1970	43			
1971	39			
1972	68			
1973	77			
1974	189			
1975	86		506	
1976	79		585	
1977	106		691	
1978	56		749	
1979	55		801	
1980	190	–2	981	13
1981	291	–2	1,280	15
1982	191	–2	1,347	13
1983	350	–1	1,704	15
1984	401	–1	2,066	15
1985	163	–1	1,999	16
1986	263	–1	2,289	15
1987	352	170	2,692	184
1988	1,105	24	3,854	212
1989	1,775	50	5,534	258
1990	2,444	140	8,209	404
1991	2,014	167		
1992	2,113	147		
1993	1,804	233		
1994	1,366	493		
1995	2,068	886	17,452	2,173
1996	2,336	931		
1997	3,746	390	13,009	1,951
1998	6,941	130	19,978	2,073
1999	3,562	344	21,717	2,312
2000	2,813	52	24,468	2,439
2001	3,759	171	28,227	2,610

Sources: a. International Financial Statistics and Balance of Payments Yearbook, various years.
b. World Investment Report, various years.

1994. Surprisingly, FDI inflows have not been affected by plummeting economic growth caused by the financial crisis. Instead, it has increased by 42 per cent in 1998.

Japan has been the largest home country of FDI in Thailand, accounting for some 36 per cent of the total in 1987–92. Other important source countries include the United States and the NIEs, especially Taiwan and Singapore. The manufacturing sector is the main recipient of FDI; its share increased from 20 per cent in 1983 to 53 per cent in 1993. Among the manufacturing industries, the electrical and electronics sector had the largest share, capturing 45 per cent in 1993. The sector distribution changed somewhat in the aftermath of the financial crisis, with financial institutions, machinery and automobile industries as the largest recipients (UN 1999).

International Labour Migration[10]

Thailand has a long history of labour export. Despite the respectable economic growth in 1960–95 (averaged above 7 per cent), the progress did not bring about much structural changes in the economy. Pernicious income inequality persisted between rural and urban areas while one third of the people lived below poverty line as late as the mid-1970s. The lack of employment opportunities for the low-educated, unskilled labour in the domestic market began to push workers abroad in the 1970s. In 1982, the number of registered Thai workers overseas surpassed 100,000 for the first time. It then fluctuated around this size until 1994 when it jumped to over 169,000, and reached the all time high of 202,000 in 1995 (Table 4.5).

In the early years, Thai workers went almost exclusively to the Middle East, accounting for more than 95 per cent in 1980 and 1982. The share of the Middle East fell steadily to less than 10 per cent in 1995, with the number down to 20,000 as compared to 114,000 in 1982. The decline, however, was more than offset by the increase in the number of workers in East and Southeast Asia. In 1982 Asian countries took a miniscule 3,206, or 2.7 per cent of the total Thai workers overseas. As the labour shortage problem was exacerbated by the currency appreciation after the mid-1980s, firms in Japan and the NIEs turned to cheap foreign workers in addition to moving offshore. In consequence, unskilled and hard-working Thai workers became much welcomed in the 3-D jobs such as construction, textile industry, metal processing, and machine operations. The share of Thai workers in the Asian countries rose to 19 per cent in 1988, and

TABLE 4.5
International Labour Migration: Thailand and Malaysia

Year	Thailand		Malaysia	
	Inward	Outward	Inward	Outward
1976		1,287		
1977		3,870		
1978		14,715		
1979		10,567		
1980		21,484		
1981		26,740		
1982		108,518		
1983		68,512		
1984		75,021	500,000	
1985		69,685		
1986		85,662		
1987		85,512		
1988		118,957		
1989		48,844		
1990	169,829	63,024	1,000,000+	
1991	175,250	63,849		
1992		81,718	483,784	
1993		137,950	588,518	
1994		169,764	696,328	
1995		202,296	767,352	
1996		185,436	1,336,972	
1997	164,313	183,689	1,929,525	
1998	116,657	191,735	1372,382	
1999	102,767	202,416	873,287	
2000	102,025	137,802	979,445	
2001			904,548+	

Note: +: As of July 2001.
Sources: a. Malaysia: Kanapathy (2000), Chandra and Manning (1999), Kassim (2002).
              b. Thailand: Soonthorndhada (2001), Tsai and Tsay (2000).

increased linearly to the highest 89 per cent in 1995 and 1997. The major receiving countries were Singapore, Brunei Darussalam, and Taiwan.

Taiwan stands out as the most spectacular case for the Thai labour export in recent years. It hosted less than 3,000 Thais before the market was formally opened in 1992. The number increased by five-fold to 10,938 in 1992 and ballooned to over 120,000 in 1995. As of 1999, about a half

(47 per cent) of the 295,000 foreign workers in Taiwan were from Thailand. Concurrently, Taiwan took 57 per cent of the 202,000 Thais registered for working abroad. After the financial crisis, the Thai government actively encouraged the export of labour to meliorate the aggravating unemployment problem as well as to earn the badly needed foreign exchange. The policy was not as effective as expected, since most of the receiving countries were also inflicted by the crisis. The total number of Thai workers overseas did increase from 184,000 in 1997 to 192,000 in 1998, and the 202,000 in 1999. In the same period, the size of the Thai labour force in Taiwan increased from 133,000 to 140,000, before reaching the peak of 143,000 in 2000.

It should be noted that the data discussed above include only the workers registered with the government authority. Those migrating on their own or with agents are excluded. Given the widespread appearance of illegal Thai workers, a recent study (Chalamwong 1998) puts the total number at 300,000. Nearly 40,000 of them are in Japan, while some 8,000 and 6,000 are in Malaysia and Taiwan, respectively.

Thailand is an interesting case in the context of ILM. As the country exports a growing number of workers, it is receiving probably an even larger amount of workers from the neighbouring less developed countries. The majority of them came from Myanmar, followed by China, Laos and Cambodia. Although some migrants have been granted work permits, most of them work illegally along the Thailand-Myanmar border, especially in *Changwat* Ranong. As expected, they are mainly engaged in unskilled jobs in farming, construction, and cottage manufacturing. The number was estimated to be 200,000 to 300,000 in the early 1990s, and jumped to one million in 1996. However, the size was cut almost by half after the crisis due to the economic slump as well as the crackdown by the government.

Malaysia (Country in Stage Two)

Economic Development

Malaysia has been one of the most open and dynamic economies in the developing world. After the independence in 1957, the economic development could be roughly divided into three phases: market-led development (1957–70), state-led development (1971–85), and adjustment and liberalization (1986–) (World Bank 1993). Like many developing countries, Malaysia embarked on the import-substitution strategy during the first phase of development. As a consequence, both foreign and domestic private investment focused on a wide range of import-substituting commodities such as foods, textiles, wood products and chemicals. While the government did protect the import-competing industries, the protection was generally limited compared to other developing countries. As in the case of Thailand, Malaysia switched to export manufacturing in the late 1960s when the import substitution strategy gradually encountered the familiar limits. The average annual growth rate in per capita GDP was 3 per cent during 1960–70. The per capita GDP reached US$386 in 1971 (in 1995 dollar), next only to Singapore among the ASEAN countries.

Following the ethnic conflicts in May 1969, the New Economic Policy (NEP) was adopted in 1970. In addition to reducing and eventually eliminating the identification of race with economic function, the NEP aimed to generate growth and employment to eradicate poverty. For that purpose, the NEP earmarked manufacturing as the growth sector to spearhead economic restructuring and employment generation. With limited potential for increase in domestic demand, it called for active promotion of exporting manufactured goods. The export-promotion co-existing with the modest import-substitution regime inherited from the 1960s became the distinctive feature of the Malaysian economy during the 1970s.

To prevent the progress made by the NEP from being undermined by the world recession, the government launched the "Look East" policy and the ill-fated Heavy Industrialization Scheme in 1981 to support heavy-industry development. Such development was to be achieved through a combination of massive injection of government funds and protection (Athukorala and Manning 1999). Much of the programme was dismantled due to the 1985–86 recession, which sent Malaysia's real per capita GDP from over US$2,000 in 1984 to US$1,606 in 1986. The rapidly worsening of fiscal imbalance to support these programmes, along with the aggravating trade deficits, eventually prompted the government to move away from the state-guided industrialization in 1986 for a more liberal phase of development.

The timing could not be better for Malaysia's reversion to a more liberal market-oriented regime. After the 1985 Plaza Accord, the drastic appreciation of the Japanese yen and currencies of some East Asian countries, along with the rising labour and other production costs, led to massive outflows of labour-intensive FDI from Japan, Korea and Taiwan to the ASEAN region. This wave of FDI was particularly beneficial to the export-oriented manufacturing like electrical and electronics products. As a result, Malaysia experienced a period of unparalleled economic growth and structural change. By the eve of the financial crisis, the real per capita GDP reached US$4,542, and Malaysia was also heralded as one of the "miracle" economies in the East Asia. While the economy contracted by 7.5 per cent in 1998, Malaysia seems to have recovered steadily from the financial crisis, with a GDP growth of 7.5 per cent in 2000 (Kanapathy 2001; Kassim 2002).

Foreign Direct Investment

Malaysia has had a long history of hosting FDI, in the estate sector back to the colonial times and then intensified with the establishment of free trade zones in the early 1970s. The FDI promotion policies since the mid-1980s together with the overall macroeconomic and political stability have made Malaysia an attractive host country.[11] It is generally agreed that the rapid economic growth since 1986 has been made possible only with the massive inflows of FDI (UN 1998). While the strong growth has led to rising domestic labour costs and thus fuelled outflows of FDI (particularly in the 1990s), the size has been relatively small compared to inward FDI. By 2001, the total outward stock of FDI, US$18,955 million, was only 35 per cent of that of the inward stock. Malaysia remains definitely a net FDI receiving country. The focus of the following discussion is thus placed on the inflows of FDI.

Malaysia has maintained the essentially free market trade and industrial policies of the colonial government after its independence. As a result, with a notable deviation in 1975–85, its policy towards FDI has generally been very open and liberal. The Pioneer Industries Ordinance (PIO) of 1958, which gave generous tax incentives and tariff protection to selected pioneer industries, was widely regarded as the cornerstone of Malaysia's FDI policies. In 1968 the PIO was replaced by the Investment Incentive Act (IIA) to broaden the scope of incentives for export-oriented manufacturing. The favourable environment has promoted both local and foreign investment in the 1960s. By 1970, the total stock of inward FDI reached US$1,255 million, which was higher than most of the neighbouring countries.

The generally intervention-free FDI regime was changed by the ethnic conflict in 1969. The NEP of 1970 required that foreign ownership be reduced to 30 per cent of a firm by 1990. The promulgation of the Guidelines for the Regulation of Acquisition of Assets, Mergers and Takeovers (GRAMT) in 1974 and the Industrial Co-ordination Act (ICA) in 1975 are of particular relevance to FDI.[12] Before its revision in 1986, the ICA was the single most powerful instrument in restructuring the Malaysian economy. Along with GRAMT, it marked the end of unintervened and unrestricted entry of FDI into Malaysia.

As a result of the restructuring, the foreign ownership in the Malaysian economy fell during the 1970s and the first half of the 1980s. However, the decline in foreign ownership was accompanied by an increase in the value of FDI (UN 1998). The stock of foreign capital in 1985 was around six-fold that of 1970 (Table 4.6). Two developments were important in facilitating inward FDI during this period of generally less favourable investment climate. First, a Free Trade Zone was set up in 1972 under the Trade Zones Act of 1971, which augmented the IIA of 1968. Besides employment creation, free trade zones, currently known as Free Zones (FZs), were established to attract export-oriented FDI as the government's development policy switched from import substitution to export promotion.[13]

Second, the Federal Industrial Development Authority (the Malaysian Board of Investment) was renamed as the Malaysian Industrial Development Authority (MIDA) in 1979 in recognition of the agency's increasing importance in international activities. One of the most important missions of the MIDA is to undertake industrial promotion activities overseas. Since 1978, it has become the principal agency responsible for evaluating investment project applying for incentives under IIA and is the one-stop agency for foreign investors.

The second oil crisis and the world recession in 1982 and 1985 hit Malaysia hard, especially in the export sector. As a result, the government abandoned the intervention and state-led industrialization strategy. The NEP was declared to be "in abeyance" and aggressive drives for FDI were mounted. In 1986, the government revised and liberalized the ICA of 1975 and introduced the Promotion of Investment Act (PIA) to replace the IIA of 1968.[14] These efforts and the remarkable economic performance have rewarded Malaysia with an upsurge of inward FDI (Table 4.6).

The ambivalent attitudes towards FDI developed in the mid-1970s and early 1980s finally went away. This change was encouraged by the success in pursuing outward-looking development strategy as well as recognizing the substantial contribution of FDI to the industrial performance. A series

TABLE 4.6
Realized Foreign Direct Investment, Malaysia (US$ Millions)

Year	Flow		Stock	
	Inward	Outward	Inward	Outward
1965	49			
1966	56			
1967	43			
1968	30			
1969	80			
1970	94			
1971	100			
1972	114			
1973	172			
1974	571			
1975	350			
1976	381			
1977	406			
1978	500			
1979	573			
1980	934		5,169	
1981	1,265			
1982	1,379			
1983	1,261			
1984	797			
1985	695		7,388	
1986	489			
1987	423			
1988	719			
1989	1,668			
1990	2,332		10,318	2,671
1991	3,998			
1992	5,183	514		
1993	5,006	1,464		
1994	4,581	2,329		
1995	5,816	2,488	28,732	11,143
1996	7,296	3,768		
1997	6,324	2,675		
1998	2,714	863		
1999	3,895	1,422		
2000	3,788	2,026	52,748	18,688
2001	554	267	53,302	18,955

Sources: a. International Financial Statistics and Balance of Payments Yearbook, various years.
b. World Investment Report, various years.

of liberalization measures have thus been introduced in the 1990s.[15] The FDI inflows peaked in 1996 to reach US$7,296 million, and subsided only after the devastating financial crisis.

International Labour Migration

Malaysia has long been a significant labour importer and exporter. It exported labour during the period of labour surplus in the 1960s and even in the late 1970s when the labour market began to tighten. On the other hand, the use of migrant workers to ease labour shortage could be traced back to the colonial period in the rubber and tin industries (Nayagam 1992; Athukorala and Manning 1999). Even though the government took some positive action as early as 1953 to restrict the inflows of migrants, increasing numbers of foreign workers have remained a salient feature accompanying Malaysian economic expansion and structural transformation.[16]

It is believed that Malaysia passed the "turning point" as predicted by the IMDP and became a net labour importer in the late 1980s or early 1990s. Despite the importance of ILM, however, there was "not even a vaguely precise figure in the public domain regarding the numbers involved and there was only scant reference to the role of ILM in national policy planning documents" (Athukorala and Manning 1999, p. 188). The major reasons include the large population of illegal foreign workers and the sensitivity of the racial politics. The following discussion will thus focus on the general trend as well as policy evolution instead of the quantitative aspects of ILM.

While the exact number is not known, Malaysia did export some of its surplus labour abroad, mainly to Singapore during the 1960s and to the Middle East in the 1970s. The out-migration essentially came to an end as the economy expanded in the late 1980s and early 1990s. As for labour import, the amount was limited by 1970. However, there were two significant waves of inflows after 1970: the first one occurred in the 1970s and was in fact ushered in by the NEP; the second wave coincided with the rapid FDI-assisted growth since the late 1980s. In each case, the government attempted to regulate the inflows of workers to achieve the competing goals of economic growth and economic restructuring, yet the efforts time and again succumbed to market pressure. To date it is estimated that around 20 per cent of the total workforce consists of foreign labour (Kanapathy 2001).

The first wave of foreign worker inflow started with the implementation of the NEP, which induced a sharp increase in rural to urban labour migration.[17] With the movement and redistribution of the workforce, labour market imbalance developed in rural agriculture and construction sectors. In the face of the shortage of local labour, the employers were forced to hire foreigners. Most of them were illegal unskilled workers from Indonesia and the Philippines. The number was small initially, estimated to be around 50,000. Having been restricted to the rural areas and were viewed as temporary migrants, they did not attract much attention. Despite the overall high unemployment rate, the import of foreign workers continued to increase. By 1984, the government's estimate of illegal migrant workers was about 500,000.

The government's response to the large number of illegal foreigners was to curb further unauthorized inflows, to deport those already in the country, and to regulate the inflows via bilateral agreements with major sending countries.[18] However, the agreements generally failed to stem the entry of illegal foreign workers in the face of continued excess demand for unskilled workers.

The second wave of labour inflows started in the late 1980s, ushered in by the rapid growth following the liberalization of the economy. As annual GDP growth rate sustained around 8 per cent in 1988–97, the unemployment rate declined drastically from 6.3 per cent to 2.4 per cent. Consequently, widespread labour and skill shortages developed and wages escalated. Beside the general tightening of the labour market due to the booming economy, the labour shortage problem was also the consequence of labour market segmentation. With higher education attainment and standard of living, increasing numbers of Malaysians tended to shun the 3-D jobs. The ever-widening imbalance in the labour market thus provided the setting for rapid labour inflows.

It was estimated that the stock of foreign workers had increased to around 1 million in 1990, over 1.5 million in 1995, and close to 2 million by the eve of the 1997 financial crisis (Athukorala and Manning 1999). The number of legally employed foreign workers seems to have declined between 1997 and 2000 due to the government's deliberate measures to reduce foreign workers. Afterward, the size of all migrant workers appears to be on the rise again. Currently, the estimated number of foreign workers is around 2 million, most of them are illegal (FEER 2002).

Summary and Concluding Remarks

This chapter puts together two strands of literature on international factor movements (that is, ILM and FDI) to form an investment-migration-development path (IMDP). The basic thesis is that both FDI and ILM are integrated parts of the global or regional development process. The two movements are the outcomes of market forces generated to equilibrate factor rewards across countries at different stages of economic development. While this phenomenon had been sufficiently visible in the Western development history, it is most clearly demonstrated in the East and Southeast Asian flying geese pattern of development. We have applied the IMDP framework to highlight this development-FDI-ILM nexus by examining the experiences of Indonesia, the Philippines, Thailand and Malaysia, which are at different stages on the development ladder.

The major results are summarized in Figure 4.2 to Figure 4.6, which depict the relationship between the net outward FDI stock and net outward ILM at different development levels as indicated by the GDP per capita. At a relatively low level of economic development, both Indonesia and the Philippines are still in Stage I of the IMDP, exporting workers while receiving net FDI inflows (see Figure 4.2 and Figure 4.3, respectively). Although Figure 4.4 shows that Thailand is also in Stage I of the IMDP, the result might be caused by the lack of appropriate statistics on illegal labour inflows. Various studies have suggested that, being at a relatively higher level of economic development than its neighbours, Thailand might well have crossed the turning point A in Figure 4.1 before the financial crisis (Vasuprasat 1994). On the other hand, as the most developed country among the four, Malaysia has clearly moved into the second stage of the IMDP (Figure 4.5). Specifically, it locates somewhere between the two turning points A and B in Figure 4,1, a net importer of both workers and FDI.

Figure 4.6 pools all the data of the four countries. The figure can be seen as depicting the relationship between FDI, ILM and the development process of a representative country. In this sense, it reveals that the IMDP does exist. When real per capita GDP (in 1995 US dollar) is less than US$500, the country will be a net exporter of workers and a net importer

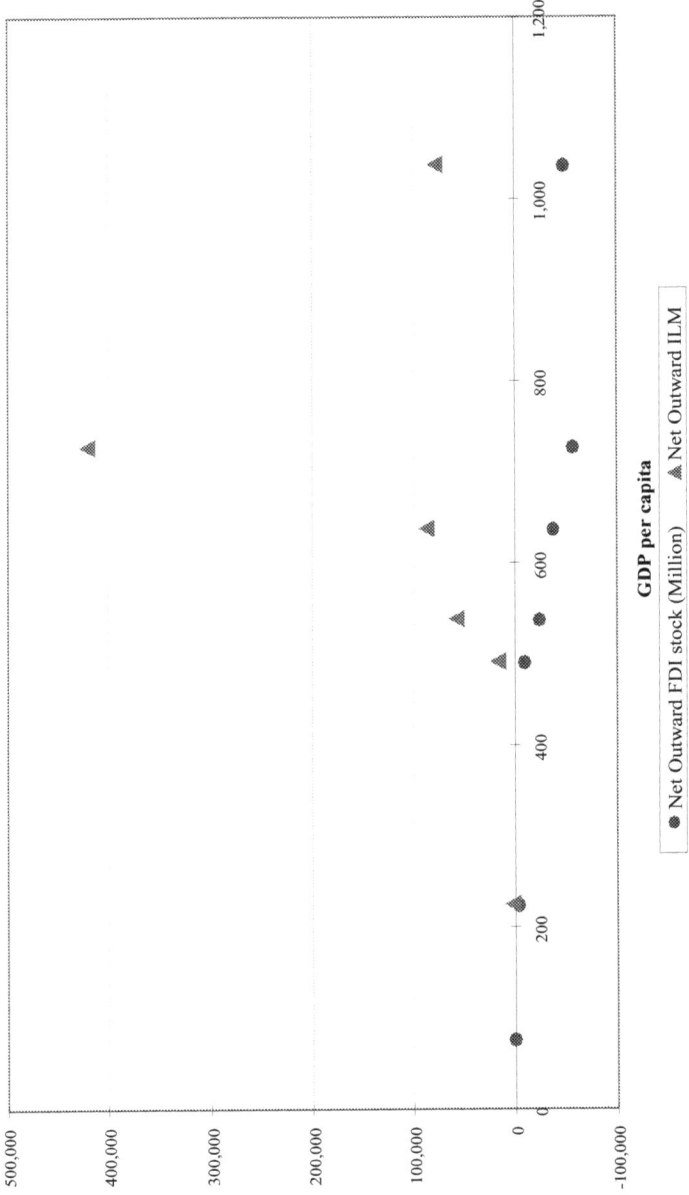

FIGURE 4.2
Investment-Migration-Development Path (IMDP), Indonesia

FIGURE 4.3
Investment-Migration-Development Path (IMDP), the Philippines

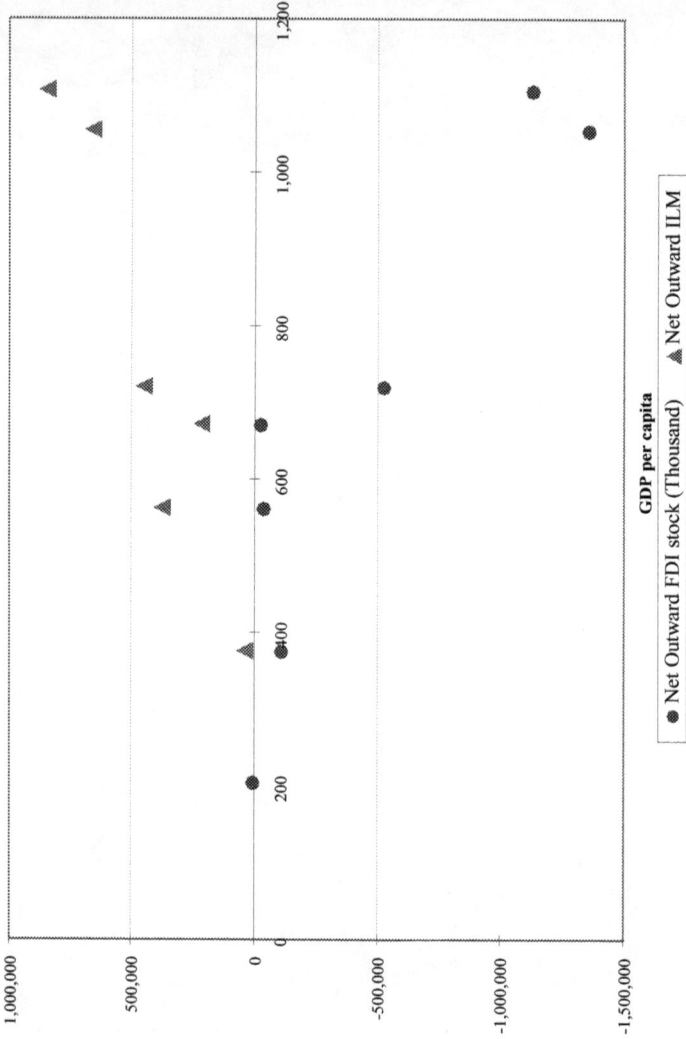

GDP per capita

● Net Outward FDI stock (Thousand)   ▲ Net Outward ILM

FIGURE 4.4
Investment-Migration-Development Path (IMDP), Thailand

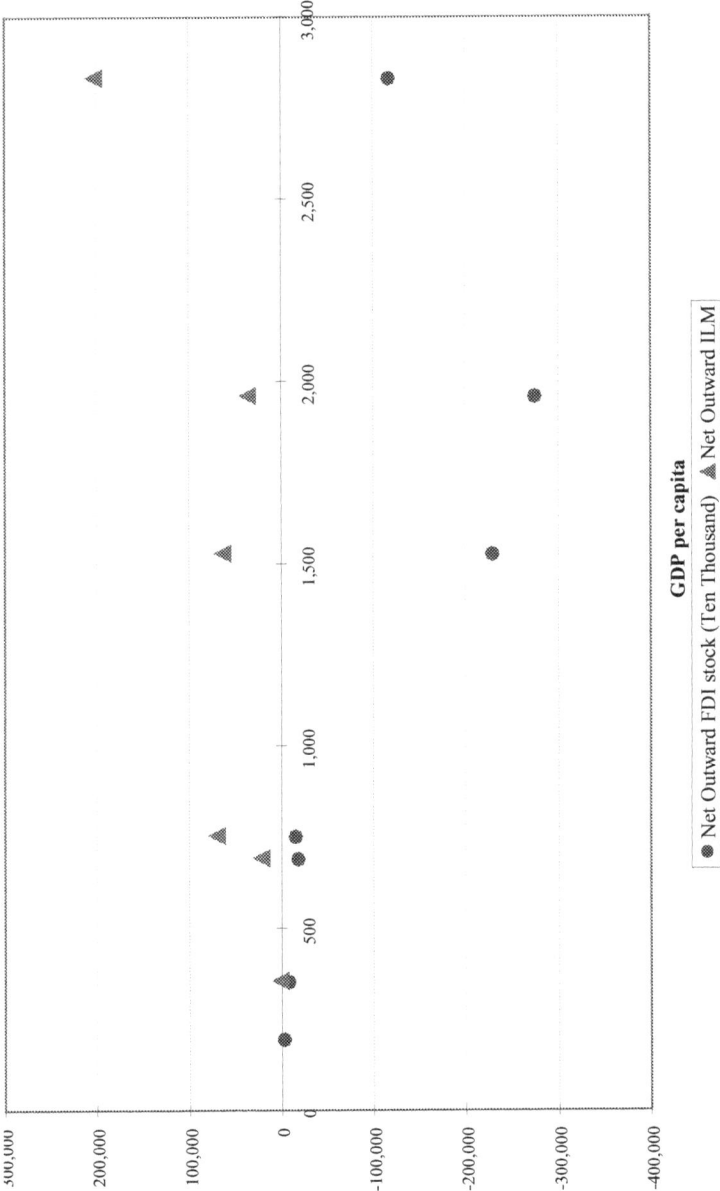

GDP per capita

● Net Outward FDI stock (Ten Thousand) ▲ Net Outward ILM

FIGURE 4.5
Investment-Migration-Development Path (IMDP), Malaysia

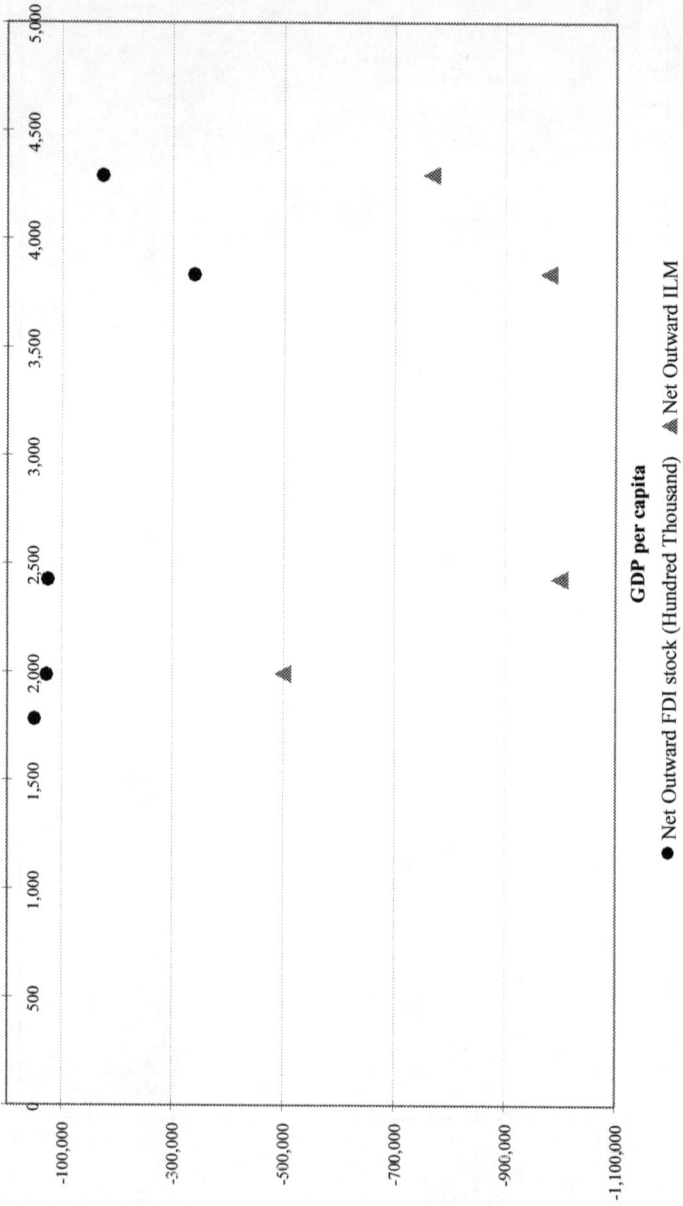

GDP per capita

● Net Outward FDI stock (Hundred Thousand)   ▲ Net Outward ILM

FIGURE 4.6
Investment-Migration-Development Path (IMDP), Pooled Data

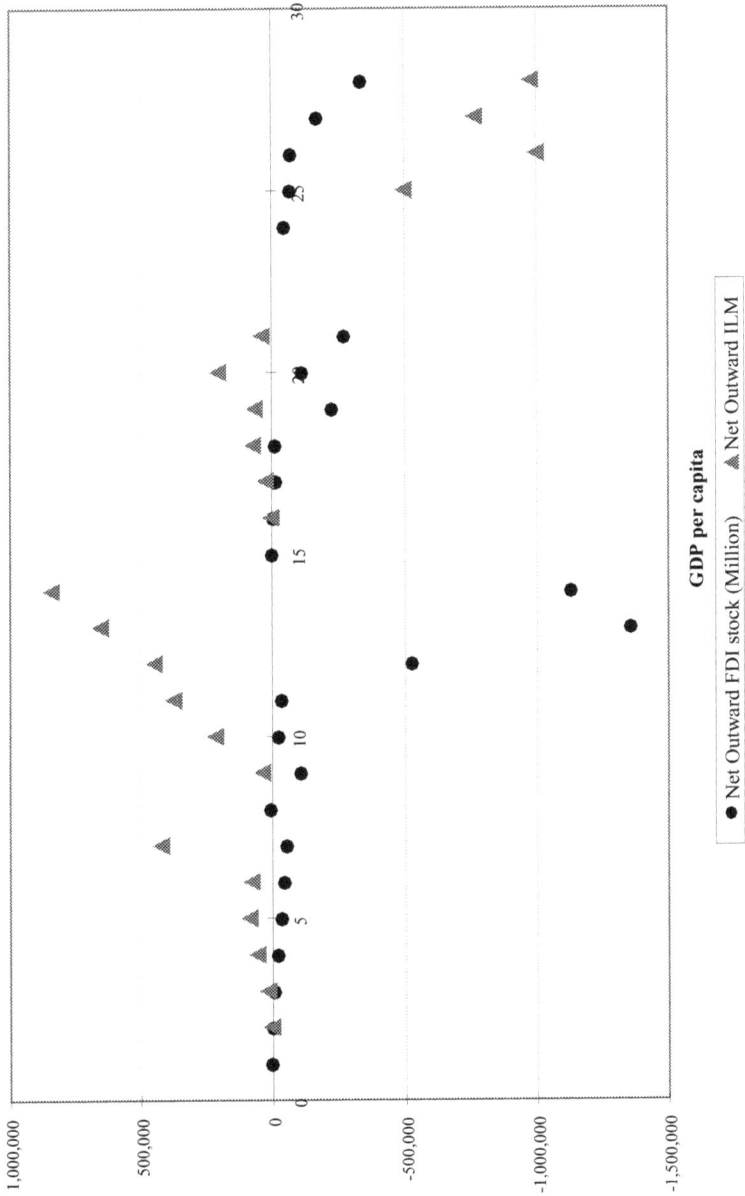

GDP per capita

● Net Outward FDI stock (Million)   ▲ Net Outward ILM

of foreign capital. However, the magnitude of each of them would be rather small as suggested by the IMDP. The magnitudes of both labour outflow and FDI inflow will then grow with the rise in the level of economic development. As real per capita GDP increases to some point in the range of US$1,500–US$2,000, the country reaches the first turning point and becomes a net importer of foreign workers.

Although Figure 4.6 does not give rise to the second turning point, the trend of the data on net outward FDI and net outward ILM seems to suggest that such a point should be at a level of per capita GDP above US$5,000. It is believed that a more complete IMDP figure will emerge if some data from more developed countries like Taiwan and Japan were added. In consequence, the empirical evidence of the four countries generally corroborates the prediction of the IMDP, despite the differences in their attitudes and policies towards FDI and ILM. This finding in turn supports our basic argument that both FDI and ILM reflect the working of market mechanism.

Like Dunning's IDP, the IMDP is not intended to be normative. It simply describes systematic relationships between patterns of ILM and FDI on the one hand, and economic development on the other. Nevertheless, given the strong policy expectations involved in almost all the discussions surrounding FDI and ILM, it is inevitable to touch upon some normative implications. In this respect, it is astonishing to find that FDI and ILM have been treated extremely asymmetrically both in a global/regional context and in a national context. Following international trade, foreign direct investment has been greatly liberalized under the GATT/WTO framework (and in essentially all regional arrangements) in the past two decades. However, population flows across country borders continue to be under tight controls. There are no comparable international institutions like WTO in trade and FDI, which endeavour to the improvement of ILM. In fact, there are no signs for one to come in the foreseeable future.

At the national level, the asymmetry in policies with respect to FDI and ILM is equally striking if not worse. Contrary to the late 1960s and 1970s, today developing countries, and developed ones as well, not only are receptive to, but also indeed are, competing for inward FDI. It is true that some countries are still worrying about losing scarce foreign exchange or being hollowed out due to massive outward FDI. But, in general, the trend toward further capital deregulation and liberalization is clear-cut and irreversible. In sharp contrast, public hostility to immigrants in general, and unskilled labour in particular shows no sign of waning. Importation of unskilled workers remains a political taboo virtually in most countries.

The IMDP thesis introduced in this chapter and the experiences of Thailand and Malaysia suggest that there is no way for countries at a higher position of the development ladder to escape the ILM problem. The same implication was also learned from the experiences of Taiwan and Japan (Tsai and Tsay 2000). There is no lasting "exceptionalism" to the market forces. If the turnaround of FDI policy in the 1980s provides any lesson for the other type of international factor movement, it would be for the labour-receiving countries to think about ILM more pragmatically and more in economic terms. In an age of declining costs of communication and transportation, if unskilled workers cannot come in through the front door, they will come in through the side door. If they cannot come in through the side door, they will always find the back door.

Notes

[1] A comprehensive discussion of the IMDP (Investment-Migration-Development Path) framework can be found in Tsai and Tsay (2000).

[2] It is noteworthy that the data could in fact seriously understate the remittances since much of the money is transferred through unofficial channels (UN 1996).

[3] It is theoretically possible to have NOI (Net Outward Investment) curve changing sign at a lower level of development than the net labour export curve. But this possibility implies that there exists a range of development in which a country is a net exporter of labour and capital, which seems non-existent in practice.

[4] While FIL represented very much an open-door policy, it also reflected the very alive, strong and deep-rooted scepticism towards FDI. This was witnessed in the requiring of a phase-down of foreign ownership over time, minimum US$1 million and licensing requirement as well as the closing of some industries to foreign investors.

[5] It should be noted that the role of the BKPM is not as important as first seen since three important sectors of FDI, namely oil, gas and financial sector, are outside the control of the BKPM.

[6] Table 60 of ILO (1974) provides FDI data of 1966–72. However, the data do not include reinvested earnings of foreign firms, resulting in a net outflow every year.

[7] American investors were granted privileged status and exempted from the phase-out provisions under the Laurel-Langley Agreement. A salient feature

of the limited amount of FDI during this early post-war period was the preponderant role of American capital. In 1970 the American investors held 76 per cent of total FDI, reflecting the special post-colonial relationship between the United States and the Philippines (ILO 1974).

[8] For instance, in the new Medium-Term Philippine Development Plan (2001–04), the government explicitly recognizes overseas employment as a "legitimate option for the country's work force. As such, government shall fully respect labour mobility, including the preference for overseas employment". (Go 2002, p. 8).

[9] The experience is just like what happened in Taiwan in the 1950s.

[10] This sub-section is based on Tsay (2002).

[11] This is clear for the new FDI from Japan and Taiwan after the 1985 Plaza Accord.

[12] The GRAMT aimed at discouraging foreign firms that confer no visible benefits to the national economy and would perpetuate the imbalances existing in the structure of ownership and control of companies and business. The ICA dealt exclusively with manufacturing sector. To ensure that the equity ownership complied with the NEP goals, it required both domestic and foreign manufacturing firms, existing or new, with shareholders' funds of RM2.5 million and above or engaging seventy-five or more full-time employees, to obtain an operating license.

[13] Firms in the FZs enjoy tax holidays, exemption from import and export duties, 100 per cent foreign ownership, unrestricted and tax-free remittance of profits and dividends, and other incentive packages such as the provision of infrastructure.

[14] Aside from providing more generous incentives to manufacturing, the PIA extended these incentives to the agriculture and tourism sectors, and to small and medium scale industries. Moreover, the 30 per cent foreign ownership requirement under the NEP was allowed to be negotiable and flexible. Specifically, the 30 per cent rule was interpreted as a national target rather than to be implemented on an individual company basis, and was waived for some new investments.

[15] Among these, equity ownership requirement for FDI was further liberalized in 1992, with 100 per cent foreign ownership permitted if companies export 80 per cent or a project has 50 per cent value-added. In 1994, R&D incentives were expanded to cover contract R&D, in-house R&D and R&D companies, and in 1995, the financial sector was further liberalized to allow foreign banks to operate in Malaysia.

[16] In 1953, the government introduced the Immigration Act to restrict the free flow of migrants into the country. The Employment Restriction Act of 1968 further required employers in identified industries to obtain work permits for

non-citizens they employed (Nayagam 1992). For Policy evolution of foreign labour management after 1984, see Table 10 in Kanapathy (2001) and Kassim (2002).

[17] The NEP supported the development and growth of manufacturing and services industries on the one hand, and initiated a land development scheme aiming at a redistribution of the population in the country on the other. Both targets were achieved to some extent, resulting in rapid growth of the manufacturing and services sectors and a sharp increase in rural-urban migration. The manufacturing sector expanded some 11 per cent per annum in 1970–80 while services employment increased by 5 per cent annually during the same period (Kanapathy 2001). That urban jobs offered higher wages and better working conditions, in addition to planned employment restructuring under the NEP, induced the better educated young people to migrate from rural to the urban areas.

[18] In 1984, the Medan Agreement was signed between Malaysia and Indonesia, which allowed Indonesia to supply six specific categories of workers whenever requested by Malaysia (Kanapathy 2001). Similar agreements were later signed with the Philippines, Thailand and Bangladesh for supplying workers for the plantations and other selected sectors.

References

Athukorala, Prema-chandra. "Statistics on Asian Labor Migration: Review of Sources, Methods and Problems". In *International Labor Migration Statistics and Information Network in Asia*. New Delhi: International Labour Organization, 1993, pp. 44–113.

Athukorala, Prema-chandra and Chris Manning. *Structural Change and International Migration in East Asia: Adjusting to Labor Scarcity*, Oxford University Press, 1999.

Chalamwong, Yongyuth. "The Impact of the Crisis on Migration in Thailand". *Asian and Pacific Migration Journal* 7, nos. 2–3 (1998): 297–312.

Dixon, Chris. *The Thai Economy: Uneven Development and Internationalisation*, London: Routledge, 1999.

Dunning, John H. and John Cantwell. *IRM Directory of Statistics of International Investment and Production*, Institute for Research and Information on Multinationals. New York: New York University Press, 1987.

Dunning, John H. and Rajneesh Narula. "The Investment Development Path Revisited". In *Foreign Direct Investment and Governments: Catalysts for Economic Restructuring*, edited by John H. Dunning and Rajneesh Narula. Routledge: London, 1996, pp. 1–41.

Far Eastern Economic Review (FEER). "Wanted: More Workers". 12 September 2002, pp. 24–25.

Firdausy, Carunia Mulya. "International Labor Migration Policy and Development Strategy in Indonesia". In *Proceedings of the International Workshop on International Migration and Structural Change in the APEC Member Economies*, edited by Yasuko Hayase and Ching-Lung Tsay. Institute of Developing Economies, JETRO, Japan, 2001.

Freeman, Gary P. and Jongryn Mo. "Japan and the Asian NICs as New Countries of Destination". In *International Trade and Migration in the APEC Region*, edited by Peter J. Lloyd and Lynne S. Williams. Melbourne: Oxford University Press, 1996, pp. 156–73.

Go, Stella P. "Recent Trends in Migration Movements and Policies: The Movement of Filipino Professionals and Managers". Paper presented at the Workshop on International Migration and Labour Markets in Asia, Tokyo, Japan, 4–5 February 2002.

Hill, Hal. *The Indonesian Economy since 1966: Southeast Asia's Emerging Giant*. Melbourne: The Cambridge University Press, 1996.

Hill, Hal and Arsenio M. Balisacan. *The Philippine Economy: Development, Policies and Challenges*. Oxford University Press and Ateneo, forthcoming.

International Labour Office (ILO). *Sharing in Development: A Programme of Employment, Equity and Growth for the Philippines*. Geneva: International Labor Office, 1974.

Kanapathy, Vijayakumari. "International Migration and Labor Market Adjustment in Malaysia: The Role of Foreign Labor Management Policies". In *Proceedings of the International Workshop on International Migration and Structural Change in the APEC Member Economies*, edited by Yasuko Hayase and Ching-Lung Tsay. Institute of Developing Economies, JETRO, Japan, 2001.

Kassim, Azizah. "Economic Slowdown and Its Impact on Cross-National Migration and Policy on Alien Employment in Malaysia". Paper presented at the Workshop on International Migration and Labour Markets in Asia, Tokyo, Japan, 4–5 February 2002.

Nayagam, James. "Migrant Labor Absorption in Malaysia". *Asian and Pacific Migration Journal* 1, no. 3–4 (1992): 477–94.

Nazara, Suahasil. "International Migration: Indonesian Case". *Proceedings of the International Workshop on International Migration and Human Resources Development in the APEC Member Economies*. Institute of Developing Economies, JETRO, Chiba, Japan, 2000.

Pang, Eng Fong. "An Eclectic Approach to Turning Points in Migration". *Asian and Pacific Migration Journal* 3, no. 1 (1994): 81–91.

Sauvant, Karl P., Padma Mallampally and Persephone Economou. "Foreign Direct Investment and International Migration". *Transnational Corporations* 2, no. 1 (1993): 33–69.

Soeprobo, Tara Bakti. "Recent Trends of International Migration in Indonesia". Paper presented at the Workshop on International Migration and Labour Markets in Asia, Tokyo, Japan, 4–5 February 2002.

Soonthorndhada, Kusol. "Changes in the Labor Market and International Migration since the Economic Crisis in Thailand". *Asian and Pacific Migration Journal* 10, nos. 3–4 (2001): 401–27.

Stahl, Charles W. and Reginald T. Appleyard. "International Manpower Flows in Asia: An Overview". *Asian and Pacific Migration Journal* 1, nos. 3–4 (1992): 417–76.

Sussangkarn, Chalongphob. "Labour Market Adjustment and Migration in Thailand". *ASEAN Economic Bulletin* 12, no. 2 (1995): 237–54.

Tan, Edita A. "Labor Market Adjustments to Large Scale: Emigration: The Philippine Case". In *Proceedings of the International Workshop on International Migration and Structural Change in the APEC Member Economies*, edited by Yasuko Hayase and Ching-Lung Tsay. Institute of Developing Economies, JETRO, Japan, 2001.

Tsai, Pan-Long and Ching-Lung Tsay. "Economic Development, Foreign Direct Investment and International Labor Migration: The Experience of Japan, Taiwan and Thailand". Paper presented at the Symposium on Experiences and Challenges of Economic Development in Southeast and East Asia, Taipei, Taiwan, October 2000.

Tsay, Ching-Lung. "Labor Migration and Regional Changes in East Asia: Outflows of Thai Workers to Taiwan". *Southeast Asian Studies* 40, no. 3 (2002): 138–60.

United Nations (UN). *World Investment Report 1992: Transnational Corporations as Engines of Growth*. New York: United Nations Publication, 1992.

United Nations (UN). *Foreign Direct Investment, Trade, Aid and Migration*. Geneva: United Nations Publication, 1996.

United Nations (UN). *Foreign Direct Investment in Selected Asian Countries: Policies, Related Institution-Building and Regional Cooperation*, Development Papers no. 19, New York, 1998.

United Nations (UN). *World Investment Report 1999: Foreign Direct Investment and the Challenge of Development*. New York and Geneva: United Nations Publication, 1999.

United Nations (UN). *World Investment Report 1999: Foreign Direct Investment and the Challenge of Development*. New York and Geneva: United Nations Publication, 2002.

Vasuprasat, Pracha. "Turning Points in International Labour Migration: A Case Study of Thailand". *Asian and Pacific Migration Journal* 3, no. 1 (1994): 175–202.

Vernon, Raymond. "International Investment and International Trade in the Product Cycle". *Quarterly Journal of Economics* 80 (1966): 190–207.

World Bank. *The East Asian Miracle: Economic Growth and Public Policy*. New York: Oxford University Press, 1993.

Yoshida, Yoshio. "The Impact of International Labor Migration on Remittances in the Philippines". In *A Study on Trade, Investment and International Migration in the APEC Member Economies*, edited by Hayase, Yasuko. APEC Study Centre, IDE-JETRO, Japan, 2001, pp. 217–52.

5

Impact of Remittances on the Indonesian Economy

Sukamdi, Elan Satriawan and Abdul Haris

Martin (2001) argued that flow of remittances — one of the most important contributions of migrants to their home countries — to the developing countries has become increasingly important. More than sixty per cent of the world's flow, which exceeds US$100,000 per year, goes to developing countries.

However, large amounts of remittances without the necessary conducive economic environment in the sending country may generate inflationary pressures, push the demand for imports and subsequently reduce or even eliminate the gain in foreign exchange contributed by the remittances. Massey et al. (1998) mentioned that over-reliance on remittances for development strategy may harm the economy itself. As with money from other sources, the more important issue is the utilization of the money (remittances) for development purposes in the sending country. It is unfortunate that policy-makers frequently consider sending labour abroad as the centrepiece of their development strategy. Poor macroeconomic policies (resulting in, for example, high inflation and uncertainty) do not encourage the productive utilization of the remittances.

Furthermore, Glytsos (2002) argued that remittances are a risky source of finance. The only party that may benefit from the process, according to this view, is the international capitalists. Hermele (1997) was of the view that the process of international migration is merely conducted to satisfy "the need and strategies of transnational capital".

International migration may also harm the sending countries because migration is a selective process, and only the "relatively better part" of the society will migrate. Therefore, the sending countries may suffer loss of important human capital and it will retard national economic development, especially if the loss of human capital cannot be compensated by the gain from remittances (see Hermele 1997). This phenomenon is what is often called the "brain drain", to describe the outflow of skill and educated workers from the countries or regions with less established incentive systems and lower wages, to ones with well established incentive systems and higher wage rates. This is especially faced by developing countries where the wage rate is lower and incentive systems for labour are not yet well set.

In other words, sending labour abroad is not a substitute for sound macroeconomic policies. To have positive contribution to the sending countries' development, the policy of sending labour abroad should be accompanied by proper domestic economic policies and public investment. It should be mentioned, however, that in a labour surplus country, especially those with zero and negative marginal productivity, sending labour abroad is a very important complement to the domestic economic development strategy.

This chapter does not attempt to discuss the benefit and cost of international migration on the economic development of the sending countries. Rather, it focuses on remittances as one important aspect of international migration on the development of the sending countries. Indonesia is the focus because it is a very large and heterogeneous country with policies favouring the sending of labour abroad as one of its economic development strategies; yet there has been little discussion on the role of remittances in the Indonesian economy. The next section discusses the role of remittances in the context of international resource flows. This section is followed by discussions on measuring the impact of remittances. The examination of the role of remittances in the Indonesian economy is preceded with a discussion on the trend of emigration from Indonesia.

This chapter is closed with some suggestions for maximizing the benefit of sending labour abroad, to the Indonesian economy.

Remittances as One of International Resource Flows

Globally, official aids have been declining in most of the 1990s because of the end of the Cold War, financial difficulties of donor countries, and rising doubt about the usefulness of aid. Official development finance (ODF) to developing countries has declined from US$55.2 billion in 1990 to US$ 38.6 billion in 2000. The countries having the largest amount of aid include Indonesia, Ghana, Rwanda, Mozambique, and Pakistan. On the other hand, remittances and private financial flow have grown very fast in the 1990s. Remittances to developing countries have almost doubled from US$33 billion in 1991 to US$65 billion in 1999. Remittances to developing countries constituted 62.1 per cent of total world remittances in 1999, compared to 57.8 per cent in 1988. Four countries (Indonesia, Columbia, Peru, and particularly Mexico) have received a very large private resource flow (Gammeltoft 2002).

Therefore, as argued by Nyberg-Sorenson et al. (2002a), remittances have formed a very large percentage of the world financial flows and they are much larger than the global overseas development finance. Athukorala (O'Neill 2001) argued that large amounts of remittances are never officially recorded, being sent through private channels or brought in by the migrants themselves. As an example, in 1982 about sixty per cent of the remittances in the Philippines were not recorded. There are two reasons for the under-representation of the "official" remittances (Puri and Ritzema 1999). First is the imprecision in accounting, and the second is the migrant labour use of informal ways to send money to their home country, such as through friends. Taylor (1999) showed that micro-level studies have indicated the existence of a substantial clandestine and in-kind transfer and statistics on remittances usually do not include them. If the remittances through informal channels are considered, the amount of remittances are surely higher than foreign aid and they become a more stable source of income to developing countries, compared to the sources from private flows and foreign direct investment. (See Table 5.1 for list of some studies on unofficial remittances.)

TABLE 5.1
Unrecorded Remittances as a Percentage to Total Remittances

Country	Source	Estimation Period	Estimate (%)
Bangladesh	Mahmud (1989)	1981–86	20
Korea	Hyun (1989)	1980–85	8
India	ESCAP (1987)	1983	40
Egypt	Adams (1992)	1985–86	33
Pakistan	ILO-ARTEP (1987)	1986	43
Sri Lanka	Rodrigo and Jayatissa (1989)	1980–85	13
Sudan	Choucri (1984)	1984	85
Thailand	Tingrabadh (1989)	1977–86	18
Tonga	Brown and Connel (1993)	1992–93	43
Western Samoa	Brown and Walker (1994)	1992–92	42

Source: Athukorala (1993) and other sources, as quoted in Puri and Ritzema (1999).

Gammeltoft also found that the absolute amount of total resource flows into low-income countries is lower than those to middle-income countries. The higher the income of the countries, the lower is the amount of aid and the higher is the amount of private resource flows. Aid in low-income countries is large in both the size and percentage to the total international resource flow. On the other hand, the lower middle-income countries receive the largest remittances, but the contribution of the remittances is much higher in the low-income countries.

Nyberg-Sorenson et al. (2002b) argued that remittances to developing countries have a more direct impact, compared to other resource flows. Furthermore, the benefit of remittances in developing countries is more likely to go to the better-off households in the better-off communities of the better-off countries. The benefit of remittances also goes beyond the remittance-receiving households. The non remittance-receiving households also benefit from the remittances because of the existence of trade and services between non-migrants and migrants and their families.

Measuring the Impact of Remittances

Taylor (1999) noted several ways to measure the impact of remittances on the economy. First is the direct impact on the economy, measured by indicators such as the ratio of remittances to merchandise export and remittances per capita. Labour service is seen as an export and the remittances are part of the payment to the sending countries for the export of the labour services. In Turkey and Mexico, the ratios to exports in 1994 were 14 per cent and 12 per cent, respectively. The ratio was more than 100 per cent in Dominican Republic, more than 75 per cent in Egypt, El Salvador, and Jordan, more than 50 per cent in Yemen and Greece. Remittances per capita was highest in New Zealand ($411), followed by Portugal ($407).

Gammeltoft used the ratio of remittances to the national income. With this indicator, remittances are very important in El Salvador, the Dominican Republic, Pakistan, and Sri Lanka. Mexico and Colombia receive the largest absolute amount of remittances, but the amount is less significant compared to the size of their economies.

Another indicator of the direct effect is through the contribution of the remittances to the supply of foreign exchange, that is, the improvement of the balance of payment. In 1985, OECD (as cited in Glytsos 2002) argued that the addition of foreign exchanges is the most important positive contribution to the sending countries. Ratanakomut (2000) showed that remittances helped to overcome the trade deficit during 1987 and 1992 in Thailand. However, he also argued that the positive effect of remittances to Thailand's balance of payment has been substantially offset by the social cost in the migration process, and the opportunity cost because of the rising labour shortages. Furthermore, the migrant workers have had to spend an enormous amount of money (such as for recruitment fees and transportation expenses) before they arrive in the destination countries.

Second is the indirect impact, through the stimulation of the economy. This is the multiplier effect of remittances. Taylor argued that the multiplier is largest when the remittances go to rural households, where the community favours goods produced domestically using the relatively labour-intensive technologies and consumes less imported goods. In South Korea, between 3 per cent and 7 per cent of the growth of the GNP in 1976–81 had been attributable, both directly and indirectly, to the remittances. Massey et al. (1998) noted that every dollar contributed by a Mexican migrant had resulted in an increase of between US$2.69 and US$3.17 in Mexico's GNP.

Massey et al. (1998) found that remittances in the Philippines were used to buy basic necessities and pay debts. The remaining money was then used for housing, education, and land. However, this spending can also be seen as investment in human capital (improving the basic necessities, housing, and education) and in physical investment (buying land). Furthermore, this spending has a multiplier effect in the areas where the migrants returned. Remittances have been the most important determinant of the recovery of the Philippine's economy after the end of the regime in 1985. The use of remittances for consumption is also seen in Thailand. One third of the remittances from the Thai workers in the Gulf States is spent on housing, 21 per cent for repaying debts, 18 per cent on consumer goods, 6 per cent on farm investment, and 5 per cent on vehicles. The rising demand for houses has become an important stimulus for the Thai economy and skills enhancement.

Massey et al. also mentioned that many Asian countries (especially Korea, Thailand, and Indonesia) have favourable macroeconomic policies, resulting in economic environments conducive to productive investment and incorporating international labour migration in their development planning. Some Asian countries have also encouraged the repatriation of remittances for development purposes.

Many local studies show that remittances are used for consumption. However, the facts in Asian countries do not consistently support the view that income generated from remittances is mainly used for consumption rather than for saving. Some studies have shown that in Sri Lanka for example, there is no significant difference in the consumption pattern between households that receive remittances and those that do not. Others even found that households with remittances save more than non remittance-receiving households. The explanation as to why those households save more is that the households assume that the remittance-generated income is just transitory which may lead them to save it rather than to consume it. (See Puri and Ritzema 1999.)

Massey et al. (1998) concluded that the remittances have also greatly benefited those who are not the ones receiving the remittances. The remittances may be initially spent on consumption, but it has induced other economic activities and the creation of new jobs. In addition, spending on schooling and housing are often categorized as consumption, though in fact, better schooling and housing are investments in human capital.

The linkages between remittances-receiving households and non remittances-receiving households have amplified the initial benefit received by the remittances-receiving households. As an illustration, a rural remittances-receiving household may spend the money for consumption in the urban areas. This creates employment opportunities in urban areas. In turn, the rising income in urban areas may be partly spent back to the rural areas by spending on agricultural products or through domestic remittances by rural workers working in urban areas. In other words, examination of the full effect of remittances should go beyond the observation of the remittances-receiving households and even beyond the socio-economic sector or region where the households receive the remittances. Computable general equilibrium models (CGE) can be employed to measure the full impact of the remittances.

The measurement of the impact of the remittances on the economy should also be seen in the development context of the society. Taylor found that poor public service and infrastructure have reduced the potential of the contribution of remittances to the economy. Remittances will have greater impact on society where local institutions already exist to utilize the savings for production by other members of the society. An analysis of the development impact of remittances needs to consider the initial conditions under which people go abroad. Poor families obviously need more time than the better-off to gain from production.

Trends and Patterns of Indonesian Labour Emigration

The outflow of Indonesian workers to neighbouring countries has a long history. But, the significant increase of the outflows was notable during the New Order era, especially since the First Five Years Development Plan (*Pelita* I). In *Pelita* I, there were only 5,625 Indonesians working overseas and the number increased to 17,042 in the Second Five Years Development Plan (*Pelita* II). This number further increased dramatically in the Third Five Years Development Plan (*Pelita* III) to 295,037, and finally in *Pelita* V it reached 641,000 (Alatas 1995). In spite of a sharp increase in the number of international migrants, there are two other interesting phenomena. First, the increase of female international migrants has been higher than that of males. Second, the number of illegal migrants is getting higher especially those going to nearby countries such as Singapore and Malaysia (see Dwiyanto 2001).

Table 5.2 shows the trend and pattern of Indonesian labour international migration. First, international labour migration from Indonesia continued

TABLE 5.2
Number of Indonesian Workers Overseas, 1995–97

Country	1995			1996			1997		
	Male	Female	Male & Female	Male	Female	Male & Female	Male	Female	Male & Female
Malaysia*	11,079 29.0%	18,633 22.9%	29,712 24.9%	5,090 12.9%	33,562 18.6%	38,652 17.6%	194,207 85.7%	123,478 44.7%	317,685 63.2%
Other Asian Countries	18,024 47.3%	20,700 25.4%	38,724 32.4%	24,396 61.9%	32,022 17.7%	56,418 25.6%	22,331 9.9%	35,301 12.8%	57,632 11.5%
Middle East and Africa	5,505 14.4%	42,019 51.6%	47,524 39.8%	7,447 18.9%	115,117 63.7%	122,564 55.7%	8,775 3.9%	117,572 42.5%	126,347 25.1%
Europe and America	3,535 9.3%	12 0.0%	3,547 3.0%	2,500 6.3%	28 0.0%	2,528 1.1%	1,312 0.6%	1 0.0%	1,313 0.3%
Total	38,143 31.9%	81,364 68.1%	119,507 100.0%	39,433 17.9%	180,729 82.1%	220,162 100.0%	226,675 45.1%	276,352 54.9%	502,977 100.0%

Sources: 1995, 1996, 1997 Annual Reports, Dirjen Binapenta, Depnaker.
* Including Serawak and Sabah.

to increase during the period 1995–97. In 1997 the number of labour migrants was more than four times compared to that in 1995. Second, the number of female migrants was always higher in the period 1995–97. Interestingly, most female migrants preferred to work in Middle East than other countries. In 1995 for instance, more than half of female migrants went to Middle East and Africa. This figure was even higher in 1996, and it finally decreased to 42.5 per cent in 1997. In this year more female migrants resided in Malaysia, reaching almost 45 per cent. Third, Malaysia was becoming the main destination for Indonesian migrants, switching from Middle East which was very dominant in 1995 and 1996. This pattern remained the same in the following years.

In 1997/98 Malaysia was still the most preferred country for Indonesian migrants, followed by Saudi Arabia. However, as can be seen in the previous period, female labour migrants tended to prefer Saudi Arabia as the destination country while male labour migrants tended to work in Malaysia. The number of female migrants leaving for Saudi Arabia again surpassed those leaving for Malaysia. The main reason is because the highest employment opportunity for Indonesian workers in Saudi Arabia is that of housemaid. Research done by Sukamdi et al. (2001) shows that all return female migrants from Saudi Arabia preferred to re-migrate to Saudi Arabia working in the same job as housemaid.

International migration may not have increased the status of the women in terms of occupational mobility. This is unlike the Philippines' case, where female migrants are very likely to work in higher status jobs when they leave their country for the second time. That is why the Indonesian labour has always received unchanging wages compared to those from the Philippines or Thailand. Even in the same occupation such as foreign domestic helpers, Indonesian workers receive lower wages compared to the Philippine and Thai workers. As cited by Soeprobo and Wiyono (2002), Indonesian workers are the worst affected by wage violation.

In 1999 the number of Indonesia overseas workers was 427,619 and increased to 435,119 in 2000 (Table 5.3). As of 1 January 2001 alone, the number of Indonesian labour overseas was 12,463, most of whom went to Malaysia and Saudi Arabia. In the period 1999–2001, it is clear that Malaysia was still the major destination followed by Saudi Arabia. Female migrants dominated labour market in the Asia Pacific and Middle East and Africa,

TABLE 5.3
Indonesian Labour Emigration and Main Destinations

Destination	1999		2000	
	Male	Female	Male	Female
South Korea	9,278	1,800	5,527	1,162
Malaysia	80,124	89,053	106,659	85,041
Taiwan	5,822	23,550	5,390	45,118
Singapore	3,206	31,623	2,722	22,985
Hong Kong	42	12,720	6	21,703
Brunei	1,620	4,857	1,108	3,162
Japan	3,353	35	3,359	52
Other Countries	684	1	90	2
Total Asia Pacific	104,129	163,639	124,861	179,225
Arab Emirates	386	17,198	183	9,375
Saudi Arabia	14,473	116,684	10,748	103,319
Other Countries	697	5,198	328	5,212
Middle East and Africa	15,556	139,080	11,259	117,906
America (North, Central and South)	3,504	15	1,508	1
Europe	1,639	57	321	38
Total by gender	124,828	302,791	137,949	297,170
TOTAL		427,619		435,119

Source: Ministry of Manpower.

but not in other destination regions. However it is very interesting to find out that the sex composition of Indonesian labour migrants overseas varies among countries. In the Asia Pacific region for instance, female labour migrants were more in all countries except South Korea and Japan. The number of Indonesian female labour emigrants to Middle Eastern and African countries were mostly higher than male.

Table 5.4 shows that the number of Indonesian emigrants fluctuated in all major destination areas except Taiwan, where the number consistently increased in the period 1996–2000. The highest number of Indonesian workers entering Malaysia was in 1997, which then dropped to less than 100,000 the following year. It increased again in 1999 and 2000. Among the main destination countries, the number of Indonesian

TABLE 5.4
Number of Indonesian Migrant Workers in Selected Countries, 1996–2000

Countries	1996	1997	1998	1999	2000
Malaysia	38,652	317,685	95,033	169,177	170,067
Singapore	29,065	31,928	42,031	34,829	20,456
Taiwan	8,888	9,445	14,109	29,372	41,620
Saudi Arabia	115,209	116,844	177,404	131,157	108,734

Source: Tara Bakti H. Soeprobo and Nurhadi Wiyono, 2002.

workers decreased only in Malaysia in the period 1997–98. This period was the beginning of the economic crisis in Southeast Asia. If we believe that push factors worked as driving factors for Indonesian workers abroad, then we can expect that there should be an influx of out-migration from Indonesia to neighbouring countries, especially Malaysia, since Indonesia was worst hit by the crisis. However, we have to bear in mind that all these figures refer to the official data which do not necessarily represent exactly the number of outflow international migration from Indonesia. Many Indonesian workers abroad enter the destination countries by illegal means. Some data show that nearly 700,000 Indonesian migrants in Malaysia were illegal (Kassim 1997; Hugo 1992). *Kompas* (cited by Keban 2000) estimated that 58.36 per cent of Indonesian workers in Malaysia were illegal. Vermonte (2002) provided a higher number — more than 400,000 out of 600,000, or more than two-thirds of Indonesian migrants in Malaysia were illegal.

Research on illegal workers are important in understanding not only the reasons why the workers opt for illegal migration, but also the issues related to remittances. Ananta (2000) gave a clear picture of how the illegal process provides higher significant benefits for the recruiters than the legal one, but not for the migrants. Several cases in Indonesia show that the workers have to pay higher costs when they go through illegal rather than legal procedures (Mantra et al. 1999). Nevertheless, they use the illegal procedure mostly because it is a simpler process.

Illegal emigrants, especially to Malaysia, are now discouraged by the law, the Immigration Act (Amended), which caused hundreds of thousands of migrants to return home before 1 August 2002. The law consists of several punishments for illegal migrants such as RM 10,000 fine (US$2,631), five years imprisonment, and six strokes of the cane. While this may not affect the legal migrants, it is clear that in the near future the flow of illegal emigrants from Indonesia to Malaysia will slow down. There are two arguments that the flow of Indonesian labour to Malaysia will not slow down or may even increase. First, the two countries are relatively close, reducing the obstacle of distance. Second, a more important factor is the social and cultural similarities between these two countries, which may reduce the obstacles for migrants to adapt to the new environment.

The increasing number of Indonesian labour migrants indicates that the remittances they send home is likely to have a high impact on the sending country's economy, especially after Indonesia was hit by the economic crisis since mid-1997. The crisis has resulted in a large depreciation in the value of the rupiah, but this depreciation has become a blessing. The very weak rupiah has resulted in much larger values for their foreign-earned remittances.

In the following section, we examine the impact of remittances on the Indonesian economy based on limited existing data.

Macroeconomic Impacts

Though the Government of Indonesia recognizes the advantage of sending large numbers of labour — particularly unskilled labour — abroad, there has been little concern on the impact of remittances on the Indonesian economy, among both academicians and policy-makers. Not surprisingly, the statistics on remittances is also limited. As also found in many other countries, we believe that the remittances in Indonesia have been under-reported. In some regions in Indonesia the unofficial remittances can be much larger than the official ones.

The fact that Indonesia is a very large country, with a population of about 206 million in 2000, adds to the problem of recording the remittances. The province of East Nusa Tenggara, for example, is known for the international outflow of labour. Approximately 10,000 migrants from East Nusa Tenggara are estimated to have worked in Malaysia and they were able to send their remittances in the amount of 120 billion rupiah per year, which is much higher than the province budget of only 80.4 billion rupiah (Dwiyanto 2001). It means that the role of remittances in the province is significant. The problem is that the local government has never included the remittances in their economic development planning and the official statistics has under-reported the remittances. We speculate that unrecorded remittances may have constituted a large proportion of total remittances and it may be even larger than the official statistics. With this limitation, we present the picture of the macroeconomic impact of remittances on the national economy and two provincial economies.

Indonesia has used labour migration as one of its important development policies and the rising emigration is expected to be accompanied by rising remittances. As shown in Gammeltoft (2002), during 1990–99 the total international resource flows to Indonesia constituted foreign direct investment (30 per cent), aid (24 per cent), remittances (8 per cent), and other private flows (38 per cent). El Salvador had the largest (66 per cent) contribution of remittances to the total international resource flow, while most of the total international resource flows to Rwanda were in the form of aid (98 per cent). The largest FDI contribution was seen in Columbia (43 per cent), and the largest percentage of other private inflows was found in Mexico (44 per cent).

Table 5.5 shows that the total remittances officially recorded in 1999 was more than 110 times those in 1983. The number of labour migrants had also increased, but the number in 1999 was only less than twenty times that in 1983. In other words, the total remittances had grown much faster than the number of migrants. Therefore, the per capita remittances (per migrant) had also risen, becoming US$2,593 in 1999, more than seven times the number in 1983. These remittances per capita are higher than the average labour wages in Indonesia. This huge difference between average labour wage and the remittances per capita may have become an important motivation for Indonesians to work overseas.

Interestingly, the declines in the migrants in 1986–87 and 1992–95 were not accompanied by similar declines in the remittances in the same period. It is possible that the migrants had enjoyed rising earnings because of the economic boom in the receiving countries. The remittances declined in 1990, 1991 and 1997 while the number of migrants kept rising.

The latest data on remittances show that in the first three months of 2004, about US$425.2 million was sent home by almost 294,000 workers (*Jakarta Post*, 2004). Therefore, per capita remittances per month was around US$482, more than double that in 1999.

TABLE 5.5
Per Capita Remittances in 1983–99

Year	Labour Migrants	Remittances (US$ Millions)	Per Capita Remittances (in US$)	Average Monthly Nominal Wage in Indonesia
1983	29,291	10	341.402	–
1984	46,014	53	1,151.823	–
1985	54,297	61	1,123.451	–
1986	68,360	71	1,038.619	–
1987	61,092	86	1,407.713	–
1988	61,419	99	1,611.879	–
1989	84,074	167	1,986.345	–
1990	86,264	166	1,924.325	–
1991	149,782	130	867.928	–
1992	172,157	229	1,330.181	–
1993	159,995	346	2,162.568	–
1994	141,287	449	3,177.929	–
1995	120,603	651	5,397.876	–
1996	220,162	796	3,615.519	–
1997	502,977	725	1,441.418	241,837
1998	899,622	959	1,066.003	282,251
1999	427,619	1,295.50	3,029.566	346,950

Source: Data on remittances are compiled from IMF Balance of Payment Statistics Year Book. Annual, as quoted in *Migration News* <http://migration.ucdavis.edu>.
Note: US$1.00 was about Rp. 8,000 in 1999.

FIGURE 5.1
Per Capita Remittances in 1983–99

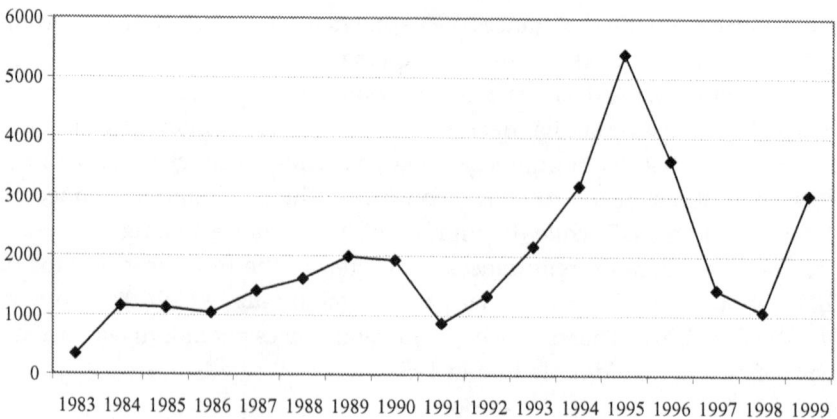

Table 5.6 presents month-by-month data on migrants for the year 2000. The number of migrants have been fluctuating, reflecting the "season" of sending labour abroad. February, June and October are the months with small numbers of migrants, while April, August and December are the peaks.

The per capita remittances have declined several times, in 1985–86, 1990–91, and 1996–98. The economic crisis hitting East and Southeast Asia since 1997 may explain the decline in per capita remittance during 1996–98. The much smaller number of migrants in 1999 and 2000 compared to the previous years may be because some contracts were not renewed and demand for new migrants could have declined. Interestingly, the remittances in each of 1999 and 2000 was higher than that in the preceeding years. A deeper study should be done to examine the correlation between trends in number of migrants and remittances on the one hand, and economic trends in the receiving countries on the other hand.

Some micro studies, however, show different pictures. The remittances per capita can be very high. The economy of the poor may be relying mostly on remittances. A study by Hernawati (1996) for instance, found that the average remittance sent from Malaysia to Indonesia was 231,400

TABLE 5.6
Number of Out-Migrants by Month: Indonesia, 2000

Period	Labour Migrants
January	29,338
February	17,215
March	26,385
April	37,710
May	30,115
June	22,129
July	31,870
August	68,490
September	36,483
October	27,431
November	49,385
December	58,568
Total	435,119

Source: Ministry of Transmigration and Manpower.

rupiah per month or 2,776,800 rupiah per year. A much higher number was found by the PSC-GMU team (Tamtiari 2000) that, in 1998, the average monthly payment sent to their homes was 3,840,552 rupiah. Therefore, the magnitude of the remittances per capita could be much larger than the Indonesian income per capita and the remittances have become an important source of income for the migrants and their families. In other words, remittances should have had a significant role in the individual or household economy.

Measured by the percentage of remittances to the GDP (Gross Domestic Product), remittances have not played an important role in the Indonesian economy. In most of the 1983–2000 period, the percentage was always less than 0.50 per cent, with the highest at only 1.15 per cent in 1998. The next highest percentages were in the two years preceding 1998 (see Table 5.7). This percentage is very small, compared to, for example, India, Tunisia, and even Lesotho. As quoted in O'Neill (2001), in 1989 India's overseas labour's remittances constituted about 1 per cent of the value of GDP, while the Indonesian figure was only about 0.22 per cent. In Tunisia, the percentage of remittances to the GDP value in 1989 was even higher than 4.8 per cent. But the most impressive example is the case of Lesotho, where Lesotho migrant labour abroad sent money to their country, constituting about 169.6 per cent of the GDP value.

The contribution of the remittances to the national economy is also not important if we measure the percentage of remittances to exports and imports. Table 5.7 shows that remittance as a percentage of exports tended to rise, but was always below 2.75 per cent. The highest percentage was 2.66 per cent (in 1999), followed by 1.96 per cent (in 1998), and 1.83 per cent (in 2000). Its percentage to imports was on average larger than that to exports, but the highest percentage was only 5.40 per cent (in 1999), followed by 3.51 per cent in 1998, and 3.39 per cent in 2000. The last three years of the period 1983–2000 saw the highest percentages to exports and imports. The percentages may have been higher if the data on remittances for 2000 had included the data on December 2000. Yet, whatever the data on December 2000, the percentages are still relatively very small compared to, for example, the Philippines, Sri Lanka, and Bangladesh. As shown in Table 5.8, the percentage to exports was 22.3 per cent in the Philippines (1993) and 19.8 per cent in Sri Lanka (1993), while the percentage to imports in the Philippines was 14.4 per cent and in Sri Lanka, 15.6 per cent. In 1993 the percentage to exports in Bangladesh was 44.1 per cent;

TABLE 5.7

**Indonesian Worker's Remittances as Percentage of GDP,
Export and Import 1983–2000**

Year	Workers' Remittances (US$ Millions)	Percentage of Remittance to GDP	Percentage of Remittance to Export	Percentage of Remittance to Import
1983	10	0.013	0.047	0.061
1984	53	0.062	0.242	0.382
1985	61	0.077	0.328	0.595
1986	71	0.129	0.480	0.662
1987	86	0.157	0.502	0.695
1988	99	0.154	0.515	0.747
1989	167	0.220	0.754	1.021
1990	166	0.213	0.647	0.760
1991	130	0.148	0.446	0.503
1992	229	0.230	0.674	0.839
1993	346	0.304	0.940	1.221
1994	449	0.377	1.121	1.404
1995	651	0.491	1.433	1.602
1996	796	0.512	1.598	1.854
1997	725	0.725	1.357	1.739
1998	959	1.149	1.963	3.508
1999	1,295.50	0.341	2.662	5.397
2000	1,135.30	0.286	1.827	3.387

Source: Remittances in the period of 1983–1998 are quoted from <http://migration.ucdavis.edu/Data/
remit.on.www/remittances.html> downloaded on 18 November 2002. Remittances for 1999
and 2000 are from the Ministry of Labour and data on Export and Import are from the
Statistical Year Book of Indonesia, 2000.

and to imports, 28.2 per cent. It may be noted that the pattern of remittances as percentages of exports and imports in Indonesia is different from that in other countries. In other countries, the percentages to exports are always larger than that to imports. However, in Indonesia, the percentages to imports are always larger than those to exports.

The macro-picture of remittances for Indonesia as a whole may not necessarily be similar to that of the regions in Indonesia. At the province of West Nusa Tenggara, for example, the direct contribution of remittances to the macro-economy is very large. Table 5.9 indicates that in 1998 remittances to West Nusa Tenggara was about 443 million rupiah in total

TABLE 5.8
Flow of Workers' Remittances and its Share in Imports and Exports of Goods in Selected Labour-Exporting Countries

Country	1980			1985			1990			1993		
	Remittances	As Percentage of Exports	Imports	Remittances	As Percentage of Exports	Imports	Remittances	As Percentage of Exports	Imports	Remittances	As Percentage of Exports	Imports
Bangladesh	286	36.1	12.2	502	50.2	22	779	46.6	23.9	1,004	44.1	28.2
India	2,715	32.7	19.5	2,427	25.6	16.1	2,263	12.4	9.7	–	–	–
Indonesia	–	–	–	61	0.3	0.5	166	0.6	0.8	346	0.9	1.2
Korea, Rep.	100	0.6	0.5	265	1	1	597	0.9	0.9	605	0.7	0.8
Pakistan	2,108	82.1	38.7	2,573	97.2	43.8	2,175	40.4	26.9	1,602	23.7	17.2
Philippines	613	10.6	7.9	805	17.4	15.8	1,460	17.8	12	2,542	22.3	14.4
Sri Lanka	139	13.1	7.5	233	17.7	12.7	369	19.9	15.9	551	19.8	15.6
Thailand	348	5.4	4.2	809	11.5	9.6	774	3.4	2.6	–	–	–

Source: Puri and Ritzema (1999), Table 2.

TABLE 5.9
Remittances sent to West and East Nusa Tenggara
(in Indonesian Rupiah Monthly), in 1998

Province	Total Remittances	No. of Respondents	Per Capita Remittances
West Nusa Tenggara	442,947,996	310	1,428,864.50
East Nusa Tenggara	131,539,100	296	444,388.85
Total	574,487,096	606	947,998.51

Source: Mantra et al., 1999.

per month (or equivalent to US$39,201). The Director of Bank of Indonesia branch of Mataram, the capital of West Nusa Tenggara, reported that in the first quarter of 2002, the total remittances sent by 21,900 international migrants was 146.70 billion rupiah. It increased sharply to 171.69 billion rupiah in the second quarter per month remittances inflow (Kompas 2002). This amount was much larger than the local revenue of West Nusa Tenggara, which was only 61 billion rupiah in 2001.

It should be noted that the mentioned amounts of remittances were only those sent through two major banks in Mataram, the Mandiri bank and BNI bank. The amount would have been larger if we include the remittances sent through other banks and informal channels, including those by illegal migrants. The remittances produced by illegal migrants may be larger than those by legal migrants.

As reported in Dwiyanto (2001), in 1995 total remittances to West Nusa Tenggara was about 111.106 billion rupiah and it constituted 3.79 per cent of the gross regional domestic product. This contribution to the macro-economy is larger than that at the national level.

Remittances sent to East Nusa Tenggara were relatively smaller. The amount in 1998 was only about 131.5 million rupiah (or equivalent to US$11,641) per month. Yet, Tamtiari (1999) calculated that the average amount of remittances sent by illegal migrants from East Lombok, an island in the West Nusa Tenggara province, was as high as 299,324 rupiah per month, more than the 283,151 rupiah per month by legal migrants.

East Java is another illustration. Bank of Indonesia in the East Java branch reported that in the fiscal year of 2002 the migrants contributed as much as 181.64 billion rupiah to the East Java's income, more than those sent to East Nusa Tenggara (*Jakarta Post*, 8 March 2003). Yet, this amount was less than the 193.68 billion rupiah in the preceding year. However, this amount of money is only limited to that from Besuki, part of the East Java province. We can expect that there would be much higher remittance flow to East Java if the calculation is based on the whole area of the province.

West Nusa Tenggara, East Nusa Tenggara, and East Java are only three of many other provinces in Indonesia sending labour abroad. Yet, these cases have shown the important direct contribution of remittances to the macro-economy of the provinces, a different picture from the contribution of remittances to the macro-economy at the national level. Other provinces, especially those known for sources of migrants, may have similar pictures as shown in West Nusa Tenggara and East Nusa Tenggara, though others may show similar pictures with the one at the national level. East Java (especially Bawean and Tulungagung), West Java (especially Indramayu), and the western part of Central Java are also well-known sources of international migration.

Impact on Household Economy

It should be mentioned here that there has not been any study on the multiplier effect of remittances in Indonesia, or in the regions. Despite the lack of studies on the multiplier, there have been many small-scale studies and anecdotal evidences on the impact of remittances on the remittance-receiving households and non remittance-receiving households.

One of the important linkages of the "contribution" of the remittances is unfortunately through the extortion of the remittances by various individuals who "help" the migrants. The money channelled to these individuals can be much larger than those actually going to the migrants and their families. Indeed, Jones (2000) reported that labour-sending activities have been very a lucrative, multi-million-dollar business in Indonesia. It has been dealing with illicit activities such as narcotics trade. Extortion has taken place at every stage, from the time the migrants leave their villages, in the working places in the destination countries, and until they return to their own villages. Ironically, the multiplier effect through this business may be very large and the impact on economic growth may be significant. The business of sending workers abroad, and their forward and backward linkages, may have helped a large amount of individuals cope with or even prosper during the crisis that started to hit Indonesia in 1997.

The Government of Indonesia has set up the so-called "Terminal 3" in the Sukarno-Hatta international airport (the airport of the capital of Indonesia) to help the migrants, leaving from and returning to Indonesia. Unlike other passengers, all would-be migrants must go through this terminal to leave from and enter Indonesia. However, many have suspected that the creation of Terminal 3 will only aggravate the situation, strengthening the extortion of migrants.

The Jakarta Post (28 March 2003) reported that the Terminal 3 is a famous place for treating the migrants, especially when they return home and bring a lot of money, as cash cows. The individuals extorting the migrants include government officials, police officers, bank employees, non-governmental organization activists, bogus journalists and the bus drivers taking the migrants from the airport to their villages. The "robbery" can be in the form of bus drivers asking "cigarette money" (*uang rokok*) or by raising the cost of the ticket, of business persons asking the migrants to change their foreign money at low exchange rates, of strangers asking them to buy electronic goods at a very high price, and of many other ways. The extortion has become an organized crime by officials and individuals with no legal authority.

It should also be borne in mind that most of the remittances are sent through banks and mail services as well as middlemen or "*calo*" and their friends. Compared to the bank and mail services, the second channel (middlemen) is riskier, but the migrants may feel more comfortable with. Most of the remittances sent through middlemen or *calo* disappear for some unclear reasons, such as robberies or other reasons that can be used to explain why the families of the migrants did not receive the full amount of money sent by the migrants. There are a lot of stories of how returning migrants have become victims of robbery or "wrong" procedures. As an illustration, *Kedaulatan Rakyat* (3 September 2002) reported that Barningsih, 24 years old, returned home with psychological problems. Her problems were worsened by a complicated bank procedure. She could not withdraw the 15 million rupiah from her two years of working overseas.

An important approach to examining the impact of remittances on the household economy is by understanding the use of remittances by the household members. The following analysis is based on a household survey carried out by the Centre of Population and Policy Studies in three provinces, East Java, East Nusa Tenggara and West Nusa Tenggara.

The result may not represent provincial figures, but at least it can be used as a preliminary step to better understanding the impact of remittances on the economy, especially through their impact on other activities, and not necessarily by the remittance-receiving households only, in the local economy or even wider economies.

The observations of the Indonesian cases are consistent with the findings in other countries, mentioned in the beginning of the chapter. Most of the remittances are used for "unproductive" activities, such as consumption purposes and/or paying debts. Migrants from Central Lombok (in West Nusa Tenggara province), for instance, used most of their remittances to pay off their debts, to cover their daily needs, and to provide for their school children (Dwiyanto 2001). Those in East Lombok (also in West Nusa Tenggara) used their remittances mostly to build and repair their houses and finance their children's education (Haris 2000). A case study in East and West Nusa Tenggara shows that the remittances sent by migrant workers from Malaysia had been used for a variety of purposes (see Keban 1999 and Mantra 1999). The most conspicuous ones were for housing, farming, and education, in addition to fulfilment of basic needs.

After spending on subsistence needs such as food, clothing, education, and health care, they spent the remittances on expensive non-subsistent items such as unusually modern houses and expensive consumer goods. Fariani (Soeprobo and Wiyono 2002), based on her study in West Java, found that households with members working abroad, especially Saudi Arabia, usually have beautiful houses. Research by Adi (Soeprobo and Wiyono 2002) found that 58 per cent of the migrants used their remittances for non-productive activities such as to build and or renovate the house and pay off debts. A similar finding has also been found in the study done by Sukamdi, et al. (2001) in Yogyakarta and Setiadi (1998) in East Nusa Tenggara. Most of the migrant families said that they used the remittances to buy things such as refrigerators, televisions, radios, motorcycles, and houses.

We should be careful on the use of the word "unproductive" to refer to the mentioned activities. They may not use the money to engage in market-oriented production, those often-called "productive" activities. However, the migrants have been very rational is using the remittances. They prioritize the use of the remittances for subsistence needs, before spending on luxurious consumption. The ability to pay off debts will certainly increase the welfare and feeling of comfort among the households. Improvements to the condition of the house, the quality of food and clothing, and even education and health are certainly activities of human capital investment. This kind of investment does not immediately result in their profit, but the increase in human capital itself is one of the important objectives of economic development. This progress, in human capital, may not be able to be translated into economic growth, but economic growth is not the only indicator of the success of economic development.

Spending the remittances on luxury goods has raised the socio-economic status of the remittance-receiving households. Traditional customs have been transformed into more modern ones, especially in the areas of housing and construction. Housing, for example, can be regarded as monuments to show their successes as migrant workers. In short, the remittances have improved the economic status of the migrant families and they have great impact on the consumption patterns of the families.

It should also be noted that only very few migrants spent their money in the destination areas. Most of them spent the money locally. Those spending on luxurious goods, especially on housing, would have increased the aggregate demand for the local economy or even wider economy, including those in the urban areas. Yet, unlike in Thailand, the remittances have not resulted in the growth of the housing industry.

Therefore, even if we want to measure the impact of remittances on economic growth, we should also measure the extent to which the "non-productive" activities have increased the aggregate demand. During the Indonesian crisis, an increase in consumption expenditure had helped prevent the economy from collapsing, and it could even help maintain the growth rate. Indeed, the migrants, and the remittance-receiving households have particularly benefited from the crisis. The flow of the remittances has freed the origin areas from the impacts of the crisis.

Despite the possible benefits of using the remittances for "non-productive" activities, some of the remittances have been indeed used for "productive" activities, though the percentage is smaller than those used for "non-productive" activities. A survey in East Lombok shows that about 34 per cent of migrant families had invested the remittances in several productive activities such as additional capital for trade activities, agriculture and small-scale industries (Haris 2000). Several success stories of using remittances for economic activities can be found in the poor village of Jambon, Bantul District, the province of Yogyakarta. Sarjuni, for example, received about five million rupiah since his wife started working in Malaysia. He invested the money to increase his capital to develop his economic activity in selling furniture. Sarjono has a different way in investing the money. He received about fifteen million rupiah in fourteen months after his wife started working in Malaysia and spent part of the money to buy livestocks such as cows and saved part of it in the bank (see *Kedaulatan Rakyat*, 11 August 2002).

Maximizing the Benefit of Remittances

There has been inadequate attention on the role of remittances in economic development by academicians and yet the limited literature is mixed on the contribution of remittances to economic development. The debate on the measurement of the impact is one of the puzzles of assessing the impact. For the Indonesian case, the impact is small if measured in the macro-economy at the national level, but greater at some provinces. However, the impact may be greater if we measure the impact on the human capital of the migrants and their families. But, all these studies have not considered the impact, including the multiplier effect, on the aggregate demand in the local economy or provincial and even national economy.

Another debate is on the utilization of the remittances themselves, whether they are spent on "productive" or "unproductive" activities. It is not fair however, to expect that the migrants and their families should carry out "productive activities". The migrants are the source of funding and, as in other sources of funding, it is the task of the government and the society as a whole to optimize the availability of the funding. Nevertheless, the government should not expect that maximizing the remittances from migrants is a panacea to Indonesian development. Even in some areas, the opportunities to develop small-scale economic activities are limited. Furthermore, it is still important that the government also influences the use of the remittances by the migrants and the families themselves. Puri and Ritzema (1999), and also O'Neill (2001) suggested those which focus on establishing the ability of migrant labour to set up their own enterprise. This is conducted through several policies explicitly encouraging migrant labour to spend the income on capital goods through concessional rates on duty. Another policy needed to supplement previous policies is one that is designed to raise the ability and skills of migrant labour to run their enterprise, such as by establishing business counselling and training or initiating an institute on entrepreneurship development.

It should be emphasized, however, that without sound macroeconomic policy, including creating the needed infrastructure conducive for productive activities, the rising amount of remittances could harm the economy, by pushing up the inflation rate and raising imports.

The question then, is how to maximize the benefit of the remittances for the Indonesian economy at national, provincial, and local levels. It should be remembered, however, that maximizing the benefit for the economy does not necessarily mean maximizing the impact on conventional macroeconomic indicators such as economic growth, remittances per capita, percentage of remittances to the national or regional income, and percentages of remittances to export and import. Of foremost importance is the impact on the welfare of the migrants and their families. Second is the impact on non remittance-receiving households and the surrounding economy. Maximizing remittances per capita, percentage of remittances to national or regional product, for example, are only means, but not the only means, to increase the welfare of the migrants and their families.

The amount of remittances is not the only means to raise the welfare, but it is a very important means. It is urgent, therefore, to reduce or even eliminate the leakages of the remittances. The leakages come from many individuals who try to "help" the migrants from the recruitment process until when the money is sent or brought back home by the migrants. We do not deny that some of the costs are really necessary to send the migrants to the working place in other countries and to bring the money back home. However, it is suspected that there are also many unnecessary "costs" the migrants have to pay. The migrants have become victims. Such unnecessary costs should be eliminated to raise the welfare of the migrants and their families.

The effort of the Jakarta Police Headquarters in assigning Sri Suari, a very dedicated person, to be in charge of the security at the Sukarno-Hatta international airport needs to be applauded. Sri Suari has a special, and important job, to provide the maximum protection to the Indonesian workers just returning from overseas. She has found at least thirty-five cases of extortion of migrant workers returning from overseas. (*Jakarta Post*, 28 March 2003.) Finding and assigning persons such as Sri Suari should be continued and supported.

Given the high proportion of unrecorded remittances, the government should also pay attention to designing policies to minimize it. In other words, government must be concerned about redirecting the remittances from the informal channels to the official one. One thing that may work is to make it mandatory to send remittances through formal financial institutions, such as through national banks. As an example, the Philippine Government through Executive Order No. 857 (1982) requires the migrant labour to send back at least about seventy per cent of their income abroad. However such a mandatory policy may be ineffective (O'Neill 2001). Another policy option that may be more effective is through the incentive scheme. This may take form as permission for the migrant labour to deposit their income in foreign currency as long as they save in a national bank that may have higher interest, and the issuance of development bonds.

Another important issue is how government may intervene to simplify the transmittal method and reduce the transmittal cost. It is well understood that most of the Indonesian migrants are lowly-educated. Yet, it is clear that there is lack of government attention to simplify bank procedures for migrants to withdraw their money. The government has to help them in such a way that the migrants are able to transfer their money in the easiest way through a formal channel.

References

Alatas, S. *Migrasi dan Distribusi Penduduk di Indonesia*. Jakarta: Kantor Menteri Negara Kependudukan/ BKKBN, 1995.

Ananta, Aris. "Economic Integration and Free Labour Area: An Indonesia Perspective". In *Labour Migration in Indonesia: Policies and Practice*, edited by Sukamdi et al. Yogyakarta: Population Studies Centre, Gadjah Mada University, 2000, pp. 23–62.

Barham, B., and S. Broucher. "Migration, Remittances, and Inequality: Estimating the Net Effects of Migration on Income Distribution". *Journal of Development Economics* 55 (1998): 307–31.

Durand, J, W. Kandel, E.A. Parado, and D.S. Massey. "International Migration and Development in Mexican Communities". *Demography* 33, no. 2 (May 1996): 249–64.

Dwiyanto, Agus. "International Migration and Its Impact on Regional Development Affairs: A Case of Indonesia". Paper presented in Annual Meeting of APMRN, Manila, 2001.

Dirjen Binapenta. *Annual Reports 1995*. Depatemen Tenaga Kerja Republik Indonesia, 1995.

———. *Annual Reports 1996*. Departemen Tenaga Kerja Republik Indonesia, 1996.

———. *Annual reports 1997*. Departemen Tenaga Kerja Republik Indonesia, 1997.

Gammeltoft, Peter. "Remittances and Other Financial Flows to Developing Countries" *International Migration* 40, no. 5 (2002), SI 2.

Glytsos, Nicholas P. "The Role of Migrant Remittances in Development: Evidence from Mediterranean Countries". *International Migration Quarterly Review* 40, no. 1 (2002): 5–26.

Haris, Abdul. *Data Survey Migrasi Internasional Asal Lombok*. Unpublished, 2000.

Hermele, K. "The Discourse on Migration and Development". In *International Migration, Immobility and Development*, edited by Hammar, T., G. Brochman, K. Tamas and T. Faist. Oxford: Berg, 1997, pp. 133–58.

Hernawati, Titian. "Analisis mobilitas pekerja ke luar negeri dan remitan serta pengaruhnya terhadap kontribusi pendapatan rumahtangga di kabupaten Lombok Tengah Proponsi Nusa Tenggara Barat". S-2 thesis, Program Studi Pengelolaan Lingkungan Hidup, Program Pasca Sarjana, Universitas Hassanuddin, 1996.

Hugo, Graeme J. "Indonesian Labour Migration to Malaysia: Trends and Policy Implication". Paper presented at the International Conference on Migration, National University of Singapore, 1992.

Jakarta Post. "Migrant Workers Contribute Rp 181.64 Billion to E. Java Economy". 8 March 2003.

———. "A Defender of Victimized Workers". 28 March 2003.

———. "Indonesia: Remittances from Migrant Workers Up". 28 July 2004.

Jones, Sidney. *Making Money off Migrants. The Indonesian Exodus to Malaysia*. Hongkong: Asia 2000 Ltd., 2000.

Kassim, Azizah. "Illegal Alien Labour in Malaysia: Its Influx, Utilization and Reunifications". *Indonesia and the Malay World*, no. 71 (1997): pp. 50–82.

Keban, Yeremias T. *Research and Training Program on International Migration and Development Studies : A Report*. Yogyakarta: Population Studies Centre, 1999.

Keban, Yeremias, T. "International Migration, The Strategy for National

Development and Globalization". In *Labor Migration in Indonesia: Policies and Practices*, edited by Sukamdi et al. Yogyakarta: Population Studies Centre, GMU and APMRN, 2000.

Kedaulatan Rakyat. "Dusun IDT Jambon Berubah, Karena TKI, Banyak Istri Tinggalkan Anak-Suami". 11 August 2002.

Kedaulatan Rakyat. "Uang Rp. 15 Juta Belum Bisa Dinikmati, 2 Tahun di Singapura, TKI Pulang Stress". 3 September 2002.

Kompas. "Rp. 24 Milyar Sebulan, Kiriman TKI Asal NTB". 12 October 2002.

Mantra, Ida Bagoes, Kasto dan Yeremias T Keban. *Mobilitas Tenaga Kerja Indonesia ke Malaysia: studi kasus Flores Timur, Lombok Tengah, dan Pulau Bawean*. Yogyakarta: Pusat Penelitian Kependudukan, 1999.

Martin, Philip and Jonas Widgren. "International Migration: Facing the Challenge". *Population Bulletin* 57, no. 1 (2002).

Martin, Susan F. "Remittances as Development Tool". Paper presented at the "Remittances As a Development Tool: A Regional Conference" organized by the Multilateral Investment Fund of the Inter-American Development Bank, Washington, D.C., May 2001.

Massey, Douglas S., Joaquín Arango, Graeme Hugo, Ali Kouaouci, Adela Pellegrino, and J. Edward Taylor. *Worlds in Motion. Understanding International Migration at the End of the Millenium*. New York: Oxford University Press Inc., 1998.

Nyberg-Sorensen et al. "The Migration-Development Nexus. Evidence and Policy Options State-of-the-Art Overview". *International Migration Quarterly Review*. Special issue: The Migration Development Nexus 40, no. 5, 2/2002a.

Nyberg-Sorensen et al. "The Migration-Development Nexus. Evidence and Policy Options". *International Migration Quarterly Review*. Special issue: The Migration Development Nexus 40, no. 5, 2/2002b.

O'Neill, Alexander C. "Emigrant Remittances: Policies to Increase Inflows and Maximize Benefits". <http://ijgls.indiana.edu/archive/09/01/oneill.shtml>. 2001.

Puri, Shivani and Tineke Ritzema. "Migrant Worker Remittances, Micro-finance and the Informal Economy: Prospects and Issues". ILO Working Paper no. 21, 1999.

Ratanakomut, Somchai. "Issues of International Migration in South Korea". In *Thai Migrant Workers in East and Southeast Asia. 1996–1997*, edited by Supang Chantavanich, Andreas Germershausen, and Allan Beesey. Bangkok: The Asian Research Centre for Migration (ARCM), 2000.

Russell, S. "International Migration: Implication for The World Bank". World Bank Working Papers, 2001.

Setiadi. "Konteks Sosio-kultural Migrasi Internasional: Kasus di Lewotolok, Flores Timur". Paper for monthly Seminar at Population Studies Centre, Gadjah Mada University, 18 November 1998.

Soeprobo, Tara Bakti and Nur Hadi Wiyono. "The Process of the International Labor Migration from Indonesia". Paper presented at National Seminar on "Isu Kebijakan Gender dalam Pembangunan". Surakarta, 11 July 2002.

Sukamdi, Setiadi, Agus Indiyanto, Abdul Haris, and Irwan Abdullah. "Country Study 2: Indonesia". In *Female Labor Migration in Southeast Asia: Change and Continuity*, edited by Supang Chantavanich, Christian Wille, Kannika Angsuthanasombat, Maruja M.B. Asis, Allan Beesey, and Sukamdi. Bangkok: Asia Research Centre for Migration, Institute of Asian Studies, Chulalongkorn University, 2001.

Tamtiari, Wini. "Dampak Sosial Migrasi Tenaga Kerja ke Malaysia". *Populasi* 10, no. 2 (1999): 39–56.

Tamtiari, Wini. "Dampak Migrasi Tenaga Kerja Ke Malaysia (Studi Kasus Implementasi Kebijakan Migrasi di Lombok Timur, Nusa Tenggara Barat)". Thesis S2 Program Studi Ilmu Administrasi Negara Jurusan Ilmu-ilmu Sosial, Program Pasca Sarjana Universitas Gadjah Mada, 2000.

Taylor, J. Edward. "The New Economics of Labour Migration and the Role of Remittances in the Migration Process". *International Migration* 37, no. 1 (1999).

Vermonte, Philips, Jusario. "RI Must Learn from Illegal Migrant Issue". *The Jakarta Post*, August 2002.

6

Transnational Networks in Female Labour Migration

Vivienne Wee and Amy Sim

Labour Migration in Southeast Asia[1]

The major sending countries of migrant workers in Southeast Asia are Myanmar, Indonesia, Laos, Malaysia, Thailand, the Philippines and Vietnam.[2] The receiving countries of these workers in Southeast Asia are Brunei, Malaysia, Singapore and Thailand. Beyond Southeast Asia, the receiving countries are worldwide, including Canada, the European Union, Hong Kong, Taiwan, United States and countries in the Middle East. Southeast Asia is thus a region that includes both sending and receiving countries.

This implies the absence of a pan-regional perspective on labour migration. Rather, a key differentiation in perspective is between labour-exporting or sending countries and labour-importing or receiving countries. This intra-regional bifurcation has led to long-standing relations of economic co-dependency, as well as relations of conflicting interests between the former and the latter. In this context, it is noteworthy that there are countries in the region that are simultaneously sending and receiving countries — for example, Malaysia (which sends workers to Singapore in particular and receives from Indonesia in particular) and Thailand (which sends workers to Hong Kong, Singapore and Taiwan and receives workers from Burma and Laos).

The Magnitude and Nature of Female Labour Migration

Women workers form a very significant part of the labour migration from Southeast Asia. Yet no precise figures exist on the magnitude of transnational female labour migration from Southeast Asia. The International Labour Organization (ILO) gives extremely conservative estimates — for example, only 611,266 Filipinas[3] working overseas in 1999 and an unknown number of women out of 137,802 Thais working abroad in 2001 (see *International Labour Migration Statistics*: Tables 11, 12 and 13). Other estimates are much higher. For example, it is estimated that from the Philippines alone — the world's largest exporter of labour — about 4.2 to 6.4 million women are working abroad as domestic helpers and entertainers, constituting 60 per cent to 80 per cent of the estimated 7–8 million Filipino migrant workers.[4]

Just for the category of domestic helpers, the following estimates have been recorded in merely three of the receiving countries: more than 200,000 documented workers in Hong Kong in 2001 (see Sim 2003, p. 1), more than 96,000 in Singapore in 1997 (see Wong 1996, p. 128), and more than 130,000 in Malaysia in 1997 (see Jones 2000, p. 65). In addition, there are unknown numbers of undocumented domestic helpers. Estimates for transnational sex workers are also unknown. If all the sending countries in Southeast Asia and migrant women workers in all occupations were included, estimates may even reach tens of millions.

Immigrant women have been described as the "absent centre", overlooked in policy, research and action (see Glenn 1986, p. 14; Hugo 1993; Hoskyns and Orsini-Jones 1995, p. 53; Li et al. 1998; Skeldon 1998; Guest 1999). Critics of studies on international migration have focused on the neglect of the economic migration of women. Reversing this trend, substantial research has been produced, opening up discourses that focus on women as migrant workers (see Hosoda 1996, Heyzer et al. 1994, Brettell and Simon 1986; Morokvasic 1984; Phizacklea 1983).

By now, female labour migration from Southeast Asia has become a migration stream of global significance and may eventually outstrip the significance of male labour migration from the region. Lim and Oishi (1996, p. 87) note that "the 1990s have seen greater feminization of Asian labour migration". For example, numbers of male and female migrant workers from the Philippines have long been near parity.[5]

The feminization of labour migration from Indonesia is even more pronounced. In 1993–94, the recorded sex ratio of Indonesian overseas workers was 36 males per hundred females (see Hugo 1995, p. 284). Yet despite its growing significance, female labour migration is still very imperfectly known. The lack of clarity of this phenomenon stems largely from gender hierarchies, which render women's work invisible, both at home and abroad.

Ethnographic studies show that both sending and receiving countries rely heavily on women's emotional and physical labour in the work of social reproduction (see Glenn 1986, p. 15; Enloe 1990; Tung 1999; Elmhirst 1999; Anderson 2001). Migrant workers who are domestic helpers are hired not just to do housework, but also to care for the young, the old and the disabled in the developed economies of the receiving countries. This reflects a particular developmental trajectory where the economy is developed through the labour force participation of its female citizens, without the government compensating for the withdrawal of their labour in social reproduction. As a result, a labour vacuum emerges which is filled by the insertion of migrant women workers, whose work thereby fits into the prevailing gender division of labour, as well as the existing dichotomization of state and family responsibilities, respectively, for formal economic production and informal social reproduction (see Heyzer et al. 1994, p. 44).

This implies that the gender hierarchy comes to be extended across national citizenries. Migrant women workers are thus positioned in gendered relations not merely to employing families, in the case of domestic helpers, but also to the state and economy of receiving countries. Migrant sex workers further articulate this transnational gender hierarchy by maintaining male sexualities in the receiving countries through the provision of commodified sex. As noted by Hosoda (1996, p. 164), the global expansion of sex-related entertainment through the labour of migrant women workers is the result of interactions between persisting patriarchies and the transnational division of labour.

Transnational Labour Networks in Female Labour Migration

Women workers from Southeast Asia do not simply go to the receiving countries as free independent travellers. On the contrary, their entire migration process is usually facilitated by others, including individuals, enterprises and organizations. Most discussions of labour networks have focused on the informal networking that takes place among friends, relatives and people from the same sending villages, towns and provinces, assisting with the chain migration of newcomers to the recipient countries (see for example, Leahy 1990 and Lowe 2000). In contrast, the "transnational labour networks" discussed in this chapter refer not only to these informal networks, but also the relatively more institutionalized networks involving commercial agencies which facilitate female labour migration, as well as non-governmental organizations which assist, organize and represent migrant workers in sending and receiving countries. The range of services included is shown in Table 6.1.

Overlapping networks are formed around these different services and are focused on different points of a typical migration cycle. Figure 6.1 shows that transnational labour networks mediate between migrant women workers and international labour markets at almost every point of a typical migration cycle. These networks form an infrastructural backbone that enables the millions of women workers to move back and forth

TABLE 6.1
Services Provided by NGOs and Commercial Agents

Services provided by NGOs	Commercial Agents
• mediate with employers, clients, host society and/or host governments	• recruit the workers
• manage their working conditions through advocacy and intercessions	• provide training
	• find them employment
• assist them in unionizing	• arrange their passage
• provide legal assistance	• provide loans
• provide shelter	• draw up contracts
• advocate their rights	• remit their remuneration
• arrange their repatriation	• arrange their repatriation

FIGURE 6.1
Typical Migration Cycle of a Migrant Woman Worker

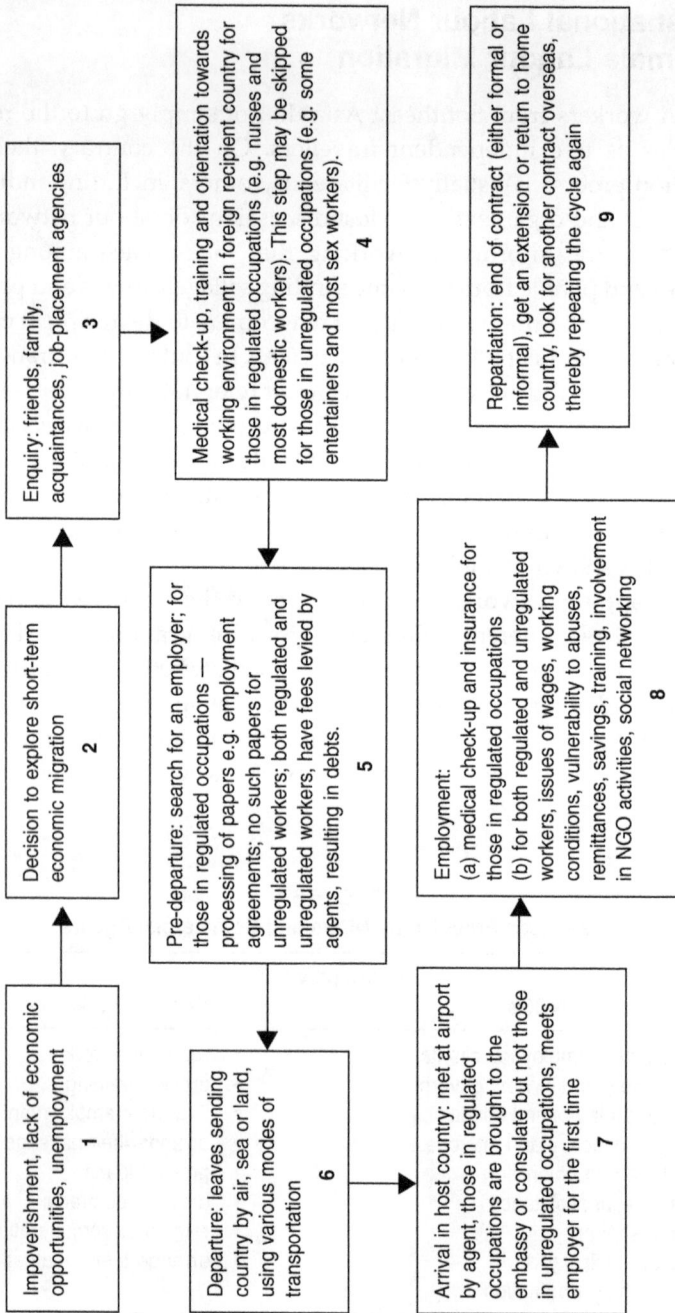

1. Impoverishment, lack of economic opportunities, unemployment

2. Decision to explore short-term economic migration

3. Enquiry: friends, family, acquaintances, job-placement agencies

4. Medical check-up, training and orientation towards working environment in foreign recipient country for those in regulated occupations (e.g. nurses and most domestic workers). This step may be skipped for those in unregulated occupations (e.g. some entertainers and most sex workers).

5. Pre-departure: search for an employer; for those in regulated occupations — processing of papers e.g. employment agreements; no such papers for unregulated workers; both regulated and unregulated workers, have fees levied by agents, resulting in debts.

6. Departure: leaves sending country by air, sea or land, using various modes of transportation

7. Arrival in host country: met at airport by agent, those in regulated occupations are brought to the embassy or consulate but not those in unregulated occupations, meets employer for the first time

8. Employment:
(a) medical check-up and insurance for those in regulated occupations
(b) for both regulated and unregulated workers, issues of wages, working conditions, vulnerability to abuses, remittances, savings, training, involvement in NGO activities, social networking

9. Repatriation: end of contract (either formal or informal), get an extension or return to home country, look for another contract overseas, thereby repeating the cycle again

Source: Adapted from Sim (2001, p. 11).

between different countries, not just from sending countries to receiving countries, but also from one receiving country to another receiving country. At the same time, these are transnational networks that cross national boundaries and serve as organizational linkages between co-dependent economies in the region — that is, between the relatively developed economies of receiving countries and the developing economies of sending countries. Furthermore, beyond passively providing services to meet workers' needs and demands, such as the demand for market access, these networks may actively shape and mobilize labour migration, based on the strategic interests of participants in such networks. Furthermore, once established, these networks inject a self-perpetuating dynamism into migration that continues long after the original, usually economic, reasons for the flow may have been reduced (Hugo 1995, p. 287).

However, despite their significance, little is known about these transnational labour networks, precisely because they are transnational and they fall between national jurisdictions. The role of transnational labour networks in female labour migration is of particular significance, because prevailing gender hierarchies in the sending countries tend to render women more reliant on the services of recruitment networks than men are. This gender-biased reliance also makes women more vulnerable to abuses inflicted on them by these networks (see Lim and Oishi 1996, p. 102).

As indicated in Figure 6.1, there are multiple points of vulnerability in the migration cycle, with unregulated migrant workers even more exposed to abuses than are regulated workers. Regulated workers are those who depart and arrive with appropriate travel documents, who have legal contracts, and whose employment is regulated by the host government (for example, through its employment ordinance). Unregulated workers are those who lack part or all of these protections. Nevertheless, even regulated workers may be vulnerable to abuses, because the nature and conditions of migrants' work isolate them and render them socially invisible. Indeed, as a general point, we agree with Anderson (2000) that the greater the degree of social invisibility is, the greater would be the degree of vulnerability of the worker working under such conditions of invisibility.

Therefore, migrant women workers are exposed to multiple vulnerabilities as a result of the multi-layered invisibilities of migrant women's work. These basically fall into two categories — first, the invisibility of the transnational labour networks that enable and manage migrant women in this work sector; and second, the invisibility of women's work in the informal reproduction of household economies and male sexualities. These multi-layered invisibilities and the corresponding vulnerabilities that are thereby structurally implied, need to be analysed as a significant dimension of gendered labour migration as a global phenomenon.

In this context, there is a critical need to map out these transnational labour networks, to understand how they are formed, how they work, and with what ramifications for whom. This entails the identification and analysis of the roles and interactions of different participants in such networks. This chapter is a preliminary report of an ongoing project on transnational labour networks in female labour migration and does not presume to give a comprehensive overview of the situation. Rather, it will outline some critical features of these networks and draw out some ramifications for workers, employers, NGOs and governments.

The rest of this chapter discusses two categories of transnational labour networks, defined in terms of their core services: labour recruitment and labour organization. A comparison is drawn between practices in the Philippines and Indonesia, with a focus on migrant domestic helpers. Some characteristics of these transnational labour networks may, however, be shared by other categories of workers, such as sex workers.

This chapter shows how, on the one hand, the invisibility of the transnational labour networks and the invisibility of migrant women's work can lead to systemic abuses. But it also shows how, on the other hand, such abuses can be curbed through the empowerment of migrant women workers in a process of civic conscientization. This is not to deny that there are structural constraints to the potential for empowerment. Nevertheless, such potential does exist, albeit in varying degrees. Different scopes for empowerment are mapped out by different contexts of state power, governance and democratization. As a result, the potential for empowerment and disempowerment varies among migrant women workers from different countries. Therefore, beyond gender differences between male migrant workers and female migrant workers, there are other structural forces that bring about uneven vulnerabilities among migrant women workers themselves. These uneven vulnerabilities show up in our comparison of Filipina and Indonesian women workers, as they interact and negotiate with the transnational labour networks that facilitate their migration and employment. Because most researchers tend to focus on either particular national streams of migrant workers or on the sending country or the receiving country, hardly any research has been done on comparing different national streams of workers across both sending and receiving countries. Our conceptual attention to transnational labour networks as the infrastructure of labour migration enables us in this chapter to attempt an analysis of this relatively unexplored area of research,[6] as it enables us to think outside the confines of national boundaries and to focus instead on labour migration as a transnational process that nevertheless interacts with national conditions.

Labour Recruitment

As of 25 April 2003, the Philippines Overseas Employment Administration (POEA) lists a total of 2,820 employment agencies that it had ever licensed to recruit Filipino workers for overseas jobs, both land-based and sea-based. The overwhelming majority of Filipina women workers are in land-based jobs. The POEA lists 1,040 currently active land-based agencies, which would be the agencies dealing with female migrant workers from the Philippines.[7]

It is less clear how many agencies there are in Indonesia involved in the recruitment of female migrant workers. Jones (2000, pp. 44–45) differentiates between three categories of recruitment agents. The first category consists of large registered companies with operating licences from the Ministry of Manpower and capable of meeting the stringent ministry requirements of 1994: by late 1998, there were just over 200 such firms. The second consists of smaller companies or individual recruiters that were certified only after July 1995 by the Ministry of Manpower, through a less stringent training course in the laws and regulations of Indonesia and Malaysia (a major destination of Indonesian workers). The third comprises the largest category by far: recruiters that have no connection with licensed recruiters or with the Ministry of Manpower; some of these may be organized as companies but are not licensed to engage in the recruitment of migrant labour.

The registered agencies in the sending countries are only the nodes of nationwide networks that extend to remote peripheries. This is one major reason why such networks are difficult to trace, because these far-flung networks shade off into community-based linkages. There is ample evidence indicating that in many cases, the first labour recruiter that a migrant woman worker comes into contact with is someone "known in the community, an individual who [can] instil confidence in the woman and convince her that taking a job abroad [is] the best thing that could happen to her" (Dias 1994, p. 141). This informal mode of recruitment tends to lead the potential worker to trust the labour recruiter and, by implication, the other people in his or her network.

In studies of legal migration in Yogyakarta, Central and West Java, the process was found to be highly organized with strong government and private recruiter involvement. Thirty-one per cent of workers leaving for the Middle East depended on the recruiter as the main source of information, much more than the nineteen per cent who depended on a government agency for information (Hugo 1995). In contrast to migrant workers who depend on family networks to reduce risks associated with migration and operate in an environment of almost total certainty, countless migrant workers depending on private recruiters have consistently been misled over issues of wages and conditions of employment (see for example, *Modern Heroes, Modern Slaves*, 1997).

In Hong Kong where the official minimum wage was — up to 31 March 2003 — HK$3,670 (US$470.57),[8] domestic workers from Indonesia were underpaid at illegal rates from HK$1,500 to HK$2,000 (US$192.33 to US$256.44) per month and not given off days, sometimes for months, in line with the misinformation that they were fed by their recruiters in Indonesia, including those licensed by the government. The Hong Kong Labour Department handled 1,786 contractual disputes involving foreign domestic helpers between January and October 2000, compared with 2,280 for the whole of 1999,[9] mostly from Indonesian domestic workers in Hong Kong, who, at 78,000, constituted the second largest ethnic group of foreign domestic workers in Hong Kong after Filipino domestic workers who numbered 148,000 in early 2003.[10] Compared to 99.5 per cent of Filipino domestic workers who received the minimum wage or more in 2001, only 91 per cent of Thai domestic workers and 52 per cent of Indonesian domestic workers received the stipulated wage.[11] With 9 per cent of Thai workers paid less than the official wage, it is clear that Indonesian workers are not singled out for exclusive discrimination, but with nearly half of them underpaid, it is equally clear that gross structural discriminants exist in the labour networks that underwrite the flow of Indonesian domestic workers to various destinations, including Hong Kong.

"The problem was worse among Indonesian migrants because employment agencies were giving them misinformation.... They are told their salary will be about HK$2,000 [US$256.44] or less. They only learn about the minimum wage when they start working in Hong Kong," said Ramon Bultron, Managing Director of the Hong Kong-based Asia Pacific Mission for Migrants. "Workers don't complain because they're afraid they'd get sent back," said Hong Kong Confederation of Trade Unions general secretary Lee Cheuk-yan.[12]

In the case of the Philippines, the recent history of strong out-migration has become entrenched as a social institution and first-time Filipino migrants are increasingly turning to employment agencies found in newspaper advertisements to assist in processing their documents and finding overseas employers, even when they have family and friends in the prospective recipient countries. Hence, is the recruiter merely meeting the migrant workers' demand for such services or do recruitment agencies have a role in conditioning such demand?

Heyzer and Wee (1994) show that the labour recruiter can also actively create demand through various inducements. They may use monetary attraction as inducements, such as promising a higher salary abroad, a "fly now, pay later" scheme, an "everything is provided for", a stepping stone to other higher-income countries, the availability of cheap consumer goods, pay increases every three to six months, and the lure of paid days-off. They also promise non-monetary inducement such as claims of "a nice country to work in" overseas, of "good and kind employers" in foreign countries, of higher status of overseas employment relative to local employment, of easy work with the use of high-tech machines, and of no adjustment required because of cultural similarities in Asia.

Such inducements interact with the aspirations of workers to obtain better-paying jobs and higher social status for themselves. As a result, recruiting agencies find two advantages — first, there is a ready demand for overseas employment among intending migrant workers, and second, the worker's lack of access to overseas labour markets renders them vulnerable to whatever is offered by the agencies.

After recruitment, the worker moves through different nodes of the recruiting network in the sending country, with the point of departure being the final place. Here a significant difference may be discerned between labour recruitment networks of domestic helpers in the Philippines and those in Indonesia. In the Philippines, after the worker has signed up with an employment agency, she is left on her own — for example, to go back to her home village or to stay somewhere in Manila — until official word is received that her visa in the receiving country is ready. At that point, she will be contacted by the agency to arrange her travel itinerary. Should she be uncontactable within the specified time period when she has to depart, the agency would simply cancel her employment and her deposit paid to the agency forfeited. It has been frequently noted that those who migrate from the Philippines are not the "poorest of the poor" and that not all who want to migrate succeed in doing so such as in those cases where no employers pick them out from the vast databases of available workers.

In Indonesia, however, many employment agencies treat the workers in a much more coercive and restrictive manner. In contrast to Filipino workers who pay a large part, if not most, of their fees before a recruiter begins processing their papers for overseas employment, Indonesian migrant workers begin paying their recruiters for the entire process, airfare and related costs only when they begin work at the point of destination. This process of repayment may cost up to seven months of wages of the standard 24-month contract (if the worker's contract is not prematurely terminated).[13] On contacting an agent, a potential Indonesian migrant worker is sent to a "training centre" some distance from their homes, usually in a town or city, for example, Jakarta, Surabaya or Batam, where they will find themselves confined for indefinite periods while awaiting departure. Information from different sources shows that the pre-departure confinement of migrant women workers for extended periods is a norm among labour recruiters in Indonesia, rather than an exception. Our own research on this point is obtained from Indonesian workers in Hong Kong, all of whom have had the experience of being detained by the labour recruiter for months, on average for six to eight months, before they departed from Indonesia. Jones (2000, pp. 66–67) corroborates this finding in her documentation of illegal detention by labour recruiters.

For example, in March 1997, 471 women were found locked up for eight months in different places in Surabaya; they had been told that they would have to pay 250,000 rupiah (US$29.23) to the labour recruiter as compensation if they wanted to return home.[14] The labour recruiter was an agency licensed by the Ministry of Manpower. In another case, in July 1997, sixty women were found confined in similar circumstances in Pontianak; what is noteworthy in this case is that enquiries about the women and their place of confinement were answered by a self-identified member of the West Kalimantan provincial police who "denied there were any problems".

Catarina Purwana Williams (2002) gave evidence of forcible detention from her field research among migrant women workers from East Nusa Tenggara. The following account of an Indonesian woman worker's experience is quoted by Chew (2003, pp. 30–31) from a field interview:

> I waited four months before I could leave for Hong Kong. I did not know that I had to wait for that long. During that time I stayed in the "training camp" of ... in Surabaya, East Java. There were around 1,000 women in this camp, all going to Hong Kong, Singapore, Malaysia and Taiwan.
>
> I could eat three times a day, but the food was not healthy. They gave us a small amount of vegetables (we were not allowed to serve ourselves) and sometimes they gave us a piece of salty fish or *tempe* or tofu only.[15] Since the food was insufficient I had to buy my own food from vendors outside the gate of the camp. We had to find roundabout ways to buy food from that vendor, since we were not allowed to leave the training camp.
>
> Many women were sick there. They had fever, colds, and many of us had skin problems since the water was not clean. I had to take a bath with ten persons in the same bathroom. The water was dirty and not enough for all of us.
>
> Many of my friends were always screaming and while I was staying in that training camp one of my friends died. She died after being sick for a long time in the camp. Actually her family was trying to take her home as she was seriously ill, but the agency did not allow it because her family refused to pay 2,000,000 rupiah [US$233.80] to the agency as guarantee that she would come back to the camp. One day later the agency brought her to the hospital but she died a day after.
>
> The agency told the women who were going to Taiwan that they should not pray; I do not know why. The agency allowed those of us going to Hong Kong to bring a prayer cloth so long as the colour is not white. According to them, Hong Kong people are afraid of white colour.
>
> The agency staff treated us very badly. They sounded like kings, commanding us to do many things for their personal needs. We had to do whatever they asked very fast, and they are shouted at us if we made a little mistake.
>
> We were not allowed to go out of the training camp. We were isolated from the community. Our families couldn't contact us since there were no telephones. If our families or relative sent a letter, the agency staff would censor it first. Often they opened our letters or did not give our letters to us.

Our families were allowed to visit us once every two weeks on Saturday between 8.30 a.m. and 3.00 p.m. only. Since many of us came from villages very far away, sometimes our families or relatives did not arrive for a visit at the right time. Then we were allowed to meet them for one to two hours only.

The agency was very strict with timing. If we were late even five minutes, they would punish us by making us do extra cleaning of the camp.

If we wanted to go back home for some important things we had to deposit a guarantee of around 1,000,000 rupiah [US$116.90] to 2,000,000 rupiah [US$233.80]. If we wanted to cancel our employment process the agency would fine us around 3,500,000 rupiah [US$409.15]. One of my friends got pregnant and since that was not allowed she had to cancel her process, for which the agency asked her to pay 3,500,000 rupiahs.

If we refused to pay, then the agency would bring us to another place, where we would have to work without any payment for an unlimited time, until our families are able to buy us out.

Almost all the women in this training camp stayed more than five to six months and some of them stayed for almost one or two years. I was lucky because they did not ask me to do part-time work. They told me because there was an employer in Hong Kong for me already. Almost all my friends there were forced to do part-time work for only 75,000 rupiah [US$8.77] to 100,000 rupiah [US$11.69] per month. They can't refuse it since this is also one of the regulations in this training camp.

In this training camp we were forced to learn Cantonese, from 8 a.m. to 5 p.m. During lunchtime we were allowed to take a rest for one hour. Those going to Hong Kong soon had to continue studying from 8 p.m. to 11 p.m.

I signed employment contract papers when I was still in the training camp. But they did not explain much about these to me; they just pointed to the places to be signed by me. So from signing these I knew that I had a contract already. But in fact I never kept any of my documents myself, including contract and passport. I just held these in my hand during my trip to Hong Kong and as soon as I arrived at Hong Kong airport, the agency staff who picked me up took all the documents away from me. However, I did not object because at that time I did not know that this is illegal in Hong Kong. I thought it was common that domestic workers were not allowed to keep their documents themselves.

As a result of such recruitment practices, Indonesian migrant workers generally start experiencing abuses inflicted by labour recruiters even before they leave the country. As shown above, these arise mostly from the detention that is inflicted on them prior to their departure, including deception, imprisonment, lack of food and health care, working without pay and sometimes even rape and assault (see for example, Jones 2000). Things do not get better on arrival. For example, in Hong Kong, recruitment agencies take migrant workers to finance companies on their arrival in order to collect the placement fees owed to the agencies. The migrant workers then pay off the loan with interests by monthly instalments, sometimes with little left to live on. If their employment contracts were to be terminated by their employers before their debts are repaid, they may go home indebted with nothing to show for months spent in "training centres" and working for their employers.[16]

Another point of contrast between labour recruiters in the Philippines and Indonesia is that there are many cases of fake or invalid travel documents being issued by the latter, while such incidents are rare among the former. Consequently, there are many more Indonesian workers deported as illegal migrants, as compared to Filipina workers (see for example, Jones 2000, pp. 39–52).

There are several reasons for the difference between labour recruitment practices in the Philippines and Indonesia. Among them is that the immigration industry in the Philippines is better regulated, with specialized government agencies set up for this purpose — specifically, the Philippines Overseas Employment Administration (POEA) and the Overseas Workers Welfare Association (OWWA). In contrast, labour migration falls under the Ministry of Manpower in Indonesia, which does not seem to view the forcible confinement of potential migrant workers awaiting departure and the abuses that occur during confinement as labour issues that fall under its purview. This illegal detention of pre-departure workers is often disguised by recruitment agencies as so-called "training" — a cover apparently accepted by the Ministry. As noted by Jones (2000, p. 52), "endemic corruption contributes to this abuse, and any effort to prevent rights violations would have to start with a determination on the part of senior government officials in Jakarta to investigate and prosecute all acts of migration-related corruption from the central government down to the municipal level".

The second reason is that women in the Philippines are better educated than Indonesian women. The literacy rate of women in the Philippines was 93 per cent in 1990, as compared to that of women in Indonesia at 81.4 per cent in 1995.[17] Furthermore, women workers from the Philippines are literate in English, as compared to those from Indonesia. Jones (2000,

p. 46) documents how Indonesian workers, who are non-literate in English, are not able to read visas in the English language and are unaware when they have been given tourist visas, rather than work visas.

The third reason is that civil society in the Philippines is much more developed than in Indonesia, with many, perhaps hundreds, of NGOs monitoring the well-being and treatment of migrant workers at home and abroad. In Indonesia, NGOs proliferated only after the fall of Suharto in 1997, with only a handful specializing in advocacy for migrant workers.

Finally, the female labour migration from the Philippines had become a large-scale phenomenon in 1978,[18] whereas such migration from Indonesia increased sharply only after the Asian financial crisis of 1997. For example, in Hong Kong, the number of Indonesian workers rose from 46,000 in 2000 to 78,000 in 2003, making up a third of the total population of domestic workers. There has been a seventy-fold increase on the numbers a decade ago.[19] This relatively recent increase means that Indonesian migrant workers are entering a labour market that is already dominated by Filipina workers and their employment agencies. Most Indonesian labour recruiters thus have no ready overseas jobs for the workers they recruit — a fact that they do not reveal to their labour recruits. To put it crudely, these labour recruiters are holding labour stock to be released only when they are able to find buyers for it.

Structural and Cultural Differentiation among Migrant Workers

The disparity between Philippine and Indonesian migrant workers continues after they arrive in the receiving countries. The relatively higher education of the Philippines and their ability to speak English are reflected not only in their higher wages but also in their greater autonomy of choice and decision-making. One important indicator of such autonomy is the migrant worker's choice of employer. All migrant workers employed as domestic helpers are restricted by their contracts to domestic work; they cannot at any time move into other sectors of employment even when their training and experience qualify them to do so. Hence, their social mobility is severely restricted (see French 1986, p. 17). However, in terms of choice and mobility within the sector of domestic work, the nationality of the employer is often perceived by migrant workers as key to an adequate level of job satisfaction and is therefore an important factor in a domestic helper's assessment of her working conditions.

As established by French (1986, p. 21), in Hong Kong, migrant domestic helpers regard the Chinese as less preferred employers, giving greater preference instead to employers who are other Asians, Americans, Canadians, Europeans and Australians. In this light, the relative distribution of migrant workers with Hong Kong Chinese employers is significant. See Table 6.2.

As shown in Table 6.2, only 77 per cent of Filipina domestic helpers have Chinese employers — a percentage that is much lower than the other two major groups of domestic helpers and the average for all these three groups. This finding is all the more significant, given that the Filipina domestic helpers form the largest group of domestic helpers in Hong Kong, at 140,000 in 1998, and 148,000 in 2003 (see Sim 2001, p. 5). Furthermore, Chinese employers are the overwhelming majority of employers in Hong Kong, with the Chinese constituting 98 per cent and other nationalities only 2 per cent of the population.

Since most employers are sourced by employment agencies, this indicates that a significant proportion of Filipinas in Hong Kong have considerable bargaining power with these agencies and are able to pick and choose their employers, according to their own preferences. In contrast, Indonesian and Thai domestic helpers in Hong Kong do not seem to have such leeway in their choice of employers.

There is evidence that Indonesian women workers elsewhere are not even able to choose their line of work. Jones (2000, pp. 65, 76–79) shows that in many cases of Indonesian women workers going to Malaysia, the Indonesian recruiter simply brings a large group of women into the country,

TABLE 6.2
Percentages of Filipina, Indonesian and Thai Domestic Helpers
with Chinese Employers

Domestic Helpers	Filipina	Indonesian	Thai	Average for These 3 Groups
Chinese Employers	77%	91%	94%	87.3%

Source: Adapted from AMC et al. (2001, p. 25).

either by illegal means or on tourist visas, and deposits them with a Malaysian agent, who will be the one to determine who goes into domestic service and who goes to the brothels.

Worse still, some Indonesian women are literally sold by Indonesian recruiters into forced prostitution. In 1992, the prices for Indonesian women sold in Tawau, Sabah, have been documented as varying from US$600 to US$800, with virgins costing more (see Jones 2000, p. 77).

Why have Filipina domestic helpers been able to assert greater autonomy of choice and decision-making? One indication is the willingness of employers of Filipina domestic workers to pay the minimum wage and to abide by other contractual obligations such as the number of off-days taken. This is a situation that has not occurred naturally but has resulted from numerous acts of labour activism on their part. Would-be employers are aware that Filipina domestic workers in Hong Kong know their legal rights. This has incidentally also earned them criticisms as being "spoilt" and "demanding" by sections of the local population in Hong Kong (see Constable 1997; French 1986; Lowe 2000). Ironically, while the Chinese are the least preferred as employers, Filipina domestic workers remain the favoured choice among the majority of Chinese employers (Lowe 2000, p. 103).

Another possible explanation for the higher level of autonomy among Filipina domestic workers lies in the development of alternative employment options — that is, an ability to find employers themselves. In Hong Kong, for example, the last fifteen years have seen the growth of an increasingly pervasive network of Filipina women workers who are able to help source for jobs for their friends and relatives. According to French (1986, p. 16), 52 per cent of Filipina workers had relatives working in Hong Kong, with 30 per cent of newcomers having more than three relatives and 12 per cent with more than eight relatives working in Hong Kong; 72 per cent had friends living and working in Hong Kong, half having more than three friends and a third with at least eight friends working in Hong Kong; 71 per cent of Filipinas arranged jobs in Hong Kong through employment agencies in the Philippines who facilitate the processing of their immigration documents, 27 per cent were hired through recommendations by relatives and 22 per cent were helped by friends already working in Hong Kong.

Lowe (2000, p. 21) reveals that the system of mutual help amongst Filipinas looking for jobs in Hong Kong has become even more pervasive and resilient as more than 95 per cent of respondents in her study had "facilitated the recruitment of their daughters, sisters, nieces, cousins and other relatives" to work in Hong Kong.

In contrast, Indonesian women workers still lack access to the labour market and are still very much controlled by the labour recruiters, with their contacts in the receiving country often limited to the employment agent and the employer. Indonesian labour recruiters are thus able to form cartels to monopolize the migrant labour market, whereas labour recruiters in the Philippines tend to be mere service providers who have to be competitive to win clients among Filipina migrant workers. While there have been improvements at transparency and accountability standards in commercial agencies servicing Filipina migrants, the resilience of monopolistic practices cannot be under-estimated.

However, the governments themselves may not be willing to allow greater market access to migrant workers — perhaps because of vested interests in labour brokerage. An example is a case in September 1999. After five years of negotiations, the Taiwan and Philippine governments signed the direct hiring scheme, which would allow employers to hire Filipinos without going through a broker. Six months later, guidelines have yet to be issued explaining exactly how this can be done. It is a concern as to whether employers and government officials are really willing to introduce the direct hiring scheme. The broker system, after all, is a very lucrative business (Asian Migrant Centre and Migrant Forum in Asia 2000, p. 251).

Monopolistic practices by Indonesian employment agencies are even more rampant, apparently with the connivance of the government. An example is the agencies' lucrative income from their monopolistic renewal of employment contracts of Indonesian migrant workers in Hong Kong. The Hong Kong government has a legal stipulation that employment agencies should charge no more than 10 per cent of one month's salary or HK$367 (US$47.06) for the renewal of employment contracts. However, our research indicates that Indonesian migrants, who are already in Hong Kong, are regularly charged between HK$3,000 to HK$13,000 (US$384.67 to US$1,666.89) by employment agencies, which have been licensed by the Indonesian Consulate for a "rubber-stamping" exercise, before the Consulate is willing to process their passports and visas. This costly and circuitous route is required of Indonesian migrants, whereas Filipina migrants in Hong Kong can simply process their own renewal of visas and employment contracts by going directly to the Philippines Consulate, at a total cost of not more than HK$500 (US$64.11).

There were two short-lived attempts in 2000 and 2002 to reform Indonesian government policies on contract renewals. These would have permitted Indonesian migrant workers in Hong Kong to process their own contract renewals and visa extensions, bypassing the agencies, and would have effectively reduced their costs to the same levels as those of Filipina migrants. However, these progressive moves proved unpopular with Indonesian employment agencies and under pressure, the Indonesian Government reversed them shortly after they were implemented.

According to a staff member of an Indonesian NGO working with Indonesian migrant workers in Hong Kong, the first policy was announced in November 2000 and reversed in January 2001, the latter after a visit to Hong Kong by the Indonesian Director-General of the Department of Labour and Manpower (in charge of migrant workers) and owners of employment agencies from Jakarta in December 2000. All subsequent renewals had again to be conducted through a list of appointed agents in Hong Kong but at the lowered rate of 10 per cent (as stipulated by Hong Kong law) of a month's salary or HK$367. In February 2001, the Indonesian Consul General in Hong Kong announced that Indonesian workers cannot change their agents, to ensure "administrative convenience" (presumably, of the consulate). Another directive, Article 69 ('Ministry decision number 104A/MEN/2002'), was issued in Jakarta on 4 June 2002 to allow all Indonesian domestic workers working overseas to renew their own employment contracts with, for example, the Hong Kong Immigration Department, without going through an employment agency. On 3 November 2002, at a meeting between leaders of the Indonesian workers' groups in Hong Kong with the Director-General of the Labour and Manpower, the workers were informed that Article 69 did not apply to Hong Kong. Therefore, after these two failed attempts at reform, Indonesian domestic workers in Hong Kong are still obliged to renew or change their employment contracts only through one of the agencies appointed by the Indonesian authorities, which will give them a "rubber stamp" without which the consulate will not process the visa/passport extension.

Another difference between labour recruiters in Indonesia and the Philippines is reflected in the contrasting charges they levy on the new migrant workers. Our research among Indonesian and Filipina domestic helpers in Hong Kong reveals that the former may be charged as much as

HK$21,000 (US$2,692.66) by their recruiters, whereas the latter are usually charged HK$6,000 to HK$7,000 (US$769.33 to US$897.55). Indonesian workers thus start their work migration process in a severe state of indebtedness, as they do not have the money to pay such exorbitant charges. In addition, Indonesian recruiters charge interest on the loans they extend to the workers; Jones (2000, pp. 55–56) notes that interest rates may be as high as 100 per cent of the loan. The wages of the workers are in most cases deducted for four to seven months to repay their loans to the labour recruiters.

In Hong Kong, as noted above, recruitment agencies take Indonesian migrant workers to finance companies on their arrival in order to collect the placement fees owed to the agencies. This is because labour recruiters are not willing to wait for payment by instalment. Instead, the Indonesian workers are forced to take on high-interest loans from the finance companies, so that the recruiters can be paid off immediately, while the finance companies will have the task of extracting repayment from the workers. This means that the workers end up paying double interest, charged by both the recruitment agency and the finance company. Enforcing debt repayment by the migrant workers requires close collaboration between the labour recruiter in the sending country and the employment agency in the receiving country. This is tantamount to a transnational money-extortion network.

'...Upon arrival in Hong Kong, the recruitment agencies will be collecting the placement fees,' said Edwina Santoyo, director of a refuge for Indonesian domestic workers. The women usually take out loans at financing companies recommended by labour agencies. The maids then paid off the loan with interest by instalment...a process made difficult when the women received far less than stipulated in their contracts. One woman said, 'Every month my employer gives me [HK]$200 [US$25.64] in cash while forcing me to sign a receipt written in English for the amount of [HK]$3,860 [US$494.94]'.[20]

Based on the legislated minimum wage for migrant domestic helpers in Hong Kong, Indonesian workers would have to forego most of their salary for an average of seven months of pay at HK$3,670 (US$470.57) each month, to pay off the loan. A large proportion of Indonesian workers in Hong Kong do not receive this minimum wage. Those who earn only HK$2,000 (US$256.44) per month are charged less by the agencies, so that they usually end up foregoing an average of four months' wages, amounting to HK$8,000 (US$1,025.78). Those who are contracted at the minimum wage of HK$3,670 (US$470.57) say that they "do not mind" the higher fees charged by the agencies, nor the longer period that they would need to pay off the loan. This is because they will net HK$67,080 (US$8,601.13) for a two-year contract, as compared to netting only HK$40,000 (US$5,128.88) for a two-year contract at HK$2,000 per month.[21] The costliest item in the package of services included by the agency is usually the one-way airfare, but this usually costs no more than about HK$4,000 (US$512.89). The agencies' fees are clearly excessive, as the other items in the package of services cost even less, such as the 2,000,000 rupiahs (US$233.80) or so needed for passport application.

In contrast, Filipina domestic helpers coming to Hong Kong are hardly ever indebted to labour recruiters and are usually financed through personal and informal means. Even if many do get caught up in debt during their stay in Hong Kong, this is usually due not to exorbitant charges levied by the agencies, but to family crises.

The financial extraction of fees by agencies is just as severe in Taiwan where there were nearly 300,000 migrant workers from Indonesia, Malaysia, Philippines, Thailand and Vietnam in 2000, the three largest groups being Thais (140,133), Filipinos (112,859) and Indonesians (46,726) (AMC 2000, p. 246). For example, after the Asian financial crisis in 1997, the Thai demand for overseas employment surged especially for jobs in Taiwan because of its high wages. Fees charged by employment agencies jumped by 100 per cent to 140 per cent, increasing from THB70,000 (US$1,649.25) first to THB90,000 (US$2,120.46), then to THB170,000 (US$4,005.32), and finally to THB180,000 (US$4,240.93).[22]

The situation of all migrant workers in Taiwan is exacerbated by a punitive structure of taxes and fees applied by the government that — together with fees levied by employment agencies — consume about twenty-one months of salary for a thirty-six month employment contract. Table 6.3 below shows how these deductions result in the migrant worker receiving no more than 25.83 per cent of the gross income she earns. So a thirty-six month contract nets her only a total sum of TWD147,364.91 (US$4,244.69).[23] This works out to an average monthly wage of TWD4,093.47 (US$117.90) or a daily average wage of TWD134.58 (US$3.88), which is only slightly more than the UN poverty threshold of US$2 per day.

For Indonesian migrant workers, if the six to eight months they spent in detention at the so-called "training centres", prior to departure, were to be added to the contracted thirty-six months, then their average wage would be even less, as they would have spent up to a total of forty-four months to earn the net total income. An Indonesian worker who has spent forty-four months to earn the net amount of TWD147,364.91 (US$4,244.69) would average a monthly wage of TWD3,349.20 (US$96.47) or a daily wage of TWD111.64 (US$3.22).

Labour Organization

French (1986) noted that in 1986, 42 per cent of Filipina domestic helpers in Hong Kong were underpaid by 10 per cent. It is significant that in 2001, a survey found that 99.56 per cent of Filipina domestic helpers received Hong Kong's legislated minimum wage of HK$3,670 (US$470.57) for domestic helpers, as compared to 52 per cent of Indonesians and 91 per cent of Thais (see AMC et al. 2001).

Equally significant is that 0.65 per cent of Filipina respondents reported earning more than HK$6,670 (US$855.24) per month, while 0.52 per cent reported earning between HK$5,670 (US$727.02) to HK$6,670. One of the respondents in our project even cited a monthly wage of HK$12,000 (US$1,538.66). These superior wages are substantially higher than the minimum wage by 50 per cent to 327 per cent. Quite obviously, these particular Filipina domestic helpers are highly valued by their employers and have achieved significant status.

Generally, Filipina domestic helpers in Hong Kong have been steadily empowered in the last fifteen years: from the 58 per cent who received the minimum wage in 1986, there has been a 41.56 per cent improvement, such that 99.56 per cent now receive the minimum wage. How has this notable success in labour rights been achieved?

Cheng (1996), Law (2002) and Sim (2001, 2003) have noted that NGOs in Hong Kong play a crucial role as advocates for migrant workers' rights. Of the sixteen NGOs in Hong Kong studied by Sim (2003) that specialize in migrant workers' issues, it is significant that ten are founded, staffed, catalyzed or led by Filipinos (see Sim 2001, 2003). This implies that a high proportion of these NGOs are closely linked to related organizations in the Philippines. A process of civic transnational networking has taken place, allowing Filipino NGOs to track and advance the well-being of migrant workers from the Philippines to Hong Kong.

TABLE 6.3
Income and Compulsory Expenditure of A Migrant Worker in Taiwan[1]

Annual gross income of migrant worker	TWD15,840 (US$456.25) × 12 months	= **TWD190,080 (US$5,475)**
Taxes and charges levied by the Taiwan Government		
Monthly tax on wages from the first to the 6th month (rate for less than a total of 183 working days)	TWD3,168 (US$91.25) × 6 months	= TWD19,008 (US$547.50)
Monthly tax on wages from the 7th to the 12th month (rate for more than 183 working days)	TWD950.33 (US$27.37) × 6 months	= TWD5,702 (US$164.22)
Total amount of taxes for the first year		= **TWD24,710 (US$711.72)**
'Forced savings'[2]	TWD5,000 (US$144.02) × 12 months	= **TWD60,000 (US$1,728.21)**
Insurance charges per month Labour	TWD215 (US$6.19) × 12 months	= TWD2,580 (US$74.31)
Health	TWD210 (US$6.05) × 12 months	= TWD2,520 (US$72.60)
Total amount of insurance charges for the first year		= **TWD5,100 (US$146.91)**
Worker's net wages after deductions in the first year		
Total deductions for taxes, 'forced savings' and insurance charges	TWD24,710 + TWD60,000 + TWD5,100	= **TWD89,810 (US$2,586.84)**
Net wages after deductions in Year 1	TWD190,080 − TWD89,810	= **TWD100,270 (US$2,888.16)**
Migrant worker's net salary per month after deductions for the first year		= **TWD8,356 (US$240.68)**

Worker's net wages after deductions in the second year

Total deductions for taxes, 'forced savings' and insurance charges	(TWD950.33 [US$27.37] × 12 months =) TWD11,403.96 (US$328.44) + TWD60,000 (US$1,728.21) + TWD5,100 (US$146.91)	= **TWD76,503.96 (US$2,203.56)**
Net wages after deductions in Year 2	TWD190,080 – TWD76,503.96	= **TWD113,576.04 (US$3,271.39)**
Migrant worker's salary per month after deductions for the second year		= **TWD9,464.67 (US$272.62)**

Time taken to pay labour broker's fee

Broker's fee	TWD180,000 (US$5,184.63)
No. of months needed to pay broker's fee	12 months at TWD8,356 = TWD100,270 (US$2,888.13) + 8.43 months at TWD9,464.67 = TWD79,787.17 (US$2,298.15)
	Total no. of months = 20.43 months to earn TWD180,057.17 (US$5,186.28)

For 20.43 months, the migrant worker has 0 income and her family receives nothing.

Worker's net wages after deductions for a standard thirty-six-month contract

12 months of Year 1	= 0
8.43 months of Year 2	= 0
3.57 months of Year 2 × TWD9,464.67 (US$272.62)	= TWD33,788.87 (US$973.24)
12 months of Year 3 × TWD9,464.67 (US$272.62)	= TWD113,576.04 (US$3,271.39)
Net income received by worker over 36 months	= (TWD33,788.87 + TWD113,576.04 =) **TWD147,364.91 (US$4,244.63)**

continued on next page

TABLE 6.3 – continued

Net average wage per month received by worker over 36 months	= (TWD147,364.91 ÷ 36 months =) **TWD4,093.47 (US$117.91)**	
Net average daily wage received by worker over 36 months	= (TWD147,364.91 91 ÷ 1095 days =) **TWD134.58 (US$3.88)**	

Apportionment of migrant worker's gross income over 36 months

Worker's gross income over 36 months	TWD15,840 (US$456.25) per month × 36 months	= TWD570,240 (US$16,425) = 100%
Taiwanese government's taxes and fees	TWD89,810 (US$2,586.84) in Yr 1 + TWD76,503.96 (US$2,203.58) in Yr 2 + TWD76,503.96 (US$2,203.58) in Yr 3	= TWD242,817.92 (US$6,993.96) = 42.58%
Broker's fee		= TWD180,000 (US$5,184.63) = 31.56%
Worker's net income after deductions over 36 months		= TWD147,364.91 (US$4,244.63) = 25.83%

Notes: 1 These computations are based on figures given by HOPE Workers Centre, as cited in AMC (2000, p. 253).
2 Many workers naively think that this money is going into their own savings account for which they will be receiving a good interest. They have no idea that on most occasions it is going to their employers. Many of the workers have never seen their savings account book. Either they are too afraid to ask, or their employers refuse to give it to them' (AMC 2000, p. 256).

The presence of these Filipino-dominated NGOs in Hong Kong has significantly empowered Filipina domestic helpers. They have become much more aware of their rights and have been able to develop their capacity to organize and manage their own labour, not just as individuals but collectively. However, the formation of domestic helpers as organized labour is hindered by the isolating nature of domestic work in individual households.

Two key factors enable Filipina domestic helpers in Hong Kong to overcome such isolation. First, our research has found that that nearly all of them, including fairly recent arrivals, possess mobile cellular telephones. The average cost for the purchase of a cellular telephone and line subscription exceeds HK$2,000 (US$256.44) or 54 per cent of the minimum monthly wage. But the possession of cellular telephones by nearly all Filipina domestic helpers testifies to the importance of this communicative device as an instrument of labour organization. In particular, it frees them from the withholding power of the employer in forbidding them to use the telephone at home.

Second, the relative autonomy of the Filipina domestic workers in Hong Kong is indicated in the number of rest days and statutory holidays they get a year. Taking an average for all domestic helpers in Hong Kong, 76.8 per cent of them get four rest days a month, roughly equivalent to the legal requirement of one rest day a week. In comparison, more than 93 per cent of Filipina domestic workers get the minimum of four rest days per month, a percentage higher than the 76.8 per cent for all domestic helpers, and certainly better than the nearly 55 per cent of Indonesian domestic workers who get three or less rest days per month (see AMC et al. 2001, p. 29). Furthermore, all migrant domestic helpers in Hong Kong are entitled to a minimum of twelve days of statutory holidays a year. According to AMC et al. (2001, p. 31), 57 per cent of Indonesian domestic workers get between zero to one day of statutory holidays a year, while 87 per cent of Filipina domestic workers get the full entitlement of twelve statutory holidays, which is above the general average of 72 per cent for all migrant domestic workers from the Philippines, Indonesia and Thailand. Apart from providing workers with leisure, these rest days and statutory holidays constitute an important temporal resource for workers to meet and congregate in large numbers in public places, providing critical opportunities for them to share experiences and organize themselves strategically.

NGOs, especially the Asian Migrant Centre (AMC) and the Asian Migrant Co-ordinating Body (AMCB), have played a key role in catalyzing migrant workers to organize themselves as pressure groups and as workers' unions — notably, the Asian Domestic Workers Union (ADWU), founded in 1989 and the Indonesian Migrant Workers' Union (IMWU), launched in January 2000. Other organizations that have been formed in Hong Kong are the Coalition for Migrants' Rights (CMR), Association of Sri Lankans in Hong Kong (ASL), Indian Domestic Workers Association (IDWA), Far East Overseas Nepalese Association (FEONA), Forum of Filipino Re-integration and Savings Groups (FFRSG), and the Thai Women Association (TWA). A regional network of migrants' organizations, the Migrant Forum in Asia (MFA), was also established in 1994, spearheaded by the Asian Migrant Centre, to represent migrants' concerns as an international bloc.

In Hong Kong, the ripple effect of Filipino-dominated NGOs across ethnic and national lines is unprecedented and has already made a significant impact on improving the lot of Indonesian workers. For example, IMWU has enhanced the autonomy of Indonesian workers against their labour recruiters and employment agents — for example, in demanding the right to hold their own passports, rather than have these impounded by the agents upon arrival. The Domestic Helpers and Migrant Workers Programme funded through Christian Action in Hong Kong has also taken up the cause of underpaid Indonesian workers since 1997 and has provided paralegal assistance to these workers in claims against their employers in the Labour Tribunal.

This has led to a backlash from recruiters and employment agents, who lobbied the Indonesian Government in Jakarta and the Indonesian consulate in Hong Kong to place obstacles in the path of the workers' autonomy. As a result, new arrivals from Indonesia are now brought immediately by the agents to the Indonesian consulate where they are advised "officially" by the consul in charge that they must stay away from NGOs in Hong Kong. To counter this information gap among migrant workers who are warned away from contact with NGOs, the International Social Service Hong Kong Branch (ISS) — an NGO — has deployed a member of its staff as an Information Ambassador to meet, greet and furnish incoming migrants with the necessary information material at the airport, six days a week.

Conclusion

This chapter illustrates that many of the abuses that arise are due to a lack of workers' empowerment. As the situation in Hong Kong shows, the empowerment of workers to organize their own labour can make a very significant difference to their well-being and job satisfaction. For example, the experience of Filipina workers in Hong Kong indicates that workers can, to some extent, provide for themselves certain necessary services, such as obtaining market access and finding employers. This implies that transnational labour networks need not be networks of external agents. These can take the form of transnational networks constituted by migrant workers themselves to organize their own labour, thereby curtailing the exploitative practices of recruiters and agents who wield arbitrary power over the workers.

As shown above, instead of contributing to the well-being of its overseas migrant workers, a government can actually institute policies that serve the financial well-being of its business and political elites. The capacity of civil society to demand governmental accountability is essential to protecting the rights of workers. Without this safeguard, regimes can evidently perpetuate self-interested policies and practices with impunity.

Therefore, even when the services of employment agents are necessary, it is crucial that the processes and costs involved be interrogated for transparency and accountability, leaving no room whatsoever for rent-seeking, monopolistic malpractices that feed on the vulnerabilities of migrant workers. Such interrogation is done most effectively by a transnational coalition of workers and NGOs, based on shared values that cross ethnic, religious and national boundaries. This process can bring about the dual outcomes of improving migrant rights and reducing institutional impediments.

Notes

[1] This chapter is based on research conducted in 2002, supported by the Southeast Asia Research Centre, City University of Hong Kong.
[2] All countries listed are mentioned in alphabetical order.
[3] We use the term "Filipina" to refer specifically to women from the Philippines. The term "Filipino" specifically refers to men from the Philippines, but can also be used to include both men and women, in the same way as the English

word "Man" is used to include men and women. We consider such usage of the term "Filipino" as patriarchal, since the term "Filipina" would never be used to include both men and women. In any case, we use the term "Filipina" as the discussion on the Philippines is focused on the women.

4   Figures derived from POEA (2002); Varona (2001); "Stop Sex Trafficking of Filipino Women and Children! A Primer on Sex Trafficking".

5   Philippines National Statistics Office (1996, 1997, 2003a, 2003b).

6   One source that sketches a comparison between Thai and Filipina domestic workers in Hong Kong is Li et al. 1998.

7   Philippines Overseas Employment Administration (2003).

8   The minimum wage for migrant domestic workers in Hong Kong was reduced by HK$400 (US$51.29) a month to HK$3,270 a month (US$419.29) for employment contracts signed on or after 1 April 2003. The respondents interviewed for this paper was all contracted prior to 1 April 2003. The exchange rate is HK$1 = US$0.128222, as of 8 May 2003.

9   "[Stop-traffic] News/Hong Kong: Indonesian maids slam exploitation in Hong Kong", <http://fpmail.friends-partners.org/pipermail/stop-traffic/2001-August/001530.html>

10   *South China Morning Post*, 24 February 2003, "10,000 maids against levy; foreign domestic workers march to the government's headquarters, as Bishop Zen holds a mass for Filipinos".

11   Earlier figures of underpayment of Indonesian domestic workers were as high as 80 per cent. (See "[Stop-traffic] News/Hong Kong: Indonesian maids slam exploitation in Hong Kong"). The situation might not be improving as a small-scale survey of 400 Indonesian domestic workers by the Asia Pacific Mission for Migrants showed that 85 per cent of the 78,000 workers were paid below the minimum wage in 2003. According to the survey, 35 per cent were paid less than HK$2,000 (US$256.44) and about 50 per cent were paid between HK$2,000 to HK$3,000 per month (US$256.44 to US$384.67).

12   *South China Morning Post*, 22 March 2003, "Few Indonesian maids get legal wage; employment agencies do not inform applicants of the minimum payment, a new study has revealed".

13   Officially registered contracts in Indonesia are usually for two years. The numbers that return before the end of a contract from the Middle East range from 10 per cent to 30 per cent in Yogjakarta to 33 per cent in Central Java (Hugo 1995: 281).

14   The exchange rate is Rp1 = US$0.0001169, as of 8 May 2003.

15   *Tempe* is a fermented bean-cake.

16   *South China Morning Post*, 7 January 2001, "Fees victory lifts helpers' campaign; Indonesian maids press for pay safeguards to end exploitation".

17   These figures are derived from *The Post-Nairobi Years: Review and Appraisal* at

<http://www.fao.org/docrep/x0175e/x0175e05.htm> and *Women's Health in Indonesia* at <http://w3.whosea.org/women2/indonesia.htm>.
18 The Labour Code of 1974 marked the formal beginning of the current wave of labour export from the Philippines. With the privatization of overseas labour recruiting agencies in 1978, labour export became a cornerstone of the Philippine national development strategy.
19 *South China Morning Post*, 23 February 2003, "Helpers who need help".
20 *South China Morning Post*, 7 Jan 2001, "Fees victory lifts helpers' campaign; Indonesian maids press for pay safeguards to end exploitation".
21 HK\$3,670 × 24 months = HK\$88,080 (US\$11,293.60) *minus* HK\$21,000 = HK\$67,080. HK\$2,000 × 24 months = HK\$48,000 *minus* HK\$8,000 = HK\$40,000.
22 These figures are cited from AMC (2000, p. 260). The exchange rate is 1 THB = US\$0.0235607, as of 8 May 2003.
23 The exchange rate is 1 TWD = US\$0.0288035, as of 8 May 2003.

References

AMC et al. *Baseline Research on Gender and Racial Discrimination towards Filipino, Indonesian and Thai Domestic Helpers in Hong Kong.* Hong Kong: Asian Migrant Centre, Asian Domestic Workers Union, Forum of Filipino Reintegration and Savings Groups, Indonesian Migrant Workers Union and Thai Women's Association, 2001.

Asian Migrant Centre and Migrant Forum in Asia. "Hong Kong". In *Asian Migrant Yearbook 2000.* Hong Kong: Asian Migrant Centre and Migrant Forum in Asia, 2000.

Anderson, B. *Doing the Dirty Work? The Global Politics of Domestic Labour.* London and New York: Zed Books, 2000.

Anderson, B. "Just Another Job? Paying for Domestic Work". In *Gender, Development and Money*, edited by Caroline Sweetman. Oxford: Oxfam GB, 2001.

Brettell, Caroline B. and Rita J. Simon. *International Migration: The Female Experience.* New Jersey: Rowman and Allanheld, 1986.

Cheng, Shu-Ju Ada. "Migrant Women Domestic Workers in Hong Kong, Singapore and Taiwan: A Comparative Analysis". *Asian Women in Migration*, special issue of *Asian and Pacific Migration Journal* 5, no. (1996): 139–52.

Chew, Lin. "Discussion Paper" written on behalf of Anti-Slavery International, for the Programme Consultation Meeting on the Protection of Domestic Workers Against the Threat of Forced Labour and Trafficking, organized by the International Labour Organization (ILO), Hong Kong, February 2003, available at <http://www.antislavery.org/homepage/resources/Anti-Slavery%20workers%20discussion%20paper%200203,pdf>

Constable, N. *Maid to Order in Hong Kong: Stories of Filipina Workers*. New York: Cornell University Press, 1997.

Dias, Malsiri. "Overview of Mechanisms of Migration". In *The Trade in Domestic Workers: Causes, Mechanisms and Consequences of International Migration 1*, edited by Noeleen Heyzer, Geertje Lucklama à Nijeholt and Nedra Weerakoon, Kuala Lumpur: Asian and Pacific Development Centre and London and New Jersey: Zed Books, 1994, pp. 135–50.

Elmhirst, Rose. "Learning the Ways of the Priyayi: Domestic Servants and the Mediation of Modernity in Jakarta, Indonesia". In *Gender, Migration and Domestic Service*, edited by Janet Henshall Momsen. London and New York: Routledge, 1999.

Enloe, C. "Just Like One of the Family: Domestic Servants in World Politics". In *Bananas, Beaches, and Bases: Making Feminist Sense of International Politics*, edited by Cynthia Enloe. Berkeley: University of California Press, 1990, pp. 117–94.

French, Carolyn. *Filipina Domestic Workers in Hong Kong: A Preliminary Survey*. Occasional Papers no. 11, Centre for Hong Kong Studies. Hong Kong: The Chinese University of Hong Kong, 1986.

Glenn, Evelyn Nakano. *Issei, Nissei, War Bride*. Philadelphia: Temple University Press, 1986.

Guest, Philip. "Mobility Transitions within a Global System: Migration in the ESCAP Region". *Asia-Pacific Population Journal* 14, no. 4 (1999): 57–72.

Heyzer, Noeleen, Geertje Lycklama à Nijeholt and Nedra Weerakoon, eds. *The Trade in Domestic Workers: Causes, Mechanisms and Consequences of International Migration 1*. Kuala Lumpur: Asian and Pacific Development Centre; London and New Jersey: Zed Books, 1994.

Heyzer, Noeleen and Vivienne Wee. "Domestic Workers in Transient Overseas Employment: Who Benefits, Who Profits?". In *The Trade in Domestic Workers: Causes, Mechanisms and Consequences of International Migration 1*, edited by Noeleen Heyzer, Geertje Lucklama à Nijeholt and Nedra Weerakoon. Kuala Lumpur: Asian and Pacific Development Centre; London and New Jersey: Zed Books, 1994, pp. 31–102.

Hoskyns, C. and M. Orsini-Jones. "Immigrant Women in Italy: Perspectives from Brussels and Bologna". *European Journal of Women's Studies* 2 (1995): 51–76.

Hosoda, N. "Filipino Women in the Japanese Entertainment Industry". In *Asia — Who Pays for Growth? Women, Environment and Popular Movements*, edited by Lele, J. and Wisdom Tettey. Aldershot and Vermont: Dartmouth Publishing Company Limited, 1996.

Hugo, Graeme. "Migrant Women in Developing Countries". In *Internal Migration of Women in Developing Countries*. New York: United Nations, 1993, pp. 47–76.

Hugo, Graeme. "International Labor Migration and the Family: Some Observations from Indonesia". *Asian & Pacific Migration Journal* 4, nos. 2–4 (1995): 274–301.

International Labour Migration Statistics at <http://www.ilo.org/public/english/ protection/migrant/ilmdb/stats.htm>

Jones, Sidney. *Making Money off Migrants: The Indonesian Exodus to Malaysia*. Hong Kong: Asia 2000; Wollongong, Australia: Centre for Asia Pacific Social Transformation Studies, 2000.

Law, Lisa. "Sites of Transnational Activism: Filipino Non-Governmental Organizations in Hong Kong". In *Gender Politics in the Asia-Pacific Region*, edited by Brenda S.A. Yeoh, Peggy Teo and Shirlena Huang. London and New York: Routledge, 2002, pp. 205–22.

Leahy, Patricia. *Female Migrant Labour in Asia: A Case Study of Filipina Domestic Workers in Hong Kong*. Hong Kong: University of Hong Kong, Master of Arts thesis, 1990.

Li, F.L.N., A.M. Findlay and H. Jones. "A Cultural Economy Perspective on Service Sector Migration in the Global City: The Case of Hong Kong". *International Migration* 36, no. 2 (1998): 131–57.

Lim, Lin Lean and Nana Oishi. "International Labour Migration of Asian Women: Distinctive Characteristics and Policy Concerns". *Asian Women in Migration*, special issue of *Asian and Pacific Migration Journal* 5, no. 1 (1996): 85–116.

Lowe, Cynthia Torda. *The Outsider's Voice: Discourse and Identity among Filipino Domestic Workers (FDWs) in Hong Kong*. Hong Kong: City University of Hong Kong. Ph.D. thesis, 2000.

Modern Heroes, Modern Slaves. Audio-visual documentary, directed by Marie Botie and Michelle Smith, produced by Productions Multi-Monde in association with the Canadian Broadcasting Corporation, 1997.

Morokvasic, Mirjana. "Birds of Passage are also Women". *International Migration Review* 18, no. 4 (1984): 886–907.

Phizacklea, Annie. *One-Way Ticket: Migration and Female Labour*. London: Routledge and Kegan Paul, 1983.

Philippines National Statistics Office. "Table 1. Number of Overseas Filipino Workers, by Region and Sex: April to September 1995–96 (in thousands)", 1996. <http://www.census.gov.ph/data/sectordata/1996/of960001.txt>

Philippines National Statistics Office. "Press Release on the 1996 Overseas Filipino Workers (OFWs)", 1997. <http://www.census.gov.ph/data/pressrelease/1997/ of9600tx.html>

Philippines National Statistics Office. "Gender Quickstat (an update of NSO's most requested sex-disaggregated statistics) as of 1st Quarter 2003", 2003*a*. <http://www.census.gov.ph/data/quickstat/qsgender.html#overseas>

Philippines National Statistics Office. "Philippines: Additional Three Persons per Minute (Results from the 2000 Census of Population and Housing, NSO)", 2003*b*. <http://www.census.gov.ph/data/pressrelease/2003/ pr0323tx.html>

Philippines Overseas Employment Administration (POEA). "Stock Estimates on Overseas Filipinos", 2002. <http://www.poea.gov.ph>

Philippines Overseas Employment Administration (POEA). "Status of recruitment agencies", 2003. <http://www.poea.gov.ph/cgi-bin/agList.asp?mode=all>; <http://www.poea.gov.ph/cgi-bin/agList.asp?mode=actLB>

Sim, Amy. *NGO Approaches to Female Labour Migration from the Philippines to Hong Kong: A Comparative Study of Two NGOs.* United Kingdom: Open University. Dissertation for the degree of Master of Science in Development Management, 2001.

Sim, Amy. "Organizing Discontent: NGOs for Southeast Asian Migrant Workers in Hong Kong". *Asian Journal of Social Science* 31, no. 3 (September 2003).

Skeldon, Ronald. "The Migration of Women in the Context of Globalization in the ESCAP Region". Unpublished paper, 1998.

South China Morning Post. "Fees Victory Lifts Helpers" campaign. Indonesian Maids Press for Pay Safeguards to End Exploitation'. 7 January 2001.

South China Morning Post. "10,000 Maids Against Levy; Foreign Domestic Workers March to the Government's Headquarters, as Bishop Zen Holds a Mass for Filipinos". 24 February 2003.

South China Morning Post. "Few Indonesian Maids Get Legal Wage. Employment Agencies Do Not Inform Applicants of the Minimum Payment, a New Study has Revealed". 22 March 2003.

"[Stop-traffic] News/Hong Kong: Indonesian Maids Slam Exploitation in Hong Kong". <http://fpmail.friends-partners.org/pipermail/stop-traffic/2001-August/001530.html>

"Stop Sex Trafficking of Filipino Women and Children! A Primer on Sex Trafficking". <http://members.tripod.com/~gabriela_p/8-articles/990601_prose.html>

The Post-Nairobi Years: Review and Appraisal. <http://www.fao.org/docrep/x0175e/x0175e05.htm>

Tung, Charlene. *The Social Reproductive Labor of Filipina Transmigrant Workers in Southern California: Caring for Those who Provide Elderly Care.* Irvine: University of California, Irvine. Ph.D. thesis, 1999.

Varona, Rex. "Trends in the Asian Migration Map". Paper presented at the seminar *On the Philippine Migration Trail: Migration and Reproductive Health,* Bangkok, Thailand, February 2001. Excerpted at <http://www.ips.org/migration/varona.htm>

Williams, Catarina Purwana. Oral presentation at *Symposium Antropologi Indonesia,* Denpasar, Bali (Indonesia) in July 2002.

Women's Health in Indonesia. <http://w3.whosea.org/women2/indonesia.htm>

Wong, Diana. "Foreign Domestic Workers in Singapore". *Asian Women in Migration,* special issue of *Asian and Pacific Migration Journal* 5, no. 1 (1996): 117–38.

7

Borders, Globalization and Irregular Migration in Southeast Asia

Maruja M.B. Asis

Introduction*

The year 2002 barely started when reports of riots by Indonesian workers in a textile factory in Nilai, Negeri Sembilan and at a construction site in Cyberjaya triggered a series of action to deal with labour migration, particularly irregular migration. The Malaysian Government immediately announced that Indonesians will be the last priority in the hiring of migrant workers, the so-called "Indonesians last" policy (*Asian Migration News*, 31 January 2002). This was followed by an announcement targeting the repatriation of 10,000 Indonesians every month, and the effectivity of amendments to Malaysia's Immigration Act of 1963 on 1 August. The amendments provide for stiffer punishments against immigration violators — irregular migrant workers as well as employers and harbourers of irregular migrants. Particularly for migrants who entered Malaysia in an irregular fashion, the punishment includes fines of RM10,000, jail terms and caning.

Sabah followed suit in announcing its intent to crack down on irregular migrants in the state, in accordance with the national objective. The campaign was launched in February and the multi-pronged approach involved inspections of workplaces, the burning of migrant settlements, and deportations.

Unlike the deportations from Peninsular Malaysia, which affected mostly Indonesians, the deportations from Sabah affected a great many Filipinos, whose presence in the state has evoked concerns beyond the economic. In the past, there were concerns that Filipinos were used for political purposes; in recent years, security issues became salient, particularly with the Sipadan kidnapping carried out by the extremist Abu Sayyaf group in 2000, and the rhetoric against "terrorism" since 11 September 2001.

Early on in 2002, Thailand also announced another plan to repatriate Burmese migrants in an irregular situation. It may be recalled that in 2001, the Thai Government experimented with a more "liberal" registration process — that is, it dropped the quotas and removed the limitations on occupations and geographical areas. Some 550,000 migrants registered (Amarapibal, Beesey and Germershausen 2003), but even then, there was a substantial number who were not registered. Thailand was able to negotiate with Burma for the repatriation of the latter's nationals, including the establishment of a repatriation centre in Myawaddy, on the Burmese side of the border (*Asian Migration News*, 15 January 2002).

While not much has been heard about Thailand's repatriation, Malaysia's campaign proceeded as planned. Malaysia offered an amnesty commencing from 20 March to 31 July for irregular migrants to leave voluntarily. In its zeal to repatriate "illegals", considerations of human rights were relegated to the background. In the Philippines, media accounts tell of congestion and deplorable conditions in the detention centres, or of deportees being shipped off in overcrowded vessels.

In the Philippines, Malaysia's actions have ignited outrage over the treatment of Filipino deportees, particularly as reports of deaths of children, sexual abuse and the rape of a 13-year-old girl surfaced. The Philippines lodged a diplomatic protest to Malaysia over the treatment of Filipino nationals and filed charges against Sabah police named by the 13-year-old girl.[1]

The dynamics between the Philippines and Malaysia are further complicated by the unresolved issues over Sabah, and there is clamour in the Philippines to reopen the claim to Sabah. In response to President Gloria Arroyo's call, the then Prime Minister Mahathir ordered the suspension of the deportation proceedings for Filipinos and allowed Filipino officials to investigate the conditions in the detention centres. Similarly, there were protests in Indonesia over the treatment of Indonesian migrants.

The strains resulting from the whole episode raises questions about the ideal of regional co-operation the Association for Southeast Asian Nations (ASEAN) aims for. Also, reinforcing border controls and more punitive sanctions seem regressive in light of moves towards more regional approaches to migration since the economic crisis in 1997. It may be recalled that Malaysia and Thailand carried out repatriation activities during the crisis to free up jobs for locals. However, the repatriations did not ease domestic unemployment, and a situation ensued where there was high unemployment and continuing labour shortages in some sectors (Battistella and Asis 1998).

The situation indicated that irregular migration was structural — there was a demand for irregular migrants — and the phenomenon was more than just the desire of individuals to migrate in any way possible. It became apparent that co-operation between countries of origin and countries of destination was necessary, and this started the holding of regional conferences in Bangkok (1999), in Manila (2000), and Bali (2002) on the specific issue of irregular migration and trafficking. All three regional conferences came up with a regional action plan and a commitment to co-operate on specific points of action. The renewed resolve to guard borders against irregular migration and the tendency towards stiffer sanctions for immigration violations underscore the difficulties of transcending national approaches. The region's experience in the last thirty years suggests that national approaches are limited in combating irregular migration, and they have even much less chance of effecting lasting changes in the context of the globalization of economies. As Tapinos and Delaunay (2000, p. 47) observed, globalization requires an international and holistic perspective:

International migration is now taking place in the context of the globalization of economies, emphasizing the interdependence of sending and host countries, as opposed to the traditional approach that focused on these countries' respective impact on each other. What is more, the economic, political and social aspects of migration are now seldom analysed as separate factors, whether to explain the reasons for emigration or its impact on the societies concerned. The debate on migration has become inseparable form the issue of human rights, the political organization and economic development of the country of origin, and the national cohesion and future of the welfare state in host societies.

Objectives

This chapter argues for the need to strengthen a regional approach to migration in general, and irregular migration in particular. Based on the experiences of two countries of origin, the Philippines and Indonesia, and two countries of destination, Malaysia and Thailand, the chapter aims to show how irregular migration results from the interaction of factors operating in both countries of origin and destination.

The first part presents an overview of migration trends and policies in Southeast Asia, particularly those influencing irregular migration. The second part discusses comparative findings from the four-country study highlighting: (a) decision-making, recruitment and deployment processes in the countries of origin, and (b) entry, employment and integration in the countries of destination. The conclusion revisits the contradictory tendencies in globalization, migration policies and migration behaviour, which in various ways contribute to the persistence of irregular migration.

Conceptual Framework

An earlier analysis pointed out that legal and authorized migration must be considered as originating from the same migration system (IOM 1999). Similar factors and processes drive legal and irregular migrations. As indicated in Figure 7.1, both migrations originate from similar determinants operating in the countries of origin and destination.

In the countries of origin, factors such as unemployment, low wages and poverty are conditions that may push people out, but they are not sufficient to lead to migration. Particularly in international labour migration, certain requirements and procedures must be met, and this is where the migration industry and other intermediaries, including social networks, step in to provide services and assistance to migrants, usually for a fee. On the other hand, in the countries of destination, there is a demand for migrant workers, and this is regulated by migration policies.

FIGURE 7.1
Dynamics of Authorized and Unauthorized Migration

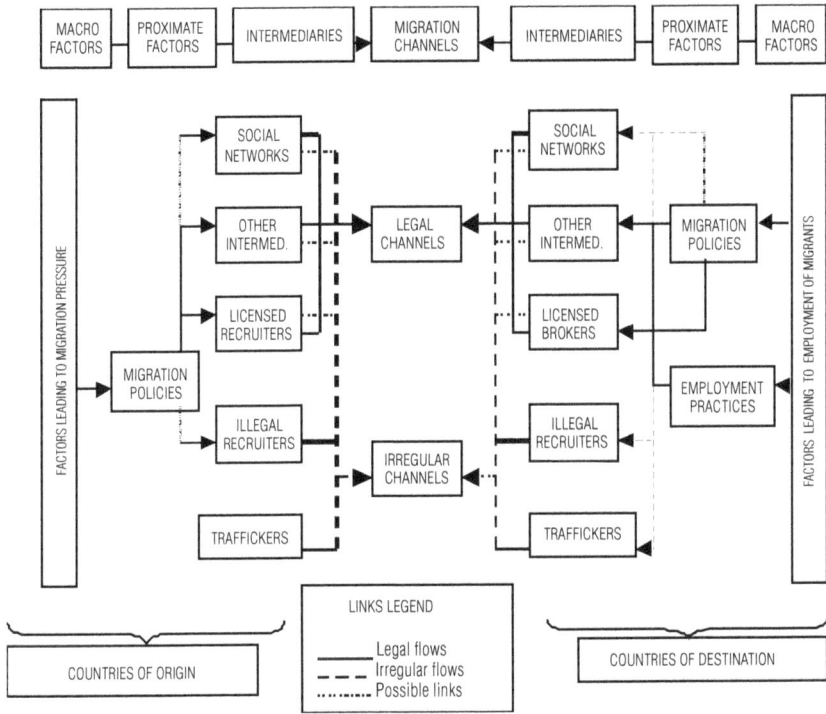

Source: Battistella and Asis (2003a: 14).

In Asia, the migration industry, labour brokers as well as social networks are also present in the countries of destination, and they link migrants to employers and provide other services to facilitate the entry and employment of migrants. Irregular migration takes place when migrants or employers access irregular channels (including traffickers). This comes about because of various reasons: migrants lack the necessary information, irregular channels are the only means to work in the intended country of destination, or migration policies are unrealistic. The migration industry, brokers and social networks, both legal and illegal, operate in both the country of origin and the country of destination, mainly to help migrants and employers to deal with the barriers of the movement of workers. The framework suggests that the migrants who come under legal and irregular channels do not come from distinct groups; the major difference between the two is that legal migrants have access to legal channels while irregular migrants have access to irregular channels.

The framework maps out the actors and factors involved and the transnational linkages between these variables that could lead to either legal or irregular migration. The linkages and inter-relatedness of variables suggest that addressing the problem at either end of the migration system, or a focus on one aspect to the exclusion of others will have limited impact.

A Note on Terminology

Irregular migration has been defined as a departure from or violation of the migration norms of the country of origin, transit, or destination; usually these norms have to do with exit, entry, employment and residence (for example, IOM 1999; Ghosh 1998). Irregular migration is commonly referred to as "illegal migration" and migrants are routinely labelled as "illegal migrants or aliens" or simply "illegals". Such language tends to draw attention to migrants as violators and obfuscates the fact that other actors or institutions could be violators and that migrants could be victims. Resolution 3449 of the UN General Assembly (9 December 1975) recommended the use of the terms "irregular migration" or "non-documented" migration. The latter term or its variant, undocumented migration, however, only refers to a sub-set of irregular migrants, that is, those who travel and/or work without documents, which excludes many other irregular migrants who carry documents. This chapter employs the terms "irregular migration" or "unauthorized migration" while references to legal migration also include regular or authorized migration.

Finally, a word about irregular migration and trafficking: sometimes these terms are used interchangeably. There is a distinction between the two, particularly with trafficking as a more specific, more exploitative type of irregular migration. Exploitation could also arise from irregular migration, but it is not a defining characteristic as it is in trafficking. The definition of trafficking has been subjected to much debate. The United Nations Protocol to Prevent, Suppress and Punish Trafficking in Persons, Especially Women and Children (adopted by the UN General Assembly in November 2000) defines trafficking as:

> the recruitment, transportation, transfer, harbouring or receipt of persons, by means of the threat or use of force or other forms of coercion, of abduction, of fraud, of deception, of the abuse of power or of a position of vulnerability or of the giving or receiving of payments or benefits to achieve the consent of a person having control over another person for the purpose of exploitation. Exploitation shall include, at a minimum, the exploitation of the prostitution of others or other forms of sexual exploitation, forced labour or services, slavery or practices similar to slavery, servitude or the removal of organs.

Migration in Southeast Asia

Population mobility has been part of Southeast Asia's history and culture. In maritime Southeast Asia, present-day Philippines, Indonesia and Malaysia were part of the greater Dunia Melayu and many historical accounts speak of extensive contacts through trade and migration (Salazar 1998*a*, p. 71). In the Philippines, for example, the ethnic groups such as the Tagalogs came from Malacca through Kalimantan, the Pampangos from Sumatera and the Bicol and Visayans from Macasar (Salazar 1998*b*, p. 113). Another indication of the importance of journeys and migrations for some groups in Indonesia can be deduced from the notion of *merantau*, and the badge of achievement conferred on individuals who had undertaken journeys (Margold 2002; Aguilar 2002). Similarly in mainland Southeast Asia, there was much exchange between Thailand and its neighbouring countries, including Yunnan, China. The cultural affinities shared by groups in the border areas of neighbouring countries attest to the history of exchanges among them.

Spontaneous population mobility in Southeast Asia ceased when countries in the region came under colonial administration. Colonial policies not only established boundaries, but also in some instances, as in the case of the British in Malaya, Chinese and Indians were "imported" as workers, thus diversifying Malaya's population. In the case of Dutch colonial policies in Indonesia, Indonesians were sent to other Dutch colonies like Surinam.

The development of independent nation-states reinforced the delineation and protection of national borders. From post-World War II and throughout the 1960s, there was not much discussion of international migration in Southeast Asia, particularly intra-regional migration. When intra-regional migration emerged in the 1970s, and especially since the 1980s, it was a reprise of old movements under changed circumstances rather than a new phenomenon.

Unlike East Asia, which is mostly a destination region (that is, with the exception of China), or South Asia, which is largely a region of origin, Southeast Asia encompasses countries of origin (the Philippines, Indonesia and Myanmar are the major source countries; Vietnam, Laos and Cambodia), countries of destination (Singapore and Brunei), and countries that are both origin and destination (Malaysia and Thailand).[2] The countries of origin are generally the less developed and more populous countries compared to the countries of destination (Table 7.1). The most recent estimate of authorized migrants in Southeast Asia is at least two million, on top of which are at least another 1.5 million to 2 million migrants in an irregular situation (Table 7.2).

Southeast Asia can be further distinguished into sub-regions which have their characteristic migration systems: the Malay Peninsula and Singapore, the Brunei-Indonesia-Malaysia-Philippines-East ASEAN Growth Area (BIMP-EAGA), and Northern ASEAN (Figure 2). In all three systems, history, geography, and cultural similarities are the major givens in considering present-day population movements.

Both legal and unauthorized migrations operate in the Malay Peninsula and Singapore. As mentioned earlier, Malaysia has been home to a large population of irregular migrants, who started coming to the country in the 1970s. The implementation of the New Economic Policy since the 1970s left some sectors (plantation, construction, services) short of workers, which were filled by migrants, mostly from neighbouring Indonesia. By the 1980s, Indonesian migrants had become a visible presence and concerns arose about the dangers of migration, especially "illegal migration". While there were concerns about the presence of migrants, employers, on the other hand, lobbied for the need to import migrant workers. An attempt to regulate the importation of migrant workers found expression in the signing of the 1984 Medan Agreement with Indonesia, followed by agreements with the Philippines in 1985 and Bangladesh and Thailand in

TABLE 7.1
ASEAN: Selected Demographic and Economic Indicators

	Mid-2002 Population (000s)[1]	Annual Population Growth Rate (%)[2]	Population Projected to 2025 (000s)[3]	Labour Force 2000 (000s)[4]	Unemployment Rate[5]	GDP Growth 2001[6]	GNP Per Capita 2002	GNP Per Capita (US$)[7]	HDI 1999[8]
Countries of Origin									
Cambodia	13,204	2.5	22,310	5,275	2.6	5.04	6	280	0.541
Indonesia	217,660	1.2	272,911	95,696	6.1	4.2	4.5	600	0.677
Lao PDR	5,536	2.3	8,721	–	–	6.0	6.5*	–	0.476
Myanmar	50,633	1.2	60,243	–	–	–	–	–	0.551
Philippines	78,744	1.9	107,703	30,908	10.1	3.1	4.2	1,050	0.749
Vietnam	80,639	1.3	105,488	–	–	6.4	6.9	370	0.682
Countries of Origin and Destination									
Malaysia	24,109	1.8	31,326	9,616	3.1	4.9	6.0	3,670	0.774
Thailand	63,430	0.8	72,122	33,973	2.4	3.5	4.5	2,010	0.757
Countries of Destination									
Brunei Darussalam	354	2.3	473	–	–	–	–	–	–
Singapore	4,157	1.7	4,998	2,192	4.4	–	–	24,150	0.876
Total	538,466	1.4	685,665	–	–	–	–	–	–

Note: * Real GDP growth.

Sources: [1,2,3]<www.unescap.org/data>; [4,5]Asian Development Bank (2001a), Tables 1 and 2 (cited in Battistella and Asis 2003a: 3). [6]Asian Development Bank (2001a), country tables; [6]Asian Development Bank (2001a), country reports; [7,8]Asian Development Bank (2001b), country reports.

TABLE 7.2
Estimates of Migrants in Selected ASEAN Countries

A. Estimates of the stock of authorized migrants (Thousands)

From	Thailand[1] 2001	Malaysia[2] 2002	Singapore[3] 2000
Indonesia	–	567.0	165.6
Philippines	–	6.5	99.3
Thailand	–	2.4	99.3
China	–		76.2
Bangladesh	–	105.0	–
Myanmar	447.1		–
Nepal	–	17.0	–
Pakistan	–	1.2	–
Other	112.5	70.9	304.6
Total	**559.6**	**770.0**	**745.0**

B. Estimates of unauthorized migrants in Malaysia and Thailand

From	Malaysia[4] 2002	Thailand[5] 2001
Bangladesh	–	–
Myanmar	–	421,719
Cambodia	–	42,119
Indonesia	–	–
Philippines	–	–
Others	–	56,159
Total	**600,000***	**520,000**

Note: * Media reports in 2002 often cite the 600,000-figure; there are also estimates citing one million unauthorized migrants in Malaysia (*Asian Migration News*, 31 May 2002; 30 June 2002). The figures vary depending on the source. In Sabah, there are some 600,000 foreigners, of whom 100,000-150,000 migrants are said to be in an irregular situation (*Asian Migration News*, 31 March 2002). In the 1997 regularization census, there were 150,000 irregular migrants; at the time, 250,000 Indonesians and Filipinos applied for work permits. Another source, the 2000 census, estimated some 600,000 foreigners in Sabah, of whom 400,000 remain unaccounted (*Asian Migration News*, 15 July 2002).

Sources: [1]Registered during September-October 2001 (*Asian Migration News*, 31 October 2001); [2]*Asian Migration News*, 31 January 2002; [3]*Asian Migration News*, 31 August 2001; [4]*Asian Migration News*, 31 May 2002; [5]Estimate from *Asian Migration News*, 31 October 2001 (cited in Battistella and Asis 2003a: 5–6).

FIGURE 7.2
Migration Systems in Southeast Asia

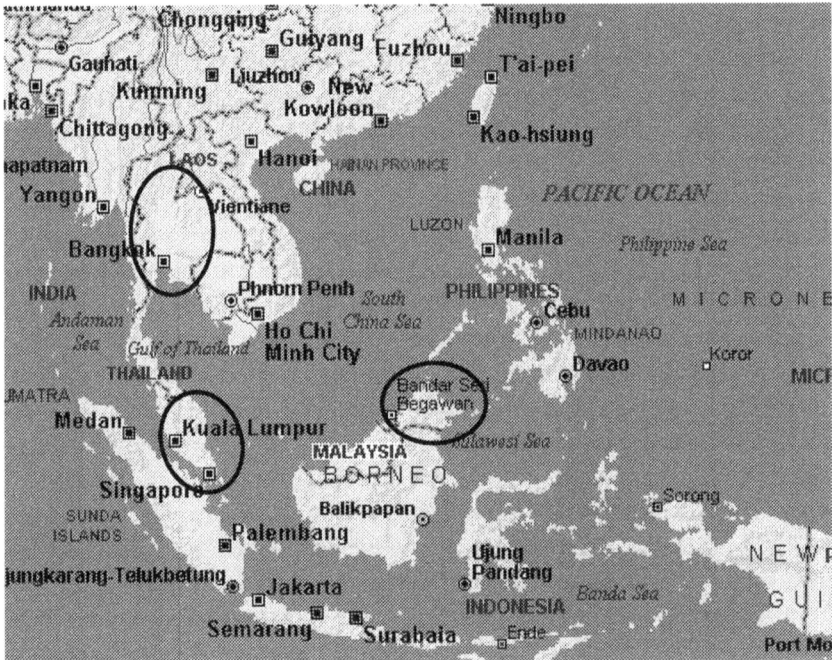

1986 (Wong and Teuku Afrizal 2003, p. 176). These agreements paved the way for a formal and legal channel of recruiting migrant workers.

However, the formal recruitment channel did not mean the end of irregular migration; rather, parallel to the formal system is the larger and unregulated channel of irregular migration, largely from Indonesia to Peninsular Malaysia, and from the Philippines (and also Indonesia) to East Malaysia, particularly Sabah. Malaysia had implemented crackdowns, deportations and regularizations, but still, these were not sufficient to curb irregular migration. Recent estimates of the migrant population in Malaysia indicate that there are some 750,000 legal migrants in the country, of whom 70 per cent are Indonesians; the estimates for irregular migrants range from 600,000 to a million. The Immigration Act (Amendment) 2002 is yet another attempt to deal with irregular migration. Malaysia's plans to recruit from Central Asian countries reflects its intent to source needed workers from more distant countries, presumably because it would be easier to regulate and rotate such workers.[3]

Singapore, on the other hand, is one destination country in the region which has managed to keep irregular migration in check. It was one of the first countries in Asia to realize its need for migrant labour and it proceeded to develop a migration policy to address and manage this need. The importation of foreign labour is supposed to be temporary, but the number of migrant workers has not only increased over the years, but the share of foreign workers in Singapore's work force is perhaps among the highest in the world — 29 per cent as of the census of 2000. Migrant workers in Singapore come from the Philippines, Indonesia and Sri Lanka (foreign domestic workers), Bangladesh, India and Thailand (construction workers), in addition to the thousands of Malaysians who cross over daily to work on the Singapore side. Apart from its compact territory, Singapore has managed to keep irregular migration low for several reasons: the policies were in place before the migrants came, migration policies generally correspond to the needs of the economy, and a generally efficient law enforcement.[4] Still reports of migrants being sneaked in lorries and cars from Malaysia, of migrants violating their social visit passes and other immigration violations have come to light, indicating the pervasiveness of irregular migration even in Singapore.

Irregular migration is very prominent in the BIMP-EAGA and Northern ASEAN migration systems. Like Malaysia, irregular migration has overshadowed authorized migration in these sub-regions. Sabah, Sarawak and Brunei are the core areas in BIMP-EAGA, to which migrants from neighbouring Indonesia (via Kalimantan) and Southern Philippines (largely from Western Mindanao and Palawan) go. The sultanate of Brunei is the only nation-member of the BIMP-EAGA configuration; the rest are sub-regions of the other member-countries. Brunei recognizes that migrant workers are and will be an essential component of its labour force, and has adopted pragmatic migration policies to suit its needs. ASEAN nationals comprise the majority of migrants in Brunei, many of whom are Malaysians (Mani 1998). Although there are also reports of immigration violations in the sultanate, they have not reached problematic proportions. Brunei's role in irregular migration in the sub-region is in providing an exit point for social visit pass holders in Sabah and Sarawak — that is, to avoid overstaying their visas, social visit pass holders exit to Brunei before or at the time of expiration of their visas, and return to Sabah or Sarawak with a new "chop".

Sabah and Sarawak are part of the Federation of Malaysia, but these two states have their own migration policies. Sabah's logging industry had attracted migrants to the state since the 1950s. Many of the old Filipino families who had settled in Sabah had gone there at a time when the state's migration and settlement policies were liberal. The arrival of refugees from the Philippines in the 1970s during the height of the Mindanao conflict in the Philippines, and the arrival of "economic migrants" thereafter contributed to the changed attitude towards migrants in the 1980s.

The discussion on irregular migration in Sabah is illustrative of the tension between economic and political concerns. The state is very much dependent on migrant workers — the plantation sector, construction and services rely heavily on irregular migrant workers — but on the other hand, concerns for ethnic balance and the fear that migrants are influencing the future of the state have contributed to the formation of negative views towards migrants. Sabah has tried policies and measures such as crackdowns, repatriations and regularizations, but irregular migration has not abated. One of the accomplishments of BIMP-EAGA was the opening of a ferry service between Zamboanga City (in Western Mindanao) and Sandakan (in Sabah), but many more prefer the familiarity, the convenience and the speed of going to Sabah *kumpit*-style. The recent amendment to the Immigration Act of 1963 may have succeeded in repatriating large numbers of migrants, but its emphasis on punishing migrants and other violators is not a durable solution to the problem of irregular migration.

Thailand is the core in the North ASEAN sub-region, drawing migrants mostly from Myanmar as well as Cambodia, Laos and Yunnan, China. Migrants were already in Thailand before policies on the recruitment and regulation of migrant workers were developed. During Thailand's march to industrialization, migrants took up the work vacated by local workers. Apart from economic reasons, the political situation in Myanmar also contributed to the influx of Burmese migrants to Thailand. With migrants already in the country, Thailand's policy focused on registering migrant workers and cracking down and repatriating those who failed to register. In attempting to regulate migrant labour, the government imposed quotas on the number of migrant workers, limited to specific industries and specific provinces. The economic crisis of 1997 prompted the government's attention to focus on the massive repatriation of Burmese migrants to ease domestic unemployment. The numerous repatriations are believed to be futile exercises, as they have not led to any significant reduction in the number of irregular migrants. Meanwhile, employers in lucrative industries — fishing-related, rice mills, agriculture, manufacturing, and services — continue to claim labour shortage, hence the need to take in migrant workers.

While countries of destination focus on controlling the entry, economic activity and stay of migrants, the countries of origin have also done their share to prevent irregular migration at their end. Contrary to the perception that only countries of destination are concerned with irregular migration, countries of origin are equally concerned in curbing irregular migration as the protection and welfare of their nationals is at stake. The Philippines, in particular, has developed specific policies and programmes to address irregular migration, mostly by trying to prevent illegal recruitment, and through various information programmes on the legal process of migration, the *modus operandi* of illegal recruiters (and of late, traffickers) and the dangers of irregular migration. The Migrant Workers and Overseas Filipinos Act of 1995 (Republic Act 8042) includes many provisions specifically addressing illegal recruitment, sanctions against errant recruiters and other violators, systems of redress, protection of victims and assistance to victims of illegal recruitment. Although these mechanisms are in place, it is acknowledged that reported cases represent only a small proportion of actual cases. Government officials and those in the recruitment industry tend to regard migrants as "willing victims" because of the latter's tendency not to pursue cases against errant recruiters.

A significant development in Republic Act 8042 is the provision of consular services and assistance to migrants in an irregular situation; in the past, only legal migrants could avail of such services.[5] The law also encourages migrants in an irregular situation to register at the consulate or embassy. There had been overtures by countries of origin like the Philippines to forge a bilateral agreement or at least a memorandum of agreement concerning the protection of its nationals. In general, countries of destination have been reluctant to discuss these issues, and even the regional discussions on irregular migration need to be more explicit on matters concerning protection. Migrants may have violated immigration regulations, but their rights as workers and as human beings should not be denied them.

Highlights from the Four-Country Study[6]

Background of the Project

A review of the literature on migration studies in the Philippines, Indonesia, Malaysia and Thailand confirmed that specific studies on irregular migration were rare in these countries. Although there are references to irregular migration in existing migration studies, these are not sufficient in understanding the various dimensions of the phenomenon. For the most part, the usual sources of data and information on irregular migration provide only a partial and selective view: data from state agencies usually focus on apprehensions and violations, particularly those committed by migrants, NGOs and migrant advocates report on violations committed against migrants, and media reports often deal with irregular migrants in unusual cases.

To advance our understanding of irregular migration beyond the descriptive stage, this study was conducted to examine some objectives. First is to review existing migration policies both in the countries of origin and countries of destination. Second is to examine specific policies on irregular migration in both countries of origin and countries of destination. Third is to investigate the dynamics of irregular migration, particularly the role played by employment agencies and intermediaries, both in the countries of origin and countries of destination. And fourth is to explore the employment mechanisms of irregular migrants and the living and working conditions they encounter.

The survey was the main instrument in collecting data in all four countries: 100 interviews with migrants who were ever in an irregular situation were carried out; in Thailand, the research team completed 327 interviews. Respondents were not selected randomly; hence the findings cannot be generalized to the larger population. Additional interviews were conducted with other players: government officials, personnel of NGOs working with migrants, the local community, and recruiters and intermediaries. Data collection took place mostly in the last quarter of 2000.

Findings from the Philippines and Indonesia

The Regulatory Context of Labour Migration

International migration has become pervasive in both the Philippines and Indonesia from the 1970s. In present-day Indonesia, migration is no longer regarded as the cultural preserve of some groups. Similarly, in the Philippines, almost all of the country's regions have been affected by international migration, although variations in the extent and other characteristics of migration remain.

In both countries, international migration has become an important part of the state's development policy, and the state is generally perceived as promoting labour migration. Between the two countries, the Philippines has developed a more codified system of regulating recruitment, deployment, monitoring the conditions of migrants abroad, and providing reintegration services and assistance.

The migration industry has been cited as one of the reasons for the continuation of migration in the region. In the Philippines, there were some 1,396 licensed agencies as of June 2002 (Battistella and Asis 2003b). In addition, there are the unlicensed agencies and licensed and unlicensed agencies that are involved in some tie-ups. The terrain of the migration industry in Indonesia has been described as involving much interface between licensed and unlicensed entities (for example, see Jones 2000 for details). The regulation of the migration industry in the Philippines has not ruled out illegal recruitment and other irregularities against migrants. The most recent development in this area was the re-affirmation of the need to regulate the industry via the new rules and regulations drafted by the Philippine Overseas Employment Administration (POEA).[7] POEA pushed for the new rules based on data indicating that 75 per cent of violations against migrants were committed by licensed agencies. No data are available on the abuses and malpractices of unlicensed agencies, but they are believed to be rampant. In Indonesia, the shades of complicity between licensed and unlicensed recruiters and agents make it difficult to trace the accountability of the different entities. In the Philippine survey, some 41 per cent of respondents claimed that they had ever been victimized by illegal recruiters, and an even higher proportion reported that they knew of others who had the same experience. On the other hand, in Indonesia, fewer respondents (13 per cent) reported that they had been victimized, in part because the intermediaries were usually part of the respondents' social networks.

Levels, Destinations, Composition and Forms of Irregular Migration

The Philippines has a larger outflow of legal migrants deployed annually, averaging about 800,000 workers (both land-based and sea-based), compared with Indonesia, which has a yearly deployment of about 300,000. In terms of irregular migration, however, the magnitude is larger in Indonesia than in the Philippines. In fact, the irregular outflows even surpass the legal ones in the case of Indonesia. Much of the irregular outflows from Indonesia are directed to Malaysia, which is understandable because of their proximity to each other. In addition, a long history of exchanges between the two countries has created well-established pathways of migration: West Malaysia is a matter of crossing the Straits of Malacca, while East Malaysia is accessible by land from Kalimantan. As for the Philippines, the destinations of irregular migrants are as global as authorized migration. Only about a quarter of Filipino irregular migrants had ever migrated to a Southeast Asian destination — Sabah. The rest went to Italy, Taiwan, Middle Eastern countries, Japan, Korea, Singapore and Hong Kong.

The gender composition of irregular migrants was markedly different in the two national groups — it was largely male (79 per cent) among Indonesians while males and females were about equally likely to have engaged in irregular migration in the Philippine sample. Another contrast is the more diverse migration history of Filipino migrants compared to their Indonesian counterparts. More Filipino migrants had left for overseas employment more than once, had ever worked abroad longer, and had gone abroad both through legal and irregular channels.

Much of irregular migration from Indonesia, destined largely for Malaysia, was undocumented migration: about 84 per cent of respondents in the Indonesian survey committed this type of irregularity (that is, they bypassed the Ministry of Manpower). Filipino migrants had engaged in various forms of irregular migration, including changing personal information, for example, changing the name, age, or marital status (n=26), using a non-working visa, mostly using tourist visa (n=50), overstaying (n=48), running away (n=16), and backdoor entry or undocumented migration (n=23). The type of irregularity is associated with certain destinations. Majority of those who changed personal information were former migrants to Taiwan who "changed names" (that is, getting a new passport using somebody else's personal information; the photograph is that of the migrant's) to be able to return to Taiwan; a few others changed their ages to meet the age requirement for domestic workers bound for Middle East countries. Those who used tourist visas went to Italy, Japan and Singapore. Usually those holding tourist visas would eventually overstay their visas (especially true for those who went to Italy and Japan). Many of those who went to Korea used a trainee visa, but they were aware that they would be actually working in Korea. The runaways were scattered in different countries; some of them were legal migrants who ran away from their employers because of difficult working conditions. Undocumented migration was very specific to Sabah.

Except for those who went to Sabah as undocumented migrants, some three quarters of Filipino migrants had to secure travel and/or work documents to reach their intended destinations. In meeting these requirements, the intervention of the migration industry was necessary. Where there were obstacles to finding work abroad, recruiters and agents offered advice that would facilitate migrants' entry.

Decision-Making Processes and Deployment

The initiative to take up migration usually came from the individual, and there was consultation with family members, who were generally supportive of the respondents' intention to migrate. In the Philippine survey, most respondents were aware of what constituted irregular practices. However, despite having a sense of what is right and wrong, nearly a quarter of respondents reported that they would engage in some irregular practices if they had to.

Indonesian respondents often mentioned family and friends as sources of information on migration. In the Philippines, the process of information-seeking involved asking family and friends to refer them to recruitment agencies, after which, the latter become the major source of information on most aspects of migration — requirements, placement fees, work opportunities abroad and so forth. The survey in the Philippines noted that despite government efforts and the initiatives of non-governmental organizations (NGOs) to disseminate migration information, migrants gravitated towards their own networks and the migration industry to obtain migration-related information.

In Indonesia, family and friends, including former migrants, are increasingly taking up the role of intermediaries. In past studies, community-based intermediaries — *calos* and *tekongs* — used to have some monopoly of knowledge and information about the ins and outs of migrating to Malaysia. The spread of migration to the general population has also made migration information more widely available. Migration incurs costs, but migrants had access to loans in the local community (family and relatives, former migrants, local elites, *calos* or *tekongs*), which made migration possible. The risks of migration are significantly reduced by the comprehensive assistance provided by intermediaries: information, documentation, transportation, and escorting migrants to their workplace in Malaysia. Compared with the arduous and long process of legal migration (also very limited prospects), irregular migration is faster and cheaper.

In the Philippines, migrants have to pay for the services provided by the recruitment agencies. Placement fees are regulated (one month's salary plus 5,000 pesos for documentation), but this is widely violated. According to survey respondents, raising the placement fee was the topmost problem they encountered while preparing for migration. The amount varies depending on the destination and the time of departure. The amount, however, appeared unimportant to migrants as they anticipated recovering their expenses once they start working abroad.

Although different systems of intermediaries were initially involved (recruitment agencies in the Philippines, community-based agents and brokers in the case of Indonesia), family and friends are emerging as important lynchpins in the migration process. This development implies more challenge for policy-making as relations and dynamics in social networks cannot be easily subjected to regulations.

Outcomes of Irregular Migration

Once in the destination countries, irregular migrants did not find it difficult to find work, that is, if they were not selective. There were no guarantees for tenure, minimum wages and work conditions. Irregular migrants were also limited to sectors — construction, plantation, services, and domestic work — which had become identified as migrants' jobs.

Common to the experience of Filipino and Indonesian migrants was their relative isolation from the local population. Their workplaces were comprised of workers of co-nationals or other migrant groups. For Indonesians, their places of residence were shared mostly with other nationals, and it was only in places of worship, where they had some interaction with the locals. Filipino migrants tended to live in neighbourhoods where locals predominated; Filipinos also attended places of worship usually frequented by other Filipinos.

Particularly in the Philippine survey, the findings underscored that irregular migration entailed a life rife with uncertainties and anxieties. There were significant variations by destination. Ever migrants to Sabah, for example, experienced the most difficulties and vulnerabilities — non-payment of wages, no contact with their family members, and high incidence of arrest. On the other hand, irregular migrants in Japan and Italy were able to find jobs, they were less subject to harassment by authorities, and most were able to work there for an extended period of time. For those who went to Italy, most of the migrants had the opportunity to regularize their status. Data from Indonesia revealed that some 46 per cent were deported back to Indonesia, suggesting that close to half returned to Indonesia prematurely. Thus, while Malaysia may be accessible to Indonesian migrants, proximity also means a higher likelihood of deportation. The survey in Malaysia confirms the risk of deportation, but this did not deter ever migrants from attempting to return to Malaysia.

Findings from Malaysia and Thailand

Ethnicity and the Local Context

Migrants in Malaysia and Thailand are predominated by Indonesians and Burmese, respectively. Proximity is a major factor in the large inflows of these groups in the destination countries. Closer examination reveals that these national groups are differentiated by ethnicity. In the case of Indonesian migrants, Wong and Afrizal (2002) identified three migrant streams, whose migration to and incorporation in Malaysia varied by ethnicity: the Aceh pattern is characteristic of migrants from Sumatra;

migrants come to Malaysia legally, usually self-organized, and most are found in ethnic business; the Lombok pattern is characteristic of migrants from East Indonesia; their entry to Malaysia is usually unauthorized, assisted by brokers, and they find work in the plantation sector; and the Bawean pattern is associated with migrants from East Java; their entry to Malaysia is legal and more expensive, usually assisted by brokers; and they are mostly in construction.

In Thailand, Burmese migrants come from three ethnic groups: Burmese, Mon and Karen. Ethnicity played a minor role in defining their conditions in Thailand; rather their location (whether they were in a border province or inland province) and the configuration of local politics were more significant factors in shaping their migration experience. The employment prospects of Burmese migrants in Thailand are dependent on the local economy. In Samutsakhon (a province near Bangkok), migrants worked in the fishing-related industries, the province's major economic sector; in Tak (a border province), migrants worked in factories, farms, construction and households. NGOs and employers' associations were more visible in Thailand than in Malaysia. Some NGOs have responded to meet the needs of migrants (for example, health) and to bring to public attention the plight of migrants in Thailand. Detailed information from the survey confirmed the low wages, poor working conditions and the precarious living conditions of irregular migrants.

Although migration to Malaysia and Thailand started out as labour migration, migrant communities have developed. In Malaysia, some neighbourhoods have become identified with Indonesian migrants; in Thailand, some migrant workers have been joined by their families, or migrants married fellow migrants (this was particularly true in Samutsakhon). The presence of children and their lack of access to education and health care raise concerns about their well being and their future.

The Role of Social Networks

The migration trail established by previous migrants was very much evident in the migration of Indonesians to Malaysia and that of Burmese to Thailand.

As mentioned earlier, ethnicity played an important part in defining the entry and incorporation of Indonesian migrants in Malaysia. Common to the Aceh, Lombok and Bawean patterns is the centrality of family and friends to the migrants' stock of social capital. Social networks were especially critical for Indonesian migrants in Malaysia as there are no NGOs to which they can turn. The survey in Malaysia noted that arranging for police protection was usually organized along ethnic lines, with the *ketua* (or head) assuming responsibility for collecting fees or contributions. Some migrants considered their employers as a source of assistance, especially for matters concerning accommodations and police protection.

In the case of Burmese migrants, ethnicity was less salient in defining their entry and incorporation in Thailand. Most migrants who went to Samutsakhon used recruiting agents (both Thai and Burmese) to enter Thailand (usually crossing the border through Ranong, Tak and Kanchanaburi); migrants bound for Samutsakhon were also more likely to travel in groups. On the other hand, very few migrants who went to Tak used recruiting agents; most had relatives already in Thailand; most travelled to Thailand by themselves.

The surveys in Malaysia and Thailand affirmed the separate lives of migrants from the local population. There was not much interaction between the local people and the migrants. Most of the people migrants worked with were their co-nationals. In the Thailand survey, migrants said they did not have problems in dealing with their employers or Thai colleagues. Data obtained from qualitative approaches, however, hinted at tensions between the migrants and local residents. Migrants who encountered problems with employers (for example, not being paid their wages) resolved the situation by moving on to another job. On the whole, most migrants expressed the view that they must accept their situation and not complain too much. Notwithstanding the difficulties they have experienced, most migrants considered themselves better off in Thailand than in Myanmar.

Shadow Institutions

Irregular migration has spawned shadow institutions in the destination countries, which capitalise on the needs and vulnerabilities of migrants. In Malaysia, the need to present some form of documentation has given rise to the business of forged documents. Protection from arrests and the threat of deportation can be secured for a fee, usually in collusion with local authorities. As described in the Malaysian survey, migrants and/or their employers pay protection money to local police to secure protection from arrests in the workplace, in the place of residence and in the local ward. Similar arrangements were observed in Thailand. Employers with political connections used their political clout to provide some protection for their workers. In Thailand, local crime syndicates were mentioned as another source of harassment for migrants.

Registration/Regularization and its Impacts

Registration or regularization, from the standpoint of the government, is an attempt to determine the number of irregular migrants and to regulate their stay. The welfare and protection of migrants is not an issue in these programmes.[8] Interviews with migrants indicated that participating in registration or regularization programmes did not improve their situation. In Thailand, respondents did not see any difference in the situation between registered and unregistered migrants. Similarly in Malaysia, respondents who had availed of regularization programmes drifted back into irregular status. The registration fees (in Thailand) and the levy (in Malaysia) were a burden to migrants, and most of all, a burden which did not offer any improvement in their status.

Putting together the findings from the different countries, several conclusions can be advanced. The study suggests that migrants exercise a measure of agency in the decision-making process. Migrants engage in information seeking, but they tend to limit their search for information to family and friends or recruiters. The decision to use irregular channels is facilitated by easier access to these channels (especially in the case of Indonesia, where agents, brokers and social networks are present in the community) than to legal channels. The participation of family members and friends as intermediaries enhances the trust that migrants invest in this type of migration. As mentioned earlier, the increasing participation of social networks in irregular migration will pose more difficulties in curbing unauthorized migration. This raises several possibilities. The involvement of family and friends may free migrants from the exorbitant fees and oppressive conditions imposed by the more formal migration industry.[9] It is also possible that social networks may transform themselves into more formalized agents of recruitment in the future.

In the region, the most common form of irregular migration is undocumented migration (Indonesia-Malaysia; Myanmar-Thailand; Philippines[Western Mindanao]-Sabah). Irregular migration from the

Philippines (except for the migration directed to Sabah) departs from the regional pattern, as Filipino migrants seek out destinations beyond Southeast Asia. Wong and Teuku Afrizal (2003) proposed to consider these movements within the framework of a regional migration system, and to consider alternative channels or mechanisms in dealing with cross-border movements.

Revisiting Globalization and Migration

The acceleration of intra-regional migration is part of the growing integration of the region's economy — and yet, migration continues to be approached gingerly in regional discussions. However, the structural role of migration in the region's life asserts itself in telling ways. Despite the insistence of countries of destination that the importation of labour is temporary, they continue to import less skilled workers. Countries of origin also articulate labour migration as a temporary solution to their economic problems, but they have not weaned themselves from promoting it. The tendency to restrict labour migration in an age of globalization inevitably leads to unauthorized migration. At the macro level, it reflects the incongruence between economic needs and political considerations. Irregular migration is symptomatic of one of several contradictions of globalization (see Castles 2000), where there is openness to the flow of goods and capital, but barriers are put up when it comes to the flow of people. The operation of factors that facilitate migration (for example, cheaper communication and transportation costs, transnational networks), the displacing consequences of globalization (which add to emigration pressures in less developing countries), and the demand for less-skilled migrant workers in the destination countries imply greater potential for population movement.[10] Demographic imperatives — particularly, the aging of the population in the more developed countries — may push destination countries towards migration as a solution to its problems. It is a solution that will require social, political, and cultural transformations on the part of receiving countries.

In the face of restrictive migration policies, irregular migration can be interpreted as an expression of the right to migrate. International law supports the right to leave a country, but not the right to enter another. By engaging in unauthorized migration, migrants breach international law.

At the same time, their action points to the inadequacy of international law in recognizing the complement of the right to migrate: the right to enter another country. Unauthorized migration is an assertion of the right to migrate, and in the process, it subverts the gate-keeping power of rich nations to regulate the entry of labour (Battistella and Asis 2003*a*).

The pervasiveness of irregular migration in the region hints that it must serve some purpose in the receiving countries (Battistella and Asis 2002a). Migration enables economies to exercise flexibility, and irregular migration, in particular, not only provides cheap labour but it also frees employers and the state of social benefits otherwise extended to their nationals and authorized migrants. Consumers in the destination countries, without their knowing it, also benefit from irregular migration because of the cheaper cost of goods and services.[11] Despite policy pronouncements to eliminate irregular migration, there must be a degree of tolerance for irregular migration given its function.

If there is an acceptable level of irregular migration, the renewed efforts towards zero irregular migration may not only be unrealistic but may be counter-productive in the long run. Building on the economic theory of illegal behaviour, Entorf (2002) examined the interplay of migrants, citizens, employers and the government. He posited that there is an equilibrium point at which the number of migrants per citizen is tolerated by irregular migrants, citizens and the government. For as long as the level of irregular migration is considered socially optimal, it will persist. This implies that attempts to reduce irregular migration below or beyond its equilibrium level leads to market disequilibrium. Excessive control beyond the equilibrium level will result in excess demand for irregular migrants. The temptation to fight irregular migration at all costs will involve pouring scarce resources that could have been better used for other urgent needs or foreign aid that would address the root causes of irregular migration (Entorf 2002, pp. 38–39). Also, the temptation to resort to ever more draconian measures will have to contend with censure from the international community over the issue of human rights.

Tolerating non-zero irregular migration should not be the end-goal of policies and measures to address the problem. There is the question of the human rights of migrant workers in an irregular situation. The statist view of irregular migrants as immigration violators overlooks the fact that there are violations against migrants and that they have rights as workers and as human beings. Migration policies and regulations focus heavily on migrants. Attention should also be given to the review of policies, the practices of the migration industry and intermediaries, and the accountability of employers towards migrant workers.

The dilemmas exposed by irregular migration compel us to approach migration in an alternative fashion. A national approach focused on migration controls will have to give way to more comprehensive and transnational arrangements. This is particularly critical in Southeast Asia where most irregular migrations are cross-border movements. Dialogue, responsibility-sharing, the promotion of human rights and commitment to narrowing inequities between developed and less developed countries should be among the guiding principles of approaching migration issues.

Notes

*   Chapter 7 is based on a research project on irregular migration in Southeast Asia, which was co-ordinated by Graziano Battistella, Scalabrini Migration Centre. Many thanks are extended to the Ford Foundation for supporting the project and to our co-operators in the three other participating countries: Rianto Adi of Atma Jaya Catholic University, Indonesia; Diana Wong and Teuku Afrizal Teuku Anwar, IKMAS, University Kebangsaan Malaysia; and Amorntip Amarapibal, Allan Beesey and Andreas Germershausen, Asian Research Centre for Migration, Chulalongkorn University, Thailand. The study was made possible because of the co-operation of migrants, government agencies, NGOs and key informants.

1   Later investigations disclosed that the victim was a Malaysian citizen, which prompted some Malaysian officials to say that the Philippines should apologize for the error. The Philippines did not issue an apology; according to some Filipino officials, taking up the cudgels for the victim was the right thing to do.

2   In the study, we examined the experiences of Malaysia and Thailand as countries of destination.

3   Shortly after announcing its Indonesians-last policy, the Malaysian Government qualified that this did not apply to Indonesians in domestic services and plantation workers. In August, due to the lobbying of the construction sector, which was seriously affected by the departure of migrants, Indonesians were put back on the list of employable migrant workers (*Asian Migration News*, 31 August 2002).

4   The Philippines and Singapore do not agree on their definition of what constitutes an irregular migrant worker. For the Philippines, workers who are not processed by the Philippine Overseas Employment Administration are irregular. Filipino workers who enter Singapore as tourists and thereafter adjust their status via a pre-approved working permit are legal migrant workers as far as Singapore is concerned, but are irregular migrant workers from the standpoint of the Philippines.

5   Some sectors see this provision as encouraging irregular migration, that is, migrants are supposedly emboldened to migrate in an irregular manner because they can count on government assistance should they encounter problems.

6   The findings are drawn from Battistella and Asis (2003a and b), Adi (2003), Wong and Teuku Afrizal (2003) and Amarapibal, Beesey and Germershausen (2003).

7   The new rules provide for the following: allowing direct hiring (that is, allowing employers or workers to deal with each other without the intervention of an agency); imposition of a placement fee equivalent to one month's salary (a different rule applies to Taiwan); increasing capitalization and other financial requirements; and increasing the minimum manpower request from fifty to a hundred (cited in Battistella and Asis 2003b, pp. 44–45). In February 2002, the recruitment agencies succeeded in getting a temporary restraining order in implementing the new rules; in May 2003, the Supreme Court allowed the POEA to implement the new rules.

8   The experiment in Thailand in 2001 included some provisions intended to provide more protection to migrants. Part of the registration fees included annual health insurance coverage and provisions for health care (*Asian Migration News*, 15 August 2001).

9   See Wee and Sim (this volume, Chapter 6).

10   The demand for highly skilled and professional migrants will also increase, but there are fewer problems anticipated in this type of migration. Since they are wanted in the countries of destination, they are offered privileges not extended to less-skilled migrant workers (for example, residence status, family reunification). The migration of the highly skilled may present some problems for countries of origin, which stand to lose skilled people who are critical to their development.

11   A recent example illustrates this point. In the wake of the deportations of irregular migrants from Malaysia, farm owners were faced with labour shortage. Without migrant workers to harvest farm produce, vegetables were left unharvested. The limited supply in the market increased the prices for consumers in Malaysia and Singapore (*Asian Migration News*, 31 August 2002).

References

Adi, Rianto. "Irregular Migration from Indonesia". In *Unauthorised Migration in Southeast Asia*, edited by Graziano Battistella and Maruja M.B. Asis. Report submitted to the Ford Foundation. Quezon City: Scalabrini Migration Centre, 2003, pp. 121–57.

Aguilar, Filomeno Jr. "Ritual Passage and the Reconstruction of Selfhood in International Labour Migration." In *Filipinos in Global Migrations: At Home in the World?* edited by Filomeno V. Aguilar, Jr. Quezon City: Philippine Migration Research Network, 2002, pp. 413–51.

Amarapibal, Amorntip, Allan Beesey and Andreas Germershausen. "Irregular Migration into Thailand". In *Unauthorised Migration in Southeast Asia*, edited by Graziano Battistella and Maruja M.B. Asis. Report submitted to the Ford Foundation. Quezon City: Scalabrini Migration Centre, 2003, pp. 229–94.

Asian Migration News. <http://www.smc.org.ph> (various issues).

Battistella, Graziano and Maruja M.B. Asis. "The Crisis and Migration in Asia". Quezon City: Scalabrini Migration Centre, 1998.

_____. "The Spectre of Unauthorised Migration in Southeast Asia". In *Unauthorised Migration in Southeast Asia*, edited by Graziano Battistella and Maruja M.B. Asis. Report submitted to the Ford Foundation. Quezon City: Scalabrini Migration Centre, 2003*a*, pp. 1–34.

_____. "Irregular Migration: The Underside of the Global Migrations of Filipinos". In *Unauthorised Migration in Southeast Asia*, edited by Graziano Battistella and Maruja M.B. Asis. Report submitted to the Ford Foundation. Quezon City: Scalabrini Migration Centre, 2003*b*, pp. 35–128.

Castles, Stephen. "Globalisation and Migration: Some Pressing Contradictions". In *Ethnicity and Globalisation*. London: Sage Publications, 2000, pp. 124–32.

Entorf, Horst. "Rational Migration Policy Should Tolerate Non-Zero Illegal Migration Flows: Lessons from Modeling the Market for Illegal Migration". *International Migration* 40, no. 1 (2002): 27–44.

Ghosh, Bimal. *Huddled Masses and Uncertain Shores: Insights into Irregular Migration*. The Hague, Martinus Nijhoff Publishers, 1998.

International Organization for Migration (IOM). "Overview of the Current Situation of Irregular or Undocumented Migration in East and Southeast Asian Region: The Need for a Policy Response Framework". A paper drafted for IOM by Graziano Battistella and Ronald Skeldon in consultation with IOM officials, and presented at the International Symposium on Migration, "Towards Regional Cooperation on Irregular/Undocumented Migration". Bangkok, 21–23 April 1999.

Mani, A. "Migration in Brunei Darussalam". In *Crossing Borders: Transmigration in Asia Pacific*, edited by Ong Jin Hui, Chan Kwok Bun and Chew Soon Beng. Singapore: Prentice Hall, 1995, pp. 441–55.

Margold, Jane. "Narratives of Masculinity and Transnational Migration: Filipino Workers in the Middle East". In *Filipinos in Global Migrations: At Home in the World?* edited by Filomeno Aguilar, Jr. Quezon City: Philippine Migration Research Network, 2002, pp. 209–36.

Salazar, Zeus. "'Malay', 'Malayan', and 'Malay Civilization' as Cultural and Anthropological Categories in the Philippines". In *The Malayan Connection: Ang Pilipinas sa Dunia Melayu*. Lunsod Quezon: Palimbagan ng Lahi, 1998a, pp. 111–44.

_____. "The Matter with Influence: Our Asian Linguistic Ties". In *The Malayan Connection: Ang Pilipinas sa Dunia Melayu*. Lunsod Quezon: Palimbagan ng Lahi, 1998b, pp. 59–80.

Tapinos, George and Daniel Delaunay. "Can One Really Talk of the Globalisation of Migration Flows?" In *Globalisation, Migration and Development*. Paris: Organization for Economic Co-operation and Development, 2000, pp. 35–58.

Wong, Diana and Teuku Afrizal Teuku Anwar. "*Migran Gelap*: Irregular Migrants in Malaysia's Shadow Economy". In *Unauthorised Migration in Southeast Asia*, edited by Graziano Battistella and Maruja M.B. Asis. Quezon City: Scalabrini Migration Centre, 2003, pp. 169–228.

8

The Silence and Violence of Forced Migration: The Myanmar-Thailand Border

Carl Grundy-Warr

Transnational Displacement as a Challenge to States

"The problem of refugees in our time is a symptom of the uprootedness or homelessness of the modern age. It is a phenomenon of the era of nation-states and of the international political economy, and it is a problem not insofar as the refugee is denied a homeland but insofar as he or she is denied the possibility of establishing a home. The system of nation-states systematically denies that possibility through its insistence upon the principle of sovereignty and the state's hegemony over questions of identity" (Xenos 1996, p. 243).

Human movement, migration, constantly shifting identities and cultural changes as a result of mobility, resettlement, the interpenetration of different cultures and so on, all relate to a world "in which human motion is more often definitive of social life than it is exceptional" (Appadurai 1996). Migrants are helping to create new human landscapes or "ethnoscapes" that transcend political spaces and rigid notions of national citizenship

(Appadurai 2000, pp. 92–93). Human migration is a truly global phenomenon and one that is offering many challenges to the way we think about our world political, cultural and economic maps. The fact is that it is far easier to be mobile now than at any other time in human history, and in a world of "flows" that is often described as being increasingly borderless, it is surprising that so many people become trapped between or within borders simply because they have moved across them.

If we begin to view human migration more as a "norm" of everyday life, then we can also consider how migrants, refugees, exiles and displaced persons can be "sources of change and transformation for the places they affect" (Soguk 1999, p. 207). One of the biggest challenges migrant pose is to the "claims to citizenship and community" based upon "territorially delineated" communities of our national geobodies. In other words, "the de-territorialized migrant subject" is central to debates about territorial sovereignty, national citizenship, state — society relations, ethnic and inter-communal relations, and numerous state "practices of inclusion and exclusion" directly affecting migrant groups (Soguk 1999, pp. 210–12). Undocumented[1] and irregular flows of people have become central elements in what Nevzat Soguk (1999, p. 215) calls "the crucible of transversal, globalizing happenings throughout the world" and one of the biggest challenges "that are now threatening to undo the practices of statecraft".

Nevertheless, Soguk (1999) also argues that the existence of large numbers of migrants and refugees simultaneously encourages states to develop policies that serve to bolster notions of citizenship, national identity and sovereignty which are central to the nation-state ideal. Numerous state agencies have an opportunity to strengthen their collective resolve to protect the domain of "legitimate" citizens against the perceived "threats" to the socio-economic and political order posed by having large numbers of "displaced" folks entering "national space". At one level, undocumented migration flows represent truly transnational phenomena that are quite beyond the capacity of states to contain, and at another level, displaced persons provide opportunities for states to demonstrate to their citizenry the advantages of being "in place" inside the "national" home. These challenges to state institutions and statecraft are very real for several of the member states of ASEAN. This chapter focuses on these issues in relation to two Southeast Asian neighbours — Myanmar and Thailand as a source and host state for large numbers of undocumented migrants and refugees.

The Problematized Figure of the Refugee and Undocumented Migrant

By far the overwhelming notion of whole categories of migrants who do not become "regularized" within host state systems is that they constitute a "problem" to be prevented, managed, reduced or eliminated. In many senses, such attitudes and responses to the phenomenon of undocumented and irregular migration are manifestations of state- and citizen-centred thinking based upon fixed territorial sovereignties (Grundy-Warr 2002). Thus, people whose very movements and existence transgress the everyday rules, regulations and documentation associated with bureaucratic nation-statehood are viewed with enormous suspicion, if not genuine contempt, by the relevant authorities, agencies and functionaries whose job it is to govern, regulate and enforce the "laws of the land". In fact, by categorizing undocumented migrants and refugees "as problems" themselves often means that their histories, cultures, and a whole myriad of issues that underlie decisions to move somewhere else in search of jobs, livelihoods or security are rarely given much consideration in host state responses and policy measures.

The official categorization of migrants is often arbitrary, vague and imprecise. For instance, the blanket categories of "regular" versus "irregular", "documented" versus "undocumented", "legal" versus "illegal", registered "refugee" versus "non-refugee", and so on and so forth, are simply that — blanket categories, homogenizing and dehumanizing labels that render the individual human being (who happens to also be a migrant without "official" documentation) helpless, powerless and voiceless (Prem Kumar and Grundy-Warr 2004). Another strong tendency relates to the politics of representation, that is the way "undocumented" and "irregular" migrants and refugees are represented (and subsequently treated) as "threats" to the "national order", as "transgressors" of territorial sovereignty, as generators of crime, as transmitters of disease, and as political troublemakers. Part of this chapter examines the way the undocumented migrants and refugees are represented in Thailand and an analysis of the way the Thai state is handling the issues of forced migration and large numbers of refugees living within her borders.

Against the backdrop of dominant state-centric representations of "irregular" and "undocumented" migrants are the numerous narratives and voices of the migrants themselves, of their motivations, hopes, fears, sacrifices, journeys and circumstances. Only by paying more attention to the socio-economic, political and cultural complexity of migration experiences, to the sheer variety of migrants, to the underlying mechanisms that generate migrations and to the diverse motivations of migrants themselves will we be able to focus on appropriate responses that incorporate notions of human dignity and security as relevant components of policy frameworks. A central argument advanced in this chapter is that we must consider the complex geopolitics of cross-border migration, particularly in contexts of protracted social, political, ethnic and military conflict. In the context of the Myanmar-Thai borderlands where the human landscape has been completely disfigured by decades of low-level warfare, insurgency, counter-insurgency, factionalism, ceasefires, broken ceasefires, warlord politics, and immense human suffering, it is absolutely essential that we try to comprehend the true nature and significance of *forced migration* (see also Grundy-Warr and Wong 2002). The real "problem" is not the figure of the undocumented migrant or the refugee, the real problems are the underlying mechanisms that generate, even necessitate, large-scale movements of people across an international boundary.

Undocumented migrants and refugees often fall between the cracks of recognition and protection within the territorial state system. A central theme of this chapter is the deafening silence about the conditions and realities of much undocumented and forced migration. As Matthew Gibney (2001, p. 1) has observed in relation to irregular forms of migration within Europe:

"... for all its contemporary salience, irregular migration remains a very poorly understood phenomenon. In the midst of all the cacophony of recent debates on asylum across Europe, there exists an important silence: the voices of migrants with irregular status themselves are rarely heard. Not only has this fact distorted most discussions of irregular migration, comforting those who prefer well worn stereotypes to an accurate appreciation of the realities of living with irregular migration status; it has also limited our understanding of this phenomenon."

He also examines how the vast majority of "irregular" and "undocumented" migrants within Europe are in effect silenced by their very predicament of being without authorized documents, which means that even those agencies seeking to represent the interests of migrants are often forced to adopt low profiles and may be viewed as slightly subversive by state agencies responsible for the surveillance, control and registering of migrants. Gibney (2001, p. 2) argues that the silence of undocumented migrants is an aspect of their lack of rights in "that they are deprived of a public stage on which they could express their grievances or explain what factors lead them to their situation". If Gibney can write about the situation within the European Union, where there exists a whole plethora of different national laws relating to migrants, differential interpretation and application of European laws by each member state, and very differing degrees of migration affecting each of those states, then what about Southeast Asia?

At least within the European Union context there is an on-going process to try to create some common guidelines to deal with undocumented and irregular migrants, including tentative steps towards defining the rights of "persons in an irregular situation" by such bodies as the Immigration Law Practitioners' Association (ILPA), the Migration Policy Group (MPG), and the European Council on Refugees and Exiles (ECRE). There is no such political-legal process to define basic *migrant rights* within Southeast Asia. The main regional association — ASEAN — is fundamentally based upon certain "cardinal principles of the Westphalian international system" such as the "doctrines of non-interference, non-intervention and pacific settlement of disputes" (Acharya 2001, p. 63), which in my view, help to explain the intense political sensitivities generated by large flows of cross-border migration within the region. Whilst undocumented migration has become a stern test of the doctrine of non-interference, hitherto the issue of undocumented migration, whether forced or largely voluntary, within and across borders of ASEAN states, has been addressed primarily in sovereignty and security terms. Realist, pragmatist and state-centred geopolitics still tend to dominate the political landscape of the region.

Terminological Chaos

Another common issue is the way in which migrants are often categorized in rather untidy and unsatisfactory ways. As noted above, terms like "regular", "irregular" and "undocumented" actually capture people from incredibly diverse cultures, societies and communities, different genders, ethnic groups and races, and people from different walks of life and class. Subtle sociological distinctions rarely enter into the picture of "regular" versus "irregular" categorizations. Even if we restrict the view to "official" notions of who is legal or not, who is regular or not, we are left with a multiple spectrum of migrants, including people who entered the country illegally without passing through official ports of entry; people who enter without proper papers or passports or visas, people who enter with valid documents, but who subsequently breach the terms of their admission, particularly those who overstay; refugees and others who seek asylum but who are deemed not to qualify for it; and so on.

The problem is compounded by the fact that many "irregular" or "undocumented" migrants have powerful motivations not to put their own cases to the official test, even if they are probably eligible for refugee status under the Geneva Convention, asylum, or, at least other forms of humanitarian assistance. Fear of being found out, arrested, punished, detained, deported or repatriated deter many migrants from attempting to escape their "irregular" lives. I know of people who live secretive and precarious lives as undocumented migrants in Thailand, always worrying that one day they will be discovered, arrested, or most frightening of all, be deported back to Myanmar to face punishment or a worse fate.

Along the Thai-Myanmar border, I have come across many different groups of migrants, including those who migrated into Thailand generations ago and now have Thai citizenship but who belong to so-called "minority" communities; those who are generations-old "minorities" with restricted or no status; more recent migrants who are considered officially to be "displaced" minorities from Myanmar and who are confined to refugee camps along the border; and recent migrants who fall into the twilight zone of "illegal", "semi-legal", mostly "irregular" migrants who are found literally in their hundreds of thousands within Thailand today. The categories are at best arbitrary because of the problems of corruption, differential application of criteria and rules, not to mention the thin line between being a refugee and being an "irregular" migrant. What unites many of the different ethnic minority migrants and other Burmese migrants from Myanmar into Thailand is the fact that they have either been compelled to move due to dire economic circumstances, often worsened by military rule; or due to fear of persecution, and/or due to becoming forcibly displaced as a result of on-going ethno-political struggles or deliberate military strategies inside the border regions of Myanmar. The next section examines the issue of forced migration and distinct groups of forced and undocumented migrants in the specific political geographic context of the Myanmar-Thai borderlands.

Forced Migrants of the Myanmar-Thai Border

At the time of writing there are around 125,000 refugees living in camps monitored by the UNHCR along the Myanmar-Thailand border. Many more migrants have not entered into refugee camps under the aegis of relevant Thai authorities and supplied by various humanitarian and refugee assistance bodies. For instance, there are tens of thousands of Shan refugees inside Thailand who have no official status as registered displaced persons because of the Thai Government's position that these people are mostly "economic migrants". Estimates of numbers of internally displaced persons inside Myanmar range from "at least 600,000" in the "border areas" to as many as between one and two million people for the country as a whole.[2]

Unfortunately, verification of numbers through surveys of affected populations are not possible in many areas, particularly border zones, where access by independent teams of observers and international agencies is either restricted in some areas or totally prohibited in others due to protracted military, ethnic and political conflicts. Similarly, figures for forcible relocations are problematic due to the patchy data available. For instance, commenting on the situation in 1997, former UN Special Rapporteur on Myanmar, Mr. Rajsmoor Lallah, estimated there to be over one million people who had been "forcibly relocated, without compensation to towns, villages or relocation camps in which they were essentially detained" (UN Economic and Social Council 1997). Since then, the Global IDP (Internally Displaced Persons) Project (http://www.db.idpproject.org) has given similar figures for internally displaced people within Myanmar. According to a January 2002 United Nations Commission on Human Rights report there are approximately 300,000 IDPs in Shan State, 100,000 to 200,000 in Karen state, 70,000–80,000 in Karenni state, 60,000–70,000 in Mon state, and 100,000 in Rakhine state. Of course, the actual figures are extremely difficult to verify.

More compelling evidence comes from studies that have focused on forcible relocations and internal displacement within particular districts or ethnic areas, and are based upon very large numbers of oral testimonies with displaced persons both "inside" affected areas and of people who have crossed over an international boundary to become refugees. For instance, the Burma Ethnic Research Group (BERG) estimated in 1998 that "approximately 30 per cent of 480,000 of the rural Karen population of Eastern Burma are currently displaced", a figure that included both internally displaced persons and refugees. The intense forced relocations in several Karen areas during the last decade have been detailed in several well-documented reports by the Karen Human Rights Group (KHRG, 2002; 2001; 2000; 1999; 1998a; 1998b).[3]

These sorts of figures are supported by a Burmese Border Consortium (BBC) (2002) report indicating that more than 2,500 villages have been destroyed by the Myanmar Army, forcibly relocated to new sites, or abandoned by fleeing villagers, affecting 633,000 individuals over the five years to the date of the report's publication. All of these people are variously categorized as "IDPs in hiding or temporary shelters" or as "IDPs in Myanmar military controlled relocation sites". In addition to these internally displaced persons are a large number of people who have fled across the border into Thailand to become refugees in camps. The BBC puts the total refugee camp population at 143,000 people, including those who reside in three Mon resettlement camps just inside the Myanmar border.

Central and southern Shan states have also experienced intensive forced relocation of villages where as many as 300,000 people were forcibly relocated by the Myanmar military in the period 1996–98 (Shan Human Rights Foundation, 1998). In that period alone there were probably 1,400 villages in central Shan state that were affected by the Myanmar Army counter-insurgency operations. In Kayah (or Karenni) state, it was reported that the wide-scale coerced displacements in 1996 affected 25,206 people; 11,669 were known to have moved to relocation sites; 4,400 were registered in refugee camps; and a further 9,137 were unaccounted for (BERG 2000). However, there have continued to be further forced relocations, and unofficial estimates of the total numbers displaced inside Karenni state are that about 70,000–80,000 persons who are adversely affected.[4]

Clearly, there have been many militarily-coerced relocations in those areas bordering Thailand that still have armed ethnic opposition to the ruling State Peace and Development Council (SPDC) of Myanmar, including groups such as the KNPP, Karen National Union (KNU), and Shan State Army (SSA). But it is important to stress that other territories and borders have been affected by forced relocations and mass displacements of people. For example, in the early 1990s there was an exodus of about 260,000 Rohingya Muslims[5] who were displaced from all but two of seventeen townships in Arakan state into Bangladesh, and other rounds of coerced displacement since then (Human Rights Watch 2000; Grundy-Warr and

Wong 2001; Burma Centrum Nederland 1995; Lambrecht 1995). Not all of the Rohingya people fled to Bangladesh, others sought refuge in Malaysia (Human Rights Watch 2000). Displaced Chin and Naga people have also fled in large numbers into India. In sum, coerced relocation and forced displacement are widespread and deeply embedded issues affecting large territories and various ethnic communities inside Myanmar.

Battle for the Borderlands, Burmanized ì Nation-Buildingî, Ceasefires and the ì Four Cutsî

The widespread forced relocations and massive displacement problem that exists is explained mostly with reference to the intensive battle for control over territory, resources and identity within Myanmar's borderlands, many of which are areas where so-called ethnic minorities form the majority of local populations. As noted above, the biggest concentrations of forced migration are found within the Myanmar-Thai border regions. Undoubtedly, the ruling military regime in Myanmar is engaged in what it sees as a long-run effort to fully integrate the unruly borderlands and the various ethnic groups within them into "the national fold". Since the collapse of the Communist Party of Burma (CPB) in the late 1980s and the military crackdown on the pro-democracy movement in 1988, the State Law and Order Restoration Council (SLORC),[6] later reformulated as the less severe sounding State Peace and Development Council (SPDC) (in November 1997), has been basing many of its internal security, martial law and order strategies around the regime's own notion of "national" security and integrity. The "Three Main National Tasks" are "Non-disintegration of the Union, Non-disintegration of National Unity" and the "Perpetuation of National Sovereignty" (Yan Nyein Aye 2000).

It is around these national tasks that the higher echelons of the SPDC has advanced its strategies to extend the regime's military and political reach into territories where prior to 1988 the regime still had only a tenuous hold. These strategies are multi-pronged and incorporate a mix of political, economic and military measures. With those ethnic political groups that sign ceasefire agreements with the SPDC there are plans to extend the so-called Border Area Development Programme (BADP) into the territories affected by the respective ceasefires. This was highlighted by Secretary 1 of the SPDC (then SLORC), Lieutenant General Khin Nyunt during a visit to Loikaw, Kayah (Karenni) state on 17 November 1993, who stated that those "national groups" (ethnic political parties) that "rejoin" "the legal community" (meaning, that sign ceasefires with the SLORC/ SPDC) would be able to gain the fruits of "development". Development in the context of the Master Plan for the Development of Border Areas and National Races (23 June 1994) refers mostly to infrastructural projects, health and education projects, eradication of poppy cultivation, and the maintenance of security, law and order (under the auspices of the ruling military). Not surprisingly, the main English-language mouthpiece of the SPDC has often covered senior military personnel visits to various "border development" projects as evidence of a new era of "national unity" that is bringing the national races out of "darkness" into a new bright era of "peace and prosperity" (*New Light of Myanmar*, 14 February 1994; 13 February 2001).

Numerous ceasefires have been signed with various ethnic political organizations since the late 1980s to the present time (Figure 8.1). To some extent these ceasefires have brought about an uncertain peace within border areas. The "military truces" should not be viewed as a sign that the military leadership of the SPDC is willing to share "national power" with the various ethnic political organizations that have signed, such as the Kachin Independence Organization (KIO) or the New Mon State Party (NMSP), but rather as temporary agreements that end open warfare and hostility *in particular areas* (Steinberg 2000; Smith 1999). Ceasefires have allowed the SPDC to forge new deals with certain ethnic leaders to undertake infrastructure schemes and to exploit natural resource wealth, such as teak and jade in Kachin territory. The end of open hostility has also enabled some limited dialogue between the SPDC and the ethnic parties involved, although the SPDC's unwillingness to countenance any moves towards a federal system or even long-term political autonomy for ethnic parties in the border areas, would seem to be a significant obstacle in the way of transforming multiple ceasefires into something resembling a lasting peace. Critics of the ceasefires argue that they are simply a vehicle for the Myanmar military to gain a stranglehold over the border regions; and that the forms of "border development" that have been implemented merely assist the process of "Burmanization" and the subjugation of ethnic cultures (Lambrecht 2000).

What about those territories that are not covered by ceasefire agreements? In these zones the SPDC continues to rely heavily on the use of military coercion and the long-established "Four Cuts" (*Pya Ley*

FIGURE 8.1
Chart of Armed Ethnic Groups, April 2002

Main Ceasefire Groups (In Order of Agreements)	Year
Myanmar National Democratic Alliance Army (Kokang)*	1989
United Wa State Party*	
National Democratic Alliance Army (eastern Shan state)*	
Shan State Army**	
New Democratic Army (Kachin)*	
Kachin Defence Army (ex-KIO 4th brigade)	1991
Pao National Organization**	
Palaung State Liberation Party**	
Kayan National Guard	1992
Kachin Independence Organization**	1994
Karenni Nationalities Peopleís Liberation Front*	
Kayan New Land Party***	
Shan State Nationalities Liberation Organization*	
New Mon State Party**	1995

Other Ceasefire Groups/Militia (Not Always Listed by Government)	
Democratic Karen Buddhist Army	1995
Mongko Peace Land Force (splinter group from Kokang)	
Shan State National Army	
Mong Tai Army	1996
Karenni National Defence Army	
Karen Peace Force (ex-KNU 16th Batallion)	1997
Communist Party of Burma (Arakan)*	
KNU 2 Brigade Special Region Group (Thandaung)	

Non-Ceasefire Groups
Arakan Liberation Party**
Arakan Rohingya National Organization
Chin National Front**
Hongsawatoi Restoration Party (breakaway group from NMSP)
Karen National Union** (1995ñ96 talks broke down)
Karenni National Progressive Party** (1995 ceasefire broke down)
Lahu National Democratic Front**
Mergui-Tavoy United Front*
National Socialist Council of Nagaland
National United Party of Arakan
Shan State Army [South] (re-formed in 1996 after MTA surrender)
Wa National Organization** (1997 talks broke down)

Source: Smith (1999), Chart 3.
Notes: * Former ally or breakaway force from the Communist Party of Burma
         **Former or present National Democratic Front member

A number of other small, armed groups exist in name. Most are affiliated to the National Council Union of Burma.

Pya) to cut off sources of food, funds, intelligence and recruits to ethnic insurgency groups. The "Four Cuts" have effectively transformed the military and political map in many parts of Myanmar. Early dress rehearsals started in the mid-1960s in the Naga Hills and Kachin Hills where many thousands of people were killed in military "scorched earth policy" (Smith 1999, p. 220). During the 1980s and 1990s, the "Four Cuts" has been widely applied in those areas deemed to be still under the influence of non-ceasefire groups, such as the Karen National Union (KNU), the Karenni National Progressive Party (KNPP), and Shan State Army (South) (SSA). These territories cover much of the borderlands near to Thailand. And it is precisely from these zones where most of the forced migrants have come from.

To the military strategists of the SPDC, the extensive border zones resemble a "vast chessboard under the *Tatmadaw*'s ... regional commands and shaded in three colours: black for entirely insurgent-controlled areas; brown for areas both sides still disputed; and white was 'free' ", meaning totally under *Tatmadaw* control (Smith 1999, p. 259). Over the years the *Tatmadaw* has been very thorough in the way it highlights zones considered to be "rebel held" or containing villages that provide some support for insurgents, then issuing orders to the village chiefs of all those villages to relocate all villagers to designated settlements or strategic hamlets (*byu hla jaywa*) within strict time periods. Any villagers disobeying such orders are likely to be regarded by the *Tatmadaw* as rebels themselves and so may be killed. When troops enter the emptied villages they often confiscate rice stores, foodstuffs, destroy fields, pollute water supplies, and sometimes plant landmines around village outskirts. All this is to "secure" these villages from insurgent forces. Of course, the forced relocation of hundreds of villages can have enormous and lasting impacts on the human landscape and livelihood security of those people directly affected, but the military goal of seizing territory and squeezing insurgent forces is very effective. As Martin Smith (1999, p. 260) observed: "For the *Tatmadaw* in the *Four Cuts* campaign there is no such thing as an innocent or neutral villager. Every community must fight, flee or join the *Tatmadaw*." There is no such thing as a halfway house.

Many different parts of the contested borderlands have been adversely affected by the "Four Cuts" and strict martial law that usually follows it within newly "pacified" zones. The important issue to stress is that forced village relocation is one of several intertwined reasons that cause widespread forced displacement within Myanmar and also contributes to large-scale cross-border forced migration, particularly into Thailand. Other precipitating military-induced causes include the associated loss of means of livelihood with the destruction of villages and fields; the requisition by the military of forced portering and other forms of forced labour (see Amnesty International 2002; various reports by the Karen Human Rights Group, KHRG). For example, one recent KHRG (2002) report on "forced displacement, massacres and forced labour in Dooplaya District" of Karen state, bluntly reports on many incidences of the military making constant labour demands on all settlements in areas the SPDC that have recently been "secured" from insurgent forces.

> "On average a village, whether it has been relocated or is still in place, has to provide two or three people per day as messengers, two or three for camp labour, one or two as camp sentries, ten or more as road sentries, three or four as porters, and a few more for whatever other *ad hoc* labour may be required. When roads or bridges are being built or repaired, one person per family is usually demanded every day until the work is completed."

If it is not labour, it is demands for food, for materials or other "taxes" that make survival very difficult for ordinary people caught in the recently "won" SPDC territories or in the still contested "brown areas".

Hazel Lang (2002, pp. 78–79) has articulated the resultant landscapes of fear that the widespread application of the "Four Cuts" has and still continues to create inside Myanmar's borderlands. As she puts it:

> "Civilians have at times been caught in the cross-fire, but they have also been routinely displaced by the ongoing process of militarized surveillance and control occurring in their areas. Sometimes a village has become a battleground, at other times a pool for the coercive recruitment of porters and labourers, as well as a setting for financial exploitation. The pattern of displacement, whether associated with direct hostilities or other factors ... has undermined the security of everyday life, resulting in the impoverishment and the destabilization of civilian livelihoods. Many have been displaced by the intersecting factors of fear and impoverishment."

A great many displaced persons stay relatively close to their old destroyed villages, trying to hide and survive (see below), whilst others eventually decide to run either to a totally different district within Myanmar or across an international boundary.

Figure 8.2 is based upon primary interviews, various reports by NGO groups examining issues if internal displacement, and available secondary

FIGURE 8.2
Different Patterns of Forced Displacement

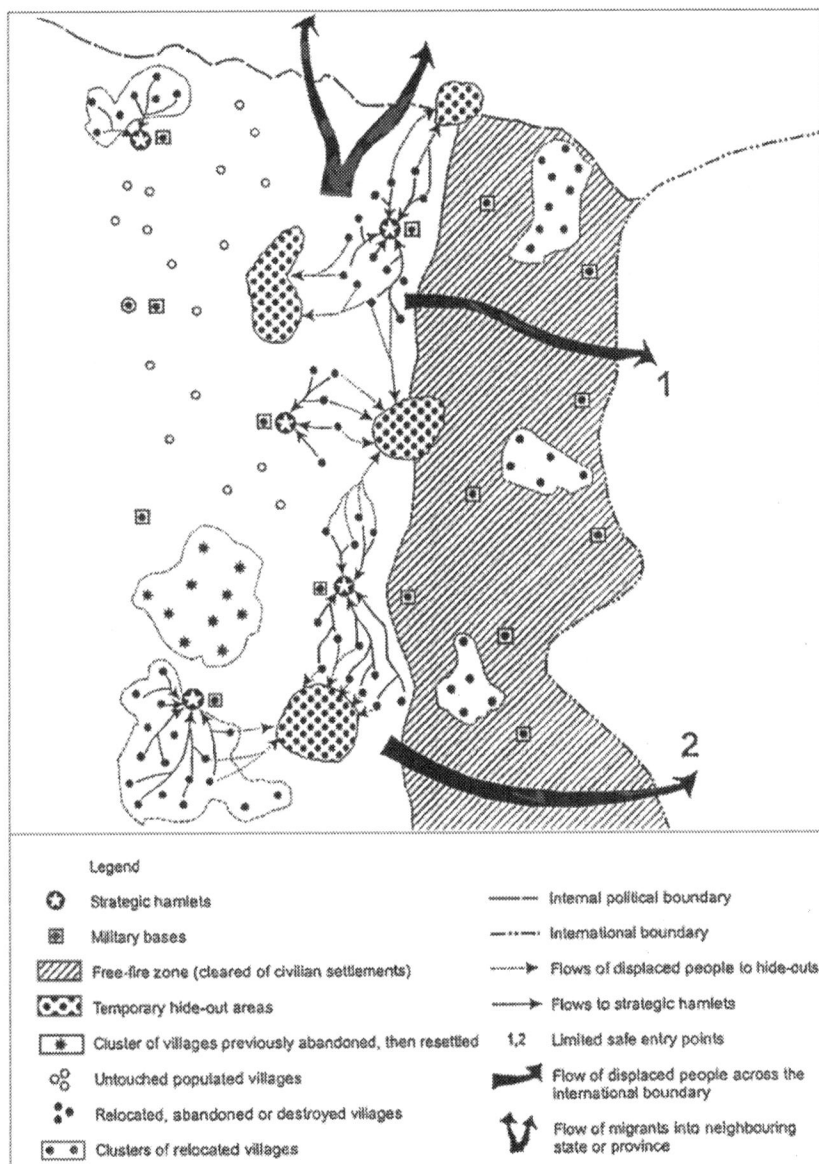

Legend

⊛ Strategic hamlets

▣ Military bases

▨ Free-fire zone (cleared of civilian settlements)

⬭ Temporary hide-out areas

▭※ Cluster of villages previously abandoned, then resettled

₀⁰₀ Untouched populated villages

⦂• Relocated, abandoned or destroyed villages

⬚ Clusters of relocated villages

— — — Internal political boundary

— ·· — International boundary

·····▶ Flows of displaced people to hide-outs

———▶ Flows to strategic hamlets

1,2 Limited safe entry points

◣ Flow of displaced people across the international boundary

⇡⇣ Flow of migrants into neighbouring state or province

Source: Authorís map.

materials. It represents something of the complexity of migration within areas designated as either "black" or "brown" zones by the *Tatmadaw*. It depicts a very complex political geography related to different *de facto* scenarios within the border zones of Myanmar. This map is essentially a diagram of the localized and often complex patterns of displacement that have occurred in different parts of the borderland. Alongside clustered zones of forced relocation where all villages have been emptied and destroyed are zones of relatively little disturbance because the *Tatmadaw* does not consider these villages to be supporting insurgents. There are different kinds of flows of displacement, flows of people who go into hiding as internally displaced persons, flows of people to relocation sites firmly under the control of the military, flows of people into neighbouring states of Myanmar and flows of people who make it to the international boundary. All of these different patterns of displacement will require urgent attention if there is ever to be peace in the war-torn borderlands and a concerted effort to rebuild communities torn apart by forced relocation and migration.

Life ì In Hidingî

For displaced persons there are many dangers. As one middle-aged woman who had spent almost one-year living hand-to-mouth in the jungle before deciding to move with her group to Thailand, put it: "We couldn't sleep at night. Every sound could be a soldier coming to kill us."[7] A farmer from Shadaw Township in Karenni state reveals the insecurity of farming in contested zones.

> "If we could find a place for farming, we were able to work the hill cultivation. But in such a dangerous situation, we could not work peacefully. We were always insecure and worried about soldiers coming" (Amnesty International 1999).

Another farmer, Soe Reh, told me that after four years in hiding with his family living off boiled roots and bamboo, foraged food, and suffering from illness and disease that killed two of his four children, he had no alternative but to become a refugee.[8] Life in jungle hideouts inevitably splits up community groups, because survival is only possible in small groups due to the constant fear of being "found". The division of village communities into smaller groupings of displaced persons is another reason why so-called "internally displaced persons" become "lost in sovereign space".

Frequent forced relocations are another source of livelihood insecurity. As one displaced person put it: "Once I was taken to become a porter for one month. When I went back, the village had already moved. The Burmese Army always makes us move. So far, I've had to move six times already. When we move to a new village, we think we can do some farming. But then the Burmese Army makes us move again and again."[9]

Proximity to abandoned villages is cold comfort for most displaced persons, because they have little opportunity of return unless the *Tatmadaw* issues orders that the areas are deemed free of insurgents. In any case, villagers who have been hiding would be considered with suspicion by the military. Even quick visits to old village sites in search of food or possessions are dangerous, due to the planting of landmines. As one report puts it:

> "Another tragedy for the people in Geh Lo is the landmines planted in the village. From 1996 to 2000 there were seven villagers and 20 buffalo injuries due to landmines in the village. The landmines were planted after June 1996 during the forced relocation time. After the *Tatmadaw* troops burned down the village they planted the landmines on every road from the forest to the village. They were trying to block people to move from place to place in order to stop them obtaining items of daily use such as salt, clothes, fish-paste, pots, medicines, and knives."[10]

Case Study of Cross-Border Migrants: The Shan or Tai Yai in Thailand

It is necessary to point out that cross-border migration is far from being a recent phenomenon. For instance, Mae Hong Son province in northwestern Thailand has long been a recipient of many Tai Yai[11] or Shan migrants from Myanmar. For many years Tai Yai people have settled, lived and worked in this province, developing their own cross-border networks of trade and travel. Utilizing the pre-existing linkages with the receiving society, the Tai Yai immigrants build and reinforce the networks with local villagers, and gradually become recognized members of the Tai Yai community in Mae Hong Son (Kaise 1999). Even so, clear distinctions have emerged between migrants who entered Thailand in the early 1960s when Thai administrative procedures were still not so strict and obtaining official Thai identification cards was more likely; immigrants who have subsequently obtained various types of identification that guarantee refuge in Thailand but do not necessarily mean that their status is the same as ordinary Thai citizens.[12]

Until the late 1980s, Thai Government policy towards Burmese immigrants was relatively liberal and a great many people were permitted to stay temporarily in Thailand. At that time the main Thai preoccupation was with refugees from Indochina, particularly Khmer refugees along the Thai-Cambodia border (Supang Chantavanich and Reynolds 1988). With growing numbers of migrants and refugees from Myanmar in the 1990s, the Thai policy became more restrictive, including occasional crackdowns on illegal migrants by the police, arrests and deportations. Obtaining "legal" documents allowing refuge has become much tighter. This means that more recent Tai Yai migrants have increasingly been viewed as "illegal immigrants", even in Mae Hong Son province (Kaise 1999). So whilst old established kinship, friend and worker networks may facilitate the continued Tai Yai immigration, the ground is much harder to establish any secure roots. In other words, political territoriality has hardened on the Thai side of the border, just as political and military conditions on the Burmese side have made everyday life increasingly tough for most Tai Yai people.

The 1990s have turned large parts of central and southern Shan State in Myanmar into landscapes of violence and fear. Peoples' lives have become marked by insecurity and flight. The quotes below are just a tiny fraction of a huge number of migrant reports and oral testimonies.

> "I have nowhere else to go and I don't know where go so I will just stay here [in Mae Hong Son]. If I am caught, I will be sent back to Burma maybe. This has happened to many people. When they are caught, they are sent back. But they just come again – over and over. Being chased by the Thai authorities is better than being chased by the Burmese military."[13]

> "I can't survive in Burma. It's very hard to survive ... under the Burmese Army. I've been arrested three times by the army to become a porter. I've been disturbed by the Burmese and I have to run all the time because we are chased by the military. My life was in danger so I just ran to Thailand, ran for my life."[14]

The Tai Yai migrants fall between the categories of political and economic, forced and voluntary, legal and illegal, "refugee" and "migrant worker" more than any other group from Myanmar. Historic social, economic and cultural ties across the political boundary, plus the Tai Yai ability to merge more easily into the human landscape than other ethnic groups, and Thai demands for supplies of very cheap labour, all mean that there are currently tens of thousands of Tai Yai migrants, who have faced forced relocation and military coercion inside Myanmar, but who have found "unofficial" toe-holds inside northern Thailand. In other words, Tai Yai migration has a distinct history and political economy that is not shared by other forced migrant communities. The fact is that the Tai Yai migrants, alongside other "illegal" and "undocumented" workers are viewed by the Thai authorities as both "a problem" and "a resource" simultaneously, constituting a common paradox of territorial statehood, variations on this theme existing in other cross-border migratory situations (see Soguk 1996). For instance, in October 2001, Mr. Kachadpai Buruspat, the National Security Council chief of Thailand, stated that the Shan people who had migrated recently to Thailand were "unacceptable" for refugee status for they had entered the country illegally for economic reasons (*Bangkok Post*, 22 October 2001).

The Tai Yai story is further complicated by the fact that the Shan State Army (SSA), another group that has refused to sign a ceasefire with the ruling military junta of Myanmar, continues to operate near to positions along the northern Thai border, and Thailand is frequently accused of assisting the SSA by Yangon. Indeed, the recent closure of the border since May until the current date has been blamed upon the SPDC alleging that the Thai Army has been supporting the SSA against the *Tatmadaw* and the United Wa State Army (UWSA), which Thailand in turn accuse of being very active in the cross-border drug trade in amphetamines and *yaa baa* (or "crazy drug" in Thai). The tit-for-tat military exchanges near to the border reflect ups and downs in inter-state diplomacy between Yangon and Bangkok. Unfortunately, the serious geopolitical situation that has led thousands of Tai Yai to flee their homelands have largely been ignored by the politicians, or else they have been obscured by Yangon's desire to rid the border areas of so-called rebels and the Thai state's primary concern about the transnational drug trade.

Forced Relocations and Rape as a Weapon of War

For many years there have been efforts by various agencies concerned about displaced persons to monitor and record what has been happening to them inside the border areas of Myanmar. However, few of these reports have ended up being reported widely in the world's media. An important exception to this has been the recent publication entitled *A Licence to Rape* by the Shan Human Rights Foundation (SHHF) and Shan

Women's Action Network (SWAN) published in May 2002. The report details 173 incidents of rape and other forms of sexual violence, involving 625 girls and women, committed by Burmese army troops in Shan state, mostly between 1996 and 2001. Undoubtedly the most significant feature of this detailed report is the evidence it provides that rape has been "officially condoned as a 'weapon of war' against the civilian populations in Shan state". It describes the incidents of rape committed by soldiers from fifty-two different battalions, 83 per cent of them being committed by officers, usually in front of their own troops.

Furthermore, 25 per cent of the rapes ended in fatality for the victims, others involved torture such as beating, mutilation and suffocation; 61 per cent were gang-rapes involving many soldiers, and some women were raped repeatedly over long periods of time. The vast majority of the reported cases were inside the territories of central Shan state where the *Tatmadaw* has had an extensive forced relocation programme, and between 1996–97, an alleged 300,000 rural people from over 1,400 villages were moved at gunpoint to relocation sites near to main roads or military barracks. In giving voice to some of the women and girls who have experienced sexual violence associated with an on-going military strategy to alter the human landscape of non-ceasefire zones near the border, the report unmasks some of the many terrible hidden aspects of forced migration. Violence against women and girls is in war zones is sadly, as Carolyn Nordstrom (1999, p. 66) notes, "largely, dangerously, invisible".

Undocumented Migrants and the Geopolitics of Inter-State Relations

The following sections provide some details regarding the different positions of Myanmar and Thailand on the current refugee crisis.

Myanmar's Position

The military regime's direct involvement in generating the refugee crisis through its "Four Cuts" counter-insurgency operations that blur distinctions between soldiers, activists and villagers; widespread, systematic forced relocations of villages in "brown" and "black" areas; and various military impositions on village life, including demands for forced labour, making normal life virtually impossible; are all denied by the military's top brass. To the SPDC, many of the "so-called" refugees living in Thailand are either armed insurgents or the families of armed insurgents. They are enemies of the Union of Myanmar who have not entered the "legal fold" by signing ceasefire agreements with the SPDC. A common accusation in the state-run newspaper, *The New Light of Myanmar*, is that Thailand is harbouring the Karen National Union (KNU) and Karenni National Progressive Party (KNPP) and their followers, who are actively using Thai soil to launch attacks against the Myanmar *Tatmadaw* from those camps. Similarly, the SPDC have accused Thailand of allowing the Shan "rebels" access to bases on the Thai side of the border to launch attacks against Myanmar forces. In such a way, the desperate situation of tens of thousands of ordinary village people who have been made homeless and stateless by the battles for political hegemony over the borderlands are apparently of little official consequence to the SPDC. Rather, "genuine refugees" caught in the crossfire are viewed as victims of "rebel propaganda" and the "brainwashing" of the KNU and KNPP.

I cannot think of a better summary of Myanmar's position on refugees than the one found in the monograph by Maung Aung Myoe (2002) entitled *Neither Friend Nor Foe*. For this reason, I shall quote two passages from this publication.

"In view of the Myanmar government, the so-called refugee camps are 'a safe haven or shelter for insurgents (KNU) when it appears that they are going to be crushed in the Tatmadaw's offensives.' As armed raids on the Tatmadaw's positions came from the refugee camps from time to time, the Myanmar government has never been convinced that these so-called refugee camps are safe places or shelters for genuinely displaced people. The Myanmar government confirmed this view when SPDC leaders let Professor Sadako Ogata, the high commissioner of the UNHCR, in October 2000. The SPDC leaders told Professor Ogata that 'Myanmar refugees living in the camps on the Thai side of the Myanmar-Thai border were either members of the ethnic insurgent groups or their relatives, and not displaced persons.' A commentator in a Myanmar newspaper said that he 'believed that a refugee camp where armed guards and armed insurgents could take refuge could be found only in Thailand' (Maung Aung Myoe 2002, p. 83).

"The Myanmar government had come to believe that, by keeping the refugee issue as evidence of alleged human rights violation by the Myanmar government, the Thai government is using it as a political and diplomatic leverage on western governments to keep pressure on the regime. Moreover, the Myanmar government believes that, by establishing refugee camps along the Myanmar-Thailand border, the Thai government not only had a buffer zone but also exploited cheap labour from the refugees and made money in collaboration with NGOs. According to a commentary which appeared in the government controlled media, 'the Thai government, which has from time to time lavishly claimed that it provides temporary shelter for the displaced persons on humanitarian grounds, has accepted refugees because it yields economic profit and political favour (from the west) and gains certain strategic importance (buffer zone)' " (Ibid, pp. 83–84).

Whilst the SPDC has at various times discussed repatriation with the Thai authorities and with the UNHCR, it is clear from the official pronouncements that the regime has a very distinct view that many of the people currently residing in the camps in Thailand are not proper refugees or displaced persons, but enemies of the state. Furthermore, the SPDC attaches distinct geopolitical and economic motivations for Thailand's assistance to the refugees, and considerable suspicion regarding the role of various "Western" NGOs along the Thai side of the border. Furthermore, the SPDC has been able to use its shield of sovereignty to great effect in keeping international and NGO humanitarian and relief agencies well and truly away from the border regions where the bulk of militarily enforced relocations of the civilian population have taken place.

Thailand's Position

Since the late 1980s, the large numbers of forced "displaced persons" entering Thailand have increasingly been perceived as "problems" to be managed and contained in "temporary" camps with the view to future repatriation. Indeed, Thailand has not ratified the 1951 United Nations Convention Relating to the Status of Refugees and the subsequent 1967 Protocol Relating to the Status of Refugees, and so the Thai state has limited legal obligations under international law regarding the treatment of displaced persons (Robinson 1998). Nevertheless, Thailand has become a refuge for refugees from all the surrounding countries of Indochina and Myanmar over the past three decades. This said, officially, Thailand's handling of refugees has been outside the parameters of international refugee law. The Ministry of Interior (MOI) defines a "displaced person" (*phuu oppayop*) as someone "who escapes from dangers due to an uprising, fighting, or war, and enters in breach of the Immigration Act", and because they enter in breach of the Immigration Act they are then *prima facie* "illegal immigrants" (Muntarbhorn undated, p. 7, cited in Lang 2002, p. 92).

As with any state apparatus, it would be misleading to define Thai policy as if all the institutions and branches of the state machinery are part of something homogenous that always acts in a co-ordinated manner. Several institutions are extremely significant in terms of making, interpreting and implementing policy measures, including the National Security Council (NSC, established in 1959), the Ministry of Interior (MOI), the Border Patrol Police (BPP), the Ministry of Foreign Affairs (MFA), and the military. Prior to 1992 it would be fair to argue that one of the most important agencies were the Royal Thai Armed Forces and BBP, although even here distinct divisions of the army and BBP responsible for separate zones of the borderlands often operated differently or applied central commands according to different interpretations or local circumstances. The NSC's role in defining border policy and in influencing broad approaches towards "displaced persons" has become more significant during the last decade.[15] According to Panitan Wattanayagorn (1998, p. 439) the NSC has become a "central institution for coordinating and integrating development in the border areas." The MOI wields bureaucratic control over the Police Department, including the BBP, the Immigration Division, provincial governors, and district officers, although each of these affect many matters of refugee camp administration and issues of border security on the ground. The BBP (established in 1953) has a very broad policing role and deals with a variety of issues, such as drug smuggling, banditry, border crime, trafficking, illegal immigration, and intelligence gathering.[16]

The Royal Thai Armed Forces still continues to be a prominent player on the ground, and regional commanders, like their counterparts in Myanmar, can significantly affect or influence events due to their strong *de facto* position. However, there have been strenuous efforts in Thailand to enhance the role of civilian institutions and the military no longer determines central policy. Rather, the Royal Thai Armed Forces is involved in numerous matters in relation to the protection of Thailand's territorial sovereignty, such as prevention of illegal entry, and it has powers to turn away displaced persons if it deems them to be security threats, and "the army is ultimately in charge of major events, such as relocations of refugee camps and repatriation on the ground" (Lang 2002, p. 97).

With respect to the large numbers of Burmese migrants, the Thai state has adopted a multi-pronged approach that ranges from relative toleration to efforts aimed at stemming the flow, or in some cases turning back would-be migrants at the border and forcible repatriation of groups of "illegal workers". As noted in the discussion of Tai Yai migration into northern Thailand, the Thai economy has continued to absorb "undocumented" workers into its economy, in some cases awarding differing types of semi-legal status in the form of ID passes, and in other cases allowing employers in some economic sectors to register employees and pay stipulated amounts for specified numbers of foreign workers (Caouette et al. 2000).

As for the people who are not migrant workers, but people who have effectively become refugees, the Thai authorities prefer to label these persons as *phuu oppayop* or *chon platthin* (displaced persons), or as *chon klumnoy* (minority people) or as *chon klumnoy phuu raysanchaat*, meaning "minority people without documents (nationality)". Officially the word "refugee" (*phuu liiphay*) is less frequently used, and the "displaced persons" and "undocumented minorities" (although a distinction here has to be made between those who are recent migrants and others who have resided in Thailand for generations) are considered to be a "temporary" nuisance. On the whole, displaced persons living in the border camps are effectively confined to the districts near to those camps with few of the people having travel permits to go to nearby Thai towns. A slight exception are those displaced persons considered to be culturally "exotic", who attract large numbers of tourists, such as the *kariang kaw yao* (Karen "long necks" in Thai), Padaung in Myanmar or Kayan as they prefer to be called. The Kayan have generally become a central feature of tourist promotion inside Thailand as indigenous "hill tribes" (*chaw khaw*, a term that covers several distinctive cultural groups) in Mae Hong Son with their villages deliberately located at some distance from the main refugee camp populations, who mostly remain hidden from tourist gaze.

Thus, the Thai state has tried as far as possible to confine displaced persons to districts close to the border by allowing camps to be established with relief being co-ordinated by the Coordinating Committee for Services to Displaced Persons in Thailand (CCSDPT), a government organization under the auspices of the Ministry of Interior. In addition, a whole plethora of NGO relief and humanitarian agencies are co-ordinated under what is called the Burmese Border Consortium.[17]

For a long while the Thai state was reluctant to give the United Nations High Commission for Refugees (UNHCR) a larger role in dealing with Burmese refugees, but by the mid-1990s there were already rapidly swelling numbers of refugees and the authorities at national and provincial levels were increasingly under pressure to cope with the situation without higher profile international support. In July 1998,[18] the Thai Government invited UNHCR to play an enhanced role in terms a advising the Government of Thailand in establishing criteria for "refugee status determination procedures", a partial recognition by the Thai authorities that certain groups of "displaced persons" could at least be considered as distinct from other "illegal immigrants". UNHCR was also to take charge of the registration and supervision of camps along the western border and to facilitate the organization of voluntary repatriations. UNHCR has also been charged with the task of monitoring and enabling the safe return of displaced persons subject to any future arrangements made with the relevant Burmese authorities.

In terms of Thai state representations of the "displaced persons" there are at least three kinds of security threats that are frequently raised, and also reported in the Thai mass media. First, is the threat of cross-border attacks involving the Myanmar Army or ethnic armies in the border zones where there are refugee camps (Images Asia and Borderline Video 1998).

Second, are the threats to Thai public health due to the spread of diseases, and to the environment as a result of illegal woodcutting and the stress of camps on local environmental resources.[19] Even so, it is important to point out that there is plenty of counter-evidence to these alleged health and environmental threats. For instance, Caouette et al. (2000) found extensive evidence to suggest that by far the biggest health risks were to women and children migrants and refugees and not to the Thai populace, and Friends Without Borders (2001) have provided detailed evidence to show that the environmental degradation associated with refugee communities exists but has been exaggerated and there are also useful examples of refugees trying to conserve local resources.

Third, there is a sense in which the continued "presence" of many displaced people on Thai soil creates the idea of "the anarchy" beyond national borders versus the relative peace, stability and order of "the domestic sphere" (Soguk 1999). Certainly, the border region, particularly the Burmese side, is viewed by many ordinary Thai people as *andharai* (dangerous) and in the popular imagination it is the home of unruly drug barons, warlords, ethnic rebels, and the armed forces of Myanmar. By extension, refugees and undocumented migrants may be viewed as transmitters of anarchy, chaos, crime and disorder into the domain of

Thailand. Simultaneously, the Thai authorities are able to play on such threats to reinforce the sanctity of national sovereignty and territorial integrity, of the need to protect national space and Thai citizens "as the constitutive element in the territory or space of the state".[20] Thus, refugees and migrants undermine territorial sovereignty at one level, but their presence can also be used by states to bolster the state-nation-citizen nexus (Soguk 1999).

Thailand's official policy over irregular migrants is often multi-stranded and containing contradictory elements. In spite of the much publicized occasional "clamp-downs" on irregular migrant workers and a whole plethora of regulations and restrictions relating to their employment and movements, the irregular flows have hardly been stemmed. For instance, *Migration News* (8 August 2002) reported that during the September–October 2001 registration of unauthorized foreign workers, Thai employers registered 568,000 migrants, and re-registered 429,000 or 76 per cent for another six months in February–March 2002. Conservative estimates suggest that there are at least a further 400,000 unregistered Burmese, whom Thai authorities are apparently trying to round up and return to Myanmar. Between February and July 2002, some 4,000 unregistered Burmese migrants were returned to Myanmar via the border town of Myawaddy opposite Mae Sot. The fact is that the Kingdom of Thailand, like so many other political economies, continues to officially restrict but unofficially (or less officially) encourage, or at least tolerate, very large numbers of undocumented migrants on her soil. Two key economic reasons are obviously the needs of various sectors for the cheap labour afforded by migrant workers, and another is the simple fact that the state earns millions of Baht from registrations of unauthorized workers. Thus, the fine line between being registered and unregistered is open to manipulation for both political and economic reasons, a situation that prevails in different forms in many countries today.

What Type of Engagement with Myanmar?

Since Mr. Thaksin Shinawatra became Prime Minister there has been a pendulum swing in relations with Myanmar away from the more critical and cool approach of the Chuan Leekpai administration to one characterized more by what is termed as "personal diplomacy" between senior Thai officials and the military generals in Yangon. For instance, former Foreign Minister, Mr. Surin Pitsuwan, was in favour of a more "flexible" approach to Myanmar when internal problems spilled across the common border, and he argued for a change in ASEAN's "constructive engagement" position. Whilst the call for "flexible engagement" with Myanmar gained little support within ASEAN (see below), it was developed out of frustration with a whole plethora of unresolved transnational problems and cross-border disputes with Myanmar, ranging from increasing numbers of undocumented migrants, the geopolitics of the drug trade, fishery disputes in the Andaman Sea, boundary and territorial conflicts, and occasional confrontations between the armies in strategic zones where non-ceasefire groups (in Myanmar) were active (Grundy-Warr and Wong 2001; Ganesan 2001). At that time the incumbent Thai government sought to add some external pressure by openly discussing Myanmar's internal political problems.

Under the new Thaksin administration, Thai policy has switched again to one of "constructive engagement" favoured by ASEAN, and one that involves little scope for open criticism of the military regime in Myanmar. This tendency has been further strengthened by events such as the Myanmar Embassy siege in … and the pathetically tragic Ratchaburi hospital siege on …, which critically moved Thai public opinion towards taking tougher positions against Burmese migrants and refugees. Also, the Thaksin government has made it clear that it would like to "mediate" between those ethnic groups that have not signed ceasefires and the ruling SPDC. Thus, Foreign Minister, Mr. Surakiat Sathirathai, has stressed Thailand's current stance of "non-interference in the affairs of neighbours" and has reaffirmed support for "national reconciliation" inside Myanmar, positions that reflect the general ASEAN line on Myanmar. The Deputy Prime Minister, General Chavalit Yongchaiyudh, is widely acknowledged as having particularly close ties with Myanmar, recently stated his approach following a disappointing refusal by Lt-Gen. Khin Nyunt, Secretary No. 1 of the SPDC, to join celebrations of the first anniversary of a Thai-Burmese Cultural and Economic Association of which Chavalit is the Thai advisory chairman: "My main job is to create peace and maintain friendship. We must be patient when our friends are not in a good mood. It is common for them to use harsh words. No problem" (*Bangkok Post*, 18 June 2002, p. 2).

Thus, the broad approach of the Thaksin government has been to try to "normalize relations" with Myanmar by giving financial help to tackle the drug problem, supply energy (gas) to Thailand, help build infrastructure in Myanmar, with the aim expressed once in a joint communiqué, to turn "the common border into a border of friendship, harmony and prosperity which will contribute to peace, stability and development" (*Bangkok Post*, 6 September 2001). It is somewhat ironic that in spite of the Thai Government's overall approach, there continues to be numerous troubles along its border with Myanmar that occasionally involve exchanges of fire between the militaries on both sides, and that the border has been completely closed on several occasions following bilateral disagreements. There is still significant doubt whether or not Thai-Myanmar relations have entered a new, peaceful era.

Of course, in any democracy there are usually dissenting and critical voices. One of these has been Mr. Kraisak Choonhaven, chairman of the Senate Foreign Affairs Committee, who referred to the above-mentioned Shan report on Burmese army rapes against Shan women, and reported that his panel had also heard convincing evidence from Shan refugees in Wiang Haeng district of Chiang Mai on 15 August 2002. Mr. Kraisak criticized the Thai Government for trying to deny entry to Burmese refugees on occasions and urged a tougher stance against Yangon (*Bangkok Post*, 7 September 2002, p. 1). Predictably, Myanmar's Labour Minister, Tin Win, later accused Mr. Kraisak of "hating" Myanmar and of supporting the Shan United Revolutionary Army (SURA), otherwise known as the Shan State Army (SSA).

It remains difficult to determine the precise meanings to be read into Thai policy towards Myanmar, partly because there has often been distinct differences in application of central policy by different ministries and also in the provinces. Nevertheless, perhaps the main problem being faced by forced migrants who remain confined to camps along the border are the pronouncements made by the National Security Council, which are often blunt and disturbing. It sometimes appears that the NSC may be willing to use these forced and marginalized migrants more as negotiating chips or pawns in the cross-border chess game with the authorities of Yangon. Certainly there have been high-level discussions about the repatriation of displaced persons, albeit on a voluntary basis, with international agencies to help build settlements in "safe areas" inside Myanmar (*Bangkok Post*, 6 September 2001). Frequent calls for early displaced person repatriation, even though there is still a far from peaceful settlement between the ethnic political representatives of those refugees and the SPDC, are interspersed with offers by Thai government officials to try to mediate with those ethnic political groups that still remain outside of ceasefires with Yangon. At times, it is difficult to chart the ebbs and flows of cross-border relations between the two states. The only thing that is certain is that many thousands of displaced persons continue to live with great uncertainty and a legal-political limbo, which leaves them at the mercy of policy changes on the part of the host state.

Refugee Insecurity Dilemma: Relocating Already Displaced People

One of the camps I have visited many times in Mae Hong Son province has been relocated by the Thai authorities. Between September 2002 and May 2003, virtually all of the camp's inhabitants were physically relocated to another site very close to the border where Karenni Camp 2 is already brimming with people. This relocation followed reports that: "The refugees have stolen produce from Thai villagers, worked for illegal loggers and damaged the environment in the vicinity. Besides, they use drugs, have arms, make bootleg liquor, and dump garbage in water resources and plantations of the villagers" (*Bangkok Post*, 7 July 2002, p. 3). In fact, the camp in question was established in 1995 when the Myanmar *Tatmadaw* presence and forced relocations began to intensify within Karenni territory leading to an exodus to Thailand.

Camp 3 co-existed beside a village called Ban Nai Soi. Whilst media reports of problems associated with a minority of the refugees may have some validity, there have definitely been local benefits derived from the presence of displaced persons. For example, refugees have sometimes provided cheap farm workers and labour for construction projects within the local district. Significantly, Mae Hong Son's tourist agencies have profited from a busy tourist trade associated with the Kayan ("long neck" women), Kayaw ("Big ear" women), and Kayah ("Big knee" women) who live as members of a showcase village just outside the former Camp 3. Indeed, these "exotic" tribes are advertised all over Thailand as being "hill tribes" and as much a part of the Thai uplands as folks who have lived there for generations. Rarely, do people like the Kayan get described as being "refugees" as this might lead to irksome questions to tour agents or even discourage tourist visitors. Quite apart from the complex politics and economics of such forms of tourism, which are not always detrimental to the refugees as some of them have managed to gain material benefits from

FIGURE 8.3
Karenni Refugee Camps Close to the Border

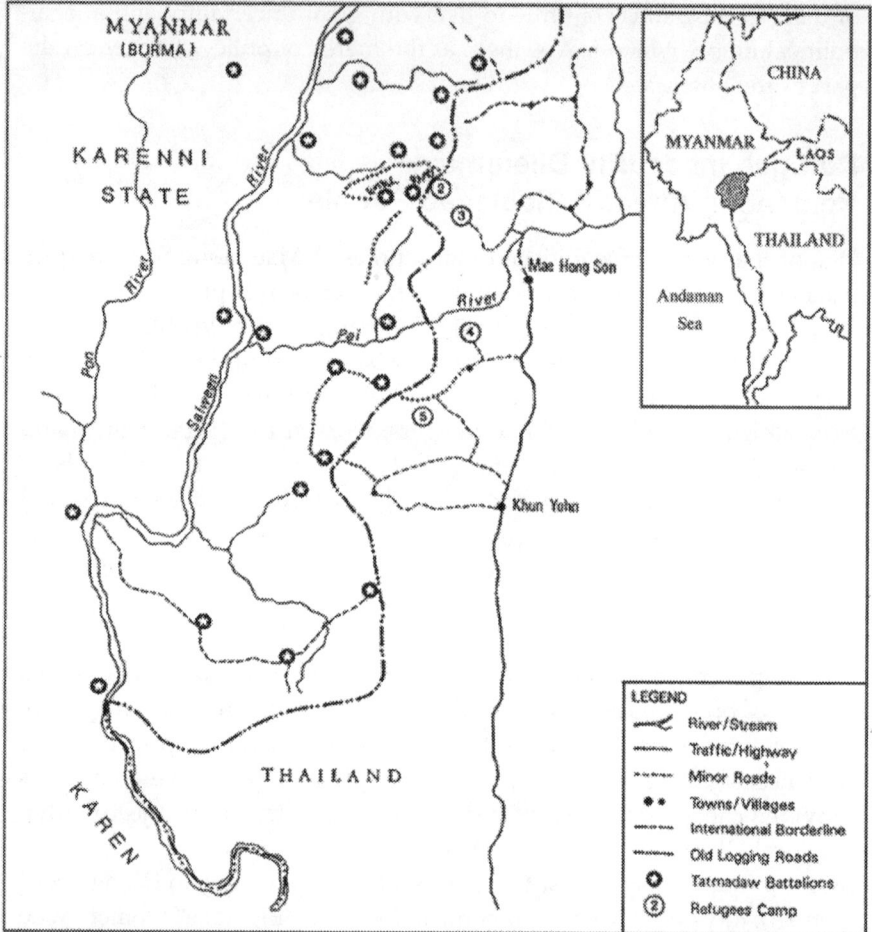

Source: Author's map.

selling aspects of their culture, the Thai agencies have undoubtedly gained most. Whilst showcasing folks deemed to be "attractive" to tourists, the Thai authorities have simultaneously tried to hide the rest. The recent relocation has successfully moved the majority of refugees even further out of sight, nearer to a border, and a difficult trek away from Nai Soi, especially during the rainy season when the existing tracks are a quagmire. But visitors to amazing Mae Hong Son can still see the "long-necks" if they want a good photo opportunity.

When I visited the Nai Soi area in September 2002, I found that only part of Camp 3 had been relocated. In all of my visits to the area over the past few years I had never known the situation to be so tense, except during a time in early 1997 following a cross-border attack on the camp by *Tatmadaw* soldiers. The refugees I spoke to were depressed and confused as to why they had to relocate. Some of them were anxious about being moved so close to the boundary, knowing that *Tatmadaw* positions lie not many kilometres away. Others were resigned to their fate as voiceless refugees who had to move whenever and wherever the authorities wished. Some of the Karenni National Progressive Party (KNPP) leaders believed that the Thai authorities were applying pressure on them due to their continued refusal to sign a ceasefire with the SPDC. Indeed, numerous travel and other restrictions had been put on the KNPP leaders, which suggested that a new tough central line was being applied locally by Thai authorities. In addition, Thailand's National Security Council (NSC) barred foreign journalists from visiting refugee camps along the border and implemented tighter scrutiny of non-governmental organizations providing relief and other services to refugee populations.[21]

One NGO officer who works for a relief organization alleged that the Camp 3 relocation was probably in response to the rape of two Karenni girls by Thai soldiers earlier in 2002, which was later publicized by a Karenni agency on the Internet (Grundy-Warr, field interview, September 2002). In many respects, the policy rationale behind the relocation of a long-established camp was the subject of intense debate, speculation and considerable anxiety on the part of ordinary refugees. The UNHCR field officers I met informed me that the relocation orders had come from the Ministry of Interior and that there was little that could be done about it, except that the UNHCR was negotiating to delay the move and to find a safe site further from the border. In fact, UNHCR was unable to do much to alleviate a distressing situation for many of the refugees. At the time of writing, the Thai authorities have made access to the large concentration of refugees now at Camp 2 extremely difficult. These refugees are more silenced than ever in their border limbo-land.

All of the images (Figures 8.4 to 8.9) included in this chapter were taken during a visit I made to Camp 3 in 1999 with a professional photographer, Ernest Goh. It is important to stress the ordinariness of life and death within such camps, as well as the enormity of the refugee predicament of being at once displaced from their "homeland" and of being considered "temporary" residents living highly circumscribed lives in a neighbouring territorial state.

Regional Silence and the Imperatives of Sovereignty

There are probably hundreds of thousands of "internally displaced persons" living inside Myanmar's extensive borderlands today. In another paper entitled "Lost in Sovereign Space" (Grundy-Warr 2002), I argued that the ruling SPDC has successfully utilized political and territorial sovereignty very skilfully in spite of the fact that some border areas are still controlled more effectively by *de facto* armed groups, such as the United Wa State Army (UWSA) in eastern Shan state, than the Myanmar Army, and in other border areas there are still no ceasefires with groups such as the KNPP, Karen National Union (KNU) and Shan State Army (SSA). In other words, the SPDC has used the convenient cloak of sovereignty to mask many of its more violent methods to achieve effective military, if not "hearts and minds", control over people living in territories along the Thai border.

Myanmar's membership of ASEAN has brought with it undoubted political and economic benefits. ASEAN's policy of non-intervention and preference for quiet diplomacy, discreet and non-confrontational relations amongst member states have produced a long-held policy of "constructive engagement" with Myanmar. Undoubtedly, several ASEAN states were quick to invest in Myanmar's increasingly open economy after 1988, albeit one still mostly controlled by the military. After years of isolation under General Ne Win's disastrous "Burmese Way to Socialism" several companies from ASEAN have invested heavily in certain sectors, particularly in Myanmar's rich natural resources. Proponents of ASEAN's

FIGURE 8.4
Village View

Plate One: Overview of Karenni Refugee Camp 3, near to Ban Nai Soi, Mae Hong Son Province, Thailand. This camp was relocated by the Thai authorities to a nearby camp closer to the border with Kayah (Karenni) State, Myanmar. Photo Ernest Goh (1999).

"constructive engagement" with Myanmar argue that embargoes, economic isolation and coercive measures against the military regime would only serve to turn it inwards and towards China, a huge regional power already holding geostrategic, military and economic influence within Myanmar. Indeed, countering China's strategic interests may have been an important reason for Myanmar's integration into the ASEAN family. Simon Tay and Goh Chien Yen (1999, p. 54) carefully considered the underlying rationale of ASEAN in accepting Myanmar into the grouping. They argued that "integration into Southeast Asia" was perceived as a way of preventing Myanmar from "slipping into potential isolation" and a means to help "the country into being a responsible member of the global community".

FIGURE 8.5
Kayah Woman

Plate Two: Profile of an elderly Kayah woman. The Kayah are the main ethnic group from Kayah state, which the Karenni National Progressive Party prefers to call Karenni state. Karenni (ìRed Kareni) is the collective term for a dozen Karen-speaking groups whose name comes from the colour of clothing of the largest sub-group, the Kayah. Photo Ernest Goh (1999).

FIGURE 8.6
Long-Neck Women

Plate Three: Kayan women carrying sticks. These so-called îlong-neck womenî, *Padaung* in Myanmar or *Kayan* as they prefer to be called, are the most photographed refugees in Thailand. They live in special îshowcaseî villages set apart from the majority of Karenni refugees. This is so the Thai tourist agencies can profit from tour groups eager to see these îexoticî guests. Whilst this form of exploitation does have its abuses, these women are able to at least bring some material benefits to an otherwise empty existence as refugees living in limbo. Photo Ernest Goh (1999).

FIGURE 8.7
A Girl Refugee

Plate Four: Refugee girl after taking a bath using water from a nearby stream. Note the typical bamboo construction and leaf roof of the refugee temporary housing. Photo Ernest Goh (1999).

This was at some political cost as the whole issue of ASEAN's constructive engagement with Myanmar and the latter's inclusion within the regional grouping exposed some serious differences in approach between ASEAN and the European Union over issues of human rights, democracy and civil liberties (also see Funston 1998).

Amitav Acharya (2001, pp. 151–57) discussed the linkages between sovereignty, non-interference and regional problem solving within ASEAN. His critical analysis reveals that ASEAN's stubborn adherence to non-interference is founded on an idea that relative regional security is based upon reducing areas of possible confrontation between members rather than exposing these areas.

FIGURE 8.8
Boys and Grave

Plate Five: Boys and grave. It is a fact that the refugee camps witness many births, deaths and marriages. The cycles of life continue albeit amongst displaced people without statehood. Photo Ernest Goh (1999).

"Apart from the issue of regime security" the reluctance of ASEAN "to endorse any departure from the norm of strict non-interference had to do with the fear that such a move would rekindle bilateral disputes and lead to regionalization of issues that are best settled bilaterally. Flexible engagement would needlessly transform bilateral issues into an ASEAN issue" (Acharya 2001, p. 154).

With regard to the specific issues of internal displacement and refugees, several of the ASEAN states have displaced populations and have implemented their own policies of forced relocation at different times. This is likely to be another reason for the regional silence on the massive forced migration problem affecting many people, particularly members of

FIGURE 8.9
Study

Plate Six: Many refugee children and young people are determined to have an education, even though it is virtually impossible for any of them to get recognized qualifications. In the Karenni camps, education is partially supported by assistance from the Jesuit Relief Service (JRS), by donations from small non-governmental agencies and by a handful of foreign volunteers. Photo Ernest Goh (1999).

ethnic communities inside Myanmar and along Thailand's borders. In effect, the principle of non-interference in internal affairs enables draconian states and regimes to commit atrocities against people within international borders (Korn 1999). That said, it is also clear that there are opportunities for ASEAN to influence the military leaders of Myanmar. Clearly, Myanmar has been unable to contain her problems within borders. The large numbers of undocumented migrants and refugees are testimony to the failure of a military regime to restore peace and order, especially in the border regions where ethnic "minorities" form the majority populations. Increasingly, ASEAN as a whole and all of the member states are now faced with numerous transnational flows and non-traditional security issues that transcend national mindsets and rigid notions of "internal affairs". Re-conceptualizing sovereign relations should be part of any process to tackle fundamental issues that are generated by preoccupations with concepts of "national" security and reconsolidation in the first place. As Acharya (2001, p. 156) argued: "In dealing with domestic issues with a clear transnational impact, such as human rights and the environment, which have increasingly crept onto ASEAN's multilateral agenda, ASEAN does need to go beyond non-interference."

Breaking the Silence

The opening quotation in this chapter, by Xenos (1996), suggests that the fundamental problem of displaced persons and refugees is that the system of nation-states systematically denies them the possibility of making a home in places other than where they were forced to leave. In this chapter, I have argued that the problem of forced migration is very much related to cycles of violence associated with struggles over national spaces, sovereignties and identities. The Karen, Karenni and Shan along the Myanmar-Thai borderlands are amongst numerous groups inside Myanmar that are either contesting their place in a national union controlled mostly by the ethnic Burman majority, or are demanding their own independence, high degrees of political autonomy or at least the basic rights of being national citizens. Nationality, homelands, sovereignty and territoriality are fundamentally a part of the problem of forced migration, both in terms of causality and the enduring problems of being without appropriate documentation, of being considered stateless and homeless.

Undocumented persons, refugees, exiles and others who transgress national boundaries and the domains of "the citizen" are effectively challenging the very foundations of nation-statehood, or as Xenos (1996, p. 244) suggests, "in their homelessness as statelessness they are often unwitting representatives of a cosmopolitan alternative to the idea of a homeland". Even so, many of the refugees I have spoken to do have definite ideas of where their "homeland" is and many have strong desires to go there in peace and dignity. Nevertheless, the enormous obstacles they face in setting up alternative homes within their states of sanctuary or exile is another dark side of the territorial and sovereignty traps created by the modern political map. There is still a strong tendency to view the displaced persons as "the problem", distracting analytical attention and policy-makers from the root causes of forced migration. In the case of forced migrants from Myanmar, efforts to break the cycle of violence requires breaking the silence of displaced persons who are literally living in jungle hideouts or in the spaces of relocation, detention centres, refugee camps, or surviving day to day in the tiny cracks of anonymity away from the scrutiny of state authorities. Breaking that silence means chipping away at the walls of indifferent sovereignty, state practices that reinforce non-interference in so-called internal affairs, and the prejudice and extremes of state-centred versions of national identity that have forced people away from their homes into legal-political limbo-land.

Notes

[1]   In this chapter, I use the term "undocumented migrant" to mean all persons who enter into a state without formal permission to be there. In practice, this category of people can cover numerous different types of migrants without "official" documentation, including persons with no official form of identification; persons without passports and visas; persons with passports but without visas allowing them entry into a particular host state; and so many registered refugees are also undocumented persons, whilst others are not. The definition of "refugee" is that used in international treaties to mean a person who is outside his or her own country and is unable to return because of a well-founded fear of persecution on the basis of race, religion, nationality, political opinion, or membership of a social group. Persons are refugees whether or not they are officially recognized by UNHCR or by a state.

[2]   The figures for "border areas" are from the United Nations General Assembly (UN GA) 20 August 2001, *Report to the General Assembly of the Special Rapporteur*

on Myanmar, UN ref: A/56/312, and the Burmese Border Consortium, August 2001, *Programme Report January to June 2001, Funding Appeal for 2002*. The figures on "internally displaced persons" (IDPs) for Myanmar are taken from the US Department of State (US DOS), 25 February 2001, *2000 Country Reports on Human Rights Practices Released by the Bureau of Democracy, Human Rights, and Labour: Burma* (Internet), section 2.d. In addition, there are various estimates in reports by the United Nations, Human Rights Watch, Amnesty International, and various ethnic human rights monitors.

3   For more information visit the Karen Human Rights Group website at <http://www.khrg.org>.

4   United Nations Commission on Human Rights (CHR), 22 January 1999, *Situation of Human Rights in Myanmar: Report of the Special Rapporteur, Mr. Rajsmoor Lallah*, submitted in accordance with Commission on Human Rights resolution 1998/63, E/CN.4/1999/35. These figures correspond with estimates given to the author by Karenni National Relief Committee members. But in practice it is notoriously difficult to come up with reliable statistics in lands where many people are literally in hiding and where large zones have been designated as "security areas" by the military.

5   The Rohingya people are not recognized as a distinct ethnic group by the Myanmar authorities. In fact, the SPDC denies them any official status as one of the "nationalities" of Myanmar, claiming that they are Bangalis who entered Myanmar mostly during British colonial rule. For instance, a press release from U Ohn Gyaw, Minister for Foreign Affairs of Myanmar, on 21 February 1992, stated: "Since the first Anglo-Myanmar war in 1824, people of Muslim faith from the adjacent country illegally entered Myanmar Naing-Ngan, particularly Rakhine State. Being illegal immigrants they do not hold immigration papers like other nationals of the country." Rohingya political leaders claim that the Rohingya are an ethnically distinct group, descendants of the first Muslims who began migrating to northern Arakan in the eighth century, though they also admit that they are a mix of Bangalis, Persians, Monghuls, Turks, and Pathans who came to the area later. Arakan is also home to Rakhine people who are Buddhist and speak a dialect of Burmese.

6   The SLORC regime was installed on 18 September 1988, and was only meant to play a temporary role, although after denying the elected government of the National League for Democracy (NLD) in 1990, it then sought to reaffirm military control inside Myanmar. As its name suggests, it set about establishing its own version of martial law and order.

7   Interview, April 2000.

8   Interview, March 2001.

9   Interview with a Shan farmer from Myanmar, who is now a seasonal worker in Mae Hong Son province, Thailand, November 2000.

10   This unpublished report was produced by a Karenni refugee called Saw May Sie Thet Win, 2001, called "The Geh Lo villagers become internally displaced in 1996".

11   The Tai Yai people are one of the many ethnic groups comprising a large part of the human flow between Myanmar and Thailand. These people are often called Shan in English, and they are a branch of the Tai ethnic groups which inhabit numerous places, spreading from southern Yunnan province in China, through the Shan states in Myanmar, to northern Thailand. Their language belongs to the Tai language family and is not mutually intelligible with Standard Thai, but can be somewhat understood by speakers of *Kammuang*, a northern Thai dialect. There are many cultural overlaps across the international boundary that now separates the Tai Yai in Myanmar from those found in Thailand. In Mae Hong Son, the Tai Yai people form a majority of the provincial population. Thus historical, cultural and social bonds transcend political spaces.

12   A common restriction on undocumented migrants is on their mobility beyond certain districts or provincial borders; certain jobs may be restricted according to type of identification; and people with less than full Thai identification documents are not allowed to own land.

13   These interviews were conducted by Wong Siew Yin, Elaine, as part of her Masters' thesis entitled *The Political Geography of Displacement in Mainland Southeast Asia: The Case of the Shans*, unpublished (2001), Department of Geography, National University of Singapore, pp. 71–72.

14   *Ibid.*, p. 76.

15   The NSC comprises nine ex-officio members and is headed in formal session by the Prime Minister (as chairperson). Other council members include the Deputy Prime Minister (vice-chairperson), Ministers of Defence, Interior, Foreign Affairs, Finance, Transport, the Supreme Commander of the Armed Forces, and the Secretary-General (who has cabinet rank and is under direct supervision of the Prime Minister). When required, senior government officials are invited to attend NSC meetings.

16   As Hazel Lang (2002, p. 96) observes: "The BPP's paramilitary police units are responsible for security on the immediate border, sometimes as a joint force with the Royal Thai Army and the Thahan Phran (paramilitary rangers). (...) Although the BPP is organizationally allied to the Police Department, it is largely autonomous nationally and in many of its field operations; in the event of external incursion, it comes under the direct control of the military's Supreme Command Headquarters.

17   Many groups have been involved in supplying relief and medical assistance to the refugee communities along the border, including the Church of Christ in Thailand (CCT), the Thailand Baptist Missionary Fellowship (TBMF), Refugee Care Netherlands (RCN), International Rescue Committee (IRC), the Jesuit Relief Service (JRS), Aide Medicale Inernationale (AMI), Handicap International

(HI), Catholic Office for Emergency Relief and Refugees (COERR), Zuid Oost Azie Refugee Care, Medicin Sans Frontieres (MSF), Tapei Overseas Peace Service, among others.

18 Nussara Sawatsawan, "Ogata Accepts Invitation", *Bangkok Post*, 25 July 1998.

19 Achara Ashayagachat, "Karenni being seen as a Threat to Forest", *Bangkok Post*, 11 March 2000, p. 2, is one of many such stories. Another case was when Thai Third Army commander, Lt. Gen. Watanachai Chaimuanwong, said that the refugees in Mae Hong Son and Tak provinces were conducting illegal activities. "Burmese refugees from many camps sneak out to fell trees for Thai and hilltribe timber poachers. There are also thieves and drug addicts among them, and they are a crime problem in towns and bordering villages," he said. His statement was made at a meeting with local administrators in the border town of Mae Sot in Tak province on 25 May 2000. He complained that the UNHCR had allowed the refugees too much freedom, and suggested that fences be erected to keep refugees inside. Supamart Kasem, "Refugees seen as a menace", *Bangkok Post*, 26 May 2000.

20 These ideas have been derived from my reading of Soguk (1999). In practice, refugees and migrants serve to simultaneously undermine aspects of statehood whilst creating opportunities for strengthening certain state tendencies and practices.

21 NSC chief Khachadpai Buruspatana told reporters: "From now on, foreign journalists will be banned from visiting camps or controlled areas as they are likely to report only on negative aspects of official work or on inaccurate and unconfirmed reports." The ban was to be strongly applied on leaders of different "resistance groups" as their views reflected poorly on Myanmar. "Thailand bans foreign journalists from Myanmar refugee camps", AFP, July 2002.

References

Acharya, Amitav. *Constructing a Security Community in Southeast Asia. ASEAN and the Problem of Regional Order*. London: Routledge, 2001.

Amnesty International. *Myanmar. Lack of Security in Counter-Insurgency Areas*, A.I. Report, ASA 16/007/2002, 17 July 2002.

Amnesty International. *Myanmar. Aftermath: Three Years of Dislocation in Kayah State*, A.I. Report, ASA 16.14.99, June 1999.

Appadurai, Arjun. "Disjuncture and Difference in the Global Cultural Economy". In *Globalization: The Reader*, edited by John Beynon and David Dunkerley. London: The Athlone Press, 2000.

Appadurai, A. "Sovereignty without Territoriality: Notes for a Postnational Geography". In *The Geography of Identity*, edited by Patricia Yager. Ann Arbor: University of Michigan Press, 1996.

Burma Centrum Nederland (BCN). *Rohingya Reader 1*. Amsterdam: BCN, 1995.

Burma Ethnic Research Group (BERG). *Conflict and Displacement in Karenni: The Need for Considered Responses*. Chiang Mai: Nopburee Press, 1999.

BERG. *Forgotten Victims of a Hidden War: Internally Displaced Karen in Burma*. Chiang Mai: Nopburee Press, 1998.

Bowles, Edith. "From Village to Camp: Refugee Camp Life in Transition on the Thailand-Burma Border". *Forced Migration Review* 2, August (1998): 11–15.

Burmese Border Consortium (BBC). *Internally Displaced People and Relocation Sites in Eastern Burma*, BBC, September 2002.

Caouette, Therese, Kritaya Archavanitkul and Hnin Hnin Pyne. *Sexuality, Reproductive Health and Violence: Experiences of Migrants from Burma and Thailand*. Institute for Population and Social Research, Mahidol University, 2000.

Chantavanich, Supang and E. Bruce Reynolds. *Indochinese Refugees: Asylum and Resettlement*. Bangkok: Institute of Asian Studies, Chulalongkorn University, 1988.

Dudley, Sandra. "Traditional Culture and Refugee Welfare in North-West Thailand". *Forced Migration Review* 6, December (1998): 5–8.

Friends Without Borders. "Taking Shelter Under Trees: Displaced Peoples and Forest Conservation". *Watershed* 7, no. 3 (November 2001–February 2002): 35–46.

Funston, J. "ASEAN: Out of its Depth?" *Contemporary Southeast Asia* 20, no. 1 (1998): 22–30.

Ganesan, N. "Thailand's Relations with Malaysia and Myanmar in Post-Cold War Southeast Asia". *Japanese Journal of Political Science* 2, no. 1 (2001): 127–45.

Gibney, Matthew J. *Outside the Protection of the Law. The Situation of Irregular Migrants in Europe*. A synthesis report commissioned by the Jesuit Refugee Service - Europe, 2001.

Grundy-Warr, Carl. "Lost in Sovereign Space: Forced Migrants in the Territorial Trap". *Asian and Pacific Migration Journal* 11, no. 4 (2002): 437–61.

Grundy-Warr, C. "Turning the Political Map Inside-Out: A View of Mainland Southeast Asia". In *The Naga Awakens: Growth and Change in Southeast Asia*, edited by Victor R. Savage, Lily Kong and Warwick Neville. Singapore: Times Academic Press, 1997.

Grundy-Warr, C. "Co-existent Borderlands and Intra-State Conflicts in Mainland Southeast Asia". *Singapore Journal of Tropical Geography* 14, no. 1 (1993): 42–56.

Grundy-Warr, Carl and Wong Siew Yin, Elaine. "Geographies of Displacement: The Karenni and the Shan across the Myanmar-Thailand Border". *Singapore Journal of Tropical Geography* 23, no. 1 (2002): 93–122.

Grundy-Warr, C. and Wong, E. "Geopolitics of Drugs and Cross-Border Relations: Burma-Thailand". *Boundary and Security Bulletin* 9, no. 1 (2001): 108–21.

Hampton, J., ed. *Internally Displaced People: A Global Survey*. London: Earthscan Publications, 1998.

Human Rights Watch (HRW). *Burmese Refugees in Bangladesh. Still No Durable Solution*. Internet version. <http://www.hrw.org>, 2000.

Images Asia and Borderline Video. *A Question of Security*. Chiang Mai: Images Asia, 1998.

Kaise, Ryoko. *Tai Yai Migration in the Thai-Burma Border Area: The Settlement and Assimilation Process, 1962–1997*. MA thesis. Programme of Thai Studies, Chulalongkorn University, Thailand, 1999.

Karen Human Rights Group (KHRG). *Information Update #2002-U3: Papun and Nyaunglebin Districts*. KHRG Report, April 2002.

KHRG. *Flight, Hunger and Survival. Repression and Displacement in the Villages of Papun and Nyaunglebin Districts*. KHRG Report, October 2001.

KHRG. *Death Squads and Displacement*. KHRG Report, No. 99-04, May 2000.

KHRG. *Continuing Fear and Hunger*. KHRG Report, May 1999.

KHRG. *Wholesale Destruction: The SLORC/SPDC Campaign to Obliterate All Hill Villages in Papun and Eastern Nyaunglebin Districts*. Chiang Mai: Nopburee Press, 1998a.

KHRG. *Uncertainty, Fear and Flight*. KHRG Report No. 99-08, November 1998b.

Korn, David D. *Exodus Within Borders*. Washington, DC: Brookings Institute Press, 1999.

Lambrecht, Curtis. *The Return of the Rohingya Refugees to Burma, Voluntary Repatriation or Refoulement*. U.S. Committee for Refugees, 1995.

Lambrecht, C. "Destruction and Violation: Burma's Border Development Policies". *Watershed* 5, no. 2 (2000): 27–32.

Lang, Hazel J. *Fear and Sanctuary. Burmese Refugees in Thailand*. Ithaca, NY: Cornell Southeast Asia Programme Publications, 2002.

Maung Aung Myoe. *Neither Friend Nor Foe. Myanmar's Relations with Thailand since 1988. A View from Yangon*. Singapore: Institute of Defence and Strategic Studies, IDSS Monograph no. 1, 2002.

Nordstrom, Carolyn. "Girls and War Zones: Troubling Questions". In *Engendering Forced Migration. Theory and Practice*, edited by Doreen Indra. New York: Berghahn Books, 2000, pp. 63–82.

Rajaram, Prem Kumar and Carl Grundy-Warr. "The Irregular Migrant as Homo Sacer: Migration and Detention in Australia, Malaysia, and Thailand". *International Migration* 42, no. 1 (2004): 33–64.

Robinson, W. Court. *Terms of Refuge: The Indochinese Exodus and the International Response*. London: Zed Books, 1998.

Shan Human Rights Foundation (SHRF). *Dispossessed. Forced Relocations and Extra-Judicial Killings in Shan State*, Chiang Mai: SHRF, April 1998.

Smith, Martin. *Burma (Myanmar): The Time for Change*. London: Minority Rights Group International, 2002.

Smith, Martin. *Burma: Insurgency and the Politics of Ethnicity*. London: Zed Books, 1999.

Soguk, Nevzat. *States and Strangers. Refugees and Displacements of Statecraft.* Minneapolis: University of Minnesota Press, 2000.

Soguk, N. "Transnational/Transborder Bodies: Resistance, Accommodation, and Exile in Refugee and Migration Movements on the US-Mexican Border". In *Challenging Boundaries. Global Flows, Territorial Identities,* edited by Michael J. Shapiro and Hayward R. Alker. Minneapolis: University of Minnesota Press, 1995.

Steinberg, David I. "The State, Power and Civil Society in Burma-Myanmar." In *Burma-Myanmar. Strong Regime Weak State?* edited by M.B. Pedersen, E. Rudland, and R.J. May. Adelaide: Crawford House, 2000.

Tay, Simon and Goh Chien Yen. "EU-ASEAN Relations: The Question of Myanmar". *Panorama,* 4/1999. Manila: Konrad-Adenauer-Stiftung, 1999.

United Nations Economic and Social Council. *Situation of Human Rights in Myanmar. Report of the Special Rapporteur.* 6 February, E/CN.4/1997/64. Geneva: UN, 1996.

Vitit Muntarbhorn. "Law and National Policy Concerning Displaced Persons and Illegal Immigrants in Thailand". Unpublished paper. Bangkok: Institute of Asian Studies, Chulalongkorn University, undated.

Wong Siew Yin, Elaine. *The Political Geography of Displacement in Mainland Southeast Asia: The Case of the Shans.* Masters thesis. Department of Geography, National University of Singapore, 2001.

Yan Nyein Aye. *Endeavours of the Myanmar Armed Forces Government for National Reconsolidation.* Yangon: U Aung Zaw, 2000.

Xenos, Nicholas. "Refugees: The Modern Political Condition". In *Challenging Boundaries. Borderlines 2,* edited by Michael J. Shapiro and Hayward R. Alker. Minneapolis: University of Minnesota Press, 1996, pp. 233–46.

9

International Migration and Conflict: Foreign Labour in Malaysia

P. Ramasamy

Introduction

Contemporary Southeast Asia is currently witnessing a massive movement of non-permanent labour, mostly the flow of contract workers from labour surplus countries such as Indonesia, Philippines, Myanmar to non-surplus countries such as Malaysia, Singapore and Thailand. While the bulk of the flow involves unskilled and semi-skilled migrants, there is also the flow of professionals from countries such as Singapore, Malaysia and Thailand to some of the newly industrializing countries outside the region. Of all the countries in Southeast Asia, Singapore has the highest ratio of foreign migrants to the local population. One of the recent trends in labour flow is the phenomenon of female labour flow from countries such as Indonesia and Philippines. Official records indicate that in the case of migrants from Indonesia and Philippines, women outnumber men (Hugo 2002, pp. 17–24).

It is estimated that there are nearly two million migrant workers constituting about 23 per cent of the total workforce in Malaysia, mainly from Indonesia and the Philippines.[1] In a more specific sense, migrants constitute the majority in sectors such as construction, plantation agriculture and domestic service. Not all the estimated two million migrants have a legal status, nearly two-thirds are illegal migrants; those who have come into the country without any valid papers attesting to their *bona fide* status. Of late, the Malaysian Government has been very concerned with the large presence of illegal migrants. There are fears that if illegal migrant flow is not systematically checked, it might contribute to the exacerbation of social and political problems. Recently the government introduced a new immigration law that provides for the mandatory caning and jail sentence for those coming illegally into the country. Before the enforcement of this new law, the government gave a general amnesty for illegals to leave the country or be voluntarily repatriated. As result of this offer, it has been estimated that nearly 300,000 illegals mostly from Indonesia and the Philippines left voluntarily and a great many were deported by the government.[2] The imposition of the new law, the harsh manner of detention, and subsequent deportation were not well received by Indonesia and the Philippines. While some politicians in Indonesia accused the Malaysian Government of inhumane treatment of their citizens, the Philippine Government dispatched a delegation with the approval of the Malaysian authorities to examine the conditions for detainees in Sabah.[3]

It is possible to speak about two major waves of migration to Malaysia.[4] One took place during the British colonial period when thousands of Indians and Chinese came into the country to work in plantations and tin mines. Although they were brought into the country temporarily, political and economic circumstances changed the outlook of the migrants. As years went by, demand for labour as result of rapid economic development, changing nature of the relationship between migrants and their homeland and the inability of many to uproot themselves from the country contributed to the emergence of a multi-racial population in the country. The second major wave of the flow of migrants began around the period when the state changed its development strategy from import substitution to export orientated industrialization. This change in strategy for the private sector development also coincided with the introduction of the New Economic Policy (NEP) that gave a major role for the state to intervene to restructure the economy and society to achieve the twin goals of the creation of a Malay entrepreneurial class and the eradication of poverty (Bowie 1991; Crouch 1994).

The flow of migrants to take advantage of the job opportunities in Malaysia began in the 1970s and has continued until today. In the beginning, the flow was mainly restricted to those from Indonesia and the Philippines, countries that have common borders with Malaysia. Later as labour demand grew, the government sought to bring in labour from Bangladesh, Thailand and Myanmar. Furthermore, the need to diversify labour sources was also determined by the country's over reliance on Indonesians and Filipinos. By the early 1980s, it was estimated that there were about 200,000 migrants in the country, mainly from Indonesia. Within a period of twenty years or so, the number of migrants jumped to about two million, a ten-fold increase. This tremendous increase of migrants was mainly a result of the flow of illegal or undocumented migrants into the country. Since many of the migrants could not afford to come through legal channels, they preferred to come by illegal means. Furthermore, the presence of numerous agents, recruiters, boatmen and corrupt officials easily facilitated the movement of illegal migrants (Zehadul Karim et al. 1999; Ariffin 2001).[5]

According to official sources, in the late 1990s, documented workers consisted of 63.9 per cent Indonesians, 27.46 per cent Bangladeshis, 2.22 per cent Filipinos, 1.91 per cent Thais, 1.62 per cent Pakistanis and 2.86 per cent others. In the domestic service sector, out of the total 111,750 domestic workers, 79,167 were Indonesians, 28,587 were Filipinos, 3,876 were Thais, and the rest Pakistanis, Indians and Sri Lankans. Plantations employed a total workforce of 137,956 (108,778 Indonesians, 11,120 Thais, 49 Filipinos, 17,366 Bangladeshis, 306 Indians and the rest from Myanmar, Nepal and Pakistan). The construction sector employed 133,414 workers (94,561 Indonesians, 6,540 Thais, 1,160 Filipinos, 27,578 Bangladeshis, 1,356 Pakistanis, 1,347 Indians and the rest were Nepalese and Sri Lankans). The service sector employed 12,485 workers (3,062 Indonesians, 1,492 Thais, 828 Filipinos, 5,803 Bangladeshis, 427 Pakistanis, 444 Indians, 39 Sri Lankans and the rest from Myanmar and Sri Lanka). And finally, the manufacturing sector employed about 107,148 (72,538 Bangladeshis, 30,568 Indonesians, 1,682 Pakistanis, 1,401 Filipinos and the rest from India, Pakistan, Myanmar and Nepal) (Ariffin 2001).

The official data only provides us a partial understanding of the nature of the migrant labour presence in the country and their sectoral distribution. Since it is estimated that there are about two million migrant workers in the country, it could be assumed that their presence in the economy is quite formidable. Given the nature of the dependence of the Malaysian economy on migrant labour, it would be difficult if not impossible for the government to get rid of illegal migrants from the country. It is not that the government has not tried, but the dependence of certain crucial sectors such as domestic services, plantation agriculture and construction on foreign workers, makes it difficult for it to adopt a restrictive policy towards the migrants. Although migrants make valuable contributions to the Malaysian economy, they are also a source of repatriation of earnings running into billion of dollars to their respective countries.[6] While it is not difficult for the government to manage and regulate the presence of legal migrants, the presence of illegal migrants imposes severe economic, political and social strains on the society. It is not that migrants are well treated in the country; they might displace local workers, but are subjected to extreme exploitation in terms of low wages, bad working and living conditions, not to mention harassment by government officials and agencies.

Since a large number of migrants have been in the country for about more than three decades, perhaps it is worthwhile to examine their impact on the economy, politics and society. We will try to find answers to such questions as: in what ways do the presence of migrants affect the opportunities of local workers and the development of the trade union movement; whether migrants drain the financial resources of the country, whether they are a damper to wage increase in the society, and to what extent do they constrain the transition of the economy from one based on cheap labour to one that is based on value added. Migrant workers come into the country for economic reasons, but in discharging their economic function, they co-exist, interact and occasionally run into conflict with the local population. What is the relationship between migrants and the local population, what is the perception of locals towards migrants, do migrants have the propensity to engage in criminal activities and what kind of social problems do migrants create in the country? We would be interested in ascertaining the impact of migrants on politics and why the government finds it difficult to get rid of illegal migrants and what are the obstacles that stand in the way. And finally, a case will be made to approach and debate the migrant issue by suggesting a regional forum.

Status of Migrants

With a considerable migrant population, Malaysia presents an interesting case to ascertain in some depth how such presence has impacted on the country. While it would be difficult to determine the full dynamics of the impact of migrants on every aspect of the Malaysian society, it is possible to sketch some of the broad trends. Migrants move across borders in search for better economic, social and even political opportunities. Countries like Indonesia and the Philippines even tend to encourage their citizens to move and locate themselves in countries such as Saudi Arabia and Malaysia so that pressure on the local job market could be reduced. Furthermore, the migration of their citizens to work in other countries also means the flow of funds from them. Such movement of funds will serve these countries to surmount their own economic problems to some extent. While sending countries might assist the movement of people, they do not, however, pay much attention to the problems faced by their citizens in the receiving countries. As has been documented, migrants in the receiving countries are subjected to much exploitation and alienation. Because of the alien status and unskilled nature of their work, they are not in a position to bargain and determine their wages in accordance with their contribution. In countries like Malaysia, migrant workers are located in very low paying sectors, subject to long hours of work, and harassment by employers and officials. The situation of illegal migrants is much worse. Due to their illegality, they cannot command wages similar to legalized workers, sometimes they are not even paid their wages, and they do not have the mechanisms available to register their grievances and often face the dim prospect of deportation by the authorities concerned.

In considering the impact of migrant workers, there is a need to reflect on their socio-economic status and how they have become victims of the differential process of development in the region. Studies on migration often give the impression that the movement of migrants from depressed economic zones to more dynamic ones takes place quite autonomously. Such imagery fails to take account of the fact that despite the economic differences between zones, movement of migrants takes place as a result of many factors. In the absence of these facilitating factors such as the role of agents, recruiters, middlemen, boatmen and corrupt officials, international migration would not have assumed the present significance. In the case of migrants moving from Indonesia and the Philippines to Malaysia, these facilitating factors play a pivotal role in the migration process. Without these parties having an economic stake in the migration process, the flow of migrants would not have assumed the present magnitude. As demonstrated by some studies, these intermediaries aiming to make quick money by facilitating the flow of labour, engage in all sort of nefarious practices. By encouraging workers to migrate, these parties impose all kinds of financial burdens on migrants. Migrants often had to sell their houses, estates and other belongings to pay for recruiters, agents, boatmen and others involved in the trafficking of human cargo. Those migrants unable to meet the financial impositions, later become indebted to their employers in Malaysia (Jones 2000; Zehadul Karim et al. 1999).

The process of exploitation of migrant workers begins from the time of their departure. Not only are they exploited by those responsible for their movement, they also become victims of corrupt officials both in Indonesia and Malaysia. Once in Malaysia, migrants are taken to their work places. The situation for illegal migrants is much worse than those with valid work permits. But in the production hierarchy in Malaysia, migrant workers are placed at the bottom end. Employers prefer foreign migrant workers not because they are hardworking, but because they can be paid low wages and be easily controlled to meet the demands of the production process. In fact about two decades ago, it was employers' argument of labour shortage in such sectors as plantations and construction that enabled the government to bring in migrant labour. Although the Malaysian Trades Union Council (MTUC) countered the argument of employers, it had no effect in influencing the government. Eventually the government bought the argument of employers by taking the necessary measures to bring in migrant labour. Apart from low wages, migrant labour does not have the option to be represented by trade unions. Although some unions have been collecting union dues, it is doubtful whether they can represent migrant workers.

Migrant workers are in a most unenviable position. They represent the surplus that could not be absorbed in their own economies. Propaganda of good income and plentiful jobs in Malaysia narrated by returned migrants and those involved in trafficking of human cargo provide them the incentives to migrate. What they earn in Malaysia is something that they could not obtain in their countries of origin. But in a relative sense, what is derived as income by migrants is perhaps not comparable to income received by locals. However, it is not so much wages but the conditions under which they work and live that are unenviable. The vast majority of migrants are employed in jobs that require little or no skill at all, jobs that are not preferred by locals. Employers prefer migrant labour for a variety of reasons. First, by employing foreign labour, employers could keep production costs down. Second, migrant labour are not inclined to create labour problems by participation in unions or taking their complaints to the industrial relations department. Third, migrant labour especially the illegals are very amenable to control and manipulation because of their undocumented nature. So in other words, the involvement of migrant labour in the Malaysian economy could be described as primitive production; production organized not so much on the basis of skills but rather on the basis of control and manipulation.

Of late, much attention has been directed at looking at the employment of foreign domestic maids by middle-class Malaysian families. To date it is estimated that there are more than 100,000 maids from Indonesia and the Philippines employed in Malaysia. Unlike the employment of migrant workers in the other sectors, the domestic service sector has been the least problematic for the state to manage and control. In fact, during economic slowdowns, the domestic service sector that employed maids was hardly touched by government policies unlike other sectors. Thus, from the beginning, the government has given much consideration not to disturb this sector. Such consideration does not stem from the fact that domestic maids are well taken care by employers, but rather, how the government views this particular sector in terms of creating and sustaining a particular middle-class conception of society. Chin seems to argue quite persuasively that the domestic service sector is very significant to the government to ensure that it obtains the consent of the growing middle-class. By bringing in maids to take care of the middle-class families, the government has given the impression that it wants to promote certain versions of the good life that might be appealing to the middle-class. In a more ideological sense, the provision of maid services to the middle-class represents an effort by the government to manufacture consent among the middle-class (Chin 1998).

Although the government has no problem in allowing the migration of maids to serve the middle-class, it, however, does not show concern in looking after the welfare of these maids. Reports about employer abuses of maids are quite common in Malaysia. Episodes such as maids running away to escape employers' cruelty, of sexual and physical assaults, of maids not being paid their salaries, and abuses get reported in the newspapers very often. However, the punishment meted out to cruel and inhumane employers is not reflective of the nature of crimes being committed against helpless maids. As the Malaysian middle-class expands, a particular version of a family has to be projected. In this respect, Indonesian and Filipino women are brought in to sustain an image, very crucial for the regime's ideological support. But then, the wage structure of maids, the lack of freedom and not to mention the abuses perpetrated against them by employers and agents, make a mockery of the Malaysian middle-class — a middle-class that seeks to sustain particular values and norms at the expense of exploiting and dehumanizing human beings on the grounds that they are members of a particular sub-altern class.

Economic Impacts

The impact of migrant labour on the economy, society and politics has not been systematically explored in Malaysia. Although there are a number of works on migrant labour, they seem more interested in providing general information about the causes of migration, the nationality of migrants, their sectoral participation in the Malaysian economy and about their nature of involvement in criminal activities. However, more pertinent questions about the impact of migrants on the economy have not been systematically and thoroughly explored and explicated. In what follows, I will try to provide a tentative assessment of the impact of migrant labour on the economy and to what extent their presence acts as a damper on the wage structure and the upward movement of Malaysia in the international production hierarchy.

Malaysia has about nine million workers. Nearly half of the population of the country are wage earners. Foreign migrant workers constitute about 23 per cent of the total workforce in the country. This provides a good indication as to the nature of the dependence of the economy on foreign migrant labour. Thus, without the contribution of foreign migrant workers, the economy would probably come to a standstill. As said earlier, this explains why the government, despite the rhetoric against migrant labour, has not been able to expel illegal migrants from the country. In fact, the biggest opposition to the government's move against foreign labour comes from employers, particularly those in the construction, plantation, manufacturing and domestic service sectors. Employers in these sectors are acutely aware that since local labour is not willing to work in these sectors, they have to count on migrant labour. Of course, the government is well aware of the employers' stand on the question of migrant labour.

Beyond employers' immediate concern, the government is also aware that it cannot afford to expel migrants on the ground of the economy's vulnerability. As it is, the country is slowly recovering from the 1997 financial crisis; for full recovery to take place, there must be some kind of economic and political stability. Moreover to get the economy functioning in full gear it cannot take any drastic action such as massive deportation exercises.

The only way for the country to reduce its intake of migrant labour is for the economy to become highly competitive based on skilled labour requirements. If such a development takes place in the near future, there will be a tendency for some of the labour intensive industries such as plantations to move to labour-cheap areas. However, for the time being, there is no clear indication that Malaysia is on the trajectory to shed its image as a cheap labour economy. One of the main reasons why migrant labour came into the country was because of the cheap labour requirement. Since employers were reluctant to raise wages in some sectors to retain the local labour force, they appealed to the government to allow for the mass migration of foreign workers. In the end, as described earlier, the government was willing to listen to employers rather than the MTUC. For the MTUC, employers' argument of the lack of labour in some sectors was an excuse not to raise wages for local workers.[7]

Can we accept the argument by some that foreign migrant workers displaced local workers in some of the sectors of the economy? There is no simple answer to this question because of the ideological position of the different parties. The employers' position is simple: foreign workers came into the country because local workers, for whatever reasons, were not willing to take up jobs in plantations, the construction sector and in the domestic service. The trade union argument is: if employers had paid fair wages and improved the living conditions, local labour would not have shied away from taking up jobs in these sectors. Since employers were not interested in improving the wage system and working and living conditions of workers, they could not attract local labour. Of course, there are others who think that the structural changes in the economy and the improvement of living conditions of Malaysians in general made it difficult for them to be situated in the low-paying sectors of the economy. Thus, it was a matter of time that Malaysian workers sought qualitative kind of labour mobility to improve their income and living standard. Thus, given this transformation, it was inevitable that a situation of labour shortage would be created. In the case of Malaysia, migrant labour was brought to fill the gap. So the real question that needs to be addressed is not so much the artificial creation of labour shortage or the lack of incentives but rather, structural changes at the level of employment.[8]

The MTUC, the Malaysian labour centre, has been in the forefront of campaigning for better wages for Malaysian workers. It was this outfit that proposed the government should introduce a minimum of RM1,200 a few years ago based on the guidelines proposed by the International Labour Organization (ILO). Although the government has not seriously commented on the proposal of minimum wage of local workers, employers have refused to concede on the question of minimum wage. Their argument is that if minimum wage were not tied to the productivity of workers, employers would not be in a position to take the financial responsibility. Of course, in the industrial relations circles, employers' opposition to wage increases of workers is well-known. The argument of the MTUC is that one of the reasons why employers have refused to concede wage increases to local labour is because of the ready availability of foreign labour. By threatening to displace local workers with foreigners, employers could prevent or stall local workers from bringing up wage and related demands. The MTUC has brought up this matter a number of times in the past to the government, but no employer has received any warnings from the government to date.

Of course, even within a similar trade, there is wage differential between locals and foreigners, but such a gap may not be very wide. The argument by the MTUC is not without merits; the employers have been cushioned against production cost increase by the ready availability of foreign labour. By using foreign labour during crucial periods, employers can prevent wage increases. This explains why whenever the government wants to adopt any drastic move against migrant labour, employers step in to ensure that their immediate benefits are not jeopardized. It is not that the philosophy of the government and employers are at odds; the difference may be only at the superficial level. At a more fundamental level, cheap labour policy has been endorsed by the government to attract multinational companies to the shores of Malaysia. In fact, cheap labour policy has been used by the government to position the economy in a particular location within the international production hierarchy. Thus, unless and until the economy emerges from this particular doldrum, it would be inconceivable for the country to shift its location to a different level in the international production hierarchy. Of course, for this to take place, other macro changes are necessary to bring about improvement in the human resource formation, the sort of area that is so crucial for qualitative changes in the economy.

If the economy is dependent on migrant labour, then how is the government going to reduce or eliminate this dependence in the near future? While bilateral agreements with the sending countries are important in terms of regulating and control the flow of labour, they are, however, not sufficient. As it is, the existing bilateral agreements with sending countries like Indonesia have not contributed to a slowing down of the flow of labour. The problem is, bilateral agreements do not address the structural problem of the economic and development differential between the sending and receiving countries. Even if the sending countries take the initiative to prevent the flow of migrants, there is no way such an initiative would be very effective. Long porous borders between countries such as Indonesia and the Philippines with Malaysia, the presence of syndicates and agents specializing in the export of labour, existence of corrupt officials and the prospect of making fast cash from the migrants makes it difficult to check the flow of labour. It has been suggested that the problem of migrant labour needs to be addressed at the regional level through certain developmental initiatives. It is only when there is more equitable economic development in the region as a whole that incentives for migration would reduce.

It is rather unfortunate that the Southeast Asian countries never gave much importance to the question of labour in addressing regional economic issues. Even though the ASEAN Free Trade Area (AFTA) was initiated in the early 1990s to reduce tariffs and non-tariff barriers to improve the flow of investments between ASEAN states and with the developed countries, no mention was made about the nature of labour flows in the region. It would have been a positive move had the members linked development with labour requirements so that it could have provided a way out to reduce dependence on foreign labour. In fact, had labour been included in the agenda of AFTA, a schedule could have been worked out between sending and receiving countries as to how they could tackle the problem of migrant labour. Even if AFTA is not the proper forum, given the contentious nature of the migrant problem, some other arrangement could be worked out to address the issue of migrant labour. However, at the end of the day, it appears that ASEAN members are not too serious about using regional economic or political forums to discuss and resolve problems that are common to them.[9] Instead when problems crop up, they try to fall back on a bilateral approach to resolve problems. Recently, given the hue and cry about the treatment of Filipino illegal migrants, the Philippine Government sought the co-operation of the Malaysian authorities to temporarily suspend the deportation of workers until a team sent by President Gloria Arroyo could ascertain the true nature of complaints of those detained in the labour camps in Sabah.

Socio-Cultural Impacts

Migrants might have come into the country for economic reasons, but their long presence in the country have a definite impact on the society. During the earlier phase of migration, thousands of Indians and Chinese came into the country as workers in the colonial economy. After some time, many of them came to regard Malaya as their home. This settlement of Indians and Chinese contributed to the creation of a multi-racial and multi-religious society. The recent phase of migration that started in the early 1970s basically involved the flow of migrants from Indonesia and the Philippines. While the majority of Indonesians entered Peninsular Malaysia, those from the Philippines moved into the state of Sabah. Apart from economic opportunities, geographical proximity between different territories in the region and cultural and religious links provided for the movement of peoples of different nationalities. In the first two decades of the flow of migrants principally from Indonesia and the Philippines, there is evidence to indicate that they were welcomed not only for economic reasons but also for political reasons. Given the nature of ethnic politics and political rivalry between Malays and non-Malays, it was felt by some people both in the government and outside, that the flow of migrants mostly of the same ethnic stock as Malays would contribute to increasing their population. This would have the effect of slowly reducing the power and the electoral strength of non-Malays in the country. In the state of Sabah, political rivalry between Muslims and non-Muslims also factored in the generous provisions given to Filipino Muslims to become permanent residents.[10]

Although it is difficult to ascertain the number of Indonesians and Filipinos who became permanent residents and citizens, some reliable sources say that it was quite considerable. The steady increase of the Malay population in the last two decades and the shrinking of the non-population were not mainly attributable to the higher birth rate among Muslims, but also to migrants taking up citizenship in the country. In recent years, foreign migrants may not be receiving the same privileges as before; the dilution of rivalry between Malays and non-Malays, the emergence of Malay opposition and the dependence of the ruling party on Chinese and Indians for electoral victory have changed the configuration of Malaysian politics to some extent. Such a change may have lessened the enthusiasm on the part of some in the government to provide any advantage for migrants. However, it has to be observed that it was the politics of the country during a particular period that could have provided for assimilation between migrants and the local Malay population.

Therefore it cannot be said that there is a high degree of compartmentalization between migrants and locals. As said earlier, there was some degree of assimilation between migrants from Indonesia and the Philippines with local Muslims. Government policy aimed at increasing the political power of Malays paved the way for migrants' integration with the local Muslims. Since migrants were of the same ethnic stock as Malays and professed the same religion, assimilation was not too difficult from a cultural angle. However, in recent years, migrants may not have had the same opportunities that they had before and this means that the government may not be encouraging migrants to make Malaysia as their home. Increased migrant presence in the country, problems with illegal labour, economic difficulties, unemployment, the tendency on the part of some segment of migrant population to engage in criminal activities and the growing class differentiation within the Malay society could have contributed to a situation where some permanent barriers could have been erected between migrants and locals.

Is there a strong link between the presence of migrants and their engagement in criminal activities? It is often assumed in Malaysia, without any scientific basis, that migrants have the tendency to engage in criminal activities. This is the reason that the government often cites for taking strong actions against migrants. Although migrants engage in crime, such engagement is not so much because they are migrants but because of certain economic circumstances. In this respect, there is no difference between migrants and locals; both categories of people engage in criminal activities under conditions of economic difficulty. It has been reasonably established that migrants have the tendency to be involved in robberies, murders and others during periods of economic difficulties. Lack of employment and non-payment of wages by employers have often been revealed as two most important factors that drive migrants to engage in crime. However, in the Malaysian context, there is a popular perception that migrants have a natural propensity to commit criminal acts. This perception, without any empirical basis, seems to be the product of a perception that migrants who engage in crimes are those illegally present in the country.

It is true that a number of migrants have been involved in criminal acts such as robberies, rapes and murders. Women migrants have been arrested for engaging in vice-related activities. The involvement of a small number of immigrants in these kinds of undesirable activities does not reflect upon the entire migrant population. The majority of them come into the country to earn a living so that they could support their families back home. However, because of the presence of a large number of illegal immigrants, it seems to be popularly assumed that migrants are not honest and will engage in all kinds of wrongdoings if ever they get the opportunity. If some migrants become involved in criminal activities, there is always the tendency to generalize. During periods of high labour demand, there will be less focus on the social ills of migrants. However, when there is economic slowdown leading to unemployment, much attention will be paid to the social problems created by migrants. It is during periods of economic slowdown that the law enforcement authorities will be directed to round up and deport migrants for their illegal presence as well as for posing social problems. In the mid-1980s and late 1990s, during periods of recession and financial crises, thousands of migrants were deported from the country not only for economic reasons but also because they were thought to be involved in undesirable social and criminal activities.

As remarked earlier, it is perhaps true that migrants may indulge in criminal activities during periods of economic slowdown as result of unemployment and loss of income. However, scientific basis for the verification of this hypothesis is not there. But the government has to come up with an acceptable rationale for the deportation of migrants during periods of economic crises. They cannot be deported just because there are no jobs; other reasons are used to reinforce the argument that the continued presence of migrants may pose not only economic but also social problems.

As result of the 1997 financial crisis, the Malaysian economy suffered as much as some of the economies of the regional countries. Although the government undertook measures to mitigate the worst effects of the crisis, economic recovery was rather slow. Not only was there high unemployment, but also foreign investors were rather slow in coming into the country. This was the time that Malaysia had a considerable presence of migrants both legal and illegal. Retrenchment exercises by some big private companies added to the problem of unemployment. Given this situation, the first priority of the government was to adopt measures to get rid of the sizeable migrant population. Economic slowdown of the country was one good reason for getting rid of illegal migrants, but it was not good enough. In this respect, the involvement of migrants in criminal and undesirable social activities were slowly highlighted to paint a negative picture of their presence in the country. It had to convince the public and obtain the mandate that it was acting in the best interests of Malaysians. Thus, before the government could introduce a tough legislation to deal with the problem posed by illegal migrants, it had to create a scenario to show that migrants in the country were troublemakers. Recently when hundreds of migrant workers went on strike and demonstrated in the town of Nilai to protest against bad working conditions and the non-payment of wages by employers, riot police were summoned to control the situation. Although there was some damage to property, demonstrators were detained to be deported. The mainstream media had a field day in highlighting the protests engaged by demonstrators and set the stage for the government to come up with more stringent measures to stem the flow of migrants.[11]

It is not that social problems of migrants are manufactured by the government for some ulterior motives. The very fact of migrant existence side by side with locals give rise to a number of social and cultural problems. Since Malaysia is a multi-ethnic and multi-cultural country, the everyday kinds of problems of co-existence can be resolved within the larger legal framework of the society. Moreover, co-existence does not imply that migrants and locals have reached a certain degree of integration or assimilation. While there was some degree of integration/ assimilation during the early period, presently there are restrictions on this. As said earlier, the government is not totally preoccupied with the Malay versus non-Malay question any more to provide encouragement for Indonesians and Filipinos to become integrated with the local Muslim population. Moreover, the growth of the Malaysian middle-class in general and Malay middle-class in particular during the period of the

NEP seems to have influenced the government to promote and sustain the values and norms of this particular class for the purpose of ideological legitimacy. From this vantage point, the migrants are now seen by the government as a particular alien sub-altern group that have been allowed into the country to support its developmental programmes in general and buttress the role of the middle-class.

The social distance between the migrants and locals have been maintained by the introduction of laws and regulations that make it difficult for the former to get married and think of eventually settling down in the country. This is why the government insists that migrants who marry locals cannot be granted permanent resident status and that they have to return to their homes upon expiry of their work permits. While there may be some difficulty in enforcing such a provision on migrants from Indonesia and the Philippines given their religious and cultural similarities, migrants of other nationalities intending to make Malaysia their home country could find it difficult. Those migrants who applied for permanent stay in the country as result of their marriage with locals have been turned down by the government. In the mid-1990s, the media reported a number of cases of Bangladeshi men harassing local women. Furthermore it was also reported that a number of Bangladeshi men had violated their terms of entry into the country by marrying local women. The government came up with the strict warning that those caught breaking the law or violating their terms of contract would be deported. In fact, a few were deported for being involved in fights with the locals. Given the negative publicity created by the media on Bangladeshi workers, the Bangladesh Government feared that their citizens might not be allowed into Malaysia any more. However, as result of the initiatives of the Bangladesh High Commission and other parties, the Malaysian Government was quite satisfied that Bangladeshi workers would not cause problems in the future.

Recent surveys of the attitudes of Malaysians towards migrant workers indicate that there is no great degree of hostility towards migrants. At work places, relationship between migrants and locals seems to be amicable. Locals do not feel that the presence of migrants might pose an economic threat. Although migrants and locals might work side by side in establishments, there is no dynamic interaction. Of course, they have been cases of locals marrying migrants, some conflict between migrants and locals and others, but beyond this, any relationship between both categories of workers is practically nil. Given the fact that migrants are here for a short period, do not command wages like Malaysians and are often subjected to abuse and discrimination, locals feel that they are one level above the migrants. And unlike locals who have the freedom of movement and job mobility, migrants are bound by their legal contracts which stipulate that changing jobs other than those specified in the contract requires obtaining the permission of relevant government authorities. Given the unequal nature of their location in economic establishments, both categories of workers do not really come together to confront and resolve problems of exploitation of employers. In this respect, the existence of migrant workers presents excellent opportunities for employers to deny material and other benefits for both segment of workers.

Political Impacts

Large-scale presence of migrants in the country would not have become a reality without the green light provided by the government. From the 1970s onwards, it was the nature of economic development that necessitated the government to bring in migrants from Indonesia and the Philippines. Of course, the high profile nature of conflict and competition between Malays and non-Malays to some extent influenced the government to allow migrants to settle in the country to sustain the population growth for the former. The initial attitude on the part of the government towards migrant labour was conditioned by economic and political factors. Of course, as long as the economy was viable and there were abundant employment opportunities, the presence of a migrant population constituted no problems for the government. In the 1970s and 1980s, complaints made by some Chinese-based political parties of the presence of large numbers of illegal immigrants, how some had acquired citizenship and their involvement in criminal activities were not taken seriously by the government. In fact, the government very often used to brush aside these complaints.

The government's position on migrant labour began to change slowly from the mid-1980s onwards. First, the recession in the mid-1980s revealed the vulnerable nature of the country's economy. Retrenchment, job losses and closing down of factories and plants necessitated the government to do some hard thinking on how to stabilize the economy. It was in this context that the government felt there was need to check and regulate the flow of large numbers of illegal immigrants in the country. For instance, the Medan Agreement reached between Malaysia and Indonesia was aimed at regulating and control the flow of labour. Second, the social problems created by migrants also influenced the government to some extent, to adopt more stringent polices in controlling the flow of migrants. Media reports of migrants engaged in robberies, murders and rapes could not be ignored by the law enforcement agencies. What is more, when victims of robberies happened to be some prominent citizens, the government was forced to intervene. Third, although the government encouraged the flow of migrants not only for economic but political reasons, there was growing realization that many groups in the country were taking advantage of the government's liberal policy by selling identity cards and even citizenships. This was particularly notorious in Sabah where local politicians were literally selling identity cards to migrants from the Philippines. This was brought to the attention of the federal government many times in the past by those groups and political parties in the opposition camp.

While the government felt that flow of migrant labour should be regulated and controlled, it found many obstacles. First, it could not adopt a tough policy because of the economy's dependence on migrant labour. It was clear by the 1990s, that sectors such as construction, plantations, domestic services and others primarily functioned on the basis of migrant labour. Without migrant labour, these sectors would be undermined, causing irreparable loss to the economy. Second, the government realized that it could not go against the wishes of employers, both local and foreign. Given the nature of dependence, employers have often impressed upon the government that getting rid of migrants would cripple the economy. On a number of occasions, it was employers' pressure that prevented the government from adopting harsh measures towards migrant labour. Recently, again it was employers' pressure that prevented the government from fully enforcing its new law on immigration. Fourth, there is dilemma for the government; that is, how to effectively curb the flow of cheap labour into the country without affecting the country's position as the provider of cheap labour for multinationals. Unless this dilemma is resolved in the coming years, attempts taken to curb the flow of migrants would not seriously materialize. Fifth, it is also realized that the flow of migrants into Malaysia cannot be seriously checked if some of the sending countries are indeed encouraging the flow, such as Indonesia and the Philippines. Recently, when the government enforced the new law to take action against illegal migrants, there was much protest from Indonesia and the Philippines.

Regional Forum

While the government may not admit it, getting rid of illegal migrants poses problems of great magnitude. As witnessed recently, it could even lead to a major diplomatic confrontation between Malaysia and countries such as Indonesia and the Philippines. Since the issue of migrant labour involves so many countries in the region, bilateral moves to resolve the problem just may not work. Even though Malaysia has bilateral agreements with Indonesia, the Philippines, and other countries, they do not seem to have an impact on the movement of migrants especially those illegal ones. It is rather strange why countries in this region have not approached the problem of migrant labour from a more regional perspective. If a regional perspective has been suggested to resolve problems of security and economic development, one wonders why the migrant labour issue has not gone beyond narrow bilateral concerns. The formation of ASEAN during the Cold War period provided a tremendous boost for the countries concerned to address security related issues. After the end of Cold War, ASEAN was transformed into a larger political mechanism for the improvement of relations between Asean countries and to undertake economic development. However, with the onset of globalization and the formation of regional blocks, the concept of AFTA (ASEAN Free Trade Area) was mooted to reduce tariff and non-tariff barriers and as the same time, to facilitate the flow of investments and trade between ASEAN countries and the developed ones.

AFTA represents a co-ordinated regional response to take advantage of globalization by removing the barriers that stand in the way of trade, technology and investment flows. But then in a typical ASEAN manner, one important issue of globalization is missing from the AFTA's larger agenda, that is, the issue of migrant labour. AFTA should not be seen as a regional mechanism merely to attract foreign capital, it should be also a forum to discuss the obstacles that stand in the way of regional integration. Now, one of the problems of regional economic integration faced by AFTA members is the existence of differential development between the member countries. This differential is the main reason for the flow of labour from one place to another in the region. Thus, without this economic differential, there would not be problems of large-scale flow of migrants, say, from Indonesia and the Philippines. While AFTA does not address the issue of economic differential in a systematic manner, it is implicitly hoped that deregulatory exercises performed by the member countries according to the schedule drawn up would equalize the level of development.

Although labour centres such as MTUC and the ASEAN Trade Union Council (ATUC) have raised the issue of linking economic development with labour rights, AFTA as whole does not seem very much concerned with incorporating the labour dimension. The traditional antipathy of ASEAN leadership towards organized labour is perhaps the main reason why AFTA has no place for labour. While the labour centres mentioned want AFTA to link economic development with labour rights, they do not, however, make a case of dealing with the major problem of abuse of migrant labour. Either AFTA or trade union centres have the answers in dealing with myriad problems of development of the region. But then focusing merely on economic development predicated on the basis of neo-liberal ideology is not enough from a social development perspective. Even if AFTA's objectives have been set and alteration might create problems, there is always the option of suggesting another regional forum for addressing not just the migrant labour issue but also the problem of labour in general.

Since the migrant labour issue has the potential to undermine the diplomatic and political relations between sending and receiving countries, it is about time that this issue is prioritized for discussion and debate in a regional forum. Such a regional forum, if it is adopted, would contribute to "regionalizing" the issue so that countries could go beyond mere bilateral concerns. It is obvious that the migrant issue is not a bilateral one and emphasis on bilateralism might contribute to more problems. As it is, as a result of Malaysia's tough policy towards migrants, there are some circles in Indonesia talking about reviving its old confrontationist policy towards Malaysia and some Filipino legislators are thinking of reviving claims over the state of Sabah. ASEAN can hardly allow such developments to undermine the spirit of political and economic solidarity of the region.

Conclusion

This chapter examined the impact of migrant labour on the Malaysian society. It was argued that although migrants are not seen to deprive job opportunities for Malaysians, they are nonetheless used by employers to prevent wage hikes and trade union rights of locals. It can be assumed that in the absence of migrant labour, trade union rights would have been enhanced. From a social-cultural perspective, it can be said that conditions for the integration/assimilation of migrants are not as before. Although there are occasional conflicts between migrants and locals, they are not major. They are often caused by the uneasy and mechanical nature of interactions between locals and migrants at their work places. Since migrants are constituted in the lowest socio-economic order, locals do not feel that migrants are a real threat to them in terms of job competition or better wages. It was argued that maintenance of social distance between migrants and locals have been assisted and sustained not only by employers for their own interests but by the government as well.

Given the class differentiation of the Malaysian society and the emergence of the middle-class, it has necessitated the government to capitalize on this class for its hegemonic role. This means, among other things, that the maintenance of social distance between migrants and locals has to be perpetuated in class terms. From a political perspective, the government is basically in a quandary as to what can be done with migrants. The political urgency to reduce their flow has been hampered by the economic dependence and employers' pressure. It is asserted that bilateral relations between sending and receiving countries may not be the best option to resolve problems of migrant labour; a regional perspective is required. Such a perspective would be able to link the political with the material so that any action to reduce the financial and social burdens of migrants have to take the larger context of equalizing development in the region.

Notes

[1] If there were nine million workers in Malaysia, then the presence of foreign migrant workers would constitute about 23 per cent.

[2] Figure provided by newspapers reports.

[3] There are real fears that if the migrant issue is not dealt with properly, a major

diplomatic row between Malaysia and Indonesia or the Philippines cannot be avoided.

[4] Within the capitalist context, it is only safe to speak about two major waves of migration into the country. Of course, there were earlier migrations within the region, but these had a different character altogether.

[5] A complete picture of the migration process has to take into account a host of factors: political, social and economic conditions in the sending countries, the presence of agents and recruiters with a vast network of connections both in the sending and receiving countries, the demand for labour in receiving countries and not to speak about historical and traditional relations between different peoples in the region.

[6] It is estimated that migrants repatriate about RM 4.5 billion every year from Malaysia to their home countries.

[7] The MTUC has been one of the most outspoken organizations that has been consistently opposed to the easy entry of foreign workers in Malaysia, especially those that come without proper documentation. But the pleas of the MTUC on the negative impact of foreign workers on the country have not received the sympathetic consideration of the government.

[8] To what extent labour shortage in the country is the creation of employers is debatable, although the unions endorse this as fact.

[9] The contentious nature of the migrant issue and the possibility that this might affect diplomatic relations between some countries have led some analysts to suggest that the resolution should take a regional approach.

[10] The problematic issue is not so much that migrants were given the right to stay permanently in Sabah, but rather, how they were used by some politicians to vote in elections.

[11] The incident in Nilai, a small town in the state of Negeri Sembilan, created much antagonism among locals against foreign migrants.

References

Ariffin, R. "Domestic Work and Servitude in Malaysia". Hawke Institute Working Paper Series, no. 11, University of South Australia, 2001.

Bowie, A. *Crossing the Industrial Divide: State, Society, and the Politics of Economic Transformation in Malaysia*. New York: Columbia University Press, 1991.

Chin, C.B.N. *In Service and Servitude: Foreign Female Domestic Workers and the Malaysian Modernity Project*. New York: Columbia University Press, 1998.

Crouch, H. *Government and Society in Malaysia*. Ithaca: Cornell University Press, 1994.

Jones, S. *Making Money Off Migrants: The Indonesia Exodus to Malaysia*. Hong Kong: Asia 2000 Ltd, 2000.

Hugo, G. "International Migration in South East Asia: Since World War II", Conference on International Migration in Southeast Asia: Challenges and Impacts, 30 September–1 October 2002, ISEAS, Singapore, 2002.

Rudnick, A. *Foreign Labour in Malaysia Manufacturing: Bangladeshi Workers in the Textile Industry*. Petaling Jaya: Insan, 1996.

Zehadul Karim, AHM, et al. *Foreign Workers in Malaysia*. Kuala Lumpur: Utusan Publications and Distributors Bhd., 1999.

10

Policies on International Migration: Philippine Issues and Challenges

Nimfa B. Ogena

Filipinos are fast becoming the most mobile race in the world today. This appears consistent with its varied cultural exposure. The present generations of Filipinos are largely of Malay descent (approximately 91.5 per cent), yet the norms and practices observed are a unique combination of the East and West. The Filipino culture is a product of centuries of colonization and migration; thanks to the Indonesians, Chinese, Spaniards, Americans, and Japanese.

The Philippine's modest economic growth is propelled by services, industry, agriculture, forestry, and fishing. Major exports include garments, semiconductors, and electronic, microcircuits, coconut products, tropical fruits, and sugar. But more than these, it is the people's hard work, resiliency, and patriotism that have helped the nation prevail over the domestic and global, political, and economic challenges it continues to face.

The Situation

The Philippines is now the second largest labour-sending country in the world, next to Mexico. Recent data show that an average of 2,500 Filipinos leave the country every day and about 7.41 million Filipinos, representing about ten per cent of the current Filipino population, are living in more than one hundred and ninety-two foreign countries in various continents of the world (CFO et al. 2002, ECMI 2002). Not included in this estimate is the likely three million migrant workers who are undocumented and illegally working abroad (Jimenez 2002).

Of the 7.41 million overseas Filipinos, roughly 3.05 million are overseas Filipino workers, 2.74 million are permanent residents, and 1.62 million are classified as irregular. The top five countries of destination for overseas Filipino workers are the Kingdom of Saudi Arabia, Hong Kong, Japan, Taiwan, and the United Arab Emirates. For the emigrants or permanent residents (including fiancées/spouses of foreign nationals), the major destination countries are the United States of America, Canada, Australia, Japan, Germany, and United Kingdom.

However, gender stereotyping of occupations of overseas Filipino workers (OFWs) exists. Women dominate in the service occupations (9 out of 10), as well as in professional and technical occupation categories (3 out of 4). In 2000, an estimated 600,000 women OFWs were domestic helpers in nineteen major destinations worldwide. There are at least 47,017 Filipino entertainers in five countries in Asia with about 95 per cent of them in Japan. The rest are in Hong Kong, Macao, South Korea, and Saipan (POEA 2000). Official statistics clearly reveal an increasing number of women both in the internal and international migrant flows. The percentage share of deployed women OFWs has steadily increased from 12 per cent in 1975, to 47 per cent in 1987, to 58 per cent in 1995, and 61 per cent in 1998 (POEA 2000).

The Philippine Overseas Employment Administration (POEA) classifies OFWs into two categories: either land-based or sea-based. Occupations in the land-based category are broader and cover almost all skill areas, from domestic helper to managers. Sea-based work pertains mostly to ship operations like navigation, engineering, and maintenance. There are also Filipino workers in large passenger vessels and they fulfil a variety of jobs, from kitchen staff to on-board entertainers. Prior to 1976, deployed sea-based OFWs outnumbered their land-based counterparts by a 2:1 ratio. This changed starting 1977 when land-based OFWs began to significantly outnumber sea-based OFWs.

In the late 1970s and early 1980s, the Middle East region was the primary destination for OFWs because of the "construction boom" spurred by the surge of millions of petro-dollars. In the late 1980s and

1990s, more than 90 per cent of OFW deployment went exclusively to two regions: Asia and the Middle East. In 1987, 71.2 per cent of OFWs went to the Middle East while 23.7 per cent went to Asia. During the same year, seven Middle East countries figured in the list of top ten host countries of deployed OFWs. Nearly 200,000 OFWs went to the Kingdom of Saudi Arabia, the nation with the largest share of OFWs in the world. In the 1990s, six of the top ten host countries were from East and Southeast Asia (POEA 2000).

Surveys have detected a selectivity-taking place in the labour migration process. Based on data cited by various studies (Ogena 2000) migration seems to be dominated by persons in their prime ages. Close to 60 per cent of migrant workers are in their early 20s and 30s. In terms of sex characteristics, an overwhelming majority (75 per cent) of the OFWs up to the early 1980s were males, a phenomenon that can easily be attributed to the demands of the construction sector in the Middle East.

In recent years, however, there is increasing feminization of migrant labour streams particularly to the countries in Asia (Japan, Hong Kong, Singapore) where the demand for domestic helper, nurses, entertainers, and other types of service workers is high (Go 1991). The documented women migrant workers from the Philippines, based on data collected by the National Commission on the Role of Filipino Women (NCRFW), have a particular profile. First, they are young, mainly in the 20–29 age group (women are generally younger than their male counterparts who are likely to be 25–39 years old. Second, they are unmarried (56 per cent were unmarried in 1992 and 1993, in contrast to most male migrant workers, 72 per cent of whom were married in 1992 and 1993; among domestic women workers, the proportion of unmarried was as high as 80 per cent) (Asis 1994). Third, about half of women migrant workers have completed some college education (one-fourth have college degrees, although more male migrant workers are college educated). Finally, most women migrant workers come from Luzon, also the region that contributes the most number of migrant men (Guerrero et al. 2001).

About one-third of the country's entire population are directly or indirectly benefiting from remittances sent by family members and relatives abroad. In 1999, the remittances of Filipino international labour migrants amounted to US$6.8 billion (POEA 2000). Not included in this estimate are remittances sent through informal channels. There is no doubt that OFW remittances have made labour export the single biggest dollar earner of the country. In the first quarter of 1999, these remittances amounted to 21 per cent of the 224.8 billion pesos gross national product (POEA 2000). A large proportion came from women migrant workers who now comprise the majority of OFWs.

The remittances of overseas Filipinos have contributed significantly in keeping the current account deficit manageable and in stabilizing the economy. It is not surprising, therefore, that the government has begun to refer to overseas workers as modern-day heroes as these funds assuage the balance of payments condition of the country.

Overseas Filipinos also send financial and material assistance to the country through government agencies and NGOs for less privilege groups and individuals, as well as under-served communities. The donations fund and support activities for relief and rehabilitation, education and scholarships, health equipment/facilities and medical missions, water and sanitation facilities, and livelihood assistance. Through the efforts of the Commission of the Filipinos Overseas, an estimated 1.041 billion pesos in donations have been sent by overseas Filipino groups through the *Lingkod sa Kapwa Filipino* (service to Filipinos) or LINKAPIL program from 1990 to 2001 for projects in seventy-one provinces. Major sources of these donations include Filipinos in the United States, Germany, Canada, Australia, and Japan.

The support of the overseas Filipinos is not limited to material/financial assistance. They also facilitate the transfer of information and technology in the country. Various opportunities are available for Filipinos overseas to visit the Philippines and share their expertise with local counterparts through lectures, workshops, and other volunteer work. These avenues include the *Balik*-Scientist Programme of the Department of Science and Technology (DOST) and the Volunteers to the Philippines Programme of the Commission of the Filipino Overseas (CFO) in the Philippines, as well as exchange programs conducted by Filipino associations overseas. Aside from these activities, partnerships for research or special projects are being encouraged between Filipinos overseas and local counterparts to pass on new knowledge and/or develop indigenous technology.

Policies

Initially conceived as a stopgap mechanism in the 1970s in response to the oil price hikes and the large demand for labour in the Middle Eastern

Countries, the Philippines quickly instituted pertinent measures to address the growing labour outflows. The 1974 Labour Code affirmed the government's explicit policy on overseas employment. It created the Overseas Employment Development Board (OEDB) and the National Seaman's Board (NSB), which are the precursors of the POEA. Their mandate was to undertake a systematic programme for overseas employment, which included the banning of direct hiring and the mandatory remittance of overseas worker's earnings. The mission of the present POEA is to ensure quality employment opportunities for OFWs.

The Overseas Workers Welfare Administration (OWWA) was created to protect the interests and well being of OFWs and their families and dependants. With funds derived from employer contributions, OWWA finances an array of programmes and services for migrant workers and their families. These include legal, livelihood, welfare, enterprise, career development and skills upgrading assistance, and benefits.

Republic Act 8042 or the Migrant Workers and Overseas Filipinos Act of 1995 spells out the benefits of overseas employment through the provision of a mechanism for full protection to migrant workers even while the migrants are still in the Philippines. More importantly, the law contains provisions on protecting OFWs in the host countries where they are susceptible to abuse and exploitation. The programmes and services provided for R.A. 8042 are anchored on the following policies. First, the dignity of the citizens, whether in the country or overseas, and Filipino migrant workers, in particular, shall be upheld. Second, Filipino migrant workers shall be provided with adequate and timely social, economic, and legal services. Third, overseas employment shall not be promoted as a means to sustain economic growth and achieve national development. The existence of the overseas employment programme rests solely on the assurance that the dignity and fundamental human rights and freedoms of the Filipino citizen shall not, at any time, be compromised or violated. Fourth, women and men shall be equal before the law; women shall have a significant role in nation-building. Fifth, an effective mechanism shall be instituted to ensure that the rights and interests of distressed overseas Filipinos, in general, and Filipino migrant workers, in particular, are adequately protected and safeguarded. Sixth, Filipino migrant workers and overseas Filipinos shall have the right to participate in the democratic decision-making process of the state and to be represented in institutions relevant to overseas employment. Seventh, the ultimate protection of all migrant workers shall lie in the possession of skills. Eighth, non-governmental organizations shall be recognized as partners in the protection of Filipino migrant workers and in the promotion of their welfare.

Through the years, legislative and policy measures promoting the welfare and protection of migrants have been pursued actively by both the executive and the legislative branches of government. Some of these are as follows. First, imposition of a minimum age requirement for those wanting to work abroad as domestic helpers to ensure that they are sufficiently mature and emotionally and psychologically ready to face the risks of overseas work. Second, enactment of Republic Act 6955, which forbids the operation of marriage bureaus and pen pal clubs matching Filipino women with foreigners for marriage. It also prohibits the advertisement, publication, printing and distribution of literature promoting mail-order brides. Third, the issuance by the Department of Foreign Affairs (DFA) of Department Order No. 15-89, which requires all Filipinos who are fiancées or spouses of foreign nationals to attend guidance and counselling sessions at the CFO prior to acquiring a passport.

Issues and Challenges

Deregulation

A current contentious issue is the deregulation of the labour export industry as mandated by Republic Act 8042, Section 29 entitled "Comprehensive Deregulation Plan on Recruitment Activities," which provides that:

> "Pursuant to a progressive policy of deregulation whereby the migration of workers becomes strictly a matter between the worker and his foreign employer, the Department of Labour and Employment, within one year from the effectivity of this Act, is hereby mandated to formulate a five-year comprehensive deregulation plan on recruitment activities taking into account labour market trends, economic conditions of the country and emerging circumstances which may affect the welfare of migrant workers."

Within a period of five years from the effectivity of this Act, POEA is expected to phase out its regulatory functions. However, there is confusion whether overseas employment should be deregulated or regulated because POEA is still expected to *regulate* private sector participation in the recruitment and overseas placement of workers by setting up a licensing and registration system despite deregulation.

Streamlining is used as the meaning and mechanism of deregulation (Opiniano 2001a). The POEA has been streamlining its regulatory functions and services since 1996 through the revision of POEA Rules and Regulations and provision of so-called "safety nets" to protect migrant workers.

The Philippine Migrants' Rights Watch (PMRW), a nine-member network of civil society groups working for migrants' rights protection, maintained that deregulation is "only sensible and effective in an environment where overseas migration is taken as an option". Fears of migrant workers being oppressed, however, remain prevalent especially with deregulation. If enforced, there is high reservation on provision of better protection for troubled migrant workers.

The recent pronouncement by the Arroyo administration toward exporting more workers has stimulated the debate. President Arroyo's admission that there is no way the economy can absorb millions of returning OFWs keep the economy afloat aggravated the fears of civil society. Deregulation was perceived as consistent with the government's aggressive move towards promoting and marketing OFWs, which necessarily translates to greater need for an upscaling of protection for OFWs. Overall, civil society fears POEA's concept of deregulation will do away with protection for overseas workers, while the overseas employment recruiters would prefer that POEA do away with all regulations.

Consequences on Families and Migrants Themselves

Behind the numbers are many stories of courage, survival, and the continuing struggle of migrant workers for recognition and protection. The large number of undocumented workers, unprotected by social and labour laws, has raised important social questions for host countries over issues of workers' welfare and human rights. Filipino labour migration affects a wide range of actors and agents, including the migrants, their families and communities, recruitment agencies and intermediaries, employers, Philippine and foreign government bodies in the Philippines and abroad, social service providers, and advocacy groups.

The 2000 Study on the Consequences of International Contract Labour Migration of Filipino Parents on their Children revealed significant sociological and psychological imprints on the children left behind by parents (NIRP Final Report 2001). Although overseas work of parents ensured that children were able to go to school and their other basic needs met, they were generally sad when the mother/father left for work abroad. Neither significant improvement on children's school performance nor influence of peers or friends was noted between children with and without parents working abroad. On health status, children with both parents working abroad were significantly healthier than children with only one parent overseas worker or no parents abroad, perhaps partly due to the higher income effect of the former.

The same survey showed that the mother's absence seems to have a stronger psychological effect on children left behind. Relative to the number of children with fathers abroad, there was a larger number of children with mothers abroad who perceived their parents' relationship was not stable; perceived that their family relationship deteriorated compared to five years earlier; did not perceive the family to be happier; viewed the family as generally sad and depressed; were often generally sad and depressed themselves; perceived that the mother or the father, in this case the father, had become more irresponsible; and claimed that many more responsibilities were delegated to the children when the mother was abroad.

The disheartening side of international migration is people trafficking, not only for labour, but also for sex. Although it is difficult to ascertain how many women have been trafficked, both undocumented and documented migrant women are especially vulnerable to the sex trade. The reported complicity of some government officials and agencies has made trafficking easier and monitoring more difficult (Beltran and De Dios 1992).

Vulnerability to HIV/AIDS infection is another real dimension of the Philippine international labour migration scene. The Philippine National AIDS Registry (PNAR) statistics in June 2002 revealed there of the 1,515 Filipinos infected with HIV/AIDS, about 407 or 27 per cent were OFWs, otherwise known as migrant workers living with HIV/AIDS (MWLWHAs). About 151 of the 408 OFWs with HIV/AIDS were seamen. Note that this figure is grossly under-estimated inasmuch as most Filipinos, whether migrant workers or not, have not taken HIV antibody tests.

To put a face to the often taken for granted statistic, allow me to quote a story that was featured in a local newspaper (Opiniano 2001b).

> Gie (not her real name), a tall stunning young beauty, likes to impersonate. This became her gate-pass to fulfil her dream of earning more from working abroad. At the tender age of 14, Gie left the country to work as an entertainer-

singer in Japan's glittery nightclubs. With this kind of job, she claimed she
endured all possible physical, sexual and emotional hardships that befall
to ladies like her. For almost two years of toiling, Gie said the club she had
worked with did not give her salary. Because of this, Gie escaped and went
home, and this time entered Malaysia as an undocumented worker. Upon
her return to the Philippines, Gie is already infected with the human
immuno-deficiency virus (HIV). As far as she can remember, Gie said she
might have been infected by Japanese men who used her upon the order of
her employer. "*Madami and nagdi-discriminate sa amin. Salot daw ako, sabi
nila, Tapos sinisisi and pagiging malandi ko* [Many discriminate against us.
They say I am a curse and they blame me for being a flirt]". Gie narrated
with tears shedding from her beautiful face. "*Care and support ang kailangan
naming, eh (dahil sa ginawa nila sa amin), parang hindi kami tao eh. Kailangan
naming eh unawa at suporta, lalo na mula sa gobyerno* [Care and support is
what we need (because of what they did to us) as human beings. We need
understanding and support especially from the government]" Gie said.

Gie represents the growing number of sea- and land-based Filipino
OFWs who are suffering from one of the most dangerous social costs of
migration: HIV and the acquired immune deficiency syndrome (AIDS).
Lamentably, Gie noted that although the pre-departure orientation seminars
(PDOS) for would-be OFWs already touch on the HIV/AIDS issue, neither
discussed in-depth are the social-cultural changes and subsequent
adjustments attendant to migration which would make migrant workers
vulnerable to HIV/AIDS, nor equally important issues relating to health,
gender and sexuality (Opiniano 2001b).

ACHIEVE, an NGO in the Philippines, noted that hostile immigration
and termination policies in some labour receiving countries contribute
to OFWs' vulnerability. Particularly affected are those working in the
entertainment and domestic work sectors. A contentious issue here is the
mandatory requirement of some countries of destination for testing of
OFWs. Oftentimes, migrant workers are subjected to these tests but
either without their permission, or through regular medical exams
without informing OFWs that their blood samples are subjected to the
HIV antibody tests.

When OFWs, particularly those with HIV, reintegrate themselves to
their families, MWLWHAs experience many personal struggles such as
alienation, stigma, depression and fear, coupled with limited employment
opportunities, financial want and even overseas work prohibition.
MWLWHAs are also experiencing discrimination, and difficulty in getting
prescribed medicines.

Reintegration of Returnees

The reintegration challenge is so immense for countries that export labour including the Philippines. Returning migrants suffer longer unemployment after their return and/or the savings from their overseas work gets depleted soon, forcing them to leave again to work abroad. To break this cycle, the government has instituted a reintegration programme that will assist returning OFWs to get back into the domestic economy. With overseas work contracts having six months to three years duration, the large volume of temporary labour migrants from the Philippines imply a huge annual labour traffic flow, some of whom opt to stay put after expiration of their contracts. This has been the government's biggest challenge as it continues to manage labour flows to maximize the economic benefits derived from international labour migration while minimizing the social costs that these exact on the individual worker, family and society.

The issue of reintegration was raised by NGOs as early as the 1990 when the Gulf War erupted and thousands of Filipino migrant workers were forced to evaluate and return home to escape from war. Without a comprehensive reintegration programme, many of the Gulf War returnees have remained dislocated, most of them had not been given their war claims; only those known to have died, been raped, and gotten injured were given compensation. Those who returned but experienced economic and psychosocial dislocation were left to fend for themselves. The first National Conference on OFW Reintegration held in April 2002 sponsored by the Overseas Workers Welfare Administration (OWWA), PMRW member Episcopal Commission on Migrants and Itinerant People (ECMI), BaliKaBayani Foundation, Atikha, and Unlad Kabayan, brought to fore the proposal of tapping and channelling migrants' remittances for the reintegration of migrants. Nevertheless, much remains to be seen pertaining to concrete measures that will address this issue perhaps through syndicated efforts from the government, NGOs and private sectors.

Human Rights Negotiation

In the face of implementing globalizing processes, labour-exporting countries have to re-negotiate for the protection of the welfare of OFWs, particularly the undocumented migrant workers (Piper and Ball 2001). After more than ten years of negotiations to reach a text that would be acceptable to everyone, the Migrant Workers Convention was adopted in 1990. The convention explicitly requires cooperation of state parties "with a view to (prevent) and (eliminate) illegal or clandestine movements". Many countries of origin have adopted a more or less regulated system to manage the exit of migrants. Everyone who enters and stays in a territory, whether authorized or not, should be guaranteed human rights protection; legal status is not a ground for discrimination.

Another twelve years passed yet only nineteen additional countries have ratified it. Quite a few of the recent signatories are major countries of origin of modern day migration, such as Mexico and Colombia in America, Egypt, Morocco and Senegal in Africa, the Philippines and Sri Lanka in Asia. Countries of destination are conspicuously absent among them are traditional countries of immigration such as the United States, Canada and Australia. As members of the European Union have reached a common policy on migration recently, unilateral ratification of international instruments by any member is discouraged even though some European countries are actively engaged in the drafting of the convention (Battistella 2002).

Battistella (2002) contends that the real issue behind the unwillingness of many countries to ratify the convention is political, rather than technical. Since the convention does not spell out an explicit responsibility for countries of origin to curb unauthorized migration, yet countries of destination have to provide protection for all migrants, even unauthorized migrants.

A recent case in point illustrates the necessity for the global ratification and adoption of the convention. Between July and October 2002, the Malaysian Government in its effort to formalize documentation of human migration flows, cracked down on illegal migrants and deported thousands of Filipino undocumented migrants. The Malaysian Government partially backed down, however, on its hard line policy as several events unfolded. The immediate replacement of deported workers in Malaysia's key economic sectors appears unlikely and crisis situation has begun to develop at the port of entry for the provision of food, transport, and shelter for the hundreds of thousands of deportees. Sadly, the deportations resulted in the death of twelve children and the rape of a thirteen-year-old deportee, which fuelled an anti-Malaysian sentiment that nearly strained diplomatic relations between the two countries (Sison 2002, Hok 2002). Following two personal appeals by the President of the Philippines, Gloria Macapagal

Arroyo, to the then Malaysian Prime Minister Mahathir Mohamad for improved conditions of Filipinos awaiting deportation and inquiry into press reports of the rape of a Filipino girl by Malaysian police, a moratorium on the arrest and deportation of Filipinos and an inquiry into the rape allegations was announced by Mahathir (Inglis 2002).

In the short-term, Malaysia is expected to continue to rely on foreign labour to fortify its economy. Hence, it will have to fall back on the co-operative management of labour flows in the region. Unlike the Philippines, Malaysia and Indonesia (the major source of Malaysia's undocumented workers) have not ratified the United Nation's International Convention on the Protection of the Rights of All Migrant Workers and Members of Their Families. Without a regional agreement among members of the Association of Southeast Asian Nations (ASEAN) countries and/or APEC countries on labour migration, conflicts of the present kind are likely to continue (Inglis 2002, Piper and Ball 2001).

In the face of globalization, human migration could be further constrained in the long-term as information technology may proxy for geographic movements. Nonetheless, as other countries begin to seriously enforce the documentation process in the entry and exit of people in their territories, a more humane treatment of persons affected would make the documentation process highly acceptable to the international community.

Concluding Remarks

The positive economic impact of overseas contract labour from the Philippines has been documented at both macro and micro levels. Mitigation of adverse political and social-psychological consequences remains as a central concern in the further improvement of its government policies. Government policy considers as a continuing challenge the improvement of protective measures for the welfare of migrants and their families. With most work contracts having a specific duration, a growing proportion of these labour migrants, specifically among those nearing retirement age, need assistance in putting their hard-earned remittances to productive purposes. Any government initiative towards the crafting of a comprehensive reintegration programme for migrants is a long overdue prospect awaited by the private sector and the NGOs alike. Finally, sending countries should find more innovative strategies that would convince receiving countries to provide human rights guarantees to everyone who enters and stays in a territory — authorized or not. As the top labour sending country in Asia, the Philippine Government is expected to proactively pursue initiatives toward attaining regional and international consensus on labour migration issues.

References

Asis, Maruja M.B. "Family Ties in World Without Borders". *Philippine Sociological Review* 42, nos. 1–4 (1994): 16–26.

Ateneo de Manila University and the Women's Education, Development, Productivity and Research Organization (WEDPRO). *The Phillipine-Belgian Pilot Project against Trafficking in Women*. Makati City, Philippines: Author, 1999.

Beltran, Mary Ruby P. and Aurora J. de Dios. *Filipino Woman Overseas Contract Workers: At What Cost?* Manila: Goodwill Trading Co., Inc., 1992.

Battistella, Graziano. Challenging the Migrant Workers Convention. *The Migrant Watch* 1, no. 2 (July 2002).

Commission on Filipinos Overseas (CFO). *Handbook of Filipinos Overseas. Sixth Edition*. Manila: CFO, 2002.

CFO, DFA, PECs, POEA, OWWA. Stock Estimates of Overseas Filipinos (as of December 2001). [One-page data sheet received from CFO], 2002.

Episcopal Commission for the Pastoral Care of Migrants and Itinerant People (ECMI), Catholic Bishops Conference of the Philippines. *Migration 2002. Situationer and Impact, Biblical Inspiration, Pastoral Challenges*, 2002.

Go, Stella. *Working in Japan: The Experience of Filipino Overseas Contract Workers*. Manila: Social Development Research Centre, De La Salle University, 1991.

Guerrero, Sylvia H., et al. *Women and Gender in Population and Development*, Quezon City: UP Centre for Women's Studies, 2001.

Hock, Kerk Kim. 2002. "Problem of Illegal Immigrants: Call on the Government to Seek the Consensus, Commitment and Cooperation of the Indonesia and Philippines Governments on Three Issues". Press Statement by DAP MP for Kota Melaka. <http://www.malaysia.net/dap/bul1714.htm> (viewed on 28 February 2003).

Inglis, Christine. "Malaysia Wavers on Labor Crackdown". *Migration Information Source*. Migration Policy Institute, Washington, D.C., 2002. <http://www.migrationinformation.org/Feature/display.cfm?ID=63> (viewed on 2/27/2003)

Jimenez, Cher. "Despite Global Woes, OFW Market Strong". *Today*, 2 May 2002, p. 1.

NIRP Final Report 2001. The Study on the Consequences of International Contract Labor Migration of Filipino Parents on Their Children. Final Scientific Report to the Netherlands-Israel Development Research Programme. University of the Philippines College of Social Sciences and Philosophy, Tel Aviv University and Friends of Filipino Migrant Workers, Inc. (KAIBIGAN). December 2002.

Ogena, Nimfa B. "International Migration, Human Resource Development and the Occupational Structure in the Philippines". *Proceedings of the International Workshop on International Migration and Human Resource Development in the APEC Member Economies.* APEC-HRD-NEDM and the Institute for Developing Economies, JETRO, Chiba, Japan. March 2000.

Opiniano, Jeremaiah. "POEA Convenes Tripartite Conference on Rules Revision: Civil Society Groups Express Fears about Deregulation of Overseas Employment". *Philippine Daily Inquirer*, 12 June, 2001*a*.

————. "OFWs, HIV and AIDS: RP's Labor Migration Policy Putting Pinoys in Inhumane Condition". Institute on Church and Social Issues. *Philippine Daily Inquirer*, 12 August, 2001*b*.

Piper, Nicola and Rochelle Ball. "Globalization of Asian Migrant Labor: The Philippine-Japan Connection". *Journal of Contemporary Asia* 31, no. 4 (2001): 533–54.

Philippine Overseas Employment Administration (POEA). *Landbased Overseas Filipino Workers by Destination and Deployment*. Official Statistics, POEA, 2000.

Sison, Marites. "Philippines: Rape Case Puts Migrant Workers Back in National Psyche". *Migration Stories*. IPS-Inter Press Service, 2002. <http://www.ipsnews.net/migration/stories/rapecase.html> (viewed on 28 February 2003).

11

Cross-border Migration in Indonesia and the Nunukan Tragedy

Riwanto Tirtosudarmo

"Boundaries do not merely obstruct people from free entrance but also create a gap between the two sides. Migration takes place because of this gap: migrants attempt to take advantage of it".

Koji Miyazaki (2000)

Migration, Borders and the State

Cross-border migration is one of the important demographic facts in the history of population movement in Southeast Asia. The boundaries separating countries, either land or sea, are always porous entities through which people and goods flow using establish routes and networks. Indonesia, currently the fourth most populous country in the world, possesses vast land and sea borders, in the north stretching as far as the Indian Ocean through the Straits of Malaka, The South China Sea, Borneo's borderland, the Celebes Sea, and the Pacific Ocean. In the east lies West Papua's borderland with Papua New Guinea, as well as the Arafuru Sea in the southeast separating Indonesia and the Australian continent. Previous studies have shown that movement within particular regions now separated by state borders is very common. For example, the movement of Minangkabau, to West Malaysia, the Sangirese to southern Mindanao in the Philippines and the West Papuans to New Guinea, as well as the Makasarese to Australia's Northern Territory.

The cross-border population movements have received more international attention recently to the extent that they tie in with issues of economic globalization. While the "traditional mobility networks" are maintained, in some areas they have been developing into new social and economic networks, products of the opening up of global market forces. Indonesia is no exception in this new development, particularly since the beginning of the 1970s as the overseas migrant workers started to flow out, particularly to the Middle East, and to our closest neighbour, Malaysia. The nature of migration flows dominated by low-paid and unskilled migrant workers provides a particular dynamic that is characterized, among other things, by its illegality and consequently for the migrants, their obvious lack of legal protection. In this chapter, the phenomena of cross-border migration will be discussed, specifically focusing on new cross-border trends, with particular emphasis on how the Indonesian Government and state is responding to these new trends, on the one hand, and the role of various non-state actors in advocating the faith of the migrant workers, on the other hand.

From the literature, we know that the modern function of boundaries is the result of the historical rise of nationalism in Europe over the past several centuries. This concept of the nation-state spread virtually worldwide through European colonialism. Under this notion, borders should be precisely defined, clearly demarcated, jealously guarded, and exclusive. This leads to a view that borders are lines separating distinct social systems, and borderlands become marginal, deriving legitimacy only through the relationship and participation in the core social systems, rather than as unique social systems.[1]

Until recently, as among others argues Asiwaju (1983, p. 3), the focus of border studies has been on the economies of states, on the conflict and diplomacy between states divided by borders, with the boundary as the point of reference, rather than on the people who inhabit the borderlands. Borderlands are generally neglected by state officials who regard such regions as fringe or marginal for economic development plans. Scholarly work has likewise been restricted by the existence of borders, either by the relative isolation of borderlands, the difficulty in obtaining government permission to conduct research there, the mistrust by borderlanders of outsiders asking a lot of questions, or by problems gaining access to relevant materials across the borders. Asiwaju further notes that just as roads and development projects decrease in importance and scale closer to the border, so too does scholarly research.

Focusing on borders between states and on the influence state activities have on life along borders, Martinez (1994) classifies borderlands into four historically related types. Each is defined in contrast to the others with no primacy of one type over the other. The first is the "alienated borderland" where cross-border interchange is non-existent because of warfare, political disputes, intense nationalism, ideological animosity, religious enmity, cultural dissimilarity, or ethnic rivalry. The second type is the "co-existent borderland" where cross-border conflict is reduced to a "manageable level" but where there is a still unresolved question about the ownership of strategic resources in the borderland. "Inter-dependent borderlands" form the third type. This is where borderlands on either side of a boundary are symbolically linked under relatively stable international relations. The people on both side, and the states, are involved in a mutually beneficial economy and on more or less equal basis; such as where one has production facilities, the other cheap labour (1994, pp. 8–9). Here significant gains from smuggling for one state might be felt as loses by the other (Collins 1985, p. 212). The fourth type is the "integrated borderland" where borderlands are economically merged, nationalism on both side's declines, and the states so linked are closely allied.

Using Martinez's classifications, borderland between Indonesia and Malaysia perhaps fall between the second and the third types: *co-existent* at the same time *inter-dependent*. It is *co-existent*, as conflict between the two countries, which occurred during the early sixties, has all but disappeared except for a lingering dispute over the islands of Sipadan and Ligitan near the border between Sabah and East Kalimantan. As we know, both countries have now brought this dispute before the International Court in The Hague.[2] The decision to bring the border dispute to The Hague reflects the political will on both sides to avoid unnecessary diplomatic backlash that could jeopardize the current good relationship. The establishment of ASEAN, and on a smaller scale BIMP-EAGA, obviously has played important roles in making the borderland's development between Indonesia and Malaysia more *inter-dependent*. However, the latest incident of mass deportation of undocumented Indonesian migrant workers from Malaysia that has already claimed a high death toll in the borderland (Nunukan) could create a new diplomatic tension and conflict if not properly solved by the countries. So, as far as the issues of borderland between Indonesia and Malaysia are concerned, as rightly argued by Asiwaju (1983, p. 3), the focus of both the authorities and the scholars has been on the economies of states, on the conflict and diplomacy between states divided by borders, with the boundary as the point of reference, rather than on the people who inhabit and cross the borderlands.

People who cross state borders to improve their economic well-being are essentially challenging the state's responsibility to protect its citizens' human security. The apparent failure of the state to protect the security of its people, while arguably exacerbated by the recent economic crisis, is generally rooted in its incomprehensible perception of human security. The dominant influence of perceptions of state security originating from a combination of strong inward-looking nationalism and military strategic interests have resulted in the inability to construct a state policy that could enhanced people's security.

The Establishment of Inward Looking Migration Policy

In Indonesia, internal migration has always been an important issue within the state's political agenda. This was mainly because both colonial and post-colonial states perceived that a range of the state's aims could be achieved through a migration policy. The state's policy on migration was formulated at the beginning of the twentieth century as a result of developments within the colonial elite class that eventually culminated in the formulation of the so-called Ethical Policy. The Ethical Policy was mostly concerned with raising agricultural productivity and had no intention of introducing drastic changes in the colonial economic structure by such means as large-scale industrialization. As Legge (1964) has argued, the measures taken by "ethical" colonial governments to improve the living standards of the indigenous population can only be seen as mere palliatives; they provided some alleviation of particular areas of hardship, but they did not achieve — and they did not attempt to achieve — any thorough-going technological changes. The importance of large-scale industrialization was actually stressed by a number of ethical reformers, but until the worldwide economic depression of the 1930s, the various plans suggested were not implemented.

From a different perspective, Kartodirdjo (1973), perceived that the rural history of Java in the nineteenth and early twentieth centuries was marked by sporadic movements of peasant unrest. Many of these erupted in more or less violent clashes with the colonial authorities. Protest movements and social unrest occurred between 1900–20 in various places in rural Java, such as in Tanggerang, Pamanukan, Sukabumi, Ciasem, Kuningan (West Java), Pekalongan, Gombong, Semarang (Central Java), Mojokerto, Sidoardjo, Kediri, and Jember (East Java).[3] Although a direct link between social unrest in rural Java and the initiation of the emigration policy cannot be established, it is not implausible to posit a cause-effect relationship. A major complicating feature of agrarian unrest in Java has been its correlation with social change in general and with the colonial impact in particular. Kartodirdjo (1973) strongly argued that the social movements had their background in the rapid penetration of a colonial economy whose impact on rural Java reached a climax during the course of the nineteenth century. The colonial rulers introduced a new legal and social relationship covering agrarian and labour matters. Excessive demands for compulsory services from the population and the levying of new taxes exacerbated popular discontent. Turning over some land to sugar cultivation and the exaction of a compulsory contribution of paddy rice had a direct bearing on some of the instances of social unrest.

As one of the three Ethical Policy objectives, Dutch colonial migration policy (*emigratie*) was therefore formulated and maintained as a result of a combination of three main factors. First were the political changes in the Netherlands which allowed the Calvinist-Catholic Coalition to come to power in 1901. The outstanding feature of the policy outcomes from this new coalition was the official abandonment of the goal of economic exploitation and the introduction of direct intervention in the economic sphere to improve the conditions of the indigenous population. The second factor was economic opportunity, particularly as seen by the Dutch capitalists after the whole archipelago was successfully brought under effective colonial control. The vast land areas on the outer islands attracted private companies looking to establish plantations. Given the scarcity of labour, Javanese were recruited as cheap labour for new economic activities. The third factor was social unrest in many parts of rural Java, resulting from simultaneous economic exploitation and population pressures. These, in turn, encouraged the colonial government to deal with social unrest by moving people to the outer islands. Emigration policy, as developed by the Dutch, therefore, can be summarized as a useful instrument to serve the many goals and interests of the state and its ruling elite. The relocation of people to ease social and political tensions is a form of demographic engineering to serve the state's economic and security purposes.

Over ten years later, after independence, the government formulated for the first time its Five-Year Development Plan from 1956–60 in which transmigration was described as an instrument to reduce population pressure in Java; provide labour in sparsely-populated provinces; support military strategy, and accelerate the process of assimilation (Hardjosudarmo 1965, pp. 128–29). The plan's most significant change in transmigration policy was its explicit reference to strategic military purposes whereas industrialization was no longer the goal. This was apparently due to increased political unrest in some regions resulting from disappointment with central government leadership. The important strategic role of transmigration was further emphasized in 1962 as a result of a change in the national constitution whereby President Sukarno proclaimed the so-called Guided Democracy system of government to replace the Parliamentary Democracy system that he considered to be a failure. The establishment of the autocratic Guided Democracy took place with the support of the central military leadership (Kuntjorojakti 1978, pp. 138–39).

Nitisastro, from a somewhat nationalist stance, criticized the Dutch assumptions that had led to enclave politics (Heeren 1979, p. 17). According to Nitisastro, the typical Dutchman's conservative politics had hampered the assimilation process among ethnic communities in the resettlement areas. Furthermore, Nitisastro argued that enclave politics were obviously in contradiction with the primary goal of Indonesian independence, building one Indonesian nation. Assimilating the Javanese with the local population was expected to bolster unification. However, this goal proved to be more difficult than the government or nationalists like Nitisastro, had anticipated. Wertheim (1959, p. 196), for example, noted from his observations in Lampung in 1956 that the assimilation of Javanese migrants resulted in neither a Sumatran nor a general Indonesian society, but rather a Javanese society modified by a Sumatran environment. This situation, according to Wertheim, led to the increasing resistance of *Sumatrans* to resettlement policies. Such resistance could seriously hamper further transmigration efforts, Wertheim argued, since the absorptive capacity of the outer islands is not only restricted by spatial and technical factors, but by social ones as well.[4]

At the beginning of the New Order, the real motive of President Suharto for the continuation of transmigration, however, is not difficult to identify. The explanation lies in the idea of harmony among the Javanese, which in the Indonesian political context can be translated into the concept of national unity and national integration, as suggested by Koentjaraningrat, the doyen of Indonesian anthropologists, and strongly endorsed by the President and the military.[5] In this context, transmigration was perceived as an instrument to accelerate the process of national integration. Government policies to relocate people from overcrowded Java to other islands were also considered as an alternative to land reform.[6] Despite this, the legacy of colonial policies, as well as the population policies of the Old Order (which were basically pronatalist and viewed the uneven distribution of population as the main population problem), could not be easily eliminated from the thinking of the ruling elite.[7]

The conventional view among the Indonesia's New Order economist-technocrats was that the rate of population growth is a significant determinant of the success of a country's economic development efforts. Compared with the problem of rapid population growth, which at the beginning of the New Order was accorded high priority; the problem of uneven population distribution between Java and outer islands had not been generally regarded by the economist-technocrats as an issue of urgency. Nitisastro (1970, p. 238), widely known as the architect of the New Order's economic development policies, strongly argued that what was needed to overcome the population problem in Indonesia was a massive development effort to create expanding employment opportunities accompanied by a rapid spread of fertility control. Yet, curiously enough, the problem of uneven population distribution and the role of transmigration as a means of overcoming it had long been a focus of government thinking, and became a very important policy within the national development plans during the New Order. The ruling elite's obsession on internal migration — a legacy of the colonial past —

emphasized the inward looking character of the state's perception of migration.[8]

Overseas Migrant Workers: Marginal Issue and Ad Hoc Policy Response

As described earlier, both in the colonial and early post-colonial periods, the state apparently gave little attention to the issue of international migration. Apart from the fact that the number of voluntary international migrants was relatively small, it had not yet become a political-economic issue in international relations. Many studies, however, have shown that labour movements from Indonesia to other countries were practised during the colonial period.[9] Following independence, particularly after the 1970s, the increasing international migration of unskilled labourers, particularly to Malaysia and Saudi Arabia, apparently had begun to attract the state's attention to the issues of international migration. It was not until the mid-1980s that the Indonesian Government began to pay more attention to the increasing number of international migrant workers, particularly those going to the Middle Eastern countries. In 1981, a private but well-connected Indonesian Manpower Supply Association (Asosiasi Perusahaan Jasa Tenaga Kerja Indonesia, APJATI) was formed to regulate the flow of workers to the Middle East. APJATI was a consortium of labour recruiting agencies, officially licensed by the Ministry of Manpower to broker job contracts with employers abroad and arrange for the conveyance of workers. As the stream of workers to the Middle East increased, the state began to see overseas employment as a useful tool to solve its own surplus labour problem, identifying it explicitly as such for the first time in the Fourth Five-Year Development Plan (1984–89).[10]

Around the mid-1980s, just as the government realized the perceived advantages of large-scale labour migration, the Indonesian press increasingly began to report cases of abuse against Indonesian women domestic workers in the Middle East, who constituted 87 per cent of the total Indonesian workforce employed there. The state's response to migrant workers to the Middle East (mostly as domestic helpers) was instigated by the increasing press reports on the violence and sexual abuse experienced by the workers in Saudi Arabia. The state's response to the issue of the negative experiences of female migrant workers shows the lack of intention to create policy measures to protect the overseas migrant workers. Instead, the state's response was primarily aimed at saving the bilateral relations with the Saudi Arabian Government and complained that the press reporting was biased against the Saudi Arabian Government. The then Minister of Labour, Retired Admiral Sudomo, a former Chief Executive of the Operation to Restore Order and Security Command (Komando Operasi Keamanan dan Ketertiban, KOPKAMTIB), in 1985, announced a ministerial decree stating that the migrant workers were not allowed to talk to the press about their experiences.

While press reports on the migrant workers in the Middle Eastern countries is more available, the slow but steady increase of cross-border movement to Malaysia seems unnoticed by the public. The flow of migration to Malaysia, both to the Malay Peninsula and Sabah as well Sarawak in Kalimantan, have a long tradition as many Malaysians originate from Indonesia. Since the early 1970s the rapid economic growth in Malaysia has increased the welfare of its population and resulted in a need for foreign labour to occupy low-wage occupations. The labour movement from Indonesia is therefore a natural economic trend as Indonesia always has a labour surplus. The Indonesian Government, as well as the public, apparently gave little attention to the labour movements to Malaysia. While in Malaysia the influx of Indonesian migrants had always become a major political issue, it attracted very little attention in Indonesia.[11] If there was any attention it most likely came from the business groups behind the labour recruitment agencies. Since the early 1980s, the Malaysian Government had begun to take serious steps in response to public demands to tackle the problem of illegal migrant workers. In 1984, for example, the Malaysian Government initiated an agreement with the Indonesian Government (Medan Agreement) to regulate migrant workers, specifically in the plantation and domestic services sectors, the largest source of employment of illegal workers from Indonesia. This policy was a failure due, among other reasons, to the reluctance of the employers, both in the plantation and domestic sectors, to support the implementation of policy regulation. Since then, several attempts to regularize the overseas migrant workers have been conducted, but not until the latest one, beginning in February 2002, has the Malaysian Government appeared seriously interested in dealing with the increasing numbers of undocumented migrants.

In Indonesia, the issue of overseas migrant workers, although it received greater attention in the so-called *"era reformasi"* (reformation era), is still generally confined in the margins of political discourse. The relatively marginal position of migrant issues also reflects the general situation of labour politics in Indonesia, a marginal issue for mainstream politicians. The efforts of the formerly suppressed labour union activists to enter mainstream politics are hampered by the fact that the political basis of the labour movement had been almost totally destroyed under three decades of New Order authoritarian regime.[12] The New Order propaganda that the labour movement is always associated with the Communist Party has significantly depoliticized labour issues. In addition, the relatively narrow base of industrialization processes in Indonesia have contributed to the small number of workers population that also limits their mobilization to play a significant role in national politics. Furthermore, the developmentalist ideology adopted by the economist-technocrats provides the New Order regime a quasi-scientific legitimation for suppressing the right for labour to freely organize.[13] The political discourse on labour during the New Order regime was therefore encapsulated into the notion of human resources within the economic development paradigm advocated by the economist-technocrats. In this regard, the replacement of the word *"buruh"* to *"pekerja"* clearly reflects the gross attempt by the state to erase the possibility of developing class-consciousness among labourers. The collapse of the New Order regime has released the state's restriction on labour forming free labour unions as well as entering national politics. Several workers' political parties were established by labour activists to articulate the political interest of labour, their political influence is however, still very slight.[14]

Since the early 1980s, compared with the issues of domestic labour, overseas migrant worker issues seemingly get more public attention, particularly as far as the press is concerned. Perhaps, the apolitical nature of the overseas migrant worker issues is less threatening for the government, which no longer suppresses the reports. Only in 1985, during the time when Sudomo became the Labour Minister, were the migrants prohibited from talking to the press regarding their problems as migrant workers in the Middle East. The press coverage on the plight of migrant workers, particularly those who work in the Middle East and Malaysia, has successfully raised their issues at the national level. In the case of migrant workers in the Middle East, the press specifically reported the human right abuses experienced by Indonesian female domestic workers. In the case of migrant labour to Malaysia, the focus of press coverage was on the various fatal risks incidents as many migrants enter Malaysia illegally. The horrifying risks experienced by illegal migrants to Malaysia ranged from the sinking of their boats before landing on Malaysian's shore and the brutal experience of enforced deportation by the authorities. It is partly because of the widely publicized press reports that the issue of overseas migrant workers has attracted major public attention since the mid-1980s. The flourishing number of non-government organizations which had taken up the cause of overseas migrant workers for their critical stand against the New Order regime, further placed the issue of migrant workers clearly at the centre of the political arena.

Emerging Role of Non-State Actors: Migrant Workers in the Reform Era

Under the systematic political subjugation of labour during the New Order regime, the articulation of labour interest through non-governmental organizations is therefore a very natural societal response to the existing political circumstances. Initially, the non-governmental organizations mainly provided assistance to the migrant workers and their families in seeking compensation as many of them were unfairly treated by their labour recruiters, particularly concerning the violation of the contract agreement. The non-governmental organization's institutional and legal assistance for welfare issues have slowly established the trust and confidence of migrant workers and their families. In a further development, non-governmental organizations have enabled scattered migrant workers to establish their own networks and organizations.[15] A significant number of local level semi-formal migrant workers organizations were established in major areas where many migrant workers resided, including various districts in West Java, East Java and West Nusa Tenggara. Many kinds of training also have been provided by the non-governmental organizations, not only related to the practical needs for improving their economic welfare but also in strengthening their political consciousness, particularly in voicing their needs and demands to government, the labour recruiters, and also their prospective employers. The sustained process of migrant worker empowerment has resulted in a significant increase in the migrant workers political clout, such as in organizing protests to the state authorities on various migrant workers issues. The migrant workers have also learned that their demands will be given more attention by the authorities if they could attract the mass media to cover their protests.

In a parallel development, the non-governmental organizations have also improved their assistance to migrant workers by establishing a national umbrella organization to defend migrant workers. In 1997 Konsorsium Pembela Buruh Migran, or Consortium In Defence of Migrant Workers (KOPBUMI) was established as an organizational forum of non-governmental organizations concerned with the improvement of the conditions of migrant workers. Along with the impetus instigating the non-governmental organizations to establish their umbrella organization was the polemics and debates surrounding the government proposal to promulgate the national law on labour (UU POKOK KETENAKERJAAN) in 1997. The content of the government proposal that was perceived as curtailing the various social, economic and political rights of the workers stimulated wide scale protests not only by labour but also academics and non-government organizations. The government proposal also overlooked the specific problems and issues of migrant workers that triggered the migrant workers related organization networks to start their campaign of protest against the proposal and further consolidated their effort to defend the political rights of the migrant workers. As protests were mounting, the government decided to pull out the new national labour law and stated that the draft should be revised. In such political circumstances then, KOPBUMI was established with the immediate target of proposing a special law for migrant workers which is obviously lacking within the government draft of national labour law. The existing policy on overseas migrant labour is generally based on various ministerial decrees which reflect the *ad hoc* circumstances of the policy.

Another important development that also contributes to the increasing public attention on the issues of overseas migrant workers is the new discourse on globalization which began around the mid-1990s. While the core of the discussion on globalization is still primarily dominated by the issues related to finance and trade regulations, it eventually also touched upon the issue of overseas migrant workers. Again in this context, the migrant workers who are largely unskilled, and many are undocumented, are generally passive participants in the margin of the playing field as the victims of the contest of globalization that is apparently an arena only for "the big and the strong".[16] International actors, primarily the transnational non-government organizations, such as International Labour Organization (ILO), International Organization for Migration (IOM), and other international NGOs — (in many instances in co-operation with national governments and local NGOs) - through various ways attempt to influence the law, regulation, protocol and covenants concerning the international migrant workers.[17] In Indonesia, the state's bureaucracy is generally very reluctant to adopt the international conventions that could improve the protection of, and strengthen the rights of the migrant workers. The reasons for this bureaucratic reluctance in addition to the fact that the issue of migrant workers is a low priority in the state's political agenda, is probably because of the strong vested interests of the bureaucratic staff who apparently benefited from the various illegal practices in the business of overseas migrant workers. The collusion between the bureaucracy and the labour recruiting agencies is an open secret and certainly hamper the genuine improvement of government regulations on migrant labour issues that are being encouraged by international agencies, such as ILO, in an attempt to change the existing fraudulent policies on overseas migrant workers.

Other major actors playing an important role in the industry of overseas migrant workers are traders and businessman. Institutionally these traders and business people act through various organizations, but most importantly they operate through the labour recruiters and suppliers agencies (Perusahaan Jasa Tenaga Kerja Indonesia or PJTKI, member of APJATI). The crux of the matter is that the government is the sole authority able to provide the license for the labour recruiting agencies to operate. The lucrative business in overseas migrant labour has obviously constituted some form of control on the association of labour recruiters and suppliers agencies Asosiasi Perusahaan Jasa Tenaga Kerja Indonesia or Indonesian Manpower Supply Association (APJATI), although this has always been contested among the different business groups behind the agencies. The business groups dealing in labour exports, which interestingly have always been dominated by the labour suppliers to the Middle East countries, are largely owned by Arab ethnic groups.[18] The rivalry between different groups to control the association has occasionally resulted in conflicts during the election of their association chairman. The New Order's state maintained its political patronage by allowing only one association and giving its approval to the candidate who is most acceptable to the interests of the government, particularly the minister of labour. Recently, a new association was established — namely, Association of Indonesian Migrant Worker Suppliers (HIMSATAKI) — whose legality is strongly denied by APJATI — the existing association. The reform era apparently will not enable the post-Suharto's government to continue the policy for allowing only one migrant labour association.

Beyond the reach of the association's control, hundreds of labour exporting agencies have been operating their business in an unrestrained manner. While certainly there are many legal recruiting-recruiting agencies operating in Indonesia, there are also many which were operating illegally. Or, in some cases, a combination of the two, in which legal recruiting agencies operate outside the legal procedures for recruiting the overseas migrant workers. The problem that will be discussed here is related to the unskilled recruiting because obviously, skilled workers are more transparently regulated as the workers are mostly professionals and highly educated. Additionally, there are far greater numbers of unskilled workers and the majority of them are females with very limited education. In many cases, the recruitment process of these unskilled workers began in their home villages, which were often beyond the reach of the state's bureaucracy, except the local village authorities which authorized the statement of residency of the prospective overseas migrant workers. It is from the village levels that the business of overseas migrant workers actually starts. The office of recruiting recruiter and suppliers agencies which are often located in nearby towns have in many ways relied on their intermediary agents who directly scout for prospective overseas migrant workers in the villages.[19]

The heavy demand for unskilled workers, such as domestic helpers for the Middle Eastern countries, and plantation workers in Malaysia, on the one hand, and the recruiting surplus in Indonesia, on the other hand, is a perfect match that will continue to sustain the overseas migrant worker industry in Indonesia. Those who are politically powerless and have limited economic opportunities, have made the position of unskilled overseas migrant workers very vulnerable to exploitation by both legal and illegal recruiting agencies which strongly control the business industry of overseas migrant workers. Furthermore, the continuing reluctance on the part of state bureaucracy to reform policies regulating migrant workers will obviously nurture the burgeoning illegal movement, which proceeds without any legal protection. In these circumstances, the increasing political awareness among the migrant workers — as can be seen from the number of semi-organization networks that are now developing with the assistance of non-governmental organizations — is very crucial for eventually strengthening the bargaining position of migrant workers in relation to state authorities as well as to the labour recruiting agencies.[20]

The decision of the Abdurahman Wahid government to implement the new national law on decentralization and regional autonomy (UU Nomor 22 Tahun 1999 tentang Pemerintah Daerah dan UU Nomor 25 Tahun 1999 tentang Perimbangan Keuangan Pusat dan Daerah) can prove to be a new opportunity to improve the policy on overseas migrant workers as the regional governments would be given the authority to regulate the movement of overseas migrant workers from their regions.[21] The fact that overseas migrant workers have significantly contributed to regional government revenues will be a strong reason for the regional government bureaucracy to obtain control of their movements. Now, under Megawati's presidency, the more fundamental problems currently facing the state and the nation to consolidate democracy in the face of popular disillusionment, along with the efforts aimed at national economic recovery will probably hamper any chances of instituting clear policy on overseas migrant workers in the near future. With the state being incapable of delivering institutional and legal protection for overseas migrant workers, on the one hand, and the likelihood of increasing demand for unskilled overseas migrant labours, on the other hand, the result will be the continuance of existing problems surrounding illegal human trafficking with all its social repercussions.

A Postscript: The Nunukan Tragedy, Will the State Learn?

The time-bomb of cross-border migration to Malaysia that has been ticking since the beginning of the 1970s exploded recently in Nunukan, a small island in the border of East Kalimantan and Sabah. With the implementation of new Immigration Act, the Malaysian Government began to arrest and fine the undocumented migrant workers. Thousands of Indonesian illegal migrant workers decided to flee from the country through various immigration gates. Nunukan, which used to be the entry point for Indonesian migrant workers via Tawau port to Sabah, this time became the "refugee camp" as massive numbers of migrant workers and their families sought shelter after being forced to leave Malaysian territory. As intensively reported by the press, the situation in Nunukan was getting worse, as the island has a very limited capacity to accommodate the migrants, who desperately needed shelter, food as well as proper medical treatment. By 5 September 2002, it was reported that seventy people had died as a result of inadequate medical facilities. While migrants continued to flow in from Malaysia, the government response was too little too late.

While the Nunukan tragedy still looms large, and as the Megawati government hurriedly tried to handle the problem, it has become starkly clear that the tragedy is yet another example of the fatal outcomes to be expected from entrusting corrupt and ignorant state bureaucracies with regulating the lucrative trade in overseas migrant workers. The Nunukan tragedy certainly will renew calls for the state to give serious attention to the plight of unprotected overseas migrant workers and their families. The question is whether the state will learn from the Nunukan tragedy. Certainly, the state will be the target of strong criticism for its lamentable performance, and in the coming months, several policy initiatives will be outlined, among others a new MOU with the Malaysian Government on migrant workers might be drawn up.[22] However, given the track record of the state bureaucracy and the underlying ignorance prevalent there, a dramatic change in the policy on overseas migrant workers is unlikely to materialize. Unless strong political pressure is brought to bear on the government from the outside, the state bureaucracy will slowly forget the tragedy and will likely return to business as usual.

A concerted effort on the part of emerging civil society actors is therefore needed if the state bureaucracy is going to change its attitude towards the plight of the common people. The Nunukan tragedy provides a rare opportunity for the various non-governmental organizations, national and transnational, concerned with overseas migrant workers, to push the government and the state to do their long neglected homework.[23]

Notes

1   The introductory part, particularly the review literature, is mostly derived from a draft paper, entitled "A Brief Review of Borderland Studies" by Reed L. Wadley (1997).
2   At the time when this chapter was being revised, the result of the International Court of Justice in The Hague, was publicized in which Indonesia had lost the

case. Unsurprisingly, as anticipated, the court decision was accepted without any difficulties and complaints from Indonesia. A little polemics occurred in the press but the public generally ignored this issue.

3   These movements have been comprehensively documented by the National Archives of the Republic of Indonesia (Arsip Nasional Republik Indonesia) in 1981.

4   Wertheim's prediction about the probability of social conflict in Lampung as a consequence of rapid population growth and social tensions between migrants and local people occurred in the so-called Lampung Affairs which broke out in February 1989.

5   "An Interview with Koentjaraningrat" (Visser 1988).

6   Land reform, which was aggressively promoted by the Indonesian Communist Party (PKI) prior to the 1965 abortive coup, was identified by the New Order as a communist policy.

7   An illustration of how the elite, particularly the military, has persistently regarded transmigration as an important undertaking is shown by a request from General Suharto to the U.S. Ambassador in Indonesia, Marshall Green, at their first meeting on 29 May 1966. In the meeting Suharto asked for US$500 million in grants or soft loans to assist the transmigration programme (Personal communication with Dr. Terry Hull, ANU, 1989).

8   For a more detailed account on the continuation of the migration policy from the colonial to the post-colonial periods, see Tirtosudarmo (1997).

9   See studies by Thompson (1947), Vredenbreght (1964), Suparlan (1995), Adam (1994), Breman (1997), Miyasaki (1998).

10 The plan set a target of 225,000 workers to be sent abroad as a way of easing the difficulties of absorbing the rapidly growing labour force.

11 On the political dimension of Indonesian illegal migration to Malaysia, see Tirtosudarmo (1996).

12 On the elaborated labour politics during the New Order's period, see Hadiz (1997).

13 In this regard, the New Order labour policy resembled the colonial policy that, according to Breman (1990, p. 144), "from the start had proven more interested in cheap than in free labor".

14 Among the new political parties establish on the basis of labour is *PBN* (Partai Buruh Nasional or Labour National Party) led by Muhtar Pakpahan who also the chairman of *SBSI*. Another minor party that is also placing labour issues in its political platform is *PRD* (Partai Rakyat Democratic or People's Democratic Party) under the chairmanship of Budiman Sudjatmiko. Both Pakpahan and Sudjatmiko were jailed in the latest period of the Suharto regime.

15 I would like to acknowledge the useful discussions on this issue with Yuniyanti Chuzaifah, an activist of *Solidaritas Perempuan* who is currently studying at Leiden University.

[16] For a comprehensive review on labour migration and globalization in Southeast Asia, see Battistella (2002).

[17] The growing importance of the so-called TANs (Transnational Advocacy Movements) on the issues related to cross-border mobility, particularly the trafficking and smuggling of women and children, is partly resulted from the fact that the civil society movements in the developing countries are often plagued by the limited capacity to initiate reform from within (see Piper and Uhlin 2002).

[18] Attempts to interview these people on their business on labour exports to Saudi Arabia by the author in 1997 was not successful as they tend to avoid being studied. Their refusal to be interviewed reflects the degree of secrecy in their business activities, particularly in exporting female labour as domestic workers to Saudi Arabia.

[19] On the role of intermediaries in the business of labour migrants in East Java, see Spaan (1994).

[20] Recently, a draft of the national law on the protection of Indonesian migrant workers and their families (UU TENTANG PERLINDUNGAN BURUH MIGRAN INDONESIA DAN ANGGOTA KELUARGANYA) was finally drafted by *KOPBUMI* and proposed to the members of parliament and to the government, as well as disseminated to those members of the public who are concerned with the fate of migrant workers. This is obviously a landmark in the context of the existing dispute about influencing the regulating policy concerning overseas migrant workers in Indonesia. The draft proposal also can be seen as a significant achievement by the migrant workers and their compatriots in what could be a long political struggle to regulate the conditions of overseas migrant workers in Indonesia.

[21] Several provinces, such as Central Java, East Java and West Nusa Tenggara, have begun to issue regulation policies concerning overseas migrant workers from the province. Among others, are the attempt to establish regional regulation on the business of overseas migrant workers in Central Java, and allocation of credit to the recruiting agencies in East Java. Another initiative, for example, has been shown recently by the opening of direct *Merpati* flight from Mataram, West Nusa Tenggara to Kuala Lumpur, Malaysia, in order to serve the heavy demand for transportation of migrant workers from West Nusa Tenggara who work in Malaysia.

[22] When this chapter was revised in May 2004, the MOU between the Indonesian and Malaysian governments on the procedures of recruitment regulation had been signed on 10 May 2004, eighteen months after the Nunukan Tragedy. Yet, the content and the substance of the new regulation is far from what is urgently needed to protect the basic rights of the Indonesian migrant workers who mostly fall under the category of so-called unskilled workers, particularly the domestic workers.

[23] The failure of the Indonesian Government in delivering sufficient protection to
the thousands of desperate migrant workers and their families in Nunukan
have become a public issue in the mass media and have galvanized the NGOs
community to strongly criticizing the government in handling the matter. In
an unprecedented moved, several NGOs have decided to establish a coalition
and took the Nunukan case to court. These NGOs have mobilized support
from the public to sue the government under the so-called Citizen Lawsuit.
The first court hearing was conducted on 31 March 2003, and followed by a
second hearing on 14 April 2003. According to Nursyahbani Katjasungkana,
one of the lawyers and the chairwoman of Women Coalition for Democracy
and Justice, in an interview with the author, the aim of the action was basically
to educate and to strengthen public awareness of their citizen rights and
responsibility so that they could respond critically to any government policies
and programmes that in the past have always been overlooked and undermined
the people's interests.

References

Adam, Asmi Warman. "Pengiriman Buruh Migran Jawa ke Vietnam tahun
1900-an" [Exporting Javanese Migrant Workers to Vietnam in the 1900s]. *Sejarah*,
no. 5 (1994): 1–6.

Arsip Nasional Republic Indonesia [National Archive of Republic of Indonesia].
*Laporan-laporan tentang Gerakan Protes di Jawa pada Abad XX [Reports on Protest
Movement in Java in the 20th Century]*. Jakarta: Arsip Nasional Republik
Indonesia, 1981.

Asiwaju, A.I. *Borderland Research: A Comparative Perspective*. Border Perspectives
Paper No. 6, El Paso: Centre for Inter-American Border Studies, University of
Texas, 1983.

Battistella, Graziano. "Workers in ASEAN, Unauthorized Migrants as Global".
Paper presented at the IUSSP Regional Population Conference on Southeast
Asia's Population in a Changing Asian Context held at Chulalongkorn
University, Bangkok, Thailand, 10–13 June 2002.

Breman, Jan. "The Civilization of Racism: Colonial and Post-colonial Development
Policies". In *Imperial Monkey Business*, edited by Jan Breman. CASA Monographs
3, 1990, pp. 123–52.

Breman, Jan. *Menjinakkan Sang Kuli: Politik Kolonial pada awal Abad ke-20* [Taming
the Coolie Beast]. Jakarta: Pustaka Utama Grafiti dan Perwakilan KITLV, 1997.

Collins, D. "Partitioned Culture Areas and Smuggling: The Hausa and the
Groundnut Trade Across the Nigeria-Niger Border from the mid-1930s to the

mid-1970s". In *Partitioned Africans: Ethnic Relations across Africa's International Boundaries, 1884–1984*, edited by A.I. Asiwaju. London: C. Hurst, 1985, pp. 195–221.

Hadiz, Vedi. R. *Workers and the State in New Order Indonesia*. London: Routledge, 1997.

Hardjosudarmo, S. *Kebijaksanaan Transmigrasi dalam rangka Pembangunan Masyarakat Desa di Indonesia [Transmigration Policy in the Context of Rural Development in Indonesia]*. Jakarta: Bhratara, 1965.

Heeren, H.J. *Transmigrasi di Indonesia [Transmigration in Indonesia]*. Yogyakarta: Gajah Mada University Press, 1979.

Kartodirdjo, Sartono. *Protest Movements in Rural Java: A Study of Agrarian Unrest in the Nineteenth and Early Twentieth Centuries*. Singapore: Oxford University Press, 1973.

Kuntjorojakti, Dorodjatun. "The Political Economy of Development: The Case Study of Indonesia under the New Order Government". Unpublished Ph.D. dissertation, University of California, Berkeley, 1978.

Legge, John. D. *Indonesia*. Englewood Cliffs, N.J.: Prentice Hall, 1964.

Martinez, Oscar J., ed. *Border People: Life and Society in the US-Mexico Borderlands*. Tucson: University of Arizona Press, 1994.

Miyazaki, Koji. "Javanese-Malay: Colonial Immigrants in Post-Colonial Era". Paper presented at the Worksop on Migration in Contemporary Southeast Asia, Singapore, 22–23 January 1998.

Miyazaki, Koji. "Culture Moves: Contemporary Migration in Southeast Asia". In *Population Movement in Southeast Asia: Changing Identities and Strategies for Survival*, edited by Abe Ken-ichi and Ishii Masako. JCAS Symposium Series 10, National Museum of Ethnology, Osaka, Japan, 2000.

Nitisastro, Widjojo. *Population Trends in Indonesia*. New York: Cornell University Press, 1970.

Nicola Piper and Anders Uhlin. "Transnational Advocacy Networks and the Issue of Female Labour Migration and Trafficking in East and Southeast Asia. A Gendered Analysis of Opportunities and Obstacles". *Asia Pacific Migration Journal* no. 2 (2002).

Spaan, E. "Taikongs and Calos: The Role of Middlemen and Brokers in Javanese International Migration". *International Migration Review* 28, no. 1 (1994): 93–119.

Suparlan, Parsudi. *The Javanese in Suriname: Ethnicity in an Ethnically Plural Society*. Monograph Series, Programme for Southeast Asian Studies, Arizona State University, 1995.

Thompson, V. *Labor Problems in Southeast Asia*. New Haven: Yale University Press, 1947.

Tirtosudarmo, Riwanto. "The Politics of Population Mobility in Southeast Asia: The Case of Indonesian Migrant Workers in Malaysia". Paper presented at the seminar on "Movement of Peoples within and from the Southeast Asian Region: Trends, Causes, Consequences and Policy Measures", conducted by Southeast Asian Studies Programme (SEASP), Indonesian Institute of Sciences, Jakarta, 5–6 June 1996.

Tirtosudarmo, Riwanto. "From *Emigratie* to *Transmigrasi*: Continuity and Change in Migration Policies in Indonesia". Working Paper Series, no. 97-05, PSTC, Department of Sociology, Brown University, 1997.

Tirtosudarmo, Riwanto. "Labor Movement and the Quest for Democracy: A Twisted Working Class in New Order's Indonesia?" Paper presented at the workshop on Discourses and Practices of Democracy in Southeast Asia, organized by Indonesian Institute of Sciences and Gajah Mada University, Yogyakarta, 16–20 March 1998.

Vredenbregt, J. "Masyarakat Perantau Pulau Bawean di Singapura" [The Baweanese in Singapore]". Unpublished Ph.D. thesis, 1964.

Visser, L. "An Interview with Koentjaraningrat". *Current Anthropology* 29, no. 5 (December 1986): 749–53.

Wadley, Reed. L. "A Brief Review of Borderland Studies". (A draft), 1997.

Wertheim, W. F. "Sociological Aspects of Inter-Islands in Indonesia". *Population Studies* 7, no. 3 (March 1959): 184–201.

12

Regional Migrant Workers Flows: Outlook for Malaysia

Bilson Kurus

Introduction

Migration has long been part and parcel of human history. However, its ascendancy into the vocabulary of governmental policies is, arguably, tied to the more recent emergence of the modern nation-states, when the broader issue of national borders and security as well as citizenship requirements became a critical concern. Since then, the issue of international migration has gradually grown in importance and even predicted to become perhaps "the most important branch of demography in the early decades of the new millennium".[1] Its currency as a rising focus of international relations is borne out by the rapidly growing volumes of articles, books and journals as well as research centres devoted to it in both the developed as well as developing countries.

One of the key factors that have been continuing to contribute to the widespread attention on migration is the fact that it is a global phenomenon. Every region of the world is affected in varying degrees and indeed all countries are likely affected in some ways either as a source, destination, or both in the international migration's equation. This reality becomes readily apparent by the very nature of migration, which has been defined as "a permanent or semi-permanent change of residence, and includes settlers, landed immigrants, temporary workers, guest workers, asylum seekers, students, and undocumented arrivals intending to stay in the short or long term — all involving the crossing of national borders".[2] In this chapter, the focus is primarily on migrant workers.

In the international movement of migrants, the Southeast Asian region has figured quite prominently both as points of origin and destination. In this respect, as a country centrally located within the Southeast Asian region and, experiencing relatively high economic growth over the past few decades, Malaysia has become a destination for migrants as well as a transit point in the international migration flows.[3] Malaysia's relative accessibility, stability and prosperity *vis-à-vis* the situation in their home regions as well as historical links would, therefore, appear to be among the key pulling factors for migrant workers to come to Malaysia, legally or otherwise.

Towards this end, this chapter begins with an overview of the Malaysian economy and labour situation. This is followed by a discussion of the salient and pertinent points of two National Development Plans in the Third Outline Perspective Plan (OPP3) and the Eight Malaysia Plan (8MP) respectively. The chapter also looks at the government and societal responses to the influx of migrant workers, with particular emphasis on undocumented migrant workers. Some of the key issues and realities that would likely influence regional co-operation are then discussed before the chapter is closed with some concluding remarks.

The Economy, Labour and Migrant Workers

As noted, one of the key attractions for migrants to enter Malaysia is the perceived conducive employment environment and opportunities within the country. Arguably, this perceived environment is the direct consequence of the generally high annual economic growth that the country has experienced over the past few decades. It would, therefore, be useful to begin with a brief overview of the economic outlook and the labour situation in Malaysia.

Malaysia's annual economic growth between 1981–2002 is depicted in Table 12.1. As can be seen, Malaysia has experienced relatively high

TABLE 12.1
Yearly Economic Growth, Malaysia: 1981–2002

Year	Gross Domestic Product (GDP)
1981	6.9%
1982	5.2%
1983	5.9%
1984	7.6%
1985	−1.0%
1986	1.2%
1987	5.2%
1988	8.7%
1989	8.8%
1990	9.8%
1991	8.7%
1992	7.8%
1993	8.3%
1994	9.2%
1995	9.5%
1996	8.6%
1997	7.8%
1998	−7.5%
1999	5.8%
2000	8.3%
2001p	0.4%
2002f	3.5%

p – preliminary
f – forecast
Sources: *Bank Negara, Statistics Department, Economic Reports.*
(As reported in the *New Straits Times,* 17 July 2002).

economic growth over the past two decades. The rapid economic growth also facilitated the gradual shift of the country's economic activities towards the manufacturing and services sectors from the primary sectors such as agriculture. And as depicted in Table 12.2, manufacturing accounts for 29.7 per cent of Gross Domestic Product (GDP) by 2001, increased from 19.6 per cent in 1980. Likewise, the services sector grew from 40.1 per cent in 1980 to 52.2 per cent by 2001. Conversely, the contribution from agriculture declined from 22.9 per cent in 1980 to 8.1 per cent in 2001.

TABLE 12.2
Contribution of Key Economic Sectors, 1980 and 2001

No.	Sector	Year	
		1980 (%)	2001 (%)
1.	Services	40.1	52.2
2.	Agriculture	22.9	8.1
3.	Manufacturing	19.6	29.7
4.	Mining and quarrying	10.1	6.5
5.	Construction	4.6	3.2
6.	Others	2.7	*

* Preliminary. No 'Others' category
Sources: Bank Negara Statistics Department, Economic Reports.
(As reported in the *New Straits Times*, 17 July 2002).

Nonetheless, the structural shifts in terms of economic activities have by and large remained unchanged with respect to its labour intensiveness. Indeed, while the agricultural sector's contribution to the national economy has declined, the opening up of agricultural estates in some states such as Sabah actually necessitated the need for more, rather than less, unskilled and semi-skilled workers. As can be seen in Table 12.3, the bulk of the migrant workers in Malaysia are distributed in five key sectors with manufacturing accounting for the largest proportion, followed by agriculture and domestic helper. Table 12.3 also indicates that the largest groups of migrant workers in Malaysia come from Indonesia and Bangladesh respectively.

Two things should be noted with respect to the figures in Table 12.3, which may also partly explain the public reactions from both Indonesia and the Philippines when Malaysia recently initiated a much tougher labour and immigration policies. First, it is clear that a sizeable number of migrant workers are involved in the manufacturing, plantation and domestic sector. This points to the important role that migrant workers play in key sectors of the Malaysian economy. The high number of migrants involved as domestic helpers also suggests that migrants fill an important gap in maintaining two-income earners households. This particular segment of the population likely forms the bulk of the rising middle-class in Malaysia. Another pertinent point to note is the actual composition of the migrant workers in the country. While Table 12.3 does indicate that

TABLE 12.3
Foreign Workers in Malaysia
by Country of Origin and Job Sectors (1 July 2001)
('000)

Nationalities	Percentage	Job Sectors	Percentage
Indonesians	73.64	Manufacturing	30.08
Bangladeshis	17.54	Plantation	25.59
Filipinos	1.90	Domestic Helper	20.40
Thais	0.80	Construction	8.57
Pakistanis	0.40	Services	7.32
Others	5.82		
Total	100.00	**Total**	100.00
	807,984		807,984

Source: As cited by Azizah Kassim, "International Migration: Prospects and Challenges in Malaysia", paper presented at the Seminar on Regional Security Risks and Challenges: The Role of Civil Society, Kota Kinabalu, Sabah, 2 July 2002, unpublished.

Indonesians and Bangladeshis form the largest recorded group nationally, as indicated in Table 12.5, the distribution is not even in that Sabah and the Federal Territory of Labuan host practically half of the total recorded migrant population in the country. In this regard, it is in Sabah and Labuan that most of the Filipino workers in Malaysia are concentrated in. Thus, Sabah occupies centre stage whenever the issue of the welfare of Filipino workers in Malaysia comes up. Likewise, the huge number of Indonesian workers in Sabah and the long land border that Sabah shares with Kalimantan also means that Sabah is directly affected by the inflow as well as outflow of Indonesian migrant workers in Malaysia.

The national employment figure as well as total number of the labour force (both locals and foreigners) for 1995 and 2002 is given in Table 12.4. As can be seen, the total employment figure increased from 7,999.2 million in 1995 to 9,271.2 million in 2000. While the figures in Tables 12.3 and 12.4 do not directly correspond with each other, a rough estimate of the recorded percentage of migrant workers in the total employed Malaysian labour force would be obtained by comparing the two tables. Thus, if the mid-2001 figure of 807,984 migrant workers is taken and compared to the total national employment figure of 9,271.2 million in 2000, migrant workers would roughly account for about 9.5 per cent of the total employed labour

TABLE 12.4
National Employment by Sector, 1995 and 2000[1]
('000)

Sector	1995 Number / %	2000 Number / %
Agriculture	1,492.7 (18.7%)	1,407.5 (15.2%)
Mining & Quarrying	40.5 (0.5%)	41.2 (0.4%)
Manufacturing	2,027.5 (25.4%)	2,558.3 (27.6%)
Construction	717.1 (9.0%)	755.0 (8.1%)
Electricity, Gas & Water	67.4 (0.8%)	75.0 (0.8%)
Transportation	395.2 (4.9%)	461.6 (5.0%)
Wholesale & Retail	1,323.5 (16.5%)	1,584.2 (17.1%)
Finance	372.8 (4.7%)	508.7 (5.5%)
Other Services[2]	1,562.5 (19.5%)	1,879.7 (20.3%)
Total Employment	**7,999.2 (100%)**	**9,271.2 (100%)**
Labour Force	8,254.0	9,572.5
Unemployment	254.8	301.3
Unemployment Rate	3.1%	3.1%

Notes: [1] Includes non-citizens
[2] Includes public, private and community services.
Source: Eighth Malaysia Plan, 2001–2005.

force in the country. However, this may not be reflective of the actual number of migrant workers in the country given the huge presence of undocumented or "illegal" immigrants in the Malaysia.

This raises one of the key difficulties in studying the situation of migrant workers in Malaysia, which is getting an accurate figure of the actual number of migrant workers in the country. The total number of migrant workers indicated in Table 12.3 (807,984) as of mid-2001, for example, is likely those that are formally registered with the relevant agencies only. Not included are obviously the huge population of so-called illegal immigrants in Malaysia. In this respect, in his meeting with President Megawati in Bali on Malaysia's new labour policy and amended Immigration Act, the then Prime Minister Mahathir Mohamad pointed out that the total number of immigrants in Malaysia stood at two million, which is approximately 10 per cent of Malaysia's population.[4] If this figure were used, then comparing that to the total labour force for 2000 (9,572.5

million), migrant workers would roughly account for about one-fifth of Malaysia overall labour force.[5]

In terms of the distribution of non-citizens in the country, Table 12.5 provides a breakdown of the national distribution. As noted, numerically the state of Sabah has the dubious distinction of having the largest number of foreigners at 614,824.[6] In terms of percentages, Sabah and Labuan both have more than one-fifth of their population comprising non-citizens. Overall, the distribution is almost evenly divided between Peninsular Malaysia and East Malaysia (Sabah, Sarawak and Labuan). However, whatever the actual numbers of migrant workers and foreigners in Malaysia today, three observations can be made. First, while it may be difficult to ascertain the exact number of foreigners in the country, there is no denying their sizeable presence in Malaysia. Second, migrant workers were an important part of the Malaysian labour force in the past and they would likely remain so into the immediate future. Finally, the distribution of the foreign population in Malaysia is not evenly distributed with respect to the various states and federal territories. Sabah and Labuan appears to comparatively bear the brunt of the foreigners' population in Malaysia.

Labour Policies and Outlook

As pointed out above, one of the key attractiveness of Malaysia for migrant workers lies primarily with the perceived availability of jobs in the country. This perception was likely facilitated by recruitment agencies, word of mouth within the migrant workers' vast networks and perhaps even by the public acknowledgment of Malaysia's rapid economic growth. Indeed, as Malaysian employers have readily turned to migrant workers, this perception may have been strengthened overtime, and this cycle no doubt facilitates the rapid growth of the migrant workers population in the country. In this regard, Malaysia has relied much on migrant workers to augment its limited manpower pool, and these trends will likely remain in place until the country's economic structure is characterized more by non-labour-intensive industries.

To be sure, Malaysia is certainly cognizant of the fact that the country's heavy dependence on migrant workers may not be sustainable indefinitely and, has consequently taken various measures to reduce its heavy dependence on migrant workers. In this context, it can be argued that the then Prime Minister Mahathir Mohamad's enunciated Vision

TABLE 12.5
Distribution of Foreign Population in Malaysia, 2000

	Total Population	Non-Citizens: Number and % Of State Pop.	Non-Citizens: % of Total Foreign Pop.
Peninsular Malaysia			
Johor	2,740,626	150,530 (5.5)	10.9
Kedah	1,649,756	25,605 (1.6)	1.8
Kelantan	1,313,014	20,795 (1.6)	1.5
Melaka	635,791	22,944 (3.6)	1.7
Negeri Sembilan	859,924	31,859 (3.7)	2.3
Pahang	1,288,376	54,800 (4.3)	3.9
Perak	2,051,236	38,345 (1.9)	2.8
Perlis	204,450	155 (1.5)	0.2
Pulau Pinang	1,313,449	48,382 (3.7)	3.5
Selangor	4,188,876	186,382 (4.5)	13.5
Terengganu	898,825	15,838 (1.8)	1.1
Federal Territory (KL)	**1,379,310**	**92,373 (6.7)**	**6.7**
Sub-Total	18,523,632	691,032	**49.9**
Sabah	2,603,485	614,824 **(23.6)**	**44.4**
Sarawak	2,071,506	62,738 **(3.0)**	**4.5**
Federal Territory (Labuan)	**76,067**	**16,150 (21.2)**	**1.2**
Malaysia	**23,274,690**	**1,384,744 (5.9)**	**100**

Source: Population & Housing Census 2000 — Population Distribution and Basic Demographic Characteristics. Department of Statistics, Malaysia, Kuala Lumpur, July 2001: various pages. (As cited by Azizah Kassim, "International Migration: Prospects and Challenges in Malaysia", paper presented at the Seminar on Regional Security Risks and Challenges: The Role of Civil Society, 2 July 2002, Kota Kinabalu, Sabah, unpublished).

2020 with its fundamental objective of achieving a developed nation status for Malaysia by the year 2020 can be construed as a policy vehicle (whether intended or otherwise) to gradually wean the country from its heavy reliance on migrant workers. Vision 2020 was publicly announced in 1990. Since then, subsequent Five-Year National Development Plans for Malaysia have stressed the need to shift the country's economic activities from labour-intensive industries towards more capital-intensive and knowledge-based industries.

Under the current Eighth Malaysia Plan (8MP), 2001–05, for example, the human resource policy thrusts place a heavy emphasis on training based on the following strategies:[7]

1. Expanding the supply of highly skilled and knowledge manpower to support the development of a knowledge-based economy;
2. Increasing the accessibility to quality education and training to enhance income generation capabilities and quality of life;
3. Improving the quality of education and training delivery system to ensure that manpower supply is in line with technological change and market demand;
4. Promoting lifelong learning to enhance employability and productivity of the labour force;
5. Optimizing the utilization of local labour;
6. Increasing the supply of S&T manpower;
7. Accelerating the implementation of the productivity-linked wage system;
8. Strengthening labour market information system to increase labour mobility;
9. Intensifying efforts to develop and promote Malaysia as a regional centre of educational excellence, and;
10. Reinforcing positive values.

What is also interesting is that item 5 above is focused specifically on the optimum utilization of local labour. In this respect, four strategies are outlined to facilitate this objective.[8] First is to increase women's participation by the setting up of community nurseries and kindergartens within residential areas as well as ensuring better access to training opportunities. Second is to encourage teleworking, part-time work and job sharing to allow women, especially those who are highly educated, the flexibility of working and at the same time be a homemaker. Third is to extend retirement age to 56 years on a trial basis. And fourth is to increase efforts to optimize the use of local labour and further to *reduce dependence on foreign labour* (emphasis added). At the same time, firms will be encouraged to take positive steps to move into higher capital-intensity production processes.

By the same token, the Third Outline Perspective Plan (OPP3), which serves as the overall development guideline for the first decade of the twenty-first century for Malaysia also places great emphasis on a skilled and expanded labour force with the following three strategies.[9] First is to provide more opportunities for Malaysians to pursue tertiary education with the expansion in education and training facilities as well as the growth in virtual learning. Second is to expect more women to participate actively in the economy with improved levels of education and expanding employment opportunities as well as the institution of more flexible working arrangements. The third is to raise the rate of women's participation in the professional and technical group.

As noted, the various strategies outlined above under both the 8MP and OPP3 are intended to create a labour force that is capable of meeting the country's overall target of moving towards more capital-intensive and knowledge-based industries. However, it is also acknowledged that in some specific sectors, the demand for foreign workers will likely remain and may in fact even rise in some cases. For example, both the 8MP and the OPP3 placed a lot of emphasis on the expanded entry of women into the labour force as among the national strategies to augment the country's human resource pool. While the effort to increase women's participation in the labour force is certainly lauded and no doubt much welcome, the rising number of working mothers already in the workplace is, not unexpectedly, prompting a rising demand for domestic helpers. In view of the fact that it is difficult to meet this demand locally, more and more foreigners are being recruited to fill the void. In this respect, the provision for more nurseries and kindergartens as well as providing more employment flexibilities for working mothers, were no doubt prompted by this particular concern.

But perhaps an even clearer indication of the future labour requirement of the country can be ascertained by looking at the projected employment by sector during the OPP3 period (2001–10). Viewed from this trajectory, the service sector is expected to continue to command the biggest share of total employment. A large portion of the jobs created is expected to come from the other services sub-sectors, which include private education and health, other business activities, recreational, cultural and sporting activities, as well as computer and related activities. At the same time, the wholesale and retail trade, hotel and restaurants sub-sector will also be an important generator of employment due to the expected expansion of the tourism industry.

By the same token, the trend in the manufacturing sector is expected to move towards greater demand for more highly skilled labour that would require skill upgrading of the labour force. The employment trend in the agriculture sector is expected to see a decline in the demand for labour, particularly for food crops, given the anticipated introduction of high technology cultivation methods and large-scale farming as well as increased mechanization. However, the oil palm, rubber and cocoa plantation sub-sectors are still expected to require substantial amount of labour until the production and harvesting processes improve to a higher level of mechanization.[10] It is likely that the construction will also continue to be dependent on a substantial amount of labour. As such, it would appear that while there are continuing attempts on the part of the government to reduce the country's heavy dependence on migrant workers, it is equally clear that the country will likely continue to rely on migrant workers to a certain degree in meeting the labour requirements in specific sectors of the economy.

To sum up then, taking a broad look at the labour situation and requirements in Malaysia in the near and immediate terms, while the demand for unskilled and semi-skilled workers is projected to be on a declining trend, the demand in some key sectors will likely still remain strong. This would suggest that while migrant workers will continue to feature in the Malaysian labour force, it is plausible that their absolute number might see a gradual decline over the coming years. However, their actual number would likely also be influenced by how successfully Malaysia can shift its economic activities toward more knowledge, capital and technology intensive industries. At the same time, the willingness of local workers to take up jobs currently dominated by migrant workers and, the reciprocal willingness of local employers to find ways to overcome the reluctance of local workers to take up these jobs, will also play a crucial role in shaping the eventual placement and number of migrant workers within the country in the years to come.

Governmental and Societal Responses

It is important to stress that the government efforts to reduce the country's heavy reliance on migrant workers coincided with rising public concerns and demands for more concrete, tangible and meaningful policies to deal with the rapid rise of the migrant workers population and its impacts on Malaysian society. As such, the enforcement of the Immigration Act 1959/1963 (Amendment) 2002 (Act A1154) that came into effect on 1 August 2002 after a lengthy amnesty period during which time undocumented immigrants can return to their country of origin without any penalties, can also be seen as a convergence of societal reactions and governmental responses toward the longstanding issue of illegal entry and the large presence of undocumented immigrants within the country.

Among others, under the new Amendment, undocumented immigrants risked being whipped and fined a maximum of RM10,000 or jailed not exceeding five years or both with whipping of not more than six strokes. Likewise, employers found hiring less then five undocumented immigrants are also liable to be fined RM10,000–RM50,000 for each worker. For five or more workers, the penalty is a similar fine per worker plus a jail term of six months to five years and whipping of up to six strokes. By the same token, locals permitting illegal immigrants to enter or remain at their premises are also liable to a fine of RM5,000–RM30,000 or imprisonment for a term not exceeding twelve months or to both for each illegal immigrant found at the premise.[11]

The tougher stance taken by the federal government is likewise being reflected at the state level. For example, *"Ops Nyah Bersapadu II"* launched in February 2002 in the state of Sabah to deal with the problem of undocumented immigrants is the latest attempt by the state government to deal with the longstanding issue.[12] The case of Sabah is particularly pertinent given that geographically, Sabah plays host to what is arguably the largest concentration of migrant workers in the East ASEAN region.

Still, one can question as to what prompted the much tougher position of the Malaysian Government towards undocumented immigrants in the country? This is a pertinent question given that the public calls for stricter control on the entry and employment of migrant workers in Malaysia have long been made over the years. In this respect, three possible explanations may be offered.

The first is the critical threshold factor. The population of immigrants in the country has reached a perceived politically critical threshold with far reaching consequences on the public sense of personal safety and national security. If one were to look at recent statements made by the political leaders of the country, there is certainly some credence to this. For example, the then Prime Minister Mahathir Mohamad pointed out during his meeting in Bali with President Megawati of Indonesia that the estimated two million immigrants in Malaysia today comprised a very sizeable portion of the country's population.[13] Mahathir echoed a common public sentiment when he also stressed that while most migrant workers were employed and caused no problems, "many of them were jobless and were involved in undesirable activities, creating anxiety among Malaysians".[14] By the same token, reacting to criticisms of Malaysia's tougher labour and immigration policies, the then Deputy Prime Minister, Abdullah Badawi, responded that "[S]uch actions are taken to deter immigrants from entering the country...we must take such measures as there have been many instances of illegal immigrants being involved in serious crimes."[15]

The second explanation is on security and control factor. Given the heavy emphasis on proper screening and documentation of workers and, the re-entry of expatriated workers (including those from Indonesia and the Philippines) upon fulfilling this requirement, it would appear that an equally plausible consideration might be the need for a greater sense of internal as well as external control over the increasing number of non-citizens entering and working in the country. By the same token, the cross-border intrusions and subsequent hostage taking incidents in Sipadan and Pandanan Islands off Sabah in April and September 2000 respectively elicited very vocal public reactions with a number of editorials and commentaries calling the incidents as a "threat to national security".[16] Likewise, cross-border crimes and extremist activities achieved added currency in the aftermath of the September 11 terrorist attacks in New York and Washington and may have also entered into the public's concern.[17] At a minimum, such incidents arguably further underlined the need for a greater sense of control over the country's vast land and sea boundaries. In this respect, Malaysia's tougher immigration and labour policies may be seen as more an attempt to get a better handle of the migrant workers population, particularly the undocumented ones, rather than a draconian attempt to purge the country of migrant workers *per se*.

The third is the manageability and diversification factor. At the same time, as the impacts of the newly implemented labour and immigration policies illustrated, heavy reliance on workers from a select few countries can also be detrimental to the well-being of the national economy when

mass repatriation, voluntary or otherwise, occurs. This factor may have
been a practical consideration as well. In this context, the government
actions can be seen not so much as an effort to reduce the country's over-
dependence on migrant workers itself as much as to "manage" and
"diversify" the presence and sources of foreign workers in the country.
This interpretation is also buttressed by the fact that workers from non-
traditional sources such as Vietnam were being sought even as
undocumented workers within the country were being sent back to their
countries of origin.

The preceding factors may or may not explain the societal and
governmental response, but whatever the actual rationales and explanations
behind the country's tougher position may be, in one way or another, they
were certainly shaped by a combination of social, economic, political and
security considerations.

Certainly, over the past few years, both the state and federal authorities
have taken various steps and measures to address the problem and, the
fact is many of these measures continue to be implemented by the relevant
authorities, albeit with some adjustments under the tougher ambit of the
amended Immigration Act. These measures include strict border control
and checking; arrest and deportation of illegal immigrants, including
whose who overstay or misuse their tourist visa; regularization
programmes; penalty for hiring foreign workers without valid work permit;
penalty for sheltering or bringing in undocumented immigrants into the
country; penalty for those renting properties to illegal immigrants;
destruction of squatter colonies and frequent operations to flush out illegal
immigrants; levy on foreign workers; limitation of foreign workers to
specific sectors of the economy; imposition of a time limit for foreign
workers to continuously stay in the country (3+1+1 for a total of five years
for unskilled and semi-skilled workers),[18] mandatory medical examination
for foreign workers; and voluntary repatriation of foreigners.

Nevertheless, it still remains to be seen just how effective the on-going
steps and measures that the Malaysian Government is currently
undertaking in controlling and reducing the number of undocumented
immigrants will be in the long-term. What is clear is that the continuing
public calls for a more effective and consistent response to the issue and,
the government publicly stated intention to resolve the longstanding
problem, clearly indicate that addressing the problem of undocumented

immigrants remains as a major challenge for the country and region in the years to come.

Issues, Realities and Regional Co-operation

International migration activities, both legal and illegal, will likely remain and indeed may increase as peoples become more conscious and better inform of the comparative as well as relative living standards within their own countries with that of other countries. Perhaps this is one of the ironies of globalization whereby better information about the relative "safety" and perceived "good life" in other countries are important contributing factors for migrants to risk lives and limbs to seek out these destinations. Indeed, it may be no coincidence that globally, countries seen as the "bastion" of democracies and human rights as well as "economic paradise" have more often than not also become the destinations of choice for international immigrants, both legal and otherwise.

While the illegal movements of migrants across borders have understandably captured the most attention, it is also well known that the legal process have sometimes been circumvented by international migration. A recent editorial in the *Irish Times*,[19] for instance, argued that so-called asylum seekers come to Ireland not only because of favourable economic conditions in the country but also because they knew very well that the 1951 Geneva Convention makes it legally obligatory for Ireland to give them sanctuary. Likewise, pointing to the case of illegal immigrants in Germany, a member of the German Bundestag (Parliament), Carl-Dieter Spranger, notes, "[T]hey abuse our generous regulations on asylum but their objective was to get the social security benefits. They claimed to be political refugees but most of the time that was not the case."[20] Also, in the case of Sabah, the Immigration Department has reported a growing trend among those who enter the state legally, to subsequently abuse their social visit pass by working illegally or overstaying.[21]

On the face of it, the illegal cross-border movements would have been much more difficult were it not for the facilitative and exploitive presence of well-organized groups and syndicates who ferry migrants across international boundaries for a hefty price, not infrequently costing migrants not only in monetary terms but tragically their very lives. By the same token, it should also be noted that many locals themselves abet both in the illegal entry of migrant workers as well as by employing them, illustrating all too clearly the two-sided nature of the issue. In this respect, abuses of the legal processes and rights, by illegal immigrants as well hosts, are no doubt also part and parcel of the international migration equation.

Looking at the Southeast Asian region, the intended economic integration of the regional countries under the ambit of the ASEAN Free Trade Area (AFTA) may well lead to additional variables in the regional migration flows in the coming years. At the same time, the emergence and successful implementation of AFTA should also provide countries in the region with both a vehicle as well as an added incentive to address the regional migrant workers' flows. Additionally, the movements of people across national borders within the region are also increasingly becoming a critical variable in intra-regional relations. Indeed, given that migrant workers flows can be expected to increase rather then decrease over the coming years, the cacophony of issues over migrants might well push the question of peoples' mobility into ASEAN's sphere of "high politics" by default. As it stands, any action undertaken by the receiving countries not unexpectedly usually elicits a public response (both positive and negative) from the source countries.[22]

This is well illustrated, for example, by the recent implementation of Malaysia's tougher labour and immigration policies. Given the huge presence of undocumented Indonesian and Filipino immigrants in the country in particular, migrant workers from both countries were the most affected and consequently, the repatriation of thousands of workers from both countries put a heavy burden on the respective capacity of both countries to absorb their returning citizens, especially given the economic difficulties that both countries also face. At the same time, the move also affected key sectors of the Malaysian economy. In this respect, while the public protestations including the burning of the Malaysian flag in both countries may be blamed on a select few, the fact that such incidents also alluded to the more unpleasant past such as "Confrontation" and "revival of the Sabah Claim" cannot but illustrate the potential of the migrant workers issue to rekindle strong public sentiments on both sides. Malaysia may see that its actions are perfectly in consonant with its national interest, but both Indonesia and the Philippines strongly felt that their citizens, who have contributed much to the economic development of Malaysia, were being unfairly treated.

More important, such incidents arguably served to underline the need to have in place a more systematic and mutually agreeable processing mechanism for migrant workers within the region. Achieving this will, however, be no easy task given the complexity of the issues involved. Nevertheless, one can begin by looking at a number of critical factors that come into play in the regional movement of migrants. To start with, the issue of regional migration is obviously a multilateral issue, for the simple reason that the nationals and governments of various countries are inevitably involved. Thus while a source country and a receiving country can take direct bilateral actions, given the multiplicity of nationalities involved in Malaysia, for example, such bilateral actions would entail more than just one source country. Second, the multiplicity of parties involved would also suggest that for such a regional mechanism to be put in place and function effectively, the co-operation of all the affected countries would be essential.

A third factor is the actual "push-pull" factors involved in both the source and receiving countries. These contributing factors must not be overlooked as part of any effort to effectively address the regional migrant workers flows. In this regard, one key challenge is to foster economic growth and development to meet an expanding labour pool on the one hand and, to foster economic growth and development in consonant with local needs and sensitivities on the other hand. However, even if most governments may desire this, it is not easily achieved and furthermore, the movement of workers across borders is also a global reality, and many would say, rights, today. It would appear then that a subsequent challenge is how to strike a mutually agreeable and manageable balance between excess labour in the source countries and the labour needs and local sensitivities in the receiving countries. At the very least, "exporting/importing" as well as "entry/repatriation" of migrant workers must not be seen as a convenient economic and policy option by any side without due regard to the attendant consequences including those on the migrant workers themselves.

At the same time, it should also be noted that any infusion of a sizeable number of people into any given society would likely induce some reactions from and implications on the affected host society. This raises the fourth factor of societal impacts on the host countries and their level of tolerance to such infusions. This is an issue that needs to be taken into account as well, as it plays a crucial role in shaping the societal response in receiving countries. A final factor is the much broader issue of the disjuncture between the calls for trade liberalization and restriction on people mobility. This is of course part and parcel of the broader discourse on globalization itself, particularly on the calls of the developed countries for freer capital and investment flows without a corresponding openness to the freer flows of workers from the developing countries.

Within the ASEAN framework, there are certainly a number of pertinent undertakings that touched on the issue of labour mobility. For example, Article 4 (Features) (e) of the 1998 Framework Agreement on the ASEAN Investment Area (AIA) notes that the AIA shall be an area where "there is freer flow of capital, *skilled labour and professionals*, and technology amongst Member States" (emphasis added).[23] What is interesting is the fact that "skilled labour and professionals" are singled out, apparently excluding the numerically larger pool of unskilled and semi-skilled workers moving within the region. To be fair, however, the AIA was initiated as part and parcel of the AFTA process, and therefore, pointed to a time (2010) when the ASEAN region would conceivably be more developed. In addition, it should also be noted that AFTA itself was drafted long before the inclusion of all ten Southeast Asian states into ASEAN. Be that as it may, there was surely also a hopeful presumption that the regional economies would by then be more capital-, technology- and knowledge-intensive requiring less unskilled and semi-skilled labour.

At the same time, as reflected by various Joint Communiqués of the Annual ASEAN Labour Ministers Meetings, there is certainly a general recognition within ASEAN of the need to come up with comparable ASEAN wide standards on human resource training and certifications.[24] Likewise, the issue of people mobility is also highlighted at the sub-regional settings such as the growth triangles. Within the Brunei-Indonesia-Malaysia-Philippines: East ASEAN Growth Area (BIMP-EAGA), for example, people mobility has been highlighted as one of the key concerns right from the start. However, despite these stated intentions, the fact remains that neither ASEAN as an organization nor as a region, currently has in place a functional regional processing mechanism to address the regional flows of migrant workers.

One could of course argue that what is needed is not necessarily any additional mechanism or more bureaucratic hassles, but just the effective implementation of existing relevant laws within the various countries involved. As it stands, the issue of migrant workers is not a new one and there are likely already more than enough national laws and regulations in place to deal with related concerns. In this case, what is needed is the political will and capacity to effectively implement such laws as they were intended in the first place. And such political will and capacity may be much easier to muster nationally rather then regionally. Be that as it may, given ASEAN's *modus operandi* of consensual decision-making as well as its sacrosanct policy of non-interference, any move towards setting up a regional mechanism or any other similar vehicle to address the regional flows of migrant workers will likely have to account for the following factors: being mutually agreeable to all the affected ASEAN countries; a recognition of the legitimate concerns of host societies, including on the key issue of proper screening and documentation; an agreement on the need to effectively address migrant labour flows both at the points of exit (source countries) and entry (receiving countries) to ensure effective matching between source and receiving countries' needs and expectations; taking into account the role of all pertinent parties in the migrant workers' flows; and a commitment to extend equal protection to both local and migrant workers alike.

These factors are by no means comprehensive, but they are certainly some of the critical considerations that need to be accounted for in any undertaking involving migrant workers. What is clear is that the issue of migrant workers is one issue that may unilaterally warrant particular attention from ASEAN and its member countries in the early years of the twenty-first century.

Concluding Remarks

Similar to other regions in the world, the Southeast Asian region has been continuing to witness the dynamic flows of migrant workers. Within the region, Malaysia stands as an integral part of the regional migration flows. And while Malaysia has taken and continues to implement various measures to shift its economic activities towards more capital- and knowledge-intensive industries, migrant workers are expected to continue to play an important role, particularly in the plantation sub-sectors as well as construction sector in the near and immediate term. At the broader regional context, it is equally likely that the export and import of migrant workers will continue to feature as a means to address continuing labour surpluses as well as needs. Given this scenario, there are quite clearly justifiable arguments in favour of greater regional co-operation towards facilitating and managing the flows of migrant workers within the region in a mutually agreeable and beneficial manner. While this may be a desired objective, however, the fact that such a mechanism has yet to materialize within the ASEAN region, likely points to the attendant political and perhaps psychological difficulties of establishing such a set-up.

As a regional organization, ASEAN has proven its viability and relevance time and again at key junctures of its existence. In this respect, the attendant issues and implications on the affected countries posed by the migrant workers flow in the region are such that its importance and priority could well rise to the fore in the first decade of the twenty-first century. As such, ASEAN would do well to tackle the issue collectively. However, any mechanism or policy towards this direction will likely have to evolve under the prevailing realities of the ASEAN framework, particularly its longstanding practice of consensual decision-making and non-interference policy. In the final analysis, any successful endeavour towards this end will have to somehow strike a fine balance between the layered needs and interests of the source as well as receiving countries, including those of the migrants themselves.

Notes

[1]   John Samuel, "Migration and Development", *Express* (1998) no. 5 (1998): 1. International Development Information Centre, CIDA, <http://www.acdi-cida.ca/xpress/dex/xpress_e.htm>.

[2]   Ibid.

[3]   It should be noted that Malaysia is also a source of migrant workers abroad, albeit in smaller number. See, for example, Susumu Watanabe, "The Economic Crisis and Migrant Workers in Japan", *Asian and Pacific Migration Journal 7*, nos. 2–3 (1998) and Joseph S. Lee, "The Impact of the Asian Financial Crisis on Foreign Workers in Taiwan", Ibid.

[4]   As reported in the *Daily Express*, 9 August 2002. To be sure, the estimated figure likely includes the dependents of migrant workers as well.

[5]   This is of course assuming that local workers are all accounted for in the 2000 figure.

[6]   For a more detailed discussion of the migrant workers situation in Sabah, see for example, Bilson Kurus, "Migrant Labour: The Sabah Experience", *Asian and Pacific Migration Journal 7*, no. 2–3 (1999).

7   Chapter 4 — "Population, Employment and Human Resource Development" in *Eight Malaysia Plan, 2001–2005,* written by Economic Planning Unit, Prime Minister Department. Cawangan Kuala Lumpur: Percetakan Nasional Malaysia Berhad, 2001.
8   Ibid.
9   Chapter 6 — *Investing in People.*
10 Ibid.
11 *Immigration (Amendment) Act 2002.*
12 Briefing by Sabah Commissioner of Police Ramli Bin Yusuff at the Seminar on Regional Security Risks and Challenges: The Role of Civil Society, Kota Kinabalu, Sabah, 2 July 2002.
13 The observations made by two visiting German Parliamentarians on the approximate nine million illegal immigrants, or over ten per cent of Germany's eighty million population in Germany, appears to parallel Malaysia's own concerns. See for example, the *Daily Express*, 29 August 2002.
14 As quoted in the *Daily Express*, 9 August 2002.
15 As quoted in the *New Straits Times*, 15 August 2002.
16 See for example, *The Sunday Times*, 30 April 2000.
17 The Bali bombings have in a sense further "localized" the security realities and challenges of the post September 11 global environment.
18 As reported in the *Daily Express*, 8 August 2002.
19 *Europe Intelligence Wire*, 30 July 2002, NewsEdge Corporation C2000 <http://www.iom.int/>.
20 As quoted in the *Daily Express*, 29 August 2002.
21 See for example, Mohd Yaakub Hj. Johari and Ramlan Goddos, "Profiles of Foreign Workers in Sabah: Policy Implications", paper presented at the Seminar on Regional Security Risks and Challenges: The Role of Civil Society, Kota Kinabalu, Sabah, 2 July 2002, unpublished.
22 For instance, accusations of mistreatment of their citizens is a frequent point of contention that is levelled against receiving countries by source countries, particularly in cases of deportation.
23 ASEAN Secretariat <http://www.aseansec.org>.
24 ASEAN <http://www.asean.or.id>.

13

Government Policies on International Migration: Illegal Workers in Thailand

Yongyuth Chalamwong

Introduction

The exceptional economic performance of Thailand from the 1980s to the 1990s, and the subsequent experience of the economic crisis in 1997, has generated worldwide recognition, and provided an interesting case study for other countries, especially in the area of labour market and international migration. Thailand has been transforming itself from an agricultural to an industrial based economy since the mid-1980s, but the experience with labour-intensive industrialization has shown that it is not sustainable in the longer run. Intense international competition from lower cost countries, such as China, Vietnam and Indonesia, has prevented the country from further expanding in this type of industrialization. The Thai industry has been slowly forced to shift to higher value added production, and this has become the dominant driving force of the countries since early 1990s.

The rapid economic growth in the late 1980s and early 1990s has caused a general tightening of the labour market in many sub-sectors. In contrast, in addition to attractive returns from working abroad, the lack of employment opportunities for low-educated workers at home has pushed many able men and women in this period to work overseas as contract and illegal workers.

The labour tightening just before the crisis has spread out everywhere, and is especially evident during the peak season of agriculture. As wages in non-agricultural activities have become more competitive, Thai workers have become more reluctant to accept menial and lower paid work. Consequently, there has been a strong pressure for illegal labour migration that, combined with the growing affluence of the country, makes Thailand a powerful magnet for migrants from neighbouring countries.

The financial crisis, which originated in Thailand since 1997, spread to many countries in Southeast Asia. The economies of the region either suffered their consequences directly due to the region's high degree of inter-dependency through trade and investment flows, or indirectly due to a slowing down of their economies. These pronounced impacts on the economy of the region extended to the labour markets, and thereby on the employment of foreign workers.

The labour market impacts of the financial crisis were significant. For those economies which were directly affected, within twelve months of the beginning of the crisis, the median increase in unemployment as officially estimated, was almost 200 per cent. For several labour receiving countries, the essential focus of immigration policy in response to the crisis has been on limiting the extent of illegal immigration and on combating the employment of illegal foreign workers. In addition, it should be acknowledged that the September 11 terrorist attacks in the United States in 2001 have given rise to economic uncertainty and high unemployment rates in many Southeast Asian countries.

Thailand's economy has been on the road to recovery from the two crises. The economic growth has slowly recovered from a negative growth in 1998 to about 1.8 per cent in 2001 and reached 4.8 per cent in 2002. However, during these periods, the number of illegal migrant workers from neighbouring countries had not decreased, as the local labour market had shrunk, and the unemployment rate remained relatively high.

This chapter reviews the recent trends on international migration and the recent development in migration policies in Thailand and its policy implications.

Profile of Illegal Aliens in Thailand

Before 1970

During the nineteenth century, the immigration from other countries was used as labour for the monarchy, supplies of warriors and repopulation (Chintayananda, Risser, and Chantavanich 1977). The immigrant groups were unskilled labour and traders, the majority of whom came from China. The unskilled labourers were used in the construction of infrastructure, such as building canals and railroads. According to Soonthornthada and Phataravanich (1977), there were 162,505 Chinese immigrants as reported by the 1909 Bangkok Census. The other groups of immigrants who came to Thailand during the same period, such as from India, Western countries, and Malaysia, were traders, or involved in religious traditions and other purposes.

According to Sonthisakyothin (2000), King Rama the Fifth realized the unruliness and lack of discipline of the aliens who entered the Kingdom of Siam. As a consequence, the Kingdom issued the Act to control the quota of the annual number of immigrants to Thailand, causing the number of immigrants to gradually decline from 10,000 to 200 per annum. During these periods, there were influxes of migrants from neighbouring countries such as Shan, Mon, Karen, Lao, Khmer, Vietnamese, Burmese and other small ethnic groups who became minorities and lived along the border of Thailand up till now.

Since World War II, the civil wars of neighbouring countries have pushed large numbers of refugees to seek shelter in Thailand. Hundreds of thousands came to Thailand for a short stay, waiting to return to their homeland and/or seeking to be resettled in third countries. But, some of them have remained in Thailand for several decades. These include 42,211 former Vietnamese war refugees who entered Thailand since 1959 and other war refugees from other Indochinese states, estimated to be about 13,000 persons. It was estimated in 1995 that the number of illegal migrants from Burma who entered Thailand along the 1800-kilometre long border before 1976 was about 48,000, and 100,356 after 1976 (Shinnavaso 1995).

Periods After 1970

In fact, Thailand has had the Immigration Act since 1950 and the Alien Employment Act since 1978. These Acts permitted professionals to enter without limit as long as the country experienced labour shortages, but restricted other type of immigrants for national security reasons. As mentioned above, the movement of undocumented, unskilled workers entering the borders from Indochina and South Asia has grown since the Second World War. Due to civil war in neighbouring countries, Thailand became a major site of refugees fleeing the conflict and devastation. Since 1980s, the country's increasing affluence brought about by the unprecedented economic boom has made Thailand a magnet for illegal workers from neighbouring countries (Chalamwong and Sevilla 1996).

The remarkable accomplishments of the economic performance of Thailand in the late 1980s and early 1990s and the success of the higher education policy have shifted the purpose of immigrants from escaping war to seeking jobs, while Thai workers have also lost their interest in local menial work. Thai businessmen have begun to welcome illegal migrant workers from Myanmar (Burma), Laos and Cambodia to replace local workers in agriculture and fishery related sectors, especially for doing the dirty, dangerous, and difficult works (Chalamwong 1998; Chintayananda, Risser and Chantavanich 1997).

It has been very difficult to obtain reliable data on the extent of illegal immigrant workers. Much of the data of its magnitude has come from the guess of many scholars in this field rather than official documents. In 1993, it was estimated that the illegal immigrants sneaking through the ten border provinces of Thailand was 200,000, and the number was estimated to increase to 400,000 in 1995. In 1996, Chalamwong's study had put the upper range of Burmese illegal workers in Thailand to be 820,000 (Chalamwong et al. 1996).

Table 13.1 shows the profile of the Thai employment during 1997 to 2001. According to recent statistics, Malaysia, Thailand and Singapore are the three major receiving countries of migrant workers in Southeast Asia because of their superior economic development positions and better working environment compared to the sending countries. At the same time, Thailand also has sent medium and low skilled workers abroad for decades.

As indicated by Sussangkarn and Chalamwong (1994), Thai workers going overseas have become a common phenomenon since the 1970s. This is due to many factors such as the imbalance in the domestic labour market, persisting income inequalities (that is, relative poverty) in Thailand, labour policy that has encouraged the export of labour, and job opportunities in the receiving countries.

TABLE 13.1
Thai Employment and Migration Profile, 1997–2001

	1997	1998	1999	2000	2001
1. Mid-year population	60.60	61.20	61.82	62.40	62.91
2. Work Force (average) (million)	32.50	32.60	32.80	33.20	33.80
2.1 Employed (million)	31.40	30.70	30.70	31.30	32.10
2.2 Unemployed (million)	0.50	1.30	1.40	1.20	1.10
2.3 Seasonally Inactive (million)	0.60	0.70	0.70	0.70	0.60
3. Working Overseas	183,671	191,735	202,416	193,041	160,252
4. Aliens Granted Work Permits	53,175	61,427	24,726	26,455	29,079
5. Remaining Aliens with Work Permits	164,313	116,657	101,772	102,612	92,811
6. Estimated Number of Illegal Migrant Workers	667,815	986,000	986,889	1,000,000	1,000,000
7. Registered Illegal Migrant Workers	293,652	90,403	99,264	99,656	568,249
	(100.00)	(100.00)	(100.00)	(100.00)	(100.00)
7.1 Burmese	253,492	78,904	89,336	97,021	451,335
	(86.32)	(87.28)	(90.00)	(97.36)	(79.43)
7.2 Laotians	11,594	1,231	1,164	1,011	59,358
	(3.95)	(1.36)	(1.17)	(1.01)	(10.45)
7.3 Cambodians	25,566	10,268	9,496	7,421	57,556
	(8.71)	(11.36)	(9.57)	(7.45)	(10.13)
8. Share of Overseas Workers	0.57	0.59	0.62	0.58	0.47
9. Share of Legal Aliens	0.51	0.36	0.31	0.31	0.27
10. Share of Illegal Aliens	2.05	3.02	3.01	3.01	2.96

Notes: 1. Open registration to all Burmese, Laos and Cambodians.
2. Unit: persons.
Sources: National Statistical Office; Labour Force Survey, various issues and Ministry of Labour and
Social Welfare; Year Book of Employment Statistics, various issues.

Table 13.1 shows the number of overseas workers increased from 183,671 in 1997 to 202,416 million in 1999 but dropped to 160,252 in 2001. The share of out-going Thai workers was 0.57 per cent of work force in 1997, which declined slightly to 0.47 per cent in 2001. The decline of the overseas workers was due mainly to economic slowdown in the receiving countries such as Taiwan and Southeast Asian countries, and fiercer competition from cheap labour exporting countries such as Indonesia and Vietnam.

Based on Investment Promotion Acts of 1977, the Alien Act of 1978 and Immigration Acts of 1978 provided temporary permits to certain types of aliens. In addition, under the Board of Investment (BOI) Act, foreign firms could bring in foreign skilled labour, technicians and their family members for a fixed period of time, subject to certain conditions.

Alien employment in Thailand appeared to decline continuously right after the crisis. The remaining aliens with work permits decreased from 164,313 or 0.51 per cent of the work force in 1997 (before the crisis) to 92,911 or 0.27 per cent of the work force in 2001 (after the crisis).

Chalamwong (2002) observed that the majority of workers who applied and received work permits have begun to increase again from every country. The largest increase in 1999 was of the Chinese from Taipei. The majority of the Chinese from Taipei were businessmen. The countries, which have continually ranked among the principal sending country, are Japan, The United Kingdom, The United States of America, India, China and Australia. These expatriates engaged in a multitude of jobs, especially in the private sector, in jobs where Thais have no expertise. The majority worked with multinational corporations owned by nationals of their home country, where they occupied positions as senior managers and top executives, and most of whom resided in Bangkok and nearby provinces. These higher-skilled manpower has been in the upper labour market, and has had some negative impacts on local Thai workers.

The utilization of foreign workers may create some negative effects as well. The obvious one is that they compete directly with the local Thai workers if the foreign workers stay in the long-term. Their long-term stay can prolong technology transfer to Thai workers, and their presence may cause some dilution of local culture, language, and ways of life (Chalamwong and Sevilla 1996). Unlike Singapore, Thailand does not have a clear-cut medium- and long-term national development goal to utilize expatriates as a means to improve the competitiveness for the country via technology transformation.

Thailand as a net receiver of migrant workers has experienced the largest migration of illegal immigrant workers from neighbouring countries. Illegal immigrant workers have become visible in Thai society since 1995, when Thailand changed the immigration policy from national security to economic security. As a result, illegal immigrants comprised almost three per cent of the country's workforce in 2001. It indicates a high level of dependence on illegal migrant workers. They have spread out all over the country as a result of hundreds of points of entry along the 1,800-kilometre border with Myanmar, several hundred kilometres of borders with Laos

and Cambodia, and poor patrols. The government has also failed to control
the spread of illegal workers. Before 1994, illegal workers could be found
generally in farming, construction and fishing in the five main border
provinces. But recently illegal workers have been found in every province
in Thailand. The Ministry of Labour and Social Welfare reported on 1 May
1999 that the number of unregistered illegal immigrants was estimated at
986,889, while the number of registered illegal migrant workers was only
99,264. In 2001, the estimated number of illegal immigrants was
approximately one million, almost 80 per cent of them from Myanmar. It
is interesting to note that the number of registered illegal migrant was
568,249, the largest number ever to be registered, as the country openly
registered all illegal migrant workers from Myanmar, Laos, and Cambodia
for the first time (Table 13.1).

As mentioned before, the illegal workers may have both negative and
positive impacts on Thai society. The negative impacts include those on
economic security, national security, and health security. They lead to
crime, disease, and more stateless babies. Illegal workers' families compete
for social infrastructure, such as public health and schooling, with Thai
citizens. Hiring cheap labour distorts wages rates and deters Thais from
entering the labour market. The positive impacts include helping the
country to solve problems of labour shortages in 3-D jobs, stimulating
new investment in labour-intensive manufacturing along the border areas,
and encouraging Thai workers to secure higher levels of employment
through undertaking appropriate training. Most foreign workers fill the
vacant positions in agriculture and related industries such as fisheries and
related activities, rice milling, and services. Employers who hired illegal
migrant workers were estimated to save about US$0.3 billion per firm per
year in labour cost from hiring illegal immigrants (Chalamwong 2002).

Illegal Migrant Workers Policy in Thailand

During the past two decades, the Thai Government has tried to find ways
to manage the large number of illegal migrants from neighbouring
countries, especially from Myanmar. The difficult task of the government
agencies was to comply with the requests of the various pressure groups.
These pressure groups from the business sector have argued that it is now
very difficult to find Thai workers for certain jobs in specific locations,
especially in the fishery sector and rubber plantations located in the

southern part of Thailand. In August 1995, the chairman of the country's most powerful industrial group — the Federation of Thai Industries (FTI) — called for the government to allow at least one million foreign workers to help alleviate the acute labour shortage faced by many industries such as textiles, footwear, frozen seafood, transport and construction industries. These moves clearly suggest an attempt to keep profits high and maintain their competitiveness in labour-intensive industries.

Notwithstanding, a recent warning came from labour groups that the alien labour issue could turn violent because of adverse consequences to local workers, according to Chalamwong and Sevilla (1996). Among the measures proposed at that time by the FTI to the government to deal with the current account deficit was the creation of a special economic zone (primarily for exports) located along the border, to be staffed with foreign labour and no minimum wage requirement. However, the government has never approved this idea, but many labour-intensive industries have decided to receive existing privileges being offered by the Board of Investment to relocate their industries in border provinces such as Mae Sot district of Tak province. According to the Tak's Chamber of Commerce, there are nearly a hundred firms established in this area during this period.

In the early part of January 1996, officials from the Ministry of Labour and Social Welfare, the National Security Council and other state agencies agreed in principle to allow illegal immigrants to work legally in Thailand to solve the country's labour shortage. The agreement expands the coverage of the original 1992 Cabinet decision to allow illegal migrants of Burmese nationality to work in specified control areas in nine provinces. In principle, the agreement requires illegal migrants to report to the immigration police first, while waiting to be repatriated, then register with the Labour and Social Welfare Ministry before being taken on by their employers. The Ministry issued two-year work permits to these illegal aliens that could be extended upon expiry. While it is possible to credit FTI's powerful lobby for this development, it probably also indicates the government's realization of the difficulty in effectively stopping labour movement through Thailand's borders.

This decision was criticized by many scholars that the transition from low-end labour-intensive operations to more capital-intensive manufacturing would therefore be retarded by the presence of a large pool of cheap labour in the neighbouring countries, which have become readily available to Thai industrialists as economic refugees (Sussangkarn and Chalamwong 1994; Poapongsakorn and Taethiengtam 1992; Wong-anan 1995*a*, *b*). Since there was no immediate economic improvement or resolution in sight to the civil strife within these neighbouring countries, it could only be expected that combined with the growing imbalances in the Thai labour market as a result of continued rapid economic expansion, the influx of migrants who cross the border to seek employment may rapidly grow to unmanageable proportions. It is instructive to note that experiences in other countries show that once an economy becomes highly dependent on foreign labour, it is difficult to suddenly stop migration because of established family and community networks in the receiving country (Martin 2002).

According to Chalamwong and Sevilla (1996), the case of Thailand clearly demonstrates two inter-related tendencies under a regime of rapid economic growth: first, the created difficulties in the adjustment of labour supply particularly for personnel with the high skills necessary to bring the country forward to a higher and more complex level of industrialization; second, the pressure to maintain competitiveness in some labour-intensive manufacturing sectors when there is clearly little or no internal comparative advantage remaining because the skill levels of the Thai workforce are generally insufficient to drive a more technologically-intensive industrialization process. In combination with developments in neighbouring countries whose own internal problems have created a large reserve pool of economically unproductive, cheap and highly accessible labour, these factors form a pattern of industrial development among labour-intensive sectors that continues to profit from the same rationale.

Managing the Flow of Illegal Workers: From National Security to Human Rights

As in most countries, a major obstacle in producing a coherent and rational immigration policy in Thailand is the number of agencies who have responsibility over immigration in various capacities. The issue of illegal migrants is politically sensitive both at the domestic and international levels. This is primarily due to the history of refugee migrations from wars and ethnic persecution that incorporated political and military elements, and stateless minorities. From a legal and political perspective, the Thai Government considers all refugees and asylum seekers to be "illegal immigrants" (Robinson 1991). Thus, because of the difficulty in differentiating economic migrants from their ethnic and national affiliations, many agencies consider the problem of illegal migrants not only a threat to the country's social stability, but also to national security that could affect relations between countries. During the early 1990s, agencies under the Ministry of Defence and the Ministry of Foreign Affairs exercised the main responsibilities for such closely labour-related issues as war and political refugees, and the control over various minorities who have no recognized nationalities, along the Thai-Myanmar border.[1]

The Secretariat of the National Security Council (NSC) is one of the main national organizations under the Prime Minister's Office dealing with migration issues that have implications for national security. During the height of civil wars within Thailand's neighbouring countries, the major focus of NSC in dealing with the influx of refugees was directly related to national security issues (that is, intelligence gathering, policing, detention, and repatriation). Since 1990 the role of NSC has changed focus from war refugees to primarily economic refugees as the tide of illegal migrants entering Thailand rapidly increased. During the early stage of solving the immigration problem, the government designated the NSC to be responsible for finding the right measures to deal with the ever-increasing number of illegal migrants in Thailand especially those along the Thai-Myanmar border.

The Ministry of Interior on the other hand, operated the Immigration Office under the Police Department that serves as the main agency responsible for dealing with all aspects concerning the entry and exit of all persons entering and leaving the country. The Ministry controls aliens by granting both short-term permits and permanent residence. It has set up rules and regulations that allow the hiring of illegal workers while they are "waiting to be repatriated". According to the law, illegal workers are sent to court to be fined about US$60[2] or detained. The court orders detention up to thirty days if the illegal worker does not have the money to pay the court's fee. However, for those waiting to be repatriated, the Immigration Act allows an employer to bail them out by depositing about US$120 to the Immigration Office in order to make them available for work. After bail is paid, illegal migrants must apply for work permit from the Ministry and pay an annual fee of US$24.

This procedure applied only to Burmese immigrants who came to Thailand after 9 March 1976 and were already in the possession of purple and orange identity cards. In practice however, few employers go to the trouble of bailing out illegal Burmese migrants from jail. However, during that period, about 2,000 Burmese illegal migrants in the eastern province of Kanchanaburi received work permits after their employers paid the US$120 bond, applied for the work permit for the illegal migrant, and paid the annual fee of 1,000 baht.

A new Ministry of Labour and Social Welfare was established in 1993. Despite its recentness, the Ministry has already compiled an expanding database of the labour market (by province) and illegal migration. Its Department of Employment has submitted a proposal to the government to deal with illegal migrants. The measure was to allow existing illegal migrants to stay and work for two years. The proposal of granting temporary work permits was approved by the Cabinet on 25 June 1996. It legalized the illegal migrants, but still retained their illegal status, so that it would allow the government to deport them when the granting periods were expired. The policy during this period also aimed to stop a new influx of illegal migrants from neighbours at the border, and at the same time utilize the nearly one million illegal migrants to solve the country's labour shortage problem.

Since the policy's aim to stop or prevent new entries has not been very effective, the NSC has recommended measures to the Ministry of Interior whose agencies are directly responsible for the problem at the point of entry. These include stricter enforcement of checkpoints along the border, increasing penalties to both the illegal migrant and employer, and improved monitoring of illegal migrants through survey and registration. However, implementation has been difficult for a number of reasons. First, it is almost impossible to completely seal the territorial borders of the country, a problem magnified by forested terrain that is undeveloped and extremely difficult to patrol. Implementation of effective border controls to check illegal migrants has been hampered not only by limited resources for surveillance, recording, and monitoring, but also by the sensitive political issues raised especially by illegal migration of minorities in the border regions who are in limbo, nationality-wise.

Second, it is difficult to come up with a clear policy on this because of opposing interests of business and Thai labour, and conflicting views among government agencies (SLDC 1995). Third, enforcement at the field level is difficult when implementing officers are understaffed and low-paid. Fourth, the cost of a sophisticated online computerized system for foreign worker registration and identification may simply be prohibitive. Such a system would necessarily be able to store, compare and retrieve fingerprint-based data, the sole basis for identifying a migrant in the absence of reliable supporting documents from their countries of origin.

Recently, in Southeast Asia, the essential focus of immigration policy has been on reducing the dependence on unskilled foreign workers and limiting the extent of illegal immigration. Thailand is no exception. In the past, as mentioned earlier, the Thai Government focused on controlling and making use of the illegal migrants by implementing the existing law and regulations. At the same time, the government tried to prevent any new influx of workers, especially from neighbouring countries. But the government has not been successful in this. Thus, in July 1999, the National Committee on Employment agreed with the conclusions of the review on illegal migrant workers' employment. The sub-committee requested the Ministry of Labour and Social Welfare to conduct a survey to estimate the demand for manual labourers among labour-intensive industries in seventy-six provinces. The results revealed that the business operators wanted to hire a total of slightly over 303,000 illegal migrant workers. Demand was the highest in the fisheries.

On the basis of this information, the Thai Government decided on 3 August 1999, to grant only 86,895 work permits to foreign workers of Myanmar, Laotian and Cambodian nationality, granting permission to stay until 31 August 2000. Potential employers were given ninety days within which to report to the provincial authorities, bringing with them the documents of the illegal immigrant workers whom they wanted to employ. They were also required to pay a 1,000 baht-deposit charge for each worker. Though registered, these foreign workers would retain their illegal status. They would be employed in eighteen labour-intensive activities. This present policy is supposed to be a final extension for the limited number of illegal migrant workers to whom it applies.

Unregistered alien workers would be arrested and deported by the immigration and border patrol police after the end of ninety days grace period. According to the 1999 measures, the illegal immigrants have been continuously coming back, getting arrested, and then deported. The statistics released by the National Security Council (NSC) indicated that there were 319,629 arrested in 1999, and this increased to 444,636 in 2000. Employers and business owners who continued to hire undocumented workers after the granting periods expired were supposed to be arrested and prosecuted. But this measure was not fully implemented, due mainly to unclear policy from the government, as indicated by the fact that only one hundred employers were arrested and prosecuted in 2000. The Ministry of Labour and Social Welfare has announced that the government hopes to keep the number of illegal migrant workers below 200,000. If the government could decrease the number of illegal immigrants, the employment situation for Thais would improve considerably. But the outcomes of the implementation by authorities concerned have not been very satisfactory (Chalamwong 2001).

During the past few years, Thailand has changed from Chuan Leekpai's to Thaksin's administration which has been in office since February 2001. However, the immigration policy of the new government also changed. There were proposals from the National Advisory Council for Labour Development and NSC's sub-committee on solving the problem of illegal migrants by setting up a permanent organization to provide proper management of illegal migrant workers. This organization called " Office of the Administrative Commission on Irregular Workers (OAW)" was finally approved by the Cabinet in the middle of 2001, based on the initiative of the NSC. This new organization was chaired by the Prime Minister or appointed Deputy Prime Minister. The MOLSW was responsible for setting up administrative offices, and played the role of secretary of the new organization. The committee consisted of twenty-nine representatives from various organizations involved. The main tasks of the committee were to propose policies, measures, master plans, set up conditions in negotiating, seek co-operation and help from other countries. It also established networks in management of foreign labour in Thailand and develops legislation and regulations. However this office just started operating in November 2001, and work has gradually progressed since then.

However, after the granting period of illegal migrants expired again in August 2001, the present government came up with a new policy of allowing all illegal migrant workers who were already residing and working in Thailand to report to the Royal Immigration Police[3]. They could then apply for temporary work permits from MOLSW before the end of October 2001. During the first stage, the alien workers were granted work permits for six months. Then, they were required to pass a physical examination before getting another six months extension. Those registered migrants who could not pass the physical check up would be deported.

There were 562,527 illegal workers reported in ten types of business occupations in the first phase of registration. These include agriculture (18.33 per cent), mining industry (0.25 per cent), brick and porcelain making factories (0.64 per cent), construction industry (8.49), food processing industry (1.1 per cent), livestock (5.28 per cent), fishery (17.7 per cent), transport (2.27 per cent), domestic workers (14.41 per cent), special business with employers (26.86 per cent), and without employers (4.68 per cent).

Out of 562,527 registered migrants, 79.82 per cent were Burmese, 10.38 per cent Laotian and 9.8 per cent Cambodian. The government seems to be happy with this emerging figure. But it was believed that there were at least 300,000–400,000 illegal workers who still did not register, especially those temporary workers who come to work in Thailand seasonally along the border provinces of the country. After the second phase registration was completed, there were only 428,468 undocumented registered workers who reported for the health check and renewal of work permits. The government intended to freeze the number of new registration to this figure.

Several questions were raised to the government about what to do next after the latest open registration expired. Can the government keep the promise that there would be no more extension of the current work permits after the one-year term is expired? The answer to this question is loud and clear: the government cannot keep up with its promises. The Cabinet has again decided to extend the 562,527 registered workers for another year, when the term of work permit was supposed to have expired on 24 September 2002. One of the main reasons for this is to allow the research institutes sponsored by OAW enough time to conduct a survey of real demand for alien workers, so that better measures can be implemented in the medium and longer run. The government is also trying to draw a medium- to long-term Master Plan for the management of illegal migrant workers, by requesting the National Economics and Social Development Board to come up with such a plan in the next five or six months.

In the short-term then, government efforts have concentrated on measures to control influx of illegal unskilled migrants at the points of entry. For reasons explained above, this has not been effective and has only resulted in growing illegal employment, leading to exploitation of foreign workers and other social problems. The estimated number of illegal migrants from neighbouring countries kept increasing from 200,000 in 1993 to more than one million in 2001.

Over the long-term, Thai policy-makers would need to take a more comprehensive view of the problem. One of the long-term policy approaches being considered is an organized recruitment arrangement that would formalize contracting of foreign unskilled workers, and make them subject to Thai labour laws. This would mean, then, that foreign unskilled labour would earn the same wages and benefits as Thais (Wong-anan 1995a) while at the same time contribute their share of taxes. Under such terms, the Ministry of Labour will need to develop a more sophisticated monitoring system for the Thai labour market, to create a standardized procedure for bringing in and keeping track of these workers as demand fluctuates. Such measures are necessary to prevent the much greater problem later on of uncontrolled growth of foreigners that may create a backlash from Thais over such issues as culture, permanent residency, social integration, welfare spending, and social stability, especially during a prolonged period of economic downturn.

There are doubts however, on whether such a highly controlled recruitment policy of temporary workers is viable or even achievable considering the steep administration costs. Such a policy is likely to entail a lack of sensitivity to considerations of human rights and equality before the law as shown by the experiences of some major labour-importing countries. Castles (1994) has also noted that government policies failed where they ignored the social nature of migration. The experiences of Germany and Western European importing countries of the 1960s have shown that temporary importing recruitment had resulted in an unintended shift to settlement and formation of new ethnic minorities in the 1970s and 1980s, creating unexpected social, cultural and political consequences for the receiving countries (Castles 1994). Thailand is no stranger to this phenomenon, harking back to its own troubles integrating Chinese immigrants from the late nineteenth century to the early 1950s.

Policy-makers must begin to think carefully about difficult choices ahead, if Thailand is to follow the path of increasing dependence on unskilled foreign workers, a trajectory that seems to be unavoidable as an economy becomes globalized (Sassen 1994). If we apply Castles' (1994) analysis to the Thai case, it appears that the choice rests on two alternatives. If Thailand were to implement a highly controlled recruitment policy that prohibits permanent settlement or denies illegal workers their basic rights, it will create a situation of marginalization and potential conflict. On the other hand, if the country is to ensure some measure of control and at the same time, respect for human rights, it must be willing to accept potentially significant shifts in culture and national identity. With increasing democratic development in Thailand, the country could place itself in a compromising position if it were to renege adherence to respect for human rights of these illegal workers. Thai workers overseas have themselves experienced abuse and unfair treatment (Ekachai 1994). It would be interesting to find out whether the recent approval by the Prime Minister of proposed amendments to the existing unfair Family Law, which allows foreign men who marry Thai women to take up Thai nationality, will be applicable in the case of illegal migrant workers (*Bangkok Post*, 1996*d*).

In view of the pitfalls of allowing illegal, unskilled workers, the Thai Government needs to examine the long-term role of Thailand in the region. As the country becomes more prosperous, Thailand also needs to play a greater role in helping its neighbours develop. For this to happen, Thailand must use its influence to support initiatives that bring peace and stability in neighbouring countries, so that economic development can take root. Economic development in these countries will, therefore, help reduce the pressure of economic refugees pouring through its borders. Moreover, Thai entrepreneurs will also be able to invest in border industrialization zones within these countries, create employment opportunities for the local population *in situ*, while at the same time benefit from low-cost importing. A JICA/NESDB (1993) study has already proposed the concept of in-bond zones on the Cambodian side, as part of the Isarn-Indochin-In-Bond Programme. There is no reason why a similar approach cannot be implemented along the Burmese side, once the problem of minorities is resolved.

Managing the problem of the increasing magnitude of foreign workers would ultimately require a more comprehensive policy approach, involving an integrated foreign, industrialization, importing and immigration policy. This will obviously require a complicated process of co-ordination, a task that may not be immediately forthcoming from the bureaucracy, especially in a country not known to have a tradition of dirigible (Christensen et al. 1993). However, if Thailand is to continue to prosper and remain an active player in the global economy, it must start to evolve a more sophisticated process of policy co-ordination and consultation to enhance its well-known consensus approach of decision-making.

Future Policies on International Migration

In 2000, the Southeast Asia economies continued the recovery from the effects of the Asian currency crisis. With this recovery has come an increase in the demand for foreign workers. An issue of growing significance in the region, as well as globally, is the increasing involvement of highly skilled workers, especially information and communication technology workers in international importing migration. The worldwide shortage of information and communication technology workers has seen increasing international competition for workers highly trained in these areas (Hugo 2002). This situation is happening within the upper importing market, while it has limited impact on the lower importing market.

International migration policies for the lower importing market in Thailand should follow the same path as that initiated in 2001 by Thaksin Shinawatra's government, when the government decided to allow illegal migrants from Myanmar, Laos and Cambodia to register openly. This new measure allowed migrant workers to work without the restrictions on number, geographical areas, and types of occupation that they had earlier faced from the previous administration. This new policy provides better management of the illegal workers, by way of knowing where they are, what they are doing and for whom they work.

In the following year, the government decided to extend work permits for those who registered during the previous year, (about 0.56 million) for another year. At the same time, the government has intended to come up with the Migration Master Plan and Implementation Plan during the next five years, so that all agencies involved with migration management should know exactly what to do. The government is also conducting a study on demand for alien workers in various occupations and areas, so that the output of this research will help the government improve management of undocumented workers in the medium- and long-terms more effectively.

Furthermore, the emigration policy of the government continued to maintain the existing market, while encouraging workers to find new markets abroad. The upgrading of Thai workers' skills is one of the main tasks to increase the opportunity of the potential Thai emigrants seeking better jobs overseas. The Department of Employment, which engages in every process of overseas employment, has a strong commitment to control and monitor the work of recruitment agencies, so that they comply with the regulations and fulfil government policies. One measure to protect the workers is to balance the import-export via government-to-government and private-to-private recruitment agencies. This policy creates concern among the Thai scholars who monitor the local importing market. It is believed that Thai emigrant workers, unskilled and semi-skilled, have escalated the importing shortages, making room for the illegal migrant workers from neighbouring countries to fill in vacancies. Without carefully judging the net benefits of such movement of importing, it is difficult to justify concerns about whether the government should limit the number of low-skilled, and semi-skilled emigrant workers, in order to lessen the labour shortage problem in the country.

Unlike Thailand, the Philippines has its policy framework contained in the new Medium-Term Philippine Development Plan as released by the Arroyo administration in November 2001, that the Philippine Government now explicitly recognizes overseas employment as a "legitimate option for the country's work force". As such, the Philippine Government shall fully recast importing mobility, including the preference for overseas employment. The Philippine Government is now actively exploring and developing "better employment opportunities and modes of engagement in overseas importing markets consistent with regional and international commitments and agreements (Go 2002). Thus, if the Thais want to follow the same direction, it should seek to actively promote international importing migration, especially of higher skilled, knowledge-based workers, as a growth strategy for Thailand, instead of limiting Thailand to exporting low-skilled workers.

In order to avoid the problem of manpower shortages, once the Thai Government starts promoting importing labour, the Thai Government should follow Singapore's manpower policies and strategies, by formulating migration policy based on information and forecasts on industry trends and needs. It should be a task of the Ministry of Labour and Social Welfare to obtain the manpower needs for the country through effective manpower planning efforts, and projections, as well as feedback from, and consultation with, government economic agencies and industries. This measure has proved to be effective in Singapore (Yap 2002).

The MOLSW (the Ministry of Labour and Social Welfare) should utilize the minimum salary criterion for Employment Pass, to attract more legal workers in the areas where the country needs them. The country should utilize a more legal channel to import more workers in the area of shortages instead of using illegal low-skilled workers. A stricter time frame for extension of illegal migrants' work permits has to be imposed, with an aim to reduce the unskilled and semi-skilled categories of work in Thailand, similar to what has been done in Malaysia (Kassim 2002). In doing this however, experiences from Malaysia have indicated two drawbacks. Firstly, in view of the high cost of recruitment, a short working period will cause substantial losses to both employers and employees. Secondly, it makes skill acquisition among foreign workers impossible and this may affect the quality of production.

Conclusion

Current and future Asian migration will affect Thailand, which experienced it both as a sending and a receiving country of migrants. According to Chantavanich and Risser (2000), Thailand needs to develop a thorough migration policy, which can accommodate both emigrants and immigrants. The Thai Government desires to protect Thai workers in the destination countries while at the same time trying to develop equal treatment for guest workers. Thailand should learn experiences from the Philippines and other Asian countries for the better protection of emigrant workers through bilateral and multilateral agreements.

With regard to immigrant workers, according to Martin (2002), experiences of the migration policies from the Asian members of the receiving countries show that the past migration management policy among importing countries has not resulted in reducing countries' dependence on migrant workers at a satisfactory level. Migrant workers and employers are becoming more and more dependent upon each other. Once immigrants become a "structural feature", it is very difficult to eliminate and the cost of elimination would be very high to employers and the country when they decide to reduce dependence on migrant workers.

Martin (2002) also recommended improving existing migration management policies in Thailand in order to maximize the economic contributions of migrant workers, in three areas. Firstly, the government should consider introducing a more flexible registration system (including registration fee and wages) to accommodate migrant workers' shifting jobs, places and employers. Secondly, a more appropriate measure should be introduced to increase awareness of responsibilities and rights on the part of both employers and migrant workers. Finally, it is necessary to co-ordinate between sending and receiving countries to help keep migrant workers, employers and recruitment agencies in legal channels.

Notes

1 Even though there was a sizable number of war refugees along the Thai-Cambodian border, the situation is less complicated because of the more homogenous nature of this group of refugees.
2 US$1 = 42baht.
3 The Royal Thai Police has shifted from the Ministry of Interior to the Office of the Prime Minister in 2001.

References

Castles, Stephen. "Causes and Consequences of Asia's New Migrations". Proceedings of the International Conference on Transnational Migration in the Asia-Pacific Region: Problems and Prospects, The Asian Research Centre for Migration, Institute of Asian Studies, Chulalongkorn University, 1–2 December 1994, pp. 1–21.

Chalamwong, Yongyuth, et al. "A Policy Study on Managing the Illegal Migrant Workers in Thailand: A Case Study of 4 Provinces". Report prepared as part of a Policy Study on the Management of Undocumented Migrant Workers in Thailand. TDRI/NESDB. April 1996 (in Thai).

Chalamwong, Yongyuth and Ramon C. Sevilla. Dilemmas of Rapid Growth: A Preliminary Evaluation of the Policy Implications of Illegal Migration in Thailand. *TDRI Quarterly Review* 11, no. 2 (June 1996): 16–24.

Chalamwong, Yongyuth. "Recent Trends in Migration Flows and Policies in Thailand". Paper presented in International Migration in Asia: Trends and Policies, Organization for Economic Co-Operation and Development, 2001.

Chalamwong, Yongyuth. "Economic Stagnation, Labour Market, and International Migration in Thailand". Paper presented at Annual Conference on "Economic, Labour Market, and International Migration", organized by The Japan Institute of Labour. Tokyo, 4–5 February 2002.

Chantavanich, Supang and Gary Risser. "Intra-Regional Migration in Southeast and East Asia: Theoretical Overview, Trends of Migratory Flows, and Implications for Thailand and Thai Migrant Workers". In *Thai Migrant Workers in East and Southeast Asia, 1996–1997*. ARCM no. 019, Bangkok, 2002.

Chintayananda, Sudthichit, Gary Risser and Supang Chantavanich. *The Monitoring of the Registration of Immigrant Workers from Myanmar, Cambodia and Laos in Thailand.* Bangkok: Asian Research Centre for Migration, Institute of Asian Studies, Chulalongkorn University, 1997.

Christensen, S., D. Dollar, A. Siamwalla and P. Vichyanond. *Thailand: The Institutional and Political Underpinnings of Growth,* (The Lessons of East Asia Series), The World Bank, 1993.

Ekachai, Sanitsuda. "When the Nets are Empty". *Bangkok Post,* 16 September 1993, p. 27.

Go, S.P. "Recent Trends in Migration Movements and Policies: The Movement of Filipino Professionals and Managers". Paper presented at Annual Conference on "Economic, Labour Market, and International Migration", organized by The Japan Institute of Labour, Tokyo, 4–5 February 2002.

Hugo, Graeme John. "International Migration and Labor Markets in Asia: Australia Country". Paper presented at Annual Conference on "Economic, Labour Market, and International Migration", organized by The Japan Institute of Labour, Tokyo, 4–5 February 2002.

Kassim, Azizah Binti. "Economic Slowdown and Its Impact on Cross-national Migration and Policy on Alien Employment in Malaysia". Paper presented at Annual Conference on "Economic, Labour Market, and International Migration", organized by The Japan Institute of Labour, Tokyo, 4–5 February 2002.

Martin, Philip. "Thailand: Improving the Management of Foreign Workers". Paper presented at National Tripartite Seminar on Future of Migration Policy Management in Thailand, organized by ILO, IOM and Ministry of Labour and Social Welfare, United Nations Conference Centre, Bangkok, 14–15 May 2002.

Poapongsakorn, Nipon and Amornthip Taethiengtam. "Foreign Workers and Labour Laws in Thailand". Paper presented at the Symposium on Law and Social Sciences, organized by the Centre for Advanced Studies, National University of Singapore, 6–8 August 1992.

Robinson, David et al. "Thailand: Adjusting to Success, Current Policy Issues". International Monetary Fund Occasional Paper 85, Washington, D.C., August 1991.

Sassen, Saskia. "Immigration in a World Economy". Proceedings of the International Conference on Transnational Migration in the Asia-Pacific Region: Problems and prospects. The Asian Research Centre for Migration, Institute of Asian Studies, Chulalongkorn University, Bangkok, 1–2 December 1994, pp. 97–113.

Secretariat of the Labour Development Council (SLDC). "Illegal Migrants in Thailand: A Case Study of Ranong". Paper submitted to a seminar organized by SLDC, Cha Praya Park Hotel, Bangkok, 17 July 1995.

Shinnavaso, Kasemarn. "Foreign Workers: Facts, Problem Identification and Recommendations". Unpublished paper 1995 (in Thai).

Sontisakyothin, Sakdina. *Major Factors Affecting Policy Charges on Illegal Migrant Workers in Thailand.* A dissertation submitted in partial fulfilment of the requirements for the degree of Doctor of Philosophy in Development Administration, School of Public Administration, The National Institute of Development Administration, 2000.

Soonthornthada, Kusol and Umarporn Phataravanich. *Processes of Hiring Illegal Migrant Workers Employment and Recommendations from Related Public and Private Sector.* Report presented at the seminar entitled Policy Options for Importing of Foreign Labor in Thailand: A Study of Interest Parties, Legal Issues, and the State Management System. Institute for Population and Social Research, Mahidol University, 26–28 May 1997 (in Thai).

Sussangkarn, Chalongphob and Chalamwong Yongyuth. "Development Strategies and Their Impacts on Labour Market and Migration: Thai Case Study". Paper presented at the OECD Workshop on Development Strategy, Employment and Migration, Paris, France, 11–13 July 1994.

Sussangkarn, Chalongphob and Chalamwong Yongyuth. "International Labour Mobility with Reference to Thailand's Industrialization Process". *Asia Club Papers no. 3* (April 1992): 165–78, Tokyo Club Foundation for Global Studies.

Wong-anan, Nopporn. "Shortages Spark Thai Debate on Importing Cheap Labour". *Asian Wall Street Journal*, 17 October 1995a, p. 1.

Wong-anan, Nopporn. "Thai Wage Board to Study Special Low-Salary Zones". *Asian Wall Street Journal*, 9 May 1995b.

Yap, Mui Teng. "Singapore's Country Report". Paper presented at Annual Conference on "Economic, Labour Market, and International Migration", organized by The Japan Institute of Labour, Tokyo, 4–5 February 2002.

www.ingramcontent.com/pod-product-compliance
Lightning Source LLC
Chambersburg PA
CBHW021544260326
41914CB00001B/159